The **BEST** Book of
HOCKEY
FACTS
& STATS

A FIREFLY BOOK

Published by Firefly Books Ltd., 2002

Text and design copyright © 2002 by Carlton Publishing Ltd

Statistics copyright © 2002 by Stats Inc.

First Printing

National Library of Canada Cataloguing in Publication Data

Weber, Dan
        The best book of hockey facts & stats / Dan Weber.

ISBN 1-55297-660-2

1. Hockey—Miscellanea. 2. National Hockey League—Miscellanea.
I. Title.

GV847.W34 2002   796.962'64   C2002-903174-5

Publisher Cataloging-in-Publication Data
(Library of Congress Standards)

Weber, Dan.
The best book of hockey facts & stats : in association with Stats Inc. / Dan Weber. –1st ed.
        [304] p. : cm.
ISBN 1-55297-660-2 (pbk.)
1. Hockey – Records. 2. Hockey – Miscellanea.
3. National Hockey League. I. Title.
796.962   21   GV847.25.W43 2002

First published in Canada in 2002 by
Firefly Books Ltd.
3680 Victoria Park Avenue
Toronto, Ontario M2H 3K1

First published in the United States in 2002 by
Firefly Books (U.S.) Inc.
P.O. Box 1338, Ellicott Station
Buffalo, New York 14205

Commissioning Editor: Martin Corteel
Project Editor: Luke Friend
Production: Sarah Corteel

Printed and bound in Canada

The BEST Book of HOCKEY FACTS & STATS

Dan Weber

STATS INC.

FIREFLY BOOKS

CONTENTS

CONTENTS

CONTENTS

CONTENTS

INTRODUCTION

For a sport that started out on the natural ice of the frozen north, there were really only a couple of ways to go. South…and west. And, now, everywhere in between. Almost all at once, it seems.

For four decades, more or less, and 25 straight years from the onset of World War II, professional hockey was content to exist in a solid Canada-USA mix of six major markets—Toronto, Montreal, New York City, Boston, Detroit and Chicago.

There were plenty of great players and teams, and their amazing stories are here. But for many sports fans, hockey was an acquired taste. Football was another story, as the NFL was beating major league baseball to the West Coast by the better part of a decade in the Fifties. The NBA was right there, too. The three professional sports leagues were combining, consolidating competitors, conquering new markets, energizing TV empires and developing their demographics.

All the while hockey waited. And watched. Content and comfortable in their historic ice palaces, mostly from the Roaring Twenties—the Forum, Maple Leaf Gardens, Chicago Stadium, the Olympia, Boston Garden and Madison Square Gardens.

As great as Gordie Howe and Maurice "Rocket" Richard might have been, they were not names all sports fans would know much about. Here you will learn of all the great names and personalities in hockey history—the top 100 past and present stars—from goalkeepers to centers, from defensemen to wingers.

And then there are the coaches, the top 15 of all time, profiled here as well, from Jack Adams and Lester Patrick to Scotty Bowman and Mike Keenan.

All the while the pace of the game is on view. Fast and furious on the ice, hockey wasn't exactly happening off it. Sure, there were some advances—helmets, goalie masks, painting the ice white, striped shirts for the officials, the Zamboni machine. But if you cared about the National Hockey League west of Chicago or south of Manhattan, well my friend, that's why they had newsreels. Or the minor leagues.

INTRODUCTION

By the time the NHL finally expanded in a serious way after the 1966–1967 season, the NBA had beaten hockey to Los Angeles by seven years, to Minneapolis by 19 and to St. Louis by 20.The irony here is that it was the NHL that had pretty much brought pro basketball into existence after WWII in order to have a second team in their arenas in the winter. Hockey was getting beaten to the punch almost everywhere by baseball, football and basketball. In California, Florida, the Pacific Northwest, the Old South, the Rockies and the Sunbelt.

Finally the NHL did get it. From six teams in 1966–1967, the league has expanded to 30 teams just 25 years later, a 500 percent increase. No major professional sports league has expanded that far that fast. The NHL these days is in Nashville, Columbus, Vancouver, Carolina, Florida, Atlanta, Colorado, Texas and Arizona. New buildings everywhere are filled with luxury boxes. And the players no longer come from just six or seven Canadian provinces and an occasional immigrant.

American college players supplement a steady diet of blue chippers from all around the world—from Australia to the Czech Republic, from Sweden to Russia, from Finland to Slovakia, from Germany to England. Many of them are profiled here.

You know hockey has arrived when sports fans in Carolina let their Charlotte Hornets pro basketball team leave the state at the same time they go giddy for a Hurricane hockey club that improbably brings the Stanley Cup finals home to Raleigh.

Players are bigger, stronger, faster, more talented now, although the group that just left the game headed by Wayne Gretzky and Mario Lemieux will be hard to beat for sheer blinding skill levels. And maybe we'll never see the likes of Gordie Howe, Howie Morenz or Maurice Richard either.

But professional hockey? You can't miss it. Coming to a neighborhood near you, whether you're a hometown fan of the Ohio State Buckeyes or the North Carolina Tar Heels, or even the Grand Ole Opry, hockey is here. And there. Darn near everywhere.

Northeast

Boston Bruins

Buffalo Sabres

Montreal Canadiens

Toronto Maple Leafs

Ottawa Senators

BOSTON BRUINS

They became the Bruins when original owner Charles Adams' secretary suggested the name after a fan contest didn't provide a suitable mascot. Adams wanted an "untamed animal whose name was synonomous with size, strength, agility, ferocity and cunning—and in the color brown" which, along with yellow, were the colors of Adams' Brookside Stores.

Bruins they were, tenacious defenders of their home turf from the beginning. Just check out the all-time Bruin best and you get the likes of Bobby Orr, Raymond Bourque and Eddie Shore. They set the mold for the Bruins, who were successful from the beginning.

Five Stanley Cups came over an equal number of decades beginning with the 1928–29 season when Shore, Cecil "Tiny" Thompson and Dit Clapper led the way for Coach Art Ross. A decade later Shore, Clapper and Thompson were still around for another Cup. In 1940–1941, Coach Ralph "Cooney" Weiland had Frank Brimsek, Bobby Bauer and Bill Cowley.

The 1969–1970 champs featured all-time defenseman Bobby Orr and super-scorer Phil Esposito and many more for Coach Harry Sinden. That nucleus remained to win again two years later for Coach Tom Johnson.

But it's been 32 long years now as the Bruins have moved from historic Boston Garden to the Fleet Center. There were those two moments when the beloved Bourque led the Bruins to Stanley Cup finals in 1988 and again in 1990, only to have them lose both times to Edmonton, managing just one win against the Oilers.

With Joe Thornton, Glen Murray and Byron Dafoe, the Bruins have a nucleus that finished on top of the Northeast with a 43–24–6–9 record in 2001–2002. Could this be the B's decade?

FRANCHISE RECORD				
	W	**L**	**T**	**Pts**
Regular Season	2287	1947	765	5762
Playoffs	238	256	6	
Stanley Cups	**5** *(1929, 1939, 1941, 1970, 1972)*			

BOSTON BRUINS

1924 – On October 11, the Bruins are granted an NHL franchise for $15,000. The team names Art Ross its first manager.

1929 – On March 28, the Bruins faced the New York Rangers in the first-ever Stanley Cup Finals between two U.S. teams. Boston won both games to win the team's first Stanley Cup title.

1931 – Art Ross becomes the first NHL coach to pull his goalic for an extra attacker in a 1–0 loss to the Canadiens in Game 2 of the Stanley Cup semifinals.

1936 – Boston's Cecil "Tiny" Thompson becomes the first NHL goaltender to receive credit for an assist in a 4–1 win over Toronto in Boston Garden January 14.

1939 – The Bruins win the Prince of Wales Trophy by clinching the regular season title. It's the first time the Prince of Wales Trophy is awarded for this reason.

1939 – For the first time, the Stanley Cup is a best-of-seven format but the Bruins go on to take the Cup in five games anyway after a 3–1 win over Toronto's Maple Leafs on April 16.

1940 – In another historic first, one line (the Bruins' "Krautline" of Milt Schmidt, Woody Dumart and Bobby Bauer) finished 1–2–3 in scoring in the NHL.

1966 – Bobby Orr signs a two-year deal for $70,000 plus a signing bonus that gives him the top pay in the NHL.

1969 – On March 2, Bruin Phil Esposito scores twice to become the first NHL player to score 100 points in a season in a 4–0 win over Pittsburgh. Bobby Hull and Gordie Howe join him later in the season as 100 point scorers.

1970 – Boston's Orr has an assist in the season's final game to become the first NHL defenseman to win the Art Ross Trophy as the league's top scorer. Orr scored 33 goals and had 87 assists for 120 points in 76 games.

BUFFALO SABRES

The Buffalo Sabres haven't ever been the very best but they've been pretty good for most of the time. Maybe that's why this past season's 35–35–11–1 mark looks so meager for the fifth-place Sabres in the bunched-up Northeast.

They grew up in hockey country and built on years of Buffalo's minor league success. So when the Sabres won their franchise in 1970, after having been passed over in 1967, they were determined to make the most of the $6 million fee that had to be paid—three times what it cost the six expansion teams just three years earlier.

George "Punch" Imlach was the man chosen by owners Seymour and Northrup Knox, to get it going. Imlach, still upset at the way Toronto dumped him, was ready. Soon players like Gil Perreault, Rick Martin and Rene Robert, along with the late Tim Horton, all set the tone for a Sabres' franchise that chose the sword as a symbol because it was "renowned as a clean, sharp, decisive and penetrating weapon on offense as well as a strong parrying weapon on defense."

After a pair of trades and a draft, Imlach had his "French Connection" line of Perreault, Robert and Martin and the Sabres were off on a streak that saw them make the playoffs 22 of 25 seasons after missing three of the first four.

After the legendary Scotty Bowman passed through as coach and GM, the Sabres keep getting top players like Pat LaFontaine, Pierre Turgeon and Alexander Mogilny. Then came a new crop of stars led by Michael Peca and Dominik Hasek, who would push the Sabres to their second Stanley Cup Finals in 1999 (Their first coming in 1975, losing to the Flyers). This time the Dallas Stars dispatched Buffalo in six games with a very controversial deciding goal.

FRANCHISE RECORD				
	W	**L**	**T**	**Pts**
Regular Season	1193	951	392	2784
Playoffs	99	110		
Stanley Cups	0			

BUFFALO SABRES

1970 – On May 22, Sabres join the Vancouver Canucks as NHL's two expansion franchises for 1970–1971 season.

1971 – Gil Perreault scores the Sabres' first hat trick against California January 29.

1975 – In one of the most memorable games in NHL history, Flyers' goalie Bernie Parent shuts out the Sabres 2–0 in a Stanley Cup playoff game at Buffalo's Memorial Auditorium on May 27. The ice was shrouded in fog so thick that neither goalie could see the other.

1974 – After just two seasons with the Sabres, defensive star Tim Horton is killed in a tragic auto accident.

1976 – In a cold war confrontation notable for its time, the Sabres scored a 12–6 win over the powerful Soviet Wings team on January 4. It's the most goals ever given up by the Soviets.

1979 – Scotty Bowman becomes the Sabres' new GM-coach.

1984 – On December 19, Bowman becomes the winningest coach in NHL history with career victory No. 691 in the Sabres' 6–3 wn at Chicago.

1990 – Sabres retire their first jersey October 17. It's the No. 11 of Gilbert Perreault who played 1,191 games, scored 512 goals, recorded 814 assists and 1,326 points in 16 seasons.

1990 – In the first game in its new $127.5 million HSBC Arena September 27, the Sabres defeat Toronto in an exhibition in the building that seats 18,090 for hockey.

1999 Sabres fall to Dallas Stars in six games in their second-ever Stanley Cup finals.

MONTREAL CANADIENS

Much has been made of the way the Montreal Canadiens, modern as they may be in their new Molson Centre digs, aren't what they used to be. They haven't been able to keep pace, for example, with that other great North American sporting dynasty—baseball's New York Yankees. But then, the Yankees are still playing in Yankee Stadium, built a year earlier than the old Montreal Forum. "The Habs"—or les Habitants—abandoned their home of 72 seasons for the new Molson Centre in 1998.

Some even speculate that the ghosts are gone, unwilling to follow the franchise to its new home, and that's the problem. It's as good as any theory to explain the significant slippage of a team that won 23—24 by its count—Stanley Cup championships in the 20th Century. A look at the Canadiens' retired numbers is like a trip through the Hockey Hall of Fame.

Goalkeeper Jacques Plante won the Hart Trophy and six Vezinas in his 12-year career in the net from 1952 to 1963. Defensemen Doug Harvey (1) won the Norris Trophy for four straight years in his 15-year career through 1961. Centers Jean Beliveau (2) (1953–1971), Henri "the Pocket Rocket" Richard (4) (1955–1975) and Howie Morenz (16) (1923–1937) gave the Habs 52 years of stellar play in the middle. Then there was right wing where Maurice "The Rocket" Richard (7) (1942–1960) and Guy LaFleur (9) (1971–1984) gave the Canadiens another 31 seasons. No wonder all those pennants fly high. But the last one was raised after the 1992–1993 season when the Canadiens dropped the Los Angeles Kings 4–1 in the finals with goalkeeper Patrick Roy, who had led the Habs to a Stanley Cup in his rookie season in 1986, rising to replace the ghost of Plante once again.

But in just two years, the Canadiens were out of the playoff picture, a finish they

FRANCHISE RECORD			
	W	**L**	**T**	**Pts**
Regular Season	2778	1769	822	6391
Playoffs	387	255		
Stanley Cups	**24** *(1916, 1924, 1930–31, 1944, 1946, 1953, 1956–60, 1965, 1966, 1968, 1969, 1971, 1973, 1976–79, 1986, 1993)*		

matched two more times in the 1990s. Then another goalie, the sensational Jose Theodore came along in 2001–2002 to lift the Habs' spirits again. Can he keep it up is a question for the new millennium. But there's another. Can the Canadiens return the Molson Centre to where the Forum was from the beginning—at the pinnacle of pro hockey in North America?

1909 – In a meeting at the Windsor Hotel December 4, the Canadiens are founded by J. Ambrose O'Brien with a $1,000 franchise fee and another $5,000 to guarantee players' salaries.

1917 – Montreal's Windsor Hotel is again the site as the National Hockey League is founded November 26 and the team changes its name to Club de Hockey Canadien and develops the famed CH logo.

1918 – Canadien goalie Georges Vezina records the first shutout in NHL history in a 9–0 romp over Toronto.

1919 – The final game of the Stanley Cup was canceled because of a worldwide influenza epidemic April 4 and no winner was declared between Montreal and the Seattle Metropolitans.

1924 – After a group of businessmen invest in its construction, the 10,000-seat Forum is opened for hockey on November 29 as the Canadiens beat their cross-town rival Maroons to the first game in the $1.2 million building that took just 159 days to complete.

1929 – Goalie George Hainsworth becomes the first in the NHL to record 20 shutouts in a season March 2, beating Boston 3–0. His 22 shutouts remain an NHL record.

1957 – The Molson family becomes the owner of the Canadiens on September as Senator Hartland de M. Molson and his brother Thomas H.P. Molson purchase the team from the Canadian Arena Company.

1968 – Renovations are started to add 2,542 seats and improve another 6,000 with corporate suites at a cost of $9.5 million.

1977 – Montreal becomes the first NHL team to win 60 games in a season with a 2–1 win over the Capitals at Washington for a 60–8–12 season mark.

1996 – With a week of activities March 11–16 the new 21,000-seat Molson Centre is opened and concludes with an open house attended by more than 151,000 fans on March 17.

TORONTO MAPLE LEAFS

If it happened in hockey, chances are it happened first in Toronto's historic Maple Leaf Gardens. From all-star games to the Zamboni machine, from a two-door penalty box to the first-ever penalty shot, from the first transcontinental radio broadcast to Foster Hewitt's famous "He shoots, he scores" call, it probably happened in the 68 years at the historic building in the middle of town.

From Hap Day to King Clancy, from Charlie Conacher to Felix Potvin, from Doug Gilmour to Darryl Sittler, from Frank Mahovlich to Dave Andreychuk, from Syl Apps to Ace Bailey, from Pat Burns to Pat Quinn, from the old Gardens to the new Air Canada Centre where 18,819 watched on February 20, 1999 as the new building was inaugurated with a 3–2 overtime victory over Montreal, a lot of hockey history has happened in Toronto.

Start with 13 Stanley Cups have happened for starters. And they often came in bunches. There were the three in a row from 1947 through 1949 for the Maple Leafs, the first NHL franchise to manage that feat. Then there were the four that came from 1962 to 1967. Frank Mahovlich, Johnny Bower and Tim Horton led those Leafs.

But it's been 35 years since that last Stanley Cup. They say Pat Quinn will soon find a way. The team's 43–25–10–4 record in 2001–2002 , good for second in the Northeast Division and just a point behind Boston, says that could be true.

FRANCHISE RECORD			
	W	**L**	**T**	**Pts**
Regular Season	2329	2275	766	5436
Playoffs	242	258	4	
Stanley Cups	**13** *(1918, 1922, 1932, 1942, 1945, 1947–49, 1951, 1962–64, 1967)*			

TORONTO MAPLE LEAFS

1917 – The Toronto Arenas are one of the founding members of the National Hockey League November 26 along with the Montreal Canadiens and Montreal Wanderers, the Quebec Bulldogs and the Ottawa Senators.

1918 – Toronto's Joe Malone finished the first NHL season with a record 44 goals in 22 games. His record stood until the 1944–1945 season when Maurice Richard broke it in his 50-goal season.

1919 – Toronto changes its name from Arenas to St. Patrick's for Ace Bailey.

1926 – A group of businessmen headed by Conn Smythe buy the Toronto St. Patrick's franchise for $160,000 and change the name and colors—to Maple Leafs and the familiar blue and white.

1934 – Toronto defeats a team of NHL all-stars in a benefit game that serves as the league's first unofficial All-Star Game February 14 at Maple Leaf Gardens.

1936 – Toronto plays the New York Americans on November 7 in the first game ever broadcast coast to coast on the radio in Canada.

1947 – In the NHL's first official All-Star Game, the Stanley Cup champion Maple Leafs lose 4–3 to a group of NHL all-stars with proceeds going to the players' pension fund.

1949 – The Maple Leafs become the first NHL team to win three straight Stanley Cups on April 16, 1949 with a 3–1 win over Detroit.

1955 – The Zamboni machine makes its NHL debut at Maple Leaf Gardens resurfacing the ice in a game with Montreal on March 10.

1963 – Separate penalty box doors are installed at Maple Leaf Gardens for the first time in the NHL for a game against Montreal November 8.

1976 – Maple Leaf Darryl Sittler sets an NHL record of 10 points in one game February 7 with six goals and four assists in an 11–4 win over Boston at Maple Leaf Gardens.

OTTAWA SENATORS

Talk about the Ottawa Senators and you're talking about two almost completely different teams—the sensational early bunch that played in the league's first decade and the reconstituted Senators outfit that has struggled to occupy the NHL spot in the capital city of Canada this last decade.

There was King Clancy, who at the age of 18, played all six positions in a 1–0 championship win over the Edmonton Eskimos in 1923.

Or how about Frank Nighbor, who won the the first Hart Trophy as the league's MVP back in 1924?.

The team won its fourth Cup by 1927. Not bad for an outfit that was from neither Toronto nor Montreal. But shouldn't that have been the case? Wasn't Ottawa where the Cup was born, the brainchild of Frederick Arthur Lord Stanley of Preston, Canada's governor general, who bought the cup in England and brought it to Ottawa in 1893?

But after Ottawa's early spurt to the top, the Senators started struggling. They took a year off in 1931–1932 and gave in completely at the end of the 1933–1934 season, moving to St. Louis and folding after a year there.

After 59 years without a team, it cost Ottawa $50 million to secure a franchise in 1991. But this was hardly a time to be trying to get going in Ottawa, it appeared. Three years saw a total of 33 wins—an average of 11 per season. Then the Senators made the playoffs in Year 5. And they upped the ante a year later with a four games to two upset of New Jersey's Devils in 1998 and went on to total a franchise record 103 the next season for their first Northeast Division title under Coach Jacques Martin and Russian-born center Alexei Yashin.

FRANCHISE RECORD				
	W	**L**	**T**	**Pts**
Regular Season	1383	947	429	3204
Playoffs	161	148		
Stanley Cups	**4** (1920, 1921, 1923, 1927)			

OTTAWA SENATORS

1922 – The Senators and the Toronto St. Patricks play 20 minutes of overtime before their game is declared a tie on February 11 in Ottawa. It's the first tie game in NHL history.

1923 – Ottawa's King Clancy, just 18, plays all six positions (including goalie) as the Senators beat Edmonton 1–0 in Game 2 to become Stanley Cup champions.

1924 – Ottawa's Frank Nighbor wins the first Hart Trophy, created for the league's MVP, on February 9.

1927 – The Senators win their fourth—and final—Stanley Cup.

1934 – After suspending operations for the 1931–1932 season, the original Senators give up and the franchise is transfered to St. Louis and becomes the Eagles.

1991 – The NHL awards the Senators—along with the Tampa Bay Lightning—a franchise for the fee of $50 million on December 16.

1992 – The Senators return to the ice in front of 10,500 at the Ottawa Civic Center against the Montreal Canadiens as Ottawa upsets the eventual Stanley Cup champs 5–3 in a nationally televised game.

1993 – The Senators finish their first season with a slumping 10–70–4 record.

1997 – The Senators finally make the playoffs in Year 5 for Coach Jacques Martin, who took over halfway through the year for Dave Allison.

1998 – The playoff highlight for the Senators came on the team's second try in a four games to two upset of heavily favored New Jersey before being eliminated four games to one by Washington in the second round.

Atlantic

New Jersey Devils

New York Islanders

New York Rangers

Philadelphia Flyers

Pittsburgh Penguins

NEW JERSEY DEVILS

When the Kansas City Scouts were created in 1974, it soon became apparent after a first-season surge that they were going absolutely nowhere—except for Colorado and New Jersey. And to many folks, the fleeing franchise was in no better shape in New Jersey than it had been in Kansas City and Denver.

Bad teams don't last long in Denver, although six years may have been more than the Rockies deserved. After several ownership changes and complicated financial dealings to pay territorial indemnity to the Philadelphia Flyers, New York Islanders and New York Rangers, the deal was done. And New Jersey had a team for native son and baseball owner John McMullen, who first had a part interest in the Yankees and then bought the Houston Astros.

But the new owner's promise to be "more agressive" than the established Rangers across the river turned out to be mighty hollow in the early going. The lowpoint was a 13–4 loss at Edmonton that caused Wayne Gretzky to make his famous comment. "They're ruining the whole league," Gretzky said. "They had better stop running a Mickey Mouse franchise and put somebody on the ice."

And soon they did, once Providence College athletic director Lou Lamoriello arrived on April 30, 1987. With the arrival of Jacques Lemaire in 1993, the Devils finally made their move to the top thanks to Lemaire's neutral zone trap defense that took them to the franchise's first Stanley Cup title in 1995. Beating the Flyers and Red Wings, the Devils surprisingly swept to the Cup with their confounding defense.

But from there, things took a turn for the worse as McMullen—in a dispute with the team's New Jersey Sports and Exposition landlords—talked of leaving for Nashville and taking his team, the best in the decade of the 1990s, with him. Only he didn't. McMullen hung in there with the Devils as Lamoriello— No. 5 in *The Hockey News'* 100 People of Power and Influence in Hockey—rebuilt with newcomers like Patrik Elias to win a second

FRANCHISE RECORD				
	W	**L**	**T**	**Pts**
Regular Season	845	1067	306	2008
Playoffs	90	74		
Stanley Cups	**2** *(1995, 2000)*			

cup in 2000 by stopping the Dallas Stars behind Conn Smythe Trophy winner Scott Stevens. With the Devils now owned by the group that owns the Yankees, Lamoriello is the ownership's man on the board of governors. And the Devils now benefit from a metropolitan New York City cable television broadcast package that should help them stay on top.

1974 – The franchise begins life as the Kansas City Scouts.

1976 – The Scouts become the Rockies with a new home in Denver.

1982 – The Colorado Rockies team that started as the Kansas City Scouts in 1974–1975 was sold to John McMullen, John Whitehead and Brendan Byrne and moved to New Jersey to become the Devils on June 30.

1984 – Meadowlands Arena hists the 36th NHL All-Star Game January 31 before a capacity crowd of 18,939.

1987 – A January 22 blizzard creates "334 Club" as a mere 334 fans make it through 15 inches of snow for 7–5 win over Calgary in a game delayed an hour and 46 minutes. Only 13 Devil players make it to the Meadowlands for the start of the game.

1988 – Mark Johnson scores winning goal in Devils' first playoff win, 3–2, against the Islanders.

1991 – Devils name Sherry Ross as the team's radio commentator.

1993 – Hall of Famer Jacques Lemaire is named the team's eighth head coach on June 28.

1995 – After a 105-day lockout, the Devils advance to their first Stanley Cup finals by beating the Philadelphia Flyers in a six-game series. The Devils go on to sweep the Red Wings in four straight.

1996 – Goalie Martin Brodeur becomes the Devils all-time leader in wins with 107 on February 15 and Dave Andreychuk becomes the 26th NHL player to record 500 goals exactly a month later.

1998 – Announcer Mike Emrick broadcasts his 2,000th NHL game at Pittsburgh April 3.

2000 – Goaltender Brodeur is the first in NHL history to record a game-winning goal (it's his second goal and first in regular season play) as the last player to touch the puck on a delayed penalty.

NEW YORK ISLANDERS

For much of the 1970s, the New York Islanders were building. For much of the 1980s, they were winning. And for much of the 1990s, they were honoring and retiring departed stars. That's the cycle in sports and the Long Island team has seen it all since being awarded an NHL franchise November 8, 1971.

Hard as it is to believe these days, the Nassau Veterans Memorial Coliseum was brand new and the spot to be on Long Island as one great player after another came in to perform for the duo of Coach Al Arbour and GM Bill Torrey. Denis Potvin got them going as the top pick in the June, 1973 draft. Original Islander, goalie Billy Smith, center Bryan Trottier and high-scoring winger Mike Bossy were all key components. By the 1980 season, they were the best team in the NHL and showed as much through four straight Stanley Cup-winning seasons that saw the Long island team perform flawlessly when it counted.

But the Islanders couldn't make it five in the "Drive for Five" season as another dynasty in the making—Edmonton's Oilers—took the Islanders down in the Finals and won the Cup in 1984. From then on it was inevitable that the stars would retire and even Arbour would move up to GM before coming back to take over one more time in 1988.

Still, there was more time spent celebrating the jerseys in the rafters than in the playoff wins and trophies won by the Islanders from then on. By 1997, they were raising a banner to celebrate Arbour's 739 regular season wins although stars still could be found on Long Island. Bryan Berard became the fourth Islander to win the Calder Trophy that year and a year later Trevor Linden was named the club's seventh captain.

Bill Stewart, Mike Milbury and islander great Butch Goring all assume duties behind the bench in a 13-month period from March, 1998 to April, 1999. During that time, the team is bought by New York Sports Ventures co-chairmen Steven Gluckstein and Howard Milstein. They would sell it to Charles Wang, founder and CEO of Computer

FRANCHISE RECORD				
	W	**L**	**T**	**Pts**
Regular Season	1039	1014	325	2411
Playoffs	131	94		
Stanley Cups	**4** *(1980–83)*			

NEW YORK ISLANDERS

Associates and CA's president and COO Sanjay Kumar on April 26, 2000. As the third team in metropolitian New York City and the only only pro team in Long Island, it's never been easy. But it looks like the Isles have gotten things going the right way. They were back in the playoffs in 2002 and trying to re-establish them selves as a force in the NHL.

....

1971 – On November 8, the NHL awards the New York Islanders a franchise for play in the 1972–1973 season.

1972 – On October 12, Islanders beat Los Angeles Kings 3–2 for the franchise's first win.

1973 – Al Arbour is named the Islanders' head coach June 10. A week later, the team selects Denis Potvin first pick overall in the draft.

1975 – In April and May, the Isles win their first-ever playoff series—against the Rangers and Penguins—before dropping a seven-game series to the Flyers.

1980 – Islanders win their first Stanley Cup, beating the Flyers as Bryan Trottier is named playoff MVP on May 24.

1981 – Islanders defeat the Minnesota North Stars 4–1 in five-game Stanley Cup finals to defend their title.

1982 – Islanders sweep Vancouver to win their third straight Stanley Cup on May 16.

1983 – Almost exactly a year later, on May 17, Islanders sweep the Edmonton Oilers for their fourth straight Cup.

1992 – In February and March, Islanders retire Dennis Potvin's No. 5 jersey and Mike Bossy's No. 22.

1994 – On June 1, Arbour announces his second retirement as head coach.

NEW YORK RANGERS

They probably have the best uniform in sports, arguably hockey's best. No team has combined the classic red, white and blue better than the Rangers have. There was always something that made the boys on Broadway seem as if they were somehow better than anybody else, even if they weren't.

It helped that they played in Madison Square Garden in each of that famous building's reincarnations. With Lester Patrick and John Hammond and Conn Smythe leading the way, the Rangers started winning right away, taking a Stanley Cup after Season No. 2 in 1928.

It was almost as if that was just the way it was supposed to be for the franchise dubbed "the classiest team in hockey." They went to the finals four times in six years. The Rangers would miss the playoffs just once in their first 16 seasons. They would fall lower than third only twice and won three regular-season titles.

From 1942–3 however, the Rangers struggled. missing the playoffs 18 times in 24 seasons. But led by coach and GM Emile Francis, the Rangers returned in the 1960s, making the playoffs nine straight seasons from 1966–67 and finally getting back to the Stanley Cup Finals in 1972, where they lost to the Bruins in six games. In 1989, a decade after the Rangers last Stanley Cup Finals apperance, the club hired Neil Smith as GM and moved into the Cup Finals 15 seasons after their last visit, only this time they won behind Captain Mark Messier and goalie Mike Richter and stars Brian Leetch and Adam Graves.

But no star eclipsed that of No. 99 Wayne Gretzky, who played out his final three seasons of an unparalleled 20-year NHL career, on the famed Garden ice from 1996 through 1999 when he skated off on April 18 for the final time as a player.

The newest chapter in Rangers history will be directed by Glen Staher, who brought five Stanley Cup titles to Edmonton in his 24 years there, who took over from Smith in

FRANCHISE RECORD				
	W	**L**	**T**	**Pts**
Regular Season	2172	2185	791	5143
Playoffs	183	195	8	
Stanley Cups	**4** *(1928, 1933, 1940, 1994)*			

2000. Sather wasted no time in bringing back Captain Messier although the Rangers missed the playoffs after a 36–38–4–4 season saw them finish fourth in the Atlantic Conference in the 2001–2002 season. But will Eric Lindros reach his potential? It's now or never for the former Flyer turned Ranger. His ability to do that will determine how soon the Rangers return to the top.

....

1926 – Rangers awarded an NHL franchise May 15.

1928 – Lester Patrick directs the Rangers to their first Stanley Cup title in only their second season.

1933 – Rangers win their second Stanley Cup.

1940 – On February 25, the Rangers played the Canadiens in the first hockey game telecast in the United States. It was broadcast on New York station W2XBS to 300 receivers in New York. They would later go on to win their third Stanley Cup that year.

1965 – On January 27, Ulf Sterner became the first Swedish-born player to play in the NHL in a 5–2 Rangers' win over Boston.

1979 – The Rangers stop the charge of the rival Islanders in the Stanley Cup semifinals before falling to Montreal 4–1 in the five-game Finals that would be the team's last championship round for 15 years.

1994 – It's 54 years between cups as Coach Mike Keenan and Captain Mark Messier lead the Rangers to the franchise's fourth Stanley Cup.

1998 – All-time great Wayne Gretzky scores his 1,000th NHL goal in a 6–3 loss to New Jersey March 7.

1999 – On April 18, after wearing the Rangers' jersey for three seasons, Gretzky skated his final NHL game of a 20-year Hall of Fame career. His jersey No. 99 is retired immediately after the game.

2000 – After a 24-year career in Edmonton and five Stanley Cups, Glen Sather replaces Neil Smith to become the Rangers' president and general manager and brings Messier back to Broadway.

PHILADELPHIA FLYERS

It's been two dozen years since they were the Broad Street Bullies, the expansion team that just would not act like the new kids on the block. They are still the orange-and-black clad Flyers of Philadelphia's not-always-so-peaceful South Philly but it's not the same somehow. And they still have the roudy fans who fill the new arena right next door to the old Spectrum.

But the echoes of that early era—much like the Kate Smith recording of "God Bless America"—just aren't the same as the real thing from the good old days when Fred Shero's boys were bashing the establishment clubs in the National Hockey League. Sure, Bobby Clarke is still here, but his days as general manager aren't producing the success his charges on the ice did three decades ago. Owner Ed Snider has prospered with his various deals and buildings and TV conglomerates but the winning is no longer the lead item for this franchise.

Gone are players like Bernie Parent, whose acquisition in a major trade for the goaltender in 1971, got the Flyers on the road to Stanley Cup success. He would go on to win a pair of Conn Smythe trophies for his championship netminding. Gone are enforcers like Dave Schultz and all the rest of the skaters who made the Flyers of Fred Shero's dump-and-chase system work so well.

But for anyone who watches hockey in Philadelphia, that may be an overstatement to say those days are gone. May be that's the problem. No one can bring those heady days back, not even the heralded Eric Lindros, the player the Flyers won in an arbitrator's decision on the most-publicized trade brouhaha in NHL history. The Flyers win the rights to 19-year-old Eric Lindros for eight players and $15 million to the Quebec Nordiques.

Rookie coach Mike Keenan would lead them to the NHL's best record in 1985 behind strongman scorer Tim Kerr and goaltender Pelle Lindbergh. After losing the Stanley Cup finals to the Oilers, Lindbergh was killed five months later in a high-speed

FRANCHISE RECORD				
	W	**L**	**T**	**Pts**
Regular Season	1383	947	429	3204
Playoffs	161	148		
Stanley Cups	**2** *(1974, 1975)*			

auto accident. After missing a year, the Flyers returned to the Cup Finals behind new goalie Ron Hextall but again lost to the Oilers, this time in seven games.

And then the intrigue set in as the combo of Ed and son Jay Snider, Clarke, Keenan and ultimately Lindros went round and round in a revolving-door effort to find a path to the top. A series of concussions to Lindros and the cancer that came to new coach Roger Neilson were just some of the obstacles that seemed to shadow the Flyers through recent years that saw a major Clarke-Lindros feud result in the center sitting out more than a season and finally departing for New York's Rangers before the 2001 season.

....

1967 – June 5 marked the date of the league's first expansion with six new teams entering the league—the Philadelphia Flyers, Minnesota North Stars, Pittsburgh Penguins, Los Angeles Kings, Oakland Seals and St. Louis Blues.

1968 – Finishing first in the West Division, the Flyers accomplish the best finish in history for an NHL expansion team in its first season.

1972 – Bobby Clarke becomes the first Flyer to receive an individual NHL award, the Bill Masterson Memorial Trophy for perseverance, dedication and sportsmanship.

1973 – On October 11, Kate Smith makes her first live appearance at the Spectrum to sing "God Bless America" before a Flyers game. The Flyers defeat Toronto Maple Leafs 2–0.

1974 – With singer Smith again performing "God Bless America" before the start of the game in her second appearance at the Spectrum, the Flyers become first post–1967 expansion team to win the Stanley Cup, knocking off the Boston Bruins 1–0 in Game 6 of the Finals.

1975 – The Flyers, aka the Broad Street Bullies, do it again, beating the Buffalo Sabres in six games.

1982 – Rookie Ron Sutter becomes the fifth Sutter brother—Brian (St. Louis), Darryl (Chicago), Brent (Islanders) and Duane (Islanders)—to play in the NHL on November 28. It's the first time that has ever happened.

1987 – Ron Hextall became the second goalie in NHL history to get credit for scoring a goal and the first to actually shoot and score in a Flyers' 5–2 win over the Bruins December 8.

1992 – In one of the most-publicized trades in hockey history, the Flyers are awarded the rights to 19-year-old Eric Lindros for eight players and $15 million sent to the Quebec Nordiques.

1996 – On March 19, Ed Snider, Pat Croce and Comcast Corporation announce the formation of Comcast-Spectacor Ventures to create a super-regional sports network in the Delaware Valley that will own and operate the NHL Flyers, the NBA Sixers, the CoreStates Spectrum and the new CoreStates Center.

PITTSBURGH PENGUINS

Anything their mates across the state could do, well so could the Penguins. It would just take the Western Pennsylvanians a few more years to match their Eastern Pennsylvania counterpart Flyers. While both of the original expansion teams entered the NHL in 1967, the Flyers had their first back-to-back Stanley Cups in 1974 and 1975. It would take the oft-times financially strapped Penguins another 17 years to catch up. But with Magical Mario Lemieux leading the Pens, catch up they did in 1991.

That Penguin team was worth waiting for as Coach Bob Johnson—with Craig Patrick in the front office as general manager—was clearly the best in all of hockey. In addition to Lemieux there were these luminaries—Ron Francis, Paul Coffey, Tom Barrasso, Mark Recchi, Kevin Stevens, Joe Mullen, Larry Murphy, Ulf Samuelsson and Bryan Trottier.

And they were good enough to come back and do it again, even the tragic death of Johnson to cancer in November 1991. Scotty Bowman led this Penguin team to the title in 1992 with a sweep of Chicago.

And then disease struck the Penguins again after Pittsburgh dominated the next season with a 56–21–7 mark and 119 points, Lemieux was diagnosed with Hodgkin's disease and missed two months of the season for treatment. Despite returning to lead the league in scoring and his Pens to a 17-game win streak, Lemieux wasn't enough to avoid a shocking second-round upset by the New York Islanders.

Jaromir Jagr would come in to take over the scoring from Lemieux, who retired in 1997. Then Lemieux returned to put together an ownership group to buy his old team in 1999 before returning to the ice the next season in one of the most amazing comebacks in the history of professional sports.

After a 42–31–9 season in 2000–2001 the Pens, with Lemieux absent with an ailing hip, dropped off to 28–41–8–5 mark this past year.

FRANCHISE RECORD				
	W	**L**	**T**	**Pts**
Regular Season	1149	1236	369	2681
Playoffs	109	99		
Stanley Cups	**2** *(1991, 1992)*			

PITTSBURGH PENGUINS

1967 – June 5 marked the date of the league's first expansion with six new teams entering the league—the Pittsburgh Penguins, Philadelphia Flyers, Minnesota North Stars, Los Angeles Kings, Oakland Seals and St. Louis Blues.

1967 – In front of a crowd of 9,307 on October 11 at the Civic Arena, the Penguins make their NHL debut in a 2–1 loss to the Montreal Canadiens.

1970 – After missing the playoffs their first two seasons, the Penguins qualify for the postseason.

1975 – After a strong 37–28–15 season, the Penguins move into the second round of the Stanley Cup playoffs and become only the second team in NHL history to blow a 3–0 lead in a seven-game series as they allow the New York Islanders to win four straight.

1975 – Later that summer, the Penguins declare bankruptcy and the Arena doors are padlocked.

1978 – On April 5, Ohio businessman Edward DeBartolo completes his purchase of the team.

1984 – Taking the first pick overall in the NHL Entry Draft in Montreal, the Penguins selected Mario Lemieux on June 9. On October 11 of that year, Lemieux scored his first NHL career goal in his first game and—as Penguin fans would begin to expect of Lemieux—did it in an especially dramatic way. He scored on his first shift and on his first shot.

1985 – Rookie Lemieux finishes his first season with 100 points.

1006 – Joe Mullen becomes the first American-born player to score 1,000 points in a two-goal, two-assist effort February 7 against the Florida Panthers.

1995 – Jaromir Jagr becomes the first European-born player to lead the NHL in scoring as he and Flyer Eric Lindros finish the season with 70 points each in the shortened season. With a 32–29 goals-scored advantage, Jagr wins the Art Ross Trophy.

1997 – Lemieux retires.

2000 – Lemieux takes over as Peguins owner.

2001 – Lemieux unretires and scores 35 goals in 43 games.

Southeast

Atlanta Thrashers

Carolina Hurricanes

Florida Panthers

Tampa Bay Lightning

Washington Capitals

ATLANTA THRASHERS

The Thrashers are not your father's Atlanta hockey team. They're named after the Georgia state bird, to begin with—the brown thrasher, and have adopted all sorts of local color—Georgia bronze and copper, Peachtree gold and a couple of shades of blue for the city and the franchise. Clearly the Thrashers don't plan to go down in flames the way the previous National Hockey League club—the doomed Flames—did in the South after eight seasons, despite playing better than anyone had a right to expect.

This new-look Thrasher team has tried to touch all the bases in becoming the third jewel in the Turner Broadcasting sports empire in Atlanta—with baseball's Braves and basketball's Hawks. As part of the TV-market-driven expansion of the NHL, dropped the puck in spanking-new $213 million Philips Arena, named after a television company. More than 1,000 state-of-the-art video monitors are set up throughout the building, all products of the Philips Electronics company.

Then there's the top man in this enterprise. Stan Kasten, already responsible for both the Braves and Hawks, became sport's first triple-threat man in assuming the club's presidency as well as a spot on the NHL's board of governors. Under Kasten, the team of GM Don Waddell and coach Curt Fraser have gone about a three-year search for a path from the bottom. From the fans, the acceptance has been strong. The team debuted with an average attendance of 17,202 in the 18,545-seat building. But on the ice, the progress is measured mostly in potential. Year 2 saw a slight improvement in the record (23–47–12) over the first year's 14–61–7. But injuries dropped the Thrashers back to 19–47–11–5 and fifth place, 30th overall, and in line for the second draft pick in this year's free-agent draft in 2001–2002.

And that draft may be where it will have to happen for the Thrashers. With young players coming on line to join 21-year-old Patrik Stefan and impressive rookies Dany

FRANCHISE RECORD				
	W	**L**	**T**	**Pts**
Regular Season	56	149	30	153
Playoffs	0	0		
Stanley Cups	**0**			

ATLANTA THRASHERS

Heatley (21) and Ilya Kovalchuk (18). In their first season, the rookie pair are already entered as a team in *The Hockey News*' 100 People of Power and Influence at No. 97. Just 16 other active players were so honored. If the Thrashers can keep Kovalchuk's healthy ego in check and he and Heatley can play together as it looks like they can, the Thrashers could be as solid as baseball's Braves.

....

1972 – Atlanta Flames give the NHL its first team in the Old South.

1973 – Flames become one of eight NHL expansion teams to set winning streak record of four games.

1974 – In their second season, the Bernie Geoffrion-coached Flames earn a spot in the playoffs. They would miss the playoffs only twice in eight seasons.

1980 – Atlanta Flames franchise sold to Calgary.The city is without a team for nearly two decades.

1997 – NHL awards a new franchise to Atlanta on June 25.

1999 – In November, Stan Kasten becomes team president and NHL governor.

1999 – Thrashers select center Patrik Stefan as the team's No. 1 pick and No. 1 overall in the NHL entry draft.

2001 – Captain Ray Ferraro scores his 400th NHL goal Dec. 28 in 5–4 win over Toronto. He is the 57th Canadian-born and 66th NHL player to reach that mark.

2002 – Atlanta rookie pair of Heatley and Kovalchuk named NHL Rookie of the Month Co-Winners.

CAROLINA HURRICANES

They aren't ever considered an official National Hockey League expansion club because the Hartford Whalers, the team that moved to Carolina five seasons ago from New England, came fully formed into the league in 1979 after a strong history in the World Hockey Association.

But just because they weren't beginners didn't mean the Whalers weren't willing to act like it. This was one interesting outfit, willing to show some of the NHL's greatest players to their fans, no matter how past their prime the players were. How else to explain a Hockey Hall of Fame line that first NHL season that included Gordie Howe, who played all 80 games that season at the age of 51, along with Bobby Hull, who played nine, and Dave Keon, who played in 76.

The best young player the Whalers ever developed became a decade-long fixture for the club two seasons later. Ron Francis came in from Sault Ste. Marie at the age of 18 to do his first star stop in New England before moving on to similar stints in Pittsburgh and Carolina. But just as the team was forced in its early WHA seasons to play in Springfield, Mass. a couple of years for lack of a satisfactory place to play in Hartford, it would move on to a sparkling new facility in the NASCAR country of North Carolina and hope for the best. But with no place of its own for the first two years of construction, and a commuting coliseum as its home ice in Greensboro, this was hardly smooth skating for the Hurricanes. With attendance down to about 8,000 a game in Greensboro, the battle in basketball country for fans' affections started slowly. But the new home helped, jumping average attendance by more than 4,000 the first year.

To this day, some may say marketing still leads the way. The top awards won by the Hurricanes this past year, it could be argued, were for things like their Nike spoof commercial featuring mascot Storny and their "going to the penalty box" song featuring sock puppets.

FRANCHISE RECORD				
	W	**L**	**T**	**Pts**
Regular Season	711	873	238	1668
Playoffs	35	49		
Stanley Cups	0			

CAROLINA HURRICANES

So they're not the Montreal Canadiens yet but under their eighth general manager, Jim Rutherford, and their 10th coach, Paul Maurice, the Hurricanes finally seem to be on their way to a home on Tobacco Road. And never moreso than at the end of the 2002 season, when the Hurricanes advanced all the way to the Stanley Cup Finals.

1979 – Hartford Whalers enter the NHL along with three Canadian teams from the World Hockey Association—the Winnipeg Jets, Quebec Nordiques and Edmonton Oilers. The four WHA teams are not considered official "expansion" teams.

1980 – Finishing fourth in the Norris Division, the first Whalers team makes the playoffs, loses 3–0 to Montreal in the first round.

1980 – Hall of Famer Gordie Howe makes the All-Star team and plays all 80 games at the age of 51 for the first Whalers team that averages 9,856 fans in 40 home games.

1980 – Howe makes NHL history for the Whalers when, on March 9, he skates on a line with his two sons—Marty and Mark. They skated one shift together in the Whalers 1–1 tie with the Bruins at Boston.

1987 – Whaler Doug Jarvis finishes 12 straight seasons and 962 straight NHL games on April 5, before playing two more games to start the next season before retiring with an NHL-record 964 straight games.

1987 – The Whalers establish a franchise-high 93 points in an 80-game schedule to win the Adams Division over Montreal, Boston, Quebec and Buffalo.

1997 – March 25, the Hartford Whalers announce they would move from Connecticut after the 1996–1997 season and become the Carolina Hurricanes for 1997–1998.

1998 – Waiting for their new arena to be built in Raleigh, the Hurricanes begin two seasons of play in the Greensboro Coliseum.

1999 – After playing the first nine games on the road, the Hurricanes finally had a Carolina home, the Entertainment and Sports Arena, where on October 29 they debuted to a sellout crowd of 18,730 with a 4–2 loss to New Jersey.

2002 – Hurricanes (35–26–16–5) finish the season with 91 points, second best in franchise history, and move on to oust the favored New Jersey Devils in Stanley Cup Playoffs first round. They eventually reach the Stanley Cup Finals losing to Detroit in five games.

FLORIDA PANTHERS

South Florida would seem the unlikeliest of locations to write the book on "How To Build an Expansion Team" but this tropical spot turned out to be the place. Even before the Panthers dropped the ice temperature to 22 degrees in the Miami Arena on September 7, 1993, to get ready for the arrival of the original 52 players on the roster, the path to the playoffs had been constructed.

With the entrepreneurial Wayne Huizenga as the owner, with Bob Clarke as the first general manager and Roger Neilson as the first coach, goaltender John Vanbiesbrouck as the first expansion draft pick and center Rob Niedermayer as the team's first free agent draft pick, the Panthers had put in place all the pieces. Only no one knew it at the time.

But sure enough, with Doug MacLean replacing Neilson behind the bench after two years and a 53–56–23 record, the Panthers were on their way to a date with history. Maybe fans should have known something was up after the most successful start for an expansion team in NHL history in 1993–1994 when they finished 33–34–17 with an expansion record nine-game unbeaten streak (5–0–4). But no one—surely no one in the NHL could have guessed what was about to happen in the Miami Arena where the "rat trick" would become a staple. It happened when a rat emerged from out of nowhere in the Panthers' locker room and headed straight for Scott Mellanby. Grabbing his stick, Mellanby swatted the rat against the wall and then went out to dispatch Calgary with two goals in a 4–3 win. Legend turned the two-goal Mellanby "rat trick" into the Miami substitute for the three-goal hat trick.

And so it went. After 50 games that season, the Panthers were an astonishing 31–14–5, enough to survive a slump heading into their first-ever postseason playoffs.

The fairy tale ended in a three-overtime thriller in the Stanley Cup Finals that saw the Colorado Avalanche send the challengers home with 4:31 left in the third overtime of a

FRANCHISE RECORD				
	W	**L**	**T**	**Pts**
Regular Season	270	301	114	675
Playoffs	13	18		
Stanley Cups	0			

scoreless game on a Uwe Krupp goal. A capacity crowd at the Miami Arena welcomed their heroes home to celebrate the season.

Brian Skrudland, the team's first captain, had said it two years earlier but his description of the franchise in South Florida held true – "We didn't know what to expect when we came down to Florida, and we certainly didn't expect to have the best fans in the National Hockey League."

....

1992 – The NHL awards an expansion franchise to H. Wayne Huizenga, chairman of the Blockbuster Corporation, to play in South Florida.

1993 – On March 1, Hall of Famer Bob Clarke named first GM and on April 19, Bill Torrey named club's first president for play beginning in 1993–1994 season. Roger Neilson named coach June 2.

1993 – Before an NHL-record crowd of 27,227 at the ThunderDome, Panthers win first NHL game as John Vanbiesbrouck, the team's first expansion draft selection, scores a 2–0 shutout. Panthers return to play before a sellout crowd of 14,372 at Miami Arena for their first NHL home game, a 2–1 loss to Pittsburgh.

1994 – Panthers complete most successful first season ever in the NHL with a 4–1 win over Islanders. Two weeks earlier, the Panthers had recorded an NHL record 74 points in a tie with New Jersey.

1995 – Doug MacLean named the Panthers' second coach July 24

1996 – The Panthers knock off Boston's Bruins for their first playoff series win and then drop Philadelphia's Flyers in six games on May 14 to advance to the conference finals against Pittsburgh. After defeating Pittsburgh 3–1 in Game 7 of the conference finals, the Panthers advance to the Stanley Cup finals in only the third year of franchise history.

1996 – In one of the great games in Stanley up history, the Colorado Avalanche end a scoreless tie with a Uwe Krupp goal with 4:31 remaining in the third overtime.

1998 – On April 10, the Panthers play their 188th and final game in Miami Arena, losing 7–3 to the Flyers, to finish with a 81–78–29 record in five seasons. On October 9, the Panthers would host the Tampa Bay Lightning in the first-ever game at National Car Rental Center.

1999 – In the biggest trade in Panthers' history January 17, the team acquires high-scoring Pavel Bure from the Vancouver Canucks. Bure would go on to set numerous scoring records with the Panthers.

TAMPA BAY LIGHTNING

From the day in May when Phil Esposito announced that he intended to vie for an NHL expansion slot in Tampa Bay to the December 6 date when the league awarded the Tampa Bay Lightning a franchise—along with Ottawa for the 1992–1993 season—the NHL had to be convinced about the club's financial and fan viability.

Hockey talk had to take a back seat to figuring finances from the start. And until the transition from insurance magnate Art Williams to the Palace Sports and Entertainment group on June 28, 1999, nothing else seemed to matter as much. Maybe that was the way it had to be after Esposito sold the NHL on Tampa Bay and his ability to attract financing to make it work. Much of the original money Esposito rounded up came from Japan and a partnership group shrouded in mystery, Kokusai Green Co., Ltd., that eventually became general partner as other financing fell off in the early years, causing the team to miss a $22.5 million franchise installment payment in 1991.

But the fans kept showing up, from the 10,425 who filled Expo Hall for the first home game in 1992. By the next year, the Lightning were drawing an amazing 805,901 fans for a 19,656 average including an NHL record 27,227 for a game against Florida in the ThunderDome in a 30–43–11 season.

The Lightning offered fireworks from the start. The team scored the most goals ever for a first-season club with 245 in a year when Brian Bradley recorded a pair of all-time expansion marks—42 goals and 86 points.

But with a 246–440–88–16 all-time regular season record, the Lightning haven't exactly set the NHL on fire with that lone playoff appearance in 1996. For the 2001–2002 season, the Lightning finished fourth in the Southeast with a 27–40–11–4 mark, bettering only Florida (22–44–10–6) and Atlanta (19–47–11–5).

FRANCHISE RECORD				
	W	**L**	**T**	**Pts**
Regular Season	246	440	88	596
Playoffs	2	4		
Stanley Cups	0			

TAMPA BAY LIGHTNING

1990 – Phil Esposito announces on May 1 that he intends to vie for an NHL expansion slot in Tampa Bay. On December 6, the league awards the Tampa Bay Lightning a franchise—along with Ottawa for the 1992–1993 season.

1991 – Lightning Partners Inc. is restructured with a Japanese company, Kokusai Green Co., Ltd, assuming the role of general partner.

1992 – Goaltender Manon Rheaume becomes the first female to play in one of the four major professional sports when she starts against St. Louis in a preseason game.

1993 – Brian Bradley, who would go on to set an NHL expansion team record for for goals with his 39th March 16, is the first Lightning player to skate in the All-Star game February 6 in Montreal.

1993 – On October 9, the Lightning set an NHL attendance record when 27,227 fans attend the first regular season game at the ThunderDome against Florida.

1996 – Lightning clinch their first Stanley Cup playoff berth April 13, going on to set a pair of attendance records—25,945 for a playoff game against Philadelphia and then later 28,183 for an all-time NHL attendance record.

1998 – Art Williams becomes franchise's second owner July 14.

1999 – The 49th NHL All Star Game is played at the Ice Palace January 24.

1999 – On June 28, current owners—Palace Sports and Entertainment—take over as Lightning's third ownership group, naming Rick Dudley general manager and VP for hockey operations.

2000 – At the age of 19 on March 10, Vincent Lecavalier is named the team's sixth captain, the second youngest in NHL history.

WASHINGTON CAPITALS

The Washington Capitals weren't exactly a hot ticket from Day One. In fact, the team that construction man Abe Pollin bought to join his Baltimore Bullets NBA franchise got off to the slowest start in NHL expansion history. They shared the new Capital Center Pollin built with his own $18 million in the Washington suburb of Landover, Maryland. Pollin finished the job in 15 months.

But attendance wasn't all that good for a team that was all that bad, recording an NHL worst-ever 19 wins (just eight in Season 1) over their first two years. The Caps gave up the most goals (446), lost the most games in a row (17) and had the worst home record (7–28–5) for a first-year NHL team.

But the Caps kept after it. Even if a player like Mike Gartner, who would be drafted in 1979 to area indifference before going on to become the franchise's first Hockey Hall of Famer, recalls how little the game mattered inside (and outside) the Beltway.

On a tour of the District of Columbia, draftee Gartner—with his parents and girl friend—recalled a limo ride designed to show them the sights. When they drove past the Capital Centre, the driver remarked: "Yeah, that's the Capital Centre," Gartner said. "They have lots of concerts there and different events. The Washington Bullets play there." The driver then added: "You know what, I think they might even have an ice hockey team there."

Gartner said "I knew very early that I was going to a place where hockey was not very high on the priority list."

With the new MCI Center in the center of town, things are better than they were outside town, clearly. They almost made it in 1998. Finally the Caps had their shot under new coach Ron Wilson. Playing in their new MCI Center home, the Caps started slowly before getting going late into their playoff run after a 40–30–12 season. With goalie Olaf Kolzig—"Olie the Goalie"—coming into his own, the Caps knocked off Boston, Ottawa

FRANCHISE RECORD				
	W	**L**	**T**	**Pts**
Regular Season	949	988	285	2191
Playoffs	67	81		
Stanley Cups	0			

and Buffalo only to run head on into a Detroit Red Wings team that dispatched the Caps in four straight.

With the team in Ted Leonsis' hands, the Caps have stayed among the winners the past three seasons, even if they've not advanced past Pittsburgh in the first round. And now ex-Penguin Jaromir Jagr is a Cap. So let the Stanley Cup pursuit begin again.

1974 – On June 11, along with the Kansas City Scouts, the Capitals officially recive their NHL franchise.

1975 – First-year Capitals set records for early futility, allowing an expansion-worst total of 446 goals for a season that saw the Caps finish with an all-time expansion worst 8-67-5 record that showed the worst home record (7-28-5) for an expansion team that was also losing a record 17 straight games.

1976 – With a second year total of just 11 wins—and a mere 19 in the first two seasons—pioneer GM Milt Schmidt and coach Jimmy Anderson, were dismissed.

1979 – Capitals select 19-year-old Mike Gartner in the free agent draft. The Toronto native would go on to become the franchise's first Hall of Fame selectee.

1980 – After six years of not coming close to a playoff berth, the Capitals fall short by a single point.

1983 – Caps make the playoffs for the first time as Gartner becomes an offensive star and newcomer Rod Langway, acquired in a trade from Montreal in 1982, anchors the defense.

1987 – In Game 7 of the division semifinals, the Caps fell to the New York Islanders in seven periods as Islander Pat LaFontaine scored the winning goal in a 3–2 final that didn't end until nearly 2 a.m. on Easter Sunday.

1996 – For the first time in 15 seasons, the Capitals miss the playoffs.

1997 – Jim Carey, Anson Carter and Jason Allison are sent to the Boston Bruins for Adam Oates, Rick Tocchet and Bill Ranford. Then new GM George McPhee brings Ron Wilson in to coach the team.

1999 – Original Caps owner Abe Pollin sells his team to a group led by America Online president Ted Leonsis.

Central

Chicago Blackhawks

Columbus Blue Jackets

Detroit Red Wings

Nashville Predators

St. Louis Blues

CHICAGO BLACKHAWKS

They've always had one of the most classic logos in all of sports, certainly in hockey. Chief Blackhawk—that was Black Hawk in two words until the mid–1980s—could not have been more proud, more distinguished, more elegant, strong and dignified.

And no arena could produce the noise level that the Chicago Stadium could, with its 18,000-plus seats closer to the ice than any where else.

So why the droughts? There were all those great players—Bobby Hull, Stan Mikita, Chuck Gardiner, Pierre Pilote, Tony Esposito, Glenn Hall and Chris Chelios—but they weren't always enough to get to the Hawks to the Stanley Cup.

It's been 41 years since the last Cup came to Chicago. And that one came after a 23-year drought. So what gives for one of the original six NHL teams in a town of great fans where hockey has always had a good home?

Well, there's always been talk of the curse, like the ones that keep down the Cubs and the Red Sox in baseball. Seems the original coach, one Pete Muldoon, was none too pleased at his firing after the first season and may have put a hex on owner Major Frederic McLaughlin Muldoon called it, a "hoodoo."

Who do? The Hawks don't, not much anymore, although the arrival of Brian Sutter as coach gives them one of *The Hockey News'* 100 People of Power and Influence. Sutter, one of just four coaches on the list, is No. 59. For 28 years straight until 1998 the Hawks had made the playoffs. And after a four-year drought, the 2001–2002 Hawks, with a 41–27–13–1 record, had no problems finding their way into the postseason.

But will it ever be the same? How do you replace Hull, the Mickey Mantle of his sport with a slap shot so fast there was nothing defenders could do about it except hope. Or Stan Mikita, the slight but oh-so-tough-and-smooth 22-year star who always seemed to be in the right place. Or goalies like Chuck Gardiner, the tragic figure who died at the height of his career at the age of 29—or Tony Esposito or Glenn Hall.

FRANCHISE RECORD				
	W	**L**	**T**	**Pts**
Regular Season	2126	2232	790	5050
Playoffs	188	218		
Stanley Cups	**3** *(1934, 1938, 1961)*			

CHICAGO BLACKHAWKS

You don't. You especially don't if you're hoping the Wirtz family will get its act together these days. Remember they ran off Hull 30 years ago because they didn't want to pay him and they still own the team.

Maybe Sutter can get the Hawks' act together. He's the best shot they've had in a long time.

....

1926 – Chicago gets an NHL franchise September 25. Team owner is Major Frederic McLaughlin, a coffee baron.

1929 – Blackhawks play their first game in Chicago Stadium December 15, beating the Pittsburgh Pirates 3–1.

1933 – First afternoon game in NHL history is played in Chicago as Detroit beats the Blackhawks 4–3 March 19.

1940 – First chartered flight in NHL history occurs as Blackhawks fly to Toronto for first round of Stanley Cup finals March 18.

1957 – CBS televises the first NHL game, introducing "Peter Puck" to the viewers on January 5 as Blackhawks lose to New York Rangers 4–1.

1959 – Montreal's Jacques Plante wears a goaltender's mask for the first time in an NHL game against the Blackhawks November 7.

1966 – Blackhawk Bobby Hull becomes the first player in NHL history to score more than 50 goals in a season when he gets his 51st on March 12 in a 4–2 win over the New York Rangers. Hull would finish the season with 54.

1995 – Blackhawks open play in United Center beating Edmonton 5–1 on January 25.

1998 – Blackhawks finish season on April 18 and fail to qualify for the playoffs for the first time since 1969, ending a 28 year qualifying streak.

2000 – On October 21, the Blackhawks play the 5,000th game in franchise history.

COLUMBUS BLUE JACKETS

One story says the Columbus team's Blue Jacket mascot is a bug that founder John McConnell said was known for its speed, aggressiveness, industry and resourcefulness. Another version says the Blue Jacket was a good, proud Midwestern type person especially in the days when the Blue Jackets helped the nation stay together in the Civil War wearing Union army's blue outfits.

If it makes any difference, the actual game-day mascot is named Stinger and if one were to call Stinger a "bug-eyed Blue Jacket," you wouldn't get any argument.

But you won't get any argument about the new downtown Nationwide Arena with 15,000 parking spaces within eight minutes walk. Or the way the team's practice facility is a part of the 18,500-seat arena complex, unique in the NHL.

And all of it privately financed. How about that? Good old Midwestern values do seem to prevail here.

Now the hockey hasn't been all that bad although there has been a bit of slippage from the debut year's 28–39–9–6 mark and 71 points to the 22–47–8–5 and 57 points of the 2001–2002 season.

That's 12 points behind expansion club Nashville and a world apart from the other three hockey havens that populate the Central Division—Detroit, St. Louis and Chicago.

The man in charge of making it happen here in Buckeye football land is Doug MacLean, who certainly made things happen in Florida football land.

MacLean did absolutely what no one thought he could do, coaching his Florida Panthers team to the Stanley Cup Finals in only their third season, one of the fastest starts in NHL history.

It won't happen that quickly here. But for now, that's all right. Hockey is the only major pro sport in town. And that seems good enough for the moment. Neither Cincinnati nor Cleveland, Columbus' rival Ohio cities have an NHL team.

FRANCHISE RECORD				
	W	**L**	**T**	**Pts**
Regular Season	50	86	17	128
Playoffs	0	0		
Stanley Cups	**0**			

COLUMBUS BLUE JACKETS

1996 – Columbus Hockey Limited, a partnership formed by five investors to land an NHL team to Columbus, submits an application and a $100,000 fee to the NHL office.

1997 – The Columbus Blue Jackets get one of four franchises awarded by the NHL June 25 to bring the league to 30 teams. Columbus will start play with Minnesota Wild in 2000–2001 season.

1998 Doug MacLean, who led the Florida Panthers to the 1996 Stanley Cup Finals, is named the Blue Jackets' president and general manager February 11.

1998 – Ground is broken for the $150 million Nationwide Arena July 23.

1999 Blue Jackets announce on December that all 30 executive suites in Nationwide Arena have been sold.

2000 – On May 4, Greg Gardner, a standout college goaltender from Niagara University, becomes the first player in Blue Jacket history to sign a contract.

2000 – A week later, Blue Jackets make the first trade in team history as they acquire center Chris Nielsen from the New York Islanders in exchange for two draft picks in the 2000 entry draft.

2000 – On October 7, the Blue Jackets play their first NHL game, losing 5–3 after leading 3–0, to the Chicago Blackhawks in front of a sellout crowd of 18,136 at Nationwide Arena.

2001 – Geoff Sanderson collects the first hat trick in team history, scoring all the Blue Jacket goals in a 3–2 win over Nashville February 10.

2001 Ron Tugnutt makes 29 saves in recording his 22nd win April 8 by a 4–3 overtime score against Chicago. That's the most wins ever for an NHL expansion goaltender.

DETROIT RED WINGS

Hockeytown is the adopted place of name where the Red Wings play. That's right. Just in case you were wondering whether they were serious about the sport here.

In a town that's just a bridge away from Canada, hockey has a home. In a town where Gordie Howe played. And Terry Sawchuk. And Ted Lindsay. This is hockey country.

It's a special place, this town where they have produced more Red Wings who are in the Hockey Hall of Fame (54) than in the Red Wings Hall of Fame (36).

It's a tough town with even tougher players. Sid Abel, Jack Adams, Al Arbour, Andy Bathgate, John Bucyk, Charlie Conacher, Alex Delvecchio, Ed Giacomin, Glenn Hall, Gordie Howe, Tommy Ivan, Red Kelly, Ted Lewis, Harry Lumley, Frank Mahovlich, Terry Sawchuk, Earl Seibert, Tiny Thompson, Norm Ullman and Cooney Weiland.

No wonder there are fan websites for every Red Wing interest under the sun. Give a town ten Stanley Cup titles (more than every other NHL team except Montreal and Toronto) and they'll give you their attention.

Not that they could help watching the wondrous Howe, the best all-around hockey player of his era.

Or currently, watching a team of superstars some have dubbed the best in the history of hockey coached until July 2002 by the man who indisputably was the best—Scotty Bowman—ever to patrol the bench area. Look at *The Hockey News* 100 People of Power and Influence. Only the Red Wings in all the NHL have three on the list—and all in the top 50: Bowman at No. 9, Steve Yzerman at No. 41 and Dominik Hasek at No. 49. Little wonder they won the Stanley Cup for the tenth time in 2002

Yzerman, with the likes of Sergei Federov, Chris Chelios, Nicklas Lidstrom, Luc Robitaille and Brendan Shanahan give the Red Wings a Who's Who roster that will clearly be a threat. And will be for a while.

Or forever, as they say here in Hockeytown.

FRANCHISE RECORD				
	W	**L**	**T**	**Pts**
Regular Season	2263	2089	794	5330
Playoffs	251	226	1	
Stanley Cups	**10** *(1936-37, 1943, 1950, 1952, 1954-55, 1997-98, 2002)*			

DETROIT RED WINGS

1926 – Jack Adams arrives to be the Red Wings coach and GM. He will remain through the 1962–1963 season.

1926 – Detroit move into brand new Olympia Stadium as their home ice and remain there into the middle of the 1979–1980 season.

1932 – After all sorts of financial problems in the preceding several years, grain millionaire James Norris purchases the team and decides to name the team Red Wings and use the familiar winged wheel as the team's logo.

1948 – Detroit's Gordie Howe makes his first of what would be a record 21 NHL All-Star Game appearances November 3 in a 3–1 win over the Stanley Cup champion Toronto Maple Leafs in Chicago Stadium.

1950 – The first televised NHL All-Star Game is played in Detroit's Olympia Stadium October 8 as the Red Wings beat the All-Stars 7–1.

1952 – Red Wing goaltender Terry Sawchuk records one of the great performances in Stanley Cup playoff history, allowing only five goals in eight games and recording four shutouts in the four games at Olympia Stadium.

1954 – Detroit's Red Kelly is named the first winner of the Norris Trophy as the NHL's top defenseman May 10.

1963 – Gordie Howe scores his 545th career goal to break the NHL record of Maurice Richard on November 10 and does so against Richard's old team, the Montreal Canadiens.

1979 – Red Wings move into Joe Louis Arena after nearly 54 seasons at the Olympia.

1993 – The legendary Scotty Bowman is hired to coach the Red Wings after Bryan Murray is fired.

2002 – The Red Wings win their tenth Stanley Cup, defeating the Carolina Hurricanes in five games. Both Scotty Bowman and Dominik Hasek decide to go out on top, retiring after the Finals.

NASHVILLE PREDATORS

When you heard that hockey had gone country, maybe you thought you knew which country. Russia, Sweden, the Czech Republic maybe. How about Nashville?

Now that's country.

And the folks who own the Nashville Predators, Gaylord Entertainment, also own some of this town's greatest country music songbooks. The combination seems to be working so far.

After a pair of opening 28-win seasons, they bumped up to 34 a year ago before sliding back to 28 again in 2001–2002. But still not a bad effort for the team of General Manager David Poile—whose father Bud was GM for both Vancouver and Philadelphia when they were expansion teams—and Coach Barry Trotz.

And the fans of middle Tennessee noticed, turning out 664,000 strong (an average of 16,202) for that first season. Here they were right dab smack in Southeastern Conference football and basketball country and filling up a new arena to 94 percent capacity.

Amazing, indeed.

And if you don't believe it, all you have to do is buy the book of Predators' owner Craig Leipold, co-authored with Vanderbilt University professor Rick Oliver.

Hockey Tonk: The Amazing Story of the Nashville Predators is its title.

Hockey in a honky-tonk town is its story.

FRANCHISE RECORD				
	W	**L**	**T**	**Pts**
Regular Season	118	164	36	282
Playoffs	0	0		
Stanley Cups	**0**			

NASHVILLE PREDATORS

1996 – Gaylord Entertainment Center, the state-of-the-art $160 million facility that would be the Predators' home opens December 18.

1997 – NHL Board of Governors awards Nashville and Leipold Hockey Holdings Inc. a franchise June 25.

1997 – Jack Diller named Predators' first president on July 1 and David Poile is named GM July 9.

1997 – Barry Trotz is named the Predators' first head coach August 6, moving up to the NHL after four years as head coach of the American Hockey League's Portland Pirates.

1998 – With the second overall pick, the Predators select David Legwand in the Entry Draft June 27.

1998 – Sellout crowd of 17,298 sees the Predators' opening NHL game at the Nashville Arena October 10. It's a 1–0 shutout of the home team by the Florida Panthers.

1998 – Predators earn their first NHL win 3–2 against the Carolina Hurricanes October 13.

1999 – On November 10, Rob Valicevic scored the team's first hat trick in a 4–2 win over Chicago.

1999 – Predators close out their first season April 17 with a 4–3 loss to New Jersey for a 28–47–7 record that drew a total of 664,000 fans (an average of 16,202 or 94 percent capacity).

2000 – Owner Craig Leipold's book (co-authored with Vanderbilt University professor Rick Oliver) Hockey Tonk: The Amazing Story of the Nashville Predators debuted in September.

ST. LOUIS BLUES

St. Louis is a great baseball town, the best anywhere. There have been occasional successes for the NFL Rams and Cardinals and the NBA Hawks but now only the Rams remain.

But what about hockey? It's still here after 35 years. What's the deal?

Well, when it comes to hockey, St. Louis is the place they paid great players to come and retire, mostly.

You know many of the names: Hall, Plante, Moore, Harvey, Hawerchuk, Stastny, Arbour and Demers.

Old as they were, they didn't waste any time. As part of the first wave of expansion teams in 1967–1968, the Blues did something that even now is hard to believe.

In each of the first three seasons, the Blues were in the NHL, they made it to the Stanley Cup finals as the best of the expansion teams. Each time they lost in four straight but what a way to start.

But that's as close as they've ever gotten.

Whenever the Blues had any money, they spent it. They spent it on coaches like Al Arbour, Scotty Bowman and Mike Keenan. They spent it on goaltenders like Glenn Hall, Jacques Plante, Grant Fuhr and Curtis Joseph.

Even Wayne Gretzky was here, if only for the blink of an eye. But the offensive talent was deep: Dale Hawerchuk, Peter Stastny, Dickie Moore, Brett Hull, Doug Gilmour, Brendan Shanahan, Brian Sutter and many more.

You want defensemen? How about Doug Harvey, Al MacInnis, Scott Stevens and Phil Housley?

And for a free-spending franchise whose owners often wondered where their next buck was going to come from, there's even better news.

The team's chairman, William J. Laurie, is married to a Walton, Nancy, of the Wal-Mart Waltons. Her late father James L. "Bud" Walton co-founded the world's most

FRANCHISE RECORD				
	W	**L**	**T**	**Pts**
Regular Season	1208	1140	410	2836
Playoffs	134	157		
Stanley Cups	0			

successful retail chain.

With the beautiful new Kiel Center to play in and a solid fan base and all that family money to fall back on, these Blues are a lot like the Mighty Mississippi that flows through here.

They just keep rolling along.

....

1967 – Owner Sid Salomon Jr. selects the team name after being awarded an expansion franchise in 1967. "The name of the team has to be the Blues," Salomon said after the W.C. Handy song of the same name.

1968 – Finishing their first season 27–31–16, good for third in the West, the expansion Blues beat Philadelphia and Minnesota in back-to-back seven-game series to reach the Stanley Cup Finals where they lose in four straight to Montreal.

1969 – Hall of Famers Glenn Hall and Jacques Plante combine to win the Vezina Trophy as the NHL's best netminders.

1976 – In the Amateur Draft, GM Emile Francis selects Bernie Federko, Brian Sutter and Mike Liut, who would go on to be the building blocks for the Blues teams of the 1980s.

1977 – Financial reverses in the 1976–1977 season force the Blues to trim their staff to three before Halston Purina chairman R. Hal Dean invests in the team.

1986 – "Monday Night Miracle" game in the Stanley Cup semifinals sees the tired Blues trailing 5–2 in an elimination game against the Calgary Flames before scoring three unlikely goals to tie and an overtime score for a win for the ages, they say, in St. Louis.

1991 – Brett Hull becomes part of the NHL's first father-son team to win the Hart Trophy (dad Bobby won in 1965 and '66) winning the MVP award after scoring 86 goals in the season.

1997 – At the end of a 17-year career that saw him play with three teams—Boston, Edmonton and the New York Rangers—before finishing up with the Blues on April 29, Craig MacTavish is the last NHL player to appear in a game without a helmet.

2000 – Blues Chris Pronger, Pavol Demitra and Coach Joel Quenneville win NHL awards—Pronger the Hart Trophy for MVP, Demitra the Lady Byng Trophy for sportsmanship and Quenneville the Jack Adams Award as Coach of the Year.

Northwest

Calgary Flames

Colorado Avalanche

Edmonton Oilers

Minnesota Wild

Vancouver Canucks

CALGARY FLAMES

The Calgary Flames may be one of the few hockey gifts the United States has ever given to Canada.

And it was a gift from the Old South—or as they like to say in Atlanta—the New South, at that.

That's because by the end of the decade of their arrival in Alberta, the Flames were Stanley Cup champs and a sign that if it could happen in Calgary, maybe it could happen anywhere. They'd only arrived in Canada in June of 1980 and were champs by the end of May, 1989.

And not only did that little Calgary club—led by Hall of Famer Lanny McDonald and high-scoring Joe Mullen—win the ultimate prize in the National Hockey League, the Flames did it on Montreal ice at the home of the Canadien franchise that had always been the gold standard. And they did it in six games.

And this was after starting out in a place that seated only 7,000 or so and was called the Corral. But they've moved considerably uptown since then. The renovated 17,139-seat Pengrowth Saddledome—the Flames brag in their media guide—is "one of the best entertainment facilities in North America."

And they soon had a good show to put there as the Flames made the playoffs the first 11 years they played in Calgary. They haven't made the playoffs for six years now, but the show still goes on in the Saddledome. And the star is clearly Jarome Iginla, the right winger who *The Hockey News* has at No. 49—and the seventh-ranked player—in their list of 100 People of Power and Influence in Hockey. This last season, the 2001–2002 Flames finished 32–35–12–3 for 79 points and fourth in the Northwest Division dominated by Colorado.

FRANCHISE RECORD				
	W	**L**	**T**	**Pts**
Regular Season	1071	944	359	2513
Playoffs	69	87		
Stanley Cups	**1** *(1989)*			

CALGARY FLAMES

1980 – The Flames changed the "A" for a "C" on their jerseys May 21 as the NHL gave up on its original foray into Atlanta and headed for Calgary and the Stampede Corral (7,242 capacity), a far cry from the 15,141-seat Omni as Nelson Skalbania and a group of Calgary businessmen buy the team.

1983 – The cozy Corral was the home of the Flames until a 6-5 playoff win April 18 over Edmonton.

1983 – The new home and the place where the Flames have played for 19 years now is the 17,139-seast Pengrowth Saddledome that debuted October 15 with Edmonton again the guests.

1989 – In a magical postseason run, the Flames beat Vancouver, Los Angeles, Chicago and Montreal on their way to the franchise's lone Stanley Cup title. Only one series, the opener against Vancouver, went the maximum seven games.

1990 – On February 25, Flame Sergei Makarov sets a franchise record with seven points in one game—a pair of goals and five assists.

1992 – Former Flame Lanny McDonald became the first Calgary player inducted into the Hockey Hall of Fame. Also that year "Badger" Bob Johnson, who coached the Flames from 1982 to 1987 was inducted into the Hockey Hall of Fame.

1993 – Guy Lapointe, a Flame assistant coach and scout, was inducted into the Hockey Hall of Fame.

1994 – Flames formally take over management of the Saddledome.

2000 – Joe Mullen, who played 345 games for the Flames, was inducted into the Hockey Hall of Fame.

2002 – Jarome Iginla becomes the first Flames player ever to lead the NHL in scoring with 96 points and his 52 goals meant he claimed both the Art Ross and Maurice Richard Trophies.

COLORADO AVALANCHE

From Quebec, Colorado got a team beginning to reach the top of its game. The payoff for all the Nordiques' moves and building was a Stanley Cup, but it came in of all places, Denver.

In its very first year in the National Hockey League, the Avalanche—led by new goalie Patrick Roy—gave Denver a professional sports champ. *Merci beaucoup*, Quebec.

But that wasn't the end of it. The Avalanche have won a division every year since coming to their own personal Rocky Mountain High. And the second time the Avalanche made it to the Stanley Cup finals in 2001, well, they won it again. And in doing so, they sent off to retirement Raymond Bourque, one of the league's all-time good guys, with a Cup after more than two decades of trying futilely to win one in Boston.

Think of how all the blue blood franchises—Montreal, Toronto, Boston, New York, Chicago come to mind—are looking enviously at the Avs recent history.

But they'd better get used to it. Two of *The Hockey News* 100 People of Power and Influence in the league this year are Avalanche players—goalkeeper Roy, at No. 13, is the top-ranked player on the list and he's joined by center Peter Forsberg at No. 53 who is considered the game's most complete superstar.

No team in hockey has two players ranked so highly. Most don't even have one in the Top 100. Credit all this talent to Michel Goulet, vice president for player personnel and another man who made that Top 100 list at No. 100. He's good. And so is his team.

FRANCHISE RECORD				
	W	**L**	**T**	**Pts**
Regular Season	815	774	235	1871
Playoffs	113	93		
Stanley Cups	**2** *(1996, 2001)*			

COLORADO AVALANCHE

1979 – As the Quebec Nordiques, the franchise that would become the Colorado Avalanche in 16 years left the World Hockey Association for the NHL.

1980 – The Nordiques make the NHL playoffs for the first time and do so for the next six seasons.

1982 – The Nordiques advance to the Conference Championship series, something they will do again in 1985.

1989 – Guy Lafleur returns to the ice for two seasons as a Nordique.

1991 – Following a fifth straight season missing the playoffs, the Nordiques draft Eric Lindros in what will become one of the most interesting chapters in NHL draft history when Lindros refused to go to Quebec and the Philadelphia Flyers beat out the New York Rangers for his services with what turned out to be seven players, many of whom would be around for the Avalanche's Stanley Cup run five years later.

1995 – NHL announces on May 25th that the Quebec Nordiques have been sold to COMSAT Entertainment Group and the team would be moved to Colorado. The name Avalanche is unveiled August 10.

1996 – On June 10, the Avalanche delivered Denver its first professional sports title, defeating the Florida Panthers in four straight to win the Stanley Cup.

1999 – The Avalanche move from McNichols Sports Arena to the new Pepsi Center October 13.

2000 – The Avalanche closed out the season with a sixth consecutive division title.

2001 – After amassing the best points total since the NHL went to a six-division format (118), the Avs stride through the playoffs to win a second Stanley Cup, with a 3–1 Game 7 defeat of New Jersey.

2002 – The franchise wins an eighth straight divisional title (seven in Colorado) but losses in the Conference Championship.

EDMONTON OILERS

They had a running start from their World Hockey Association days. They had a teen-aged Wayne Gretzky (and they knew how good he was going to be). They had a general manager and coach—Glen Sather—who clearly knew what he was doing.

And they had so many players they almost didn't know what to do with them. No wonder the Edmonton Oilers turned quickly into a dynasty team just four years into their National Hockey League life. They had Mark Messier, Grant Fuhr, Paul Coffey, Jari Kurri and the helmetless Craig MacTavish.

In fact, they still have MacTavish, another of the hot hockey coaches in the league. *The Hockey News* has MacTavish No. 55 on its list of 100 People of Power and Influence in the NHL and one of just four active coaches to make the list. He didn't do badly this past season, leading the Oilers to a 38–28–12–4 record and third place in the Northwest, almost the same as he did with the Oilers the year before.

But as much as you should never say "Never," you can say the Oilers, no matter how much they do right, will never again approach the juggernaut that won five Stanley Cups in seven seasons from 1984 through 1990. Just the way you can say there will never be another Gretzky, a player who would hold 61 NHL records and redefine the game in his image. Throw Messier into the mix and it's not fair to expect anyone to equal that.

They won't.

Sather is gone, for one thing, now trying to right the New York Rangers. And Gretzky's goal these days is to get the Phoenix Coyotes team, where he's the majority partner, to the playoffs.

But for the fans in Northlands Coliseum, where the Oilers won four of their five Cups on home ice, and the Skyreach Centre now where there's a new community ownership group in place, they still have all the jerseys and pennants to remind them of those days when Edmonton was in a hockey world all its own . . .

FRANCHISE RECORD				
	W	**L**	**T**	**Pts**
Regular Season	759	626	199	1717
Playoffs	132	78		
Stanley Cups	**5** *(1984, 1985, 1987, 1988, 1990)*			

EDMONTON OILERS

1972 – The Oilers join the World Hockey Association where they will play for seven seasons.

1979 – Oilers select Mark Messier in the NHL Entry Draft to go along with teenager Wayne Gretzky who they'd already acquired in a trade with the WHA's Indianapolis.

1980 – On February 24, Gretzky becomes the first NHL player to score 100 points in a season before his 20th birthday. Gretzky manages it in just his 61st career game.

1982 – Gretzky scores his 77th goal of the season to break the NHL mark of 76 set by Phil Esposito

1984 – Gretzky extends his NHL-record consecutive point-scoring streak to 51 in a 3–3 tie with New Jersey on January 27.

1984 – Playing in just his 424th career game December 19, Gretzky records two goals and four assists to become the fastest player in NHL history to reach 1,000 points, breaking Guy Lafleur's mark of 725 games.

1984 – After making the playoffs their first four NHL seasons, the Oilers take the first of their five Stanley Cups.

1986 – Edmonton's Paul Coffey scores his 47th and 48th goals of the season April 2 to break Bobby Orr's NHL record for most goals by a defenseman. Orr had 46 goals in 1974–1975.

1988 – In a trade that would rock the NHL world, Gretzky is sent to the big media market of Los Angeles to play for the Kings in a 10-player deal.

1990 – A 4–1 defeat of Boston mirrors the series score as Edmonton—without Gretzky—clinches a fifth Stanley Cup in seven seasons.

1993 – Oilers miss the playoffs for the first time in team history.

2002 – Despite attaining 92 points, the Oilers miss the playoffs, snapping their postseason streak at five.

MINNESOTA WILD

It's hard to believe that the NHL would be without a franchise in hockey-mad Minnesota. That was the situation after the North Stars left fro Dallas and until the NHL would award the Twin Cities an expansion franchise that took the name Wild.

Sounds like the Minnesota Wild should be representing the Sierra Club rather than competing in the wild and wooly National Hockey League and in a division where the Colorado Avalanche makes the biggest noise in the wild Northwest.

Give them time, they say. There was marginal improvement—from 25 wins and 68 points in Year One to 26 wins and 73 points this past year. But when you're a true expansion team, not a team that moved in ready to compete the way Colorado did, you take improvement anywhere you can get it. In 2001–02, the Wild's record was better than seven teams, including Mario Lemieux's Pittsburgh Peguins, conference championship finalists a year earlier.

And you talk about your uniforms. And your colors. And the place you play. For the Wild, situated as they are in the heart of the country's college hockey hotbed, that would be the brand new Xcel Energy Center in downtown St. Paul. For once, the second sister of the Twin Cities has a team that the folks from Minneapolis have to drive east to see.

On the ice Andrew Brunette and Marian Gaborik—the first ever player selected by Minnesota in the Entry Draft—are developing nicely. Brunette's experience is certainly different; he scored the Nashville Predators' first-ever goal, played in the Atlanta Thrashers' inaugural game and scored their first ever power play goal, then in 2001, he signed for his third expansion team—the Wild—although in their second season.

FRANCHISE RECORD				
	W	**L**	**T**	**Pts**
Regular Season	51	74	25	141
Playoffs	0	0		
Stanley Cups	**0**			

MINNESOTA WILD

1967 – Minnesota's first NHL team, the North Stars, debuts with a 27–32–15 record good for fourth place in the West.

1968 – North Stars advance to the playoffs and beat Los Angeles in the first round before falling to St. Louis in the second, both in seven-game series.

1981 – The North Stars reach the Stanley Cup Finals, losing in six games to the Islanders.

1991 – A second Stanley Cup Final ends in a 4–2 series defeat, this time to the Peguins.

1993 – The North Stars announce they will move to Dallas after the season.

1997 – Minnesota Hockey Ventures Group LP is formed by majority owner Bob Naegele Jr. when the partnership is awarded an NHL franchise for St. Paul, where the team will play in the new 18,064-seat Xcel Energy Center in downtown.

1998 – The team unveils its new Wild name and logo January 22, showing a sellout crowd at the Aldrich Arena, Maplewood. The name is the product of a six-month contest that drew thousands of suggestions.

1999 – Next for the Wild came the unveiling of the jersey, November, in the team's colors of Iron Range Red, Forest Green, Harvest Gold and Minnesota Wheat. At the crest of the jersey is a Minnesota Wilderness pictrogram with a wild animal, the North Star, evergreen trees, a red sky, the sun and/or moon and a stream.

1999 – Minnesota hires Doug Risebrough as the team's first executive vice president and general manager September 2.

2000 – Wild announces the hiring of Jacques Lemaire as the team's first coach June 19.

2001 – Wild finish 25–44–13 in the team's first season, good for fifth in the Northwest.

2002 – A measure of improvement in Season 2 as Wild end up 26–35–12–9 for 73 points and another fifth-place finish in the Northwest and out of the playoffs.

VANCOUVER CANUCKS

All the wonderful hockey history in the world did Vancouver little good when the National Hockey League decided to expand in the mid–1960s. Forget those championship Vancouver Millionaire and Maroon teams from the Twenties. What can you do for us now, the league asked.

Not enough, apparently. So while California and Pennsylvania got a pair of expansion franchises each with another going to Minnesota and a final one to Missouri, Vancouver had to wait.

The wait wasn't all that long as the Pacific Northwest got its team three years later in the second wave along with Buffalo. Both are still waiting on their first Stanley Cup. But at least they've each made it to the Finals twice.

And like their East Coast couterparts, Vancouver has certainly been competitive. From the first 16,500 crowd at the the Pacific Coliseum that was the largest ever to see a hockey game in Canada, to the new General Motors Place, they've always had a good place to play. And with the likes of Roger Neilson and Pat Quinn, they've often had someone to show them how. And with players like 1988 draft pick Trevor Linden, Pavel Bure and the $20 million man Mark Messier, they've always had a name or two fans across the continent could connect with.

And now with Linden back home from the New York Islanders, he's been elevated to that Top 100 list, although as *The Hockey News* notes—more for his role as the president of the National Hockey League Players Association than his diminishing 31-year-old presence on the ice.

And no doubt under General Manager Brian Burke, they aren't bad. This past year the Canucks earned 94 points on a 42–30–7–3 record, good for second in the Northwest. Then the buzzsaw that was the champion-to-be Detroit Red Wings ended Vancouver's season in a tight playoff series.

FRANCHISE RECORD				
	W	**L**	**T**	**Pts**
Regular Season	936	1220	368	2258
Playoffs	56	78		
Stanley Cups	0			

VANCOUVER CANUCKS

1915 – First Vancouver team, the Millionaires, wins the Stanley Cup two years before the formation of the National Hockey League. It's the last time that will happen here for 77 seasons and counting.

1970 – Canucks enter the league in the second wave of NHL expansion along with the Buffalo Sabres.

1981 – Roger Neilson comes in to coach the Canucks and takes them up a notch immediately.

1982 – The Canucks knock off Calgary, Los Angeles and Chicago to earn a spot in the Stanley Cup Finals against the New York Islanders where they are sent home in four games by the champs from Long Island.

1984 – Canuck Patrik Sundstrom scores a record seven points in a game February 29 at Boston.

1994 – Canucks reach the Stanley Cup Finals a second time, only to lose 4–3 to a New York Ranger team that had not won the Cup in 54 years.

1995 – Canucks move into their new arena, General Motors Place, on October 9.

1997 – Canucks sign unrestricted free agent Mark Messier on July 28.

1997 – Joining the Mighty Ducks of Anaheim, the Canucks play a two-game series in Tokyo, Japan that marks the first-ever NHL games played outside North America on October 4–5.

1999 – Twins Daniel and Henrik Sedin, both first-round picks, sign with the Canucks on July 28.

Pacific

Mighty Ducks of Anaheim

Dallas Stars

Los Angeles Kings

Phoenix Coyotes

San Jose Sharks

MIGHTY DUCKS OF ANAHEIM

It seemed like a good idea at the time. Have a popular hockey movie come to life down the street from Disneyland for the 1992–1993 season. Disney chairman Michael Eisner's kids liked hockey, didn't they?

So hockey it was in Anaheim. Baseball's Angels would become a partner in 1995 and synergy would be the watchword in Orange County.

If only it were that easy.

Only it never is. You need more than a good idea and a cool logo and mucho marketing. You need athletes. And tough guys. And a coach who can lead and a front office that can find the talent and figure out a way to get them in the building—along with the fans.

And that's important in Southern California where the entertainment and recreation choices are almost too numerous to list.

Well, the Ducks had only the player part of it going for them and only for a bit. And even when they were together, headliners Paul Kariya and Teemu Selanne always looked as they needed something else to get them over the hump. But it never happened. And then Selanne was gone, off to Pacific Division rival San Jose.

And even Duck fans were starting to hint that maybe the team ought to free Kariya, too. Send him off to where he might have a chance to be a winner at last.

Noticing Kariya's inability to make things happen all by himself, *The Hockey News* dropped him from No. 27 a year ago in its Top 100 to No. 70 this past year. He's just 27 so there's time for the smart Kariya to get some help so his talents don't go to waste. But with the top man in the Disney sports empire, Tony Tavares having been let go and then second-term GM Pierre Gauthier following him out the door after another sad season of 29–42–8–3 and a fifth-place finish, coach Bryan Murray got out from behind the bench and moved upstairs.

FRANCHISE RECORD				
	W	**L**	**T**	**Pts**
Regular Season	269	338	88	637
Playoffs	4	11		
Stanley Cups	**0**			

MIGHTY DUCKS OF ANAHEIM

Seems like a long time ago that they were counting the consecutive sellouts at the 17,320-seat Arrowhead Pond. On some nights these days it's almost easier to count the patrons. But the Ducks haven't given up completely, dealing for NHL assists leader Adam Oates after the 2001–02 season.

....

1992 – The Disney Company's *The Mighty Ducks* movie debuts, earning $51 million and becomes the inspiration for Disney's NHL team.

1993 – Team's logo and colors of purple, jade, silver, white with a duck-head face mask unveiled June 7.

1995 – The Mighty Ducks complete a club record 51 straight home sellouts at the 17,320-seast Arrowhead Pond on October 20.

1996 – First Duck to win a major NHL award is Paul Kariya who wins the Lady Byng Trophy after becoming the first Duck to also earn first-team All-NHL honors that season.

1997 – First coach Ron Wilson does not have his contract renewed and is let go at the end of the season.

1999 – Teammates Teemu Selanne and Paul Kariya finish ranked two and three respectively in the NHL scoring charts for the second time in three seasons.

1981 – The North Stars reach the Stanley Cup Finals, losing in six games to the Islanders..

2000 – Announced that head coach Craig Hartcburg has been relieved of his duties.

2001 – Head coach Guy Charron is replaced by Bryan Murray.

2002 – Murray gives up coaching duties to move to front office to replace president and general manager Pierre Gauthier who was fired.

DALLAS STARS

Doesn't it always happen this way? A team puts in a couple of decades of less-than-championsip level play in one town, then all of a sudden, that workmanlike bunch moves on to a new town. And wins a title. So maybe it didn't happen quite that quickly for the North Stars team that left Minnesota after 27 seasons and ended up the Stanley Cup champion Dallas Stars in just in six seasons.

That's hockey.

And it was the ghosts of two franchises in Dallas, actually. The Cleveland Barons had merged with the North Stars 15 years before the move. They also took Mike Modano, the team's No. 1 draft pick in 1988. He's still at it at the age of 31, and one of the league's most marketable players, says *The Hockey News* Top 100 rankings. Modano is down a bit, from No. 50 a year ago to No. 79, but still one of the top dozen or so players who matter.

Now Minnesota had shown that this team had a Stanley Cup run in it with its improbable 1991 drive from fourth place to a spot in the Stanley Cup Finals opposite the Pittsburgh Penguins, who beat them in five.

The next time it was the Stars, with players like Ed Belfour, Derian Hatcher, Joe Nieuwendyk, Brett Hull and Modano, who came home with the Cup. They almost made it two in a row, falling in six games the next year in the finals to New Jersey.

Season 2001-02 was one to forget for Dallas. Not only did the Stars see their run of five consecutive Division titles come to an end, but they also finished four points short of a playoff spot. Cup-winning coach Ken Hitchcock was let go and former LA Kings man Dave Tippett took over.

FRANCHISE RECORD				
	W	**L**	**T**	**Pts**
Regular Season	1118	1206	431	2680
Playoffs	133	127		
Stanley Cups	**1** *(1999)*			

DALLAS STARS

1968 – The North Stars debut with a 27–32–15 record good for fourth place in the West, advancing to the playoffs and beat Los Angeles in the first round before falling to St. Louis in the second, both in seven-game series.

1978 – North Stars merge with the Cleveland Barons.

1988 – Center Mike Modano is the team's first selection in the NHL Entry Draft.

1993 – North Stars announce they will move to Dallas after the season, removing the "North" from the team's name.

1996 – Stars hire Ken Hitchcock as head coach in the middle of the 1995–1996 season.

1999 – Mike Modano becomes the first Star ever to make an NHL postseason all-star team as he is selected second-team as the league's No. 8 scorer.

1999 – Goalie Ed Belfour leads the NHL in save percentage with a .919 mark.

1999 – Under Hitchcock, Stars win the franchise's first-ever Stanley Cup.

2000 – Stars return to the Stanley Cup Finals only to lose in six games to the New Jersey Devils.

2001 – Stars move into their new home, the $325-million American Airlines Arena on the edge of downtown Dallas.

LOS ANGELES KINGS

Kings indeed.

Hockey in Hollywood seemed to be a bad idea.

And then it happened. Wayne Gretzky showed up. And the Kings mattered. As good as it was for the National Hockey League to have a Wayne Gretzky playing in a major media market like Los Angeles, it was good for the major media market of Los Angeles to have Wayne Gretzky show up.

Hockey no longer seemed so other-worldly anymore.

Sure, Hall of Famer Marcel Dionne had come here in 1975 and scored more than 1,300 points but Gretzky made it all matter. And yet the Kings were always more than Gretzky, even if it took Gretzky to make people notice.

In fact, the first class of Kings Hall of Famers honored was in March of 1977. Dionne was in this group, along with Dave Taylor, Rogie Vachon, Butch Goring, broadcaster Bob Miller and trainer Pete Demers.

Now a part of the Anschutz Sports Group along with Staples Center where they play, these Kings couldn't be any more a part of the establishment.

And they might just on the edge of breaking through. If only they can figure a way to get past a Colorado team that has eliminated them in 4–3 series the past two seasons. A part of the first expansion in 1967–68, the Kings have had a major impact as missionaries for the game in the Sunbelt and in the West. And although they've only made it to the Stanley Cup Finals once, in 1993, longtime Los Angeles sports observers will tell you that the excitement those Kings generated in that run was very memorable.

Even in laid-back LA.

Hockey can do that to you.

FRANCHISE RECORD				
	W	**L**	**T**	**Pts**
Regular Season	1100	1255	402	2513
Playoffs	65	105		
Stanley Cups	0			

LOS ANGELES KINGS

1975 – Hall of Famer Marcel Dionne arrives and goes on to score more than 1,300 points in a dozen years with the Kings.

1975 – Goaltender Rogie Vachon is named Player of the Year by The Hockey News after posting a 27–14–13 record with six shutouts and a 2.24 goals against average.

1985 – Vachon is honored for his seven seasons (1971–1978) with the team as the first King to have his jersey retired on February 14.

1988 – Wayne Gretzky—along with Marty McSorley—is traded to the Kings August 9 for two players, three first-round draft picks and cash.

1989 – Gretzky becomes the first NHL player to win an award nine times as he earns the Hart Trophy June 6.

1993 – The Kings reach their first Stanley Cup Final, but the Montreal Canadiens take the spoils in six games.

1994 – Gretzky scores career goal No. 802 to pass Gordie Howe as the NHL's all-time leading goalscorer with a score against Vancouver at the Forum.

1996 – Gretzky departs Los Angeles for St. Louis before moving onto the New York Rangers to finish out his NHL career.

1999 – Kings play their first game in the new 10,110-seat Staples Center in near downtown on October 10 against the Boston Bruins.

2000 – "The Voice of the Kings" Bob Miller is honored for his nearly three decades of broadcasting with the Foster Hewitt Memorial Award at the Hockey Hall of Fame induction ceremonies on November 13.

PHOENIX COYOTES

From Manitoba to Arizona, the Coyotes have come a long way. And we're not even talking about how the Phoenix team secured a pretty good name around this game—Wayne Gretzky—as their managing partner. He may no longer be playing but *The Hockey News* designates Gretzky, 40, as their No. 3 man on the Top 100 People of Power and Influence in the National Hockey League.

Maybe it was their shared World Hockey Association roots that drew Gretzky here. Whatever it was, having him calling the shots can't hurt. See what it did for Team Canada in the Olympics.

And the former Winnipeg Jets have always seemed to have had a way of identifying talent. Dale Hawerchuk was an inspired first pick in the Entry Draft in 1981. Teemu Selanne and Nikolai Khabibulin started in the organization. So did Keith Tkachuk. But Winnipeg was always a small-market team and though their record was consistent, it was never better than average. The Jets' best NHL finish was second in their division (1982 and '85). And the franchise has yet to play a Conference Championship series.

So now if Gretzky can keep the talent coming and the Coyotes can live up to those new Southwestern-themed colors of forest green, brick red, sand, sienna and purple, all will be well in America West Arena. In fact, it hasn't been too bad here recently. The Coyotes have finished 21 games over .500 the past two seasons.

The Coyotes' total of 95 points in 2001–02 tied the second best in franchise history, but a third playoff series victory in 18 trips to the postseason proved beyond them.

FRANCHISE RECORD				
	W	**L**	**T**	**Pts**
Regular Season	762	848	237	1714
Playoffs	29	63		
Stanley Cups	0			

PHOENIX COYOTES

1971 – Winnipeg Jets open in the World Hockey Association November 1.

1979 – The Jets join the National Hockey League for their first season with three other WHA teams.

1980 – Finishing with a 20–49–11 record the first season, the Jets fail to make the fifth-place but average 13,296 fans at home.

1996 The Jets add "A Season To Remember" to their red,white and blue jerseys in their final year in the Canadian city.

1996 – The look was completely different for the new team—the Coyotes—in its new Southwestern home. Team colors became forest green, brick red, sand, sienna and purple.

1996 – Coyotes debut in America West Arena October 10 in front of a sellout crowd of 16,210.

1997 – Coyote Mike Gartner scored his 30th goal to give him an NHL record 17 seasons scoring 30 or more goals.

1997 – Gartner becomes the fifth NHL player (with Wayne Gretzky, Gordie Howe, Phil Esposito and Marcel Dionne) to score 700 goals on December 14.

1999 – For the first time in team history, four Coyotes play in an NHL All-Star Game—Nikolai Khabibulin, Teppo Numminen, Jeremy Roenick and Keith Tkachuk.

2000 – Wayne Gretzky becomes managing partner of hockey operations for the Coyotes as the NHL's greatest player assumes both an ownership and managerial role in the team.

SAN JOSE SHARKS

They've been up and they've been down. They've played in San Francisco's Cow Palace and their own Compaq Center of San Jose. They've been miserable, living through an NHL record 17-game losing streak. And they've engineered the greatest one-season turnaround in NHL history—a 58-point improvement from Season Two to Season Three. They're the San Jose Sharks, the Bay Area's gift to the National Hockey League, or is it the other way around?

They are the good fortune that the Gund brothers—George and Gordon—owners of the Cleveland Barons and Minnesota North Stars had coming their way for putting so much into the league. No wonder the NHL looked favorably toward the Gunds when the 1992 expansion came around. The Bay Area team would be theirs.

And the Gunds decided the team would be in San Jose, not San Francisco or Oakland. At last the folks down San Jose way would have a major pro sports franchise to pull for.

And now that they've managed to go 30 games above .500 over the past two seasons, finishing first in the Pacific Division in 2001–2002, There's a lot to root for. The arrival of the fabulous Finn Teemu Selanne from Anaheim in March 2001 was the trade that put the Sharks over the top and fans in Northern California cheered when it was announced he had re-signed for the 2002–03 season.

General Manager Dean Lombardi has been with the Sharks since they started play, moving from Assistant GM to Director of Hockey Operations in June 1992 and succeeding Chuck Grillio in 1996. Manager Darryl Sutter enters his 20th season in hockey with the amazing record of never having failed to make the playoffs.

FRANCHISE RECORD				
	W	**L**	**T**	**Pts**
Regular Season	311	446	100	735
Playoffs	29	38		
Stanley Cups	0			

SAN JOSE SHARKS

1990 – Brothers George and Gordon Gund are granted an NHL franchise for the Bay Area on May 9.

1991 – Playing at the Cow Palace in San Francisco, the Sharks win their first NHL game 4–3 over Calgary October 8.

1992 – Rob Gaudreau scores the team's first hat trick December 3 in a 7–5 loss to Hartford at the Cow Palace.

1993 – The 17,496-seat San Jose Arena (now the Compaq Center at San Jose) hosts its first hockey game September 30 as Sharks beat the New York Islanders 4–2 in a preseason game.

1994 – The Sharks amaze the hockey world in upsetting Detroit's Red Wings four games to three in the team's first trip to the Stanley Cup playoffs.

1995 – Showing their Silicon Valley roots, the Sharks become the first NHL team to have a home page—www.sjsharks.com—on the World Wide Web.

1996 – Owner George Gund is named winner of the NHL's Lester Patrick Trophy for outstanding service to hockey in the United States.

1997 – Sharks host their first—and the NHL's 47th—All-Star Game January 18.

1999 – Owen Nolan and Jeff Friesen record the first multiple hat tricks in the same game for the Sharks in a 7–1 romp over the Blackhawks October 4.

2000 – Sharks stun the President Trophy-winning St. Louis Blues in seven games in the first round of the Stanley Cup playoffs.

2001 – NHL superstar Teemu Selanne arrives from Anaheim.

2002 – Sharks win their first Division title and set a franchise record with 99 points becoming one of few teams ever to increase their points tally every year for seven seasons.

ED BELFOUR

Name: Edward J. Belfour
Born: April 21, 1965, Carman, Manitoba
Catches: Left
Height: 5-11
Weight: 192

"When I was growing up, you dreamed of playing in the NHL, but you also developed a craving to play for your country. There was just something so special about having the maple leaf on your sweater."

—Ed Belfour

Fated to be a National Hockey League goalie, it seems, Ed "the Eagle" Belfour has carried it out with flair. As a youngster in Manitoba, he drew pictures of Tony Esposito and wore the No. 20 of his first goalkeeping coach Vladislav Tretiak. Belfour seemd to know where he was headed.

And it looked like he was going to get there quickly. In his second year with the Chicago Blackhawks just a few of seasons after leading the University of North Dakota to an NCAA title, Belfour did it all. He played a league-high 74 games, set a record-tying mark of 43 wins, led the Hawks to a record 49 wins and the President's Trophy while winning the Calder Trophy as a the rookie of the year, the Vezina Trophy as top goaltender and the Jennings Trophy for lowest goals against average.

Then came the playoffs where all Belfour did was record a 12-4 mark, leading the Blackhawks past the Oilers and into the finale where they lost to the Pittoburgh Penguins as the Eagle recorded a league-best 2.47 GAA.

Not bad for starters. But it wasn't until 1998–1999—in a starting-over season with Dallas—that he won his first Stanley Cup after eight years in Chicago and another in San Jose. By then he'd chalked up two more Vezina Trophies (in 1992–1993, 1994–1995), five All-Star appearances and two more Jennings Trophies. He's also become just the fourth goalkeeper ever to record better than a 3.00 GAA for 10 seasons of 40 games or more.

Belfour's special Stanley Cup season was just that. He recorded nine shutouts, led the NHL with a 1.88 GAA and then went on to play flawlessly in the Stanley Cup playoffs. Belfour's career total of 58 shutouts is second only to Patrick Roy's 61 among active NHL goalies, proving how well served he's been by emulating Esposito's butterfly style.

In the summer of 2002 he signed a deal to play for the Toronto Maple Leafs.

.

CAREER TOTALS										
GPI	GS	W	L	T	Min.	GA	GAA	SA	Sv%	SHO
735	696*	364	242	100	42327	1743	2.47	18426	.905	58

JOHNNY BOWER

Name: John William Bower
Born: November 8, 1924, Prince Albert, Saskatchewan
Catches: Left
Height: 5-11
Weight: 189

"If you don't know now, you never will."

—Johnny Bower, when asked on his retirement if he'd finally say how old he was (he was 44)

To look at the first decade or so of Johnny Bower's career would be to dismiss the fearless guy from Prince Albert, Saskatchewan as one of those special players who did great in the minor leagues but just came along at the wrong time.

And so it would seem Bower did. After having his junior career delayed for four years of service in World War II, Bower then became the best player in the American Hockey League. For eight years, he led the Cleveland Barons.

And then Bower got a break, getting called up to play a full season with the New York Rangers in 1953–1954. Then it was back to the AHL and there he stayed for three more starring turns in Cleveland and Providence. So there you have it—World War II and 14 years in the minors and that should just about be it for a player's career.

Not exactly a fast start to a Hall of Fame finish. Or even to an NHL pension.

Then it happened. In 1958, Bower got a second chance in the big leagues and made the most of it even though he didn't want to really even try at the advanced age of 34.

But he made the most of it joining the then-last-place Toronto Maple Leafs. He went on to earn his first Vezina Trophy while being named NHL first-team All-Star in 1960–1961.

In his 12 NHL seasons in Toronto, Bower would go on to win another Vezina (sharing it with Terry Sawchuk in 1965) and lead the ever-improving Maple Leafs to four Stanley Cup championships. The man who looked like he'd never get a chance was inducted into the Hockey Hall of Fame in 1976.

Refusing to wear a mask despite all sorts of injures to his face and teeth, Bower developed the poke-check maneuver that had him diving head-first toward the puck, knocking it off an opponent's stick no matter the personal harm.

When he retired in 1970, he was the oldest goalie ever to play in the NHL. The man who came to the party late made up for it by not leaving until later than anyone had ever stayed.

CAREER TOTALS										
GPI	GS	W	L	T	Min.	GA	GAA	SA	Sv%	SHO
552	0*	250	195	90	32016	1340	2.51	0*	-*	37

FRANK BRIMSEK

Name: Francis Charles Brimsek
Born: September 26, 1913, Eveleth, Minnesota
Died: November 11, 1998
Catches: Left
Height: 5-9
Weight: 170

"I'll never forget the reception that first night (in Boston)—total silence. Not a sound. Wow. Then I knew I was on trial and that I'd be on the next train out of town if I had a bad night."

—Frank Brimsek

So you've just been brought into town to succeed a star player who's been sold for the big money—in 1939, anyway—of $15,000. And no one knows who you are. All they know is that you're not all that impressive a specimen at 5-feet-9 and 170 pounds. So what do you do when they just stare at you?

All Frankie Brimsek did for his Boston Bruin debut was record three straight shutouts in his first four games. The scoreless streak of 231 minutes and 54 seconds Brimsek recorded was a new National Hockey League record.

By then, even if they didn't know his name, the Boston fans had a new one for the young man from Eveleth, Minnesota—"Mr. Zero." He would become the first American-born player to make it big in the NHL.

Mr. Zero, indeed. After giving up a goal to end his first streak, Brimsek started another three shutout streak. For those of you keeping score, that was two record-breaking three-game shutout streaks as Brimsek, just 23, won seven of his first eight games.

And the Bruins? They won the Stanley Cup that 1939 season as Brimsek joined in the winning with his own Calder Trophy and Vezina Trophy for rookie of the year and top goaltender respectively.

It turns out there was no break-in period for the young Bruin. He didn't stay long. He led the Bruins to another Stanley Cup in 1941 and missed a couple of seasons for World War II. And then after a final season with Chicago's Blackhawks after having been traded from Boston in 1948–1949, he retired with 40 career shutouts.

In 1948, the year before he was traded, Brimsek was second in voting for the Hart Trophy as the NHL's Most Valuable Player.

CAREER TOTALS										
GPI	GS	W	L	T	Min.	GA	GAA	SA	Sv%	SHO
514	0*	252	182	80	31210	1404	2.70	0*	-*	40

TURK BRODA

Name: Walter Edward "Turk" Broda
Born: May 15, 1914, Brandon, Manitoba
Died: October 17, 1972
Catches: Left
Height: 5-9
Weight: 190

"He could play in a tornado and never blink an eye."
—Toronto Coach Jack Adams

It wasn't supposed to happen for Walter "Turk" Broda, not the way it did. He was headed for retirement, actually, after World War II but decided to stay another year. And another. And another.

By the time Turk Broda finally did pack it in in 1951, the formerly fat kid from Brandon, Manitoba would be able to look back on a career that saw him lead his Toronto Maple Leafs to five Stanley Cups—four after he said he was gone.

As a result, Broda would be considered one of the great goalies of all time in the National Hockey League. Even if he did have to fight in a very public way a weight problem most of his life. One way the happy Broda did that was with an outgoing sense of humor.

"The Leafs pay me for my work in practices," he once joked, "and I throw in the games for free."

He would even be suspended when he didn't hit his target weight but always it seemed he had fun with it.

Broda would lead his Maple Leafs to three straight post-war Stanley Cups from 1947 through 1949 and then a final one—his fifth—in a famed all-overtime five-game series against arch-rival Montreal that inspired this quote from Maurice Richard.

"I couldn't beat him. Toe Blake couldn't. None of the Canadiens could."

Twice times Broda was voted the NHL's best goaltender (in 1941 and 1948) and he would complete his career with 62 shutouts and a 2.53 goals-against average. Broda would be inducted into the Hockey Hall of Fame in 1967. He died five years later at the age of 58.

CAREER TOTALS										
GPI	GS	W	L	T	Min.	GA	GAA	SA	Sv%	SHO
629	0*	302	224	101	38167	1609	2.53	0*	-*	62

MARTIN BRODEUR

Name: Martin Pierre Brodeur
Born: May 6, 1972, Montreal, Quebec
Catches: Left
Height: 6-2
Weight: 205

"I have always tried to stay composed even when you have great pressure like the Olympics. When you play at this level, sometimes you get overexcited."
—Martin Brodeur

The numbers have always been in Martin Brodeur's favor. But then so have the genes.

Not a bad idea for a youngster growing up in Canada who wants to be a National Hockey League goalie to grow up with a father who was a national team goaltender himself.

Some things are better passed down from father to son the way Denis Brodeur, a 1956 bronze medalist for Canada, did with son Martin in those early days in the family's Montreal home. Denis was a longtime photographer for both the Montreal Expos and Canadiens.

So it comes naturally to Martin Brodeur, although having a goals-against average never higher than 2.45 in his career takes more than good breeding for the New Jersey Devil whose idol has been Patrick Roy.

And Brodeur just keeps getting better. His 1.88 GAA in 1996–1997 was the lowest in the league in 25 years—since Tony Esposito's 1.77.

Martin Brodeur was the first goalie since Ken Dryden to record 10 shutouts in a season and he's done that twice (1996 97, 1997 98). Only Grant Fuhr's 79 games exceeded Brodeur's 77 in 1995–96 and he led the league with 70 in 1998–99.

Not that anyone's surprised. Brodeur won the Calder Trophy in 1993–94 after a stellar rookie season.

As a result of Brodeur's netminding, the Devils have the first two Stanley Cups in franchise history (1995, 2000), both series that featured his hot goaltending. He's also played in six All-Star games and won a pair of Jennings Trophies (1997, 1998).

Then there is his famed offensive ability that resulted in Brodeur scoring a playoff goal against the Montreal Canadiens in 1997. This is a guy who truly can do it all. And that includes winning an Olympic gold medal which he did in 2002 on Team Canada ended a 50-year barren streak in Salt Lake City.

CAREER TOTALS										
GPI	GS	W	L	T	Min.	GA	GAA	SA	Sv%	SHO
592	581	324	168	85	34582	1272	2.21	14329	.911	55

BYRON DAFOE

Name: Byron Jaromir Dafoe
Born: February 25, 1971, Sussex, England
Catches: Left
Height: 5-11
Weight: 200

"They don't have me on either side (in the Canada-Europe All-Star Game). I'm thinking I could play for Mars, but I can't play for either."
- British-born Boston goalie Byron Dafoe who grew up in British Columbia

It took Byron Dafoe only 21 years to get from Great Britain—where he was born—to the National Hockey League—where he made a one-minute, 1992–93 debut with the Washington Capitals.

Of course it helped immensely that Dafoe grew up in British Columbia instead of his Sussex, England birthplace.

His traveling days were hardly over, however. After three seasons mostly in the American Hockey League, he moved on to the Los Angeles Kings for a couple of years, earning his first regular job after just 200 games in the minors. Then it was back across the country to Boston where Dafoe has just finished his fifth season with the Bruins.

Dafoe made an immediate improvement on the Bruins in his first year, elevating Boston by 30 points in his 65 games with a 2.24 goals-against average and six shutouts.

That 1998–99 season was just the start of the new-look Byron Dafoe. His GAA was down to 1.99 and his shutouts were up to a league-best 10, Martin Brodeur territory.

A knee injury in the 1999–00 season caused him to miss almost half of the next two seasons, but Dafoe came back with a strong 2001–02 campaign, recording a 2.21 GAA. four sutouts and a .907 save percentage for the playoff-bound Bruins.

Dafoe was nominated for the Vezina Trophy after his sensational 1998–99 season that saw him named a second-team All-Star, his first-ever All-Star selection.

CAREER TOTALS										
GPI	GS	W	L	T	Min.	GA	GAA	SA	Sv%	SHO
380	365	162	148	54	21610	935	2.60	9926	.906	26

KEN DRYDEN

Name: Kenneth Wayne Dryden
Born: August 8, 1947, Hamilton, Ontario
Catches: Left
Height: 6-4
Weight: 205

This was only the second time in my life I'd seen myself on television and it shattered a lot of illusions. What a sobering experience. I always thought of myself as Nureyev on ice. But on TV, I realized I was a dum truck."

—Ken Dryden

Of course Ken Dryden should have been as good as he was. He was bigger than any goaltender who came before him in the net at 6-foot-4 and 205 pounds.

And he was surely smarter. The Ivy League Cornell grad would go on to earn a law degree and even take a year off from the National Hockey League to practice as an attorney.

But when he got back to his on-ice profession, Dryden was the best there was. He has the numbers to prove it.

Numbers like six (that's how many Stanley Cups he earned with the Canadiens) and five (the number of Vezina Trophies he won as the NHL's best goalie). And another five (the number of times he was named first-team All-Star).

But as always with the cerebral Dryden, his ability to think the game was right there with his ability to play it. Since he's retired from the ice, Dryden has written a pair of critically acclaimed hockey books—*The Game* and *Home Game*.

And now he's being credited with reviving the Toronto Maple Leafs in his hometown as the team's general manager starting in 1997 after a varied career that included teaching, broadcasting, writing and a stint in the Ministry of Education.

Should we be surprised? Ever since Dryden led the Canadiens to a Stanley Cup title in his first season in 1970–71 after playing just six regular season games, he seems to have always been where the action was.

How many goaltenders have ever won a Conn Smythe Trophy as the outstanding player in the Stanley Cup playoffs before winning the Calder Trophy as rookie of the year. Or the Vezina Trophy as top goaltender?

None, until Dryden came along, although he quickly made up for that by taking home the Calder the next season and his first Vezina the season after that.

Then he went off to be a lawyer for a year. For the next four years, Montreal won the Stanley Cup, Dryden won the Vezina Trophy as the NHL's top goalie and was named first-team All-Star all four seasons.

CAREER TOTALS										
GPI	GS	W	L	T	Min.	GA	GAA	SA	Sv%	SHO
397	0*	258	57	74	23352	870	2.24	0*	-*	46

BILL DURNAN

Name: William Ronald Durnan
Born: January 22, 1916, Toronto, Ontario
Died: October 31, 1972
Catches: Right
Height: 6-0
Weight: 190

"It (being ambidextrous) was a tremendous asset and I owe that gift to Steve Faulkner, one of my coaches in a church league in Toronto when I was just a youngster. Steve showed me how to switch the stick from one hand to the other. It wasn't easy at first because I was so young and the stick seemed so heavy. But Steve kept after me and gradually the stick became lighter and I could switch it automatically."
—Bill Durnan

Quality, not quantity.

How often you were told that and paid absolutely no attention?

Bill Durnan , however, believed every word of it. He must have, because the National Hockey League Hall of Famer surely lived as if he did.

The Toronto native played seven sensational seasons in the NHL and left a legacy that many contend makes him as good as any goalie who ever played the game.

Not that Bill Durnan hadn't played a lot of hockey when he retired at the age of 35 on top of the hockey world. In the days of the original six teams, Durnan was just another potential talent who no one in the NHL knew could play.

Durnan put in 13 seasons of organized hockey on top of the seven he put in with the Montreal Canadiens.

But how he played when he finally got the chance.

Durnan didn't get to be a rookie in the NHL until he was 27 but he opened with four straight Vezina Trophies as the league's best goalie with the lowest goals-against average all four years, not to mention four first-team All-Star selections, a pair of Stanley Cups (1944, 1946). In that first season, Durnan topped the NHL in games played, wins and goals-against average in the regular season and the playoffs. He finished runner-up for the Calder Trophy for Rookie of the Year.

And for the first time in 13 seasons, Montreal had a Stanley Cup for the Forum fans to celebrate.

One other thing. Durnan did double-duty with his hockey stick, going from the right to left and back as the occasion called for him in his uniquely ambidextrous way. But by 1950 he was gone. Seven seasons, six times he was the best goalie in the NHL. Not bad.

No wonder he was inducted into the Hockey Hall of Fame in 1963.

CAREER TOTALS										
GPI	GS	W	L	T	Min.	GA	GAA	SA	Sv%	SHO
383	0*	208	112	62	22945	901	2.36	0*	-*	34

TONY ESPOSITO

Name: Anthony James Esposito
Born: April 23, 1943, Sault Ste. Marie, Ontario
Catches: Right
Height: 5-11
Weight: 190

"Tony 'O' revolutionized goaltending in the NHL with his legs-open 'butterfly' style and his spectacular flop-on-the-ice saves during the 16 years he spent in the league."
—Legends of hockey.net

It's amazing how many of the great goalies in hockey history wasted absolutely no time in showing how good they could be.

Tony Esposito, for example, surprised the National Hockey League with his Chicago Blackhawk rookie season in 1969–70. He could have been a Montreal Canadien that year. He'd played 13 games with the Canadiens the season before, but the Blackhawks claimed him in the Interleague Draft.

Then Tony Esposito put in his own claim—for the Hockey Hall of Fame. His butterfly style and quick glove hand made him tough to beat. And he was tough. At 5-feet-11 and 190 pounds, Esposito looked and acted like the football halfback he almost became.

It didn't take long for him to prove he'd picked the right sport.

Here's how the first full NHL season for the little brother of Phil Esposito went. He won an NHL best 38 games, earned both the Calder Trophy as rookie of the year and the Vezina Trophy as the best goalie, was named first-team All-Star and delivered an unbelievable modern day record of 15 shutouts.

The former Michigan Tech star from Sault Ste. Marie clearly knew how to play this game. A two-time All-American in college who led his Tech team to an NCAA title, he would only get better. In his third NHL season, Esposito's goals-against average dropped to an unbelievable 1.77.

By the time he retired in 1984 as that NHL season's only player over 40, he was third in goalie wins with 423 and his 76 shutouts were seventh-best. Four years later Tony "O" was inducted into the Hockey Hall of Fame. He is one of the few goalies to have his number retired, an honor the Blackhawks awarded him for his 15 seasons in Chicago.

CAREER TOTALS										
GPI	GS	W	L	T	Min.	GA	GAA	SA	Sv%	SHO
886	0*	423	306	151	52585	2563	2.92	1825*	.874*	76

GRANT FUHR

Name: Grant S. Fuhr
Born: September 28, 1962, Spruce Grove, Alberta
Catches: Right
Height: 5-10
Weight: 201

"He's made more big saves than any goalie over the last 15 years. He really has no weakness."
—Mark Messier

You wouldn't think it was a special blessing for a future hockey superstar to be born in Spruce Grove, Alberta.

But you'd be wrong. Just ask Grant Fuhr.

Before he played for Glen Sather and won five Stanley Cup championships, Fuhr was fortunate to play peewee hockey for Glenn Hall, a Hockey Hall of Fame goalie who would kickstart Fuhr's career.

He became the classic standup goalie with a great glove, terrific reflexes and—as teammate Mark Messier said—"unbelievable athleticism." Injuries—one listing documents 28 in all—would take their toll in his second decade and there would be weight problems to battle. But during his first decade through the 1980s, he was something special. He showed it right from the start after being drafted by Edmonton in 1981.

The Oilers' immediate improvement only prepared the way for their first Stanley Cup in 1984, and then the ones in 1985, 1987, 1988 and 1990. During that period, Fuhr won a Vezina Trophy, shared a Jennings Trophy, was named first-team All-Star a couple of times, won an All-Star Game MVP award and was ranked as high as the No. 2 goalie in hockey three different seasons.

He's been listed as high as 10th in the top 50 goalies on some surveys.

His records include most games by a goalie in a season (79), most consecutive games by a goalie (76), most playoff wins in a season (16) and most assists in a season (14).

After a six-month drug suspension by the NHL following a positive test for cocaine in 1990, Fuhr would start a decade of travels across the NHL, first to Toronto, followed by Buffalo, Los Angeles and Calgary.

CAREER TOTALS										
GPI	GS	W	L	T	Min.	GA	GAA	SA	Sv%	SHO
868	441*	403	295	114	48945	2756	3.38	24379	.886	25

CHUCK GARDINER

Name: Charles Robert Gardiner
Born: December 31, 1904, Edinburgh, Scotland
Died: June 13, 1934
Catches: Right
Weight: 176

"The reason I became a goalkeeper was that I was a poor skater."

—Chuck Gardiner

He was seven when his family moved to Winnipeg, Manitoba from Edinburgh, Scotland, but Chuck Gardiner got a nickname that would last.

The "Wandering Scotsman" is what they called the Chicago Black Hawks goaltender for his eccentric movements out of the net as he cut down the angles of the shooters. No one had ever thought to do that before.

Maybe it helped to have been born in Europe because what Gardiner did clearly worked. After a sensational junior hockey career, Gardiner got his shot with Chicago in only its second NHL season.

His first season was good. His second was sensational, with five shutouts and a 1.85 goals-against average. Observers say how smart he seemed to be in going against shooters one-on-one as he often outguessed them.

It was the combination of quick thinking and quick hands and feet that made Gardiner so tough. In 1930–31 he recorded 12 shutouts and his GAA was down to 1.73. The next year he earned a Vezina Trophy as the NHL's best goalie.

Then came 1933–34 and Gardiner's selection as team captain. It was his sixth straight season when he would play every minute except for the final playoff game when he had to be replaced before Chicago's first Stanley Cup title.

In less than two months, Gardiner was gone at the age of 29, the result of a fatal brain tumor.

Despite just seven NHL seasons, Gardiner was one of the original class of Hockey Hall of Fame inductees in 1945. In 316 regular season games, Gardiner had 42 shutouts and a 2.02 GAA.

CAREER TOTALS										
GPI	GS	W	L	T	Min.	GA	GAA	SA	Sv%	SHO
316	0*	112	152	52	19687	664	2.02	0*	-*	42

EDDIE GIACOMIN

Name: Edward Giacomin
Born: June 6, 1939, Sudbury, Ontario
Catches: Left
Height: 5-11
Weight: 180

"I remember having such an empty feeling. I had given 10 years of my life to that team."

—Eddie Giacomin on learning he'd been waived by the Rangers

Between tough times at tryouts where he was rejected as a young player due to a scary kitchen stove explosion that burned his legs badly, Eddie Giacomin would never wear a "Can't Miss" tag. He was lucky to get a chance.

Then it would be 11 long seasons—including six with the Providence Reds in the American Hockey League—before Giacomin would make it into the National Hockey League. But he made it as a 26-year-old New York Ranger rookie.

By the time he left the Rangers, Giacomin was one the best-loved Rangers of all time. Not bad for a kid from right outside Sudbury, Ontario, who had stumbled so often on the way up. When he finally made it, in his first full season in 1966–67, Giacomin helped the Rangers to their first playoff spot in five campaigns—a level they achieved in the remaining years he played in New York, including—in 1971–72—a run to the Stanley Cup Finals.

All Giacomin did his second season was record an NHL-best nine shutouts and earn a spot on the first-team All-Stars. He would go on to play an amazing 274 games between 1966–67 and 1969–70, leading the NHL in games and minutes played all four seasons and in wins the first three.

Giacomin also managed to show off his skating in front of the net, going farther out from the goal with the puck front than anyone before him.

Maybe that's why Giacomin came so close to becoming the first goalie to score in the NHL, something he managed to do twice.

He was let go by the Rangers in 1975-76 and but returned to shut out his old team for Detroit in an emotional first game that had Rangers fans rooting for Giacomin over the home team. Two years later he retired with a 289-208-97 record and 54 shutouts. In 1987 he was inducted into the Hockey Hall of Fame.

CAREER TOTALS										
GPI	GS	W	L	T	Min.	GA	GAA	SA	Sv%	SHO
610	0*	289	208	97	35693	1675	2.82	0*	-*	54

GEORGE HAINSWORTH

Name: George Hainsworth
Born: June 26, 1895, Toronto, Ontario
Died: October 9, 1950
Catches: Left
Height: 5-6
Weight: 150

"I'm sorry I can't put on a show like some of the other goaltenders. I can't look excited because I'm not. I can't shout at other players because that's not my style. I can't dive on easy shots and make them look hard. I guess all I can do is stop pucks."

— George Hainsworth

The Hockey Hall of Fame photo of George Hainsworth says it all. The large Montreal Canadiens "C" on his sweater seems almost bigger than the man wearing it. And that's just about right.

At all of 5-feet-6 and 150 pounds, the Toronto native was one of the few men who dominated the early years of hockey in the net and he did so with a style in goal that seemed almost casual and unconcerned.

And dominate the game Hainsworth did. How about just one example of his dominance. In a 44-game National Hockey League season in 1928–1929, Hainsworth recorded 22 shutouts while giving up just 43 goals. Sure, that was a different time. But 22 shutouts in 44 games is good goaltending in any era.

No wonder Hainsworth won the Vezina Trophy as the league's best goaltender the first three years that award was given from 1927 through 1929.

Aln 1000 and 1001, he won the Stanley Cup, recording a 1.05 GAA. Hainsworth was durable too, playing in all but two games in his seven-season Montreal career. After an even-up trade with Toronto for fellow netminder Lorne Chabot he was an ever-present for the Maple Leafs the next three seasons, even leading the league in minutes played in 1933–34.

His 1.93 goals-against average was tied for the best in league history when Hainsworth retired in 1937. He was selected for the Hockey Hall of Fame in 1961.

CAREER TOTALS										
GPI	GS	W	L	T	Min.	GA	GAA	SA	Sv%	SHO
465	0*	246	145	74	29087	937	1.93	0*	-*	94

GLENN HALL

Name: Glenn Henry Hall
Born: October 3, 1931, Humboldt, Saskatchewan
Catches: Left
Height: 5-11
Weight: 180

"Hall's brilliance between the pipes was recognized as he won the Conn Smythe in 1968 even though his St. Louis Blues fell to the Montreal Canadiens in the Cup finals."

- HockeySandwich.com

When they call you "Mr. Goalie," you better be good.

Glenn Hall was good. No, he was great.

He had to be after inventing, then perfecting, a style of goaltending they called "the butterfly." Not exactly the kind of reference you'd expect in a rough-and-tumble game like hockey.

The proof was in the results. And Hall had plenty of those to point to in his durable 18 National Hockey League seasons that saw him set a goaltenders' record for 502 consecutive games played.

The lifelong farmer from Humboldt, Saskatchewan was so good, he retired three times—in 1966 from the Chicago Blackhawks, and in 1969 and 1971 from the St. Louis Blues.

Someone always wanted Hall back. And no wonder, the man could flop on the ice without ever becoming one. His career 84 assists trailed only Terry Sawchuk and George Hainsworth in NHL history.

In a quick recital of Hall's honors, awards and accomplishments, Hall led the Blackhawks to their first Stanley Cup for 23 years in 1961, won the Calder Trophy as the league's best rookie with 12 shutouts when a Red Wing in 1956, won three Vezina Trophies as the NHL's best goalie, led the league in shutouts six times, was named first-team All-Star seven times (and played in 13 All-Star Games) and won the Conn Smythe Trophy in 1968 for leading St. Louis to a Stanley Cup runnerup spot.

He was inducted into the Hockey Hall of Fame in 1975 with an NHL career average of 2.49 goals-against. In the first two Goaltender Survey votes in 1994 and 1995, Hall was voted the game's No. 5 all-time goalie.

CAREER TOTALS										
GPI	GS	W	L	T	Min.	GA	GAA	SA	Sv%	SHO
906	0*	407	326	163	53484	2222	2.49	0*	-*	84

DOMINIK HASEK

Name: Dominik Hasek
Born: January 29, 1965, Pardubice, Czech Republic
Catches: Left
Height: 6-2
Weight: 180

"I am not afraid to stop the puck with my head. I try to do it sometimes even in practice; not every day but once in a while."

– Dominik Hasek

Dominik Hasek had a pretty good 16 months between February 1998 and June 1999. All he did was lead his Czech Republic team to an Olympic upset gold medal against the likes of Canada, the USA and Russia.

Then he carried his Buffalo Sabres almost all the way to a Stanley Cup. His improbable saves were the main reason the Sabres nearly won their first Cup that year against Dallas.

For that accomplishment, Hasek won the Hart Trophy as the National Hockey League's Most Valuable Player, only the fifth goalie to win it. His 1.95 goals-against average in 1993–94 had been the first below 2.00 in the NHL in 20 seasons since Bernie Parent managed it for the Philadelphia Flyers. And he was the first European to do so.

But the man from Paradubice, Czech Republic, who seemed to specialize in lifting almost hopeless causes moved to the other end of the talent spectrum. He earned his $8 million annual salary between the pipes for Detroit where he finally won the Stanley Cup that had eluded him in Buffalo.

He was "The Dominator" before he got to Detroit. In "Hockeytown" it was "The Dominator Plus", the owner of five Vezina Trophies as the NHL's best goalie and another Hart Trophy as MVP, Hasek is the first goalie ever to do that two years in a row.

In 1997–98 with 13 shutouts, Hasek came close to Tony Esposito's modern shutout record of 15. He set a new standard in the 2002 playoffs recording six shutouts, two more than the previous record.

After winning his first Stanley Cup with the 2002 Red Wings, Hasek joined the Detroit coach Scotty Bowman in retirement.

CAREER TOTALS										
GPI	GS	W	L	T	Min.	GA	GAA	SA	Sv%	SHO
581	563	288	189	80	33746	1254	2.23	16530	.924	61

CURTIS JOSEPH

Name: Curtis Joseph
Born: April 29, 1967, Keswick, Ontario
Catches: Left
Height: 5-11
Weight: 190

"I think any goalie will tell you it's a great test of character during the playoffs. But it's something to look forward to."

–Curtis Joseph

You can call him "Cujo." Everyone does.

Curtis Joseph is his real name. And everyone is getting to know that, too. The exciting goalie is listed as No. 54—and one of just 13 players—in The Hockey News 100 People of Power and Influence in Hockey for the 2001–2002 season.

Not bad. Just like the $6,575,000 annual salary the Keswick, Ontario native is pulling down these days. The former Wisconsin Badger has had career highlights of an Oilers record eight shutouts in 1997-1998, faced a single-season record of 2,382 shots in 1993-1994 and set a goalie assist record for a season with nine in 1991–1992.

Playing for St. Louis, Edmonton and now Toronto, Cujo has had spectacular seasons with each of them. In St. Louis, there was that streak of 174-plus minutes of scoreless work in slamming the Chicago Blackhawks in the playoffs.

A two-time Canadian Olympic teamer now, Joseph signed with Toronto in 1998 and followed with a super season—a 2.56 goals-against average and three shutouts. The Maple Leafs would go on to the conference finals and the All-Star Joseph was nominated for the Vezina Trophy as the NHL's best goaltender.

In 2001-2002, Joseph finished with a 29–17–5 mark, a 2.23 GAA and four shutouts.

As the top free agent in the game this year, it was no surprise that Joseph was the man tapped by the Red Wings to replace the retiring Dominik Hasek in goal.

CAREER TOTALS										
GPI	GS	W	L	T	Min.	GA	GAA	SA	Sv%	SHO
706	687*	346	260	81	41122	1908	2.78	20640	.908	36

NIKOLAI KHABIBULIN

Name: Nikolai Khabibulin
Born: January 13, 1973, Sverdlosk, Russia
Catches: Left
Height: 6-1
Weight: 205

"Nikolai is unbelievable."

– Vincent Lecavalier, Tampa Bay Lightning center

With seven shutouts—second best in the National Hockey League—and a 2.36 goals-against average, Nikolai Khabibulin tried his best to help his hapless Tampa Bay Lightning team this past season it wasn't enough.

Nor was the work of the 6-foot-1, 205-pound goalie enough to push his native Russian Olympic team over the top as it went for the gold in Salt Lake City.

But a seven-year NHL veteran of the Winnipeg Jets and then the Phoenix Coyotes before moving on to the Lightning, Khabibulin became the first goalie to record three straight shutouts for the first time since Greg Millen in 1998. He went more than 204 minutes without allowing a goal.

A native of Sverdlosk, and inspired by countryman Vladislav Tretiak, Khabibulin had his best season in 1998-1999 when he recorded eight shutouts—third-best in the NHL —in 63 games with a sizzling 2.13 GAA.

For that season, Khabibulin was named to the NHL All-Star squad for the first time.

His Olympics play this past year also earned Khabibulin a nomination for the Eurosport Sportstar Award for ice hockey. Khabibulin played every minute of every game for bronze the medal-winning Russian team in Salt Lake City with a 3-2-1 record and a 2.34 goals-against average with one shutout. He led all goalies in minutes played and saves and was named the top goaltender of the Winter Games by the International Ice Hockey Federation.

Both *USA Today* and *Sports Illustrated* named the 29-year-old Khabibulin as a candidate for MVP after the 2001–2002 season when he set franchise-best marks of 2.36 GAA, seven shutouts, most saves (1,761) and games played (70).

CAREER TOTALS										
GPI	GS	W	L	T	Min.	GA	GAA	SA	Sv%	SHO
356	344	151	146	40	20046	894	2.68	9972	.910	28

CHRIS OSGOOD

Name: Chris Osgood
Born: November 26, 1972, Peace River, Alberta
Catches: Left
Height: 5-11
Weight: 181

"To me, it doesn't really matter where we finish. Just make it and get in (the playoffs). Whoever you play against, prepare for."

– Chris Osgood

Chris Osgood knows how to handle questions from the media.

Maybe it's a legacy from his years in Detroit. But the 5-foot-11, 181-pound goalie is a must-not-miss guy in the post-game lockerroom.

When you're in Detroit, the way Osgood was, you see the National Hockey League from the top down with all its bells and whistles.

And you learn how to handle things, especially when you've won a pair of Stanley Cups (1997, 1998) as Osgood did as a Red Wing.

Then after moving on to the New York Islanders to make way for Dominik Hasek's coming to Detroit, Osgood opened this past season as the National Hockey League's Player of the Month for October. He showed the Islanders right away why he'd been the No. 2 career goalie in wins and shutouts (behind Terry Sawchuk) in Red Wing history.

A three-time NHL All-Star (1996, 1997, 1998) for the Red Wings, the Peace River, Alberta native won the Jennings Trophy twice (1995, 1996) for the lowest goals-agsinst average.

To see what kind of player Osgood could be, just check out his 1995–1996 line as Wings starter. He played 50 games with a 2.17 goals-against average while recording five shutouts. During that time, Osgood set a Wings record for longest unbeaten streak with 21 games during a 19-0-2 run.

CAREER TOTALS										
GPI	GS	W	L	T	Min.	GA	GAA	SA	Sv%	SHO
455	440	253	135	52	26218	1056	2.42	11505	.908	34

BERNIE PARENT

Name: Bernard Marcel Parent
Born: April 3, 1945, Montreal, Quebec
Catches: Left
Height: 5-10
Weight: 180

"I lost the puck in the sun."

- Bernie Parent after allowing a soft goal in a year when part of the Spectrum roof had been blown off

The bumper sticker always said it best.

"Only the Lord saves more than Bernie Parent."

Indeed, there was a near-religious fervor in Philadelphia for their beloved Flyers and the goalkeeper who led the former expansion franchise to back-to-back Stanley Cup titles in 1974 and 1975.

The Quebec native originally signed with Boston's Bruins but was allowed to come to the original Flyers in the 1967 expansion draft. He was there from the beginning, although not continuously.

Born near Montreal, the superstitious Parent took a detour to Toronto for an apprenticeship with the great Jacques Plante, where he learned to be a stand-up goalie. From there Parent then headed off to the World Hockey Association, finding himself back in Philly with a team named the Blazers for a season in 1972-1973.

Then it was back to the National Hockey League in 1973-1974 and a Flyers team ready to bloom as the "Broad Street Bullies."

Not a bad homecoming. Parent earned the Vezina Trophy with his sensational 1.89 goals-against average and amazing 12 shutouts for the Stanley Cup winning Flyers and later would be named winner of the Conn Smythe Trophy for his playoff goaltending as well.

What to do for an encore?

Why not just do it all over again?

Which is just what Parent did with a 2.02 goals-against average and a second Vezina Trophy as the Flyers won their second Stanley Cup in a row.

And there were those same dozen shutouts and the same old Conn Smythe Trophy a second straight season.

Injuries would dog Parent a bit the next several years before a serious eye injury from a stick would send him into retirement at the age of 34. His Hockey Hall of Fame induction came in 1984.

CAREER TOTALS										
GPI	GS	W	L	T	Min.	GA	GAA	SA	Sv%	SHO
608	0*	271	198	121	35136	1493	2.55	0*	-*	54

JACQUES PLANTE

Name: Joseph Jacques Omer Plante
Born: January 17, 1929, Shawinigan Falls, Quebec
Died: February 27, 1986
Catches: Left
Height: 6-0
Weight: 175

"Stressful? Do you know lots of jobs where every time you make a mistake, a red light goes off over your head and 15,000 people start booing?"

- Jacques Plante

Jacques Plante. Pioneer. Maybe nothing the great goalie did on the ice during the games will stand as tall as what Plante did to prepare himself—and the game —for his starring turn.

Which was more important—his body of work, his awards and honors, his team triumphs, his never-equalled record of five straight Stanley Cups and five straight Vezina Trophies or his development of the stand-up style of goaltending that brought the goalie's game into the modern era? Which was more important—his tough-minded refusal to be bloodied and sent off the ice with injuries or his adamant determination to overcome the game's adherence to the old ways by wearing a protective mask that took much of the blood and brutality out of the game?

It's not possible to separate any of it. That was pretty much the message in his first-of-its-kind book: *The Art of Goaltending*. Note the use of the word "art." With Plante between the pipes for the Montreal Canadiens, that's what it was. An art. Conducted by an artist.

Finally hockey figured out Plante was right. But it wasn't easy. It took an 18-game unbeaten streak in 1959 before Plante could convince his hard-headed Montreal coach Toe Blake that a relatively safe, protected goalkeeper could concentrate on stopping the puck with more than his face. Until then, goalies' masks were just for practice.

Hard to believe no one understood how foolish that was before Jaques Plante, the last goalie to win a Hart Trophy before Dominik Hasek.

The native of Shawinigan Falls, Quebec understood so much about the game. He knew that positioning himself squarely against the shooter was the way to succeed as a shot-stopper. Cut off the angles. Stand up and find the shooter.

After his glory days in Montreal, Plante got a chance to show much of the rest of the National Hockey League what he could do. He played for the New York Rangers, retired briefly, then came back with the St. Louis Blues, the Toronto Maple Leafs, the Boston Bruins and even the WHA's Edmonton Oilers.He was inducted into the Hockey Hall of Fame in 1978.

CAREER TOTALS										
GPI	GS	W	L	T	Min.	GA	GAA	SA	Sv%	SHO
837	0*	435	247	145	49493	1964	2.38	0*	-*	82

FELIX POTVIN

Name: Felix Potvin
Born: June 23, 1971, Anjou, Quebec
Catches: Left
Height: 6-1
Weight: 190

"I have always been a guy who believed in me."

– Felix Potvin

It's taken the Anjou, Quebec native a bit of time but Felix Potvin seems to have really found a place to blossom in the Southern California sun the past two seasons.

Not that he hadn't shown sparks of his 1.96 and 2.31 goals-against averages for the Kings earlier on in more than a decade with the Toronto Maple Leafs, the New York Islanders and the Vancouver Canucks.

After his first full season in 1992–1993 in Toronto, he was a finalist for the Calder Trophy and a runner-up for the Jennings Trophy. The next year he was a two-time Player of the Week and Player of the Month and a first-time All-Star as Toronto went to the conference finals a second straight season.

He became the first National Hockey League goalie to record three straight shutouts in the postseason. All that did was elevate Potvin into *The Hockey News* Top 40 Players in the NHL rankings to No. 12. He went on to lead the league in games (74) and minutes (4,271) in 1996-1997.

But the arrival of Curtis Joseph in Toronto saw Potvin pursue his playing career elsewhere, first with the Islanders and then the Canucks. In neither place was he able to reprise his Toronto success.

This past season in Los Angeles, Potvin was 31-27-8 in 71 games with a 2.31 goals-against average as the magic seems to have returned.

CAREER TOTALS										
GPI	GS	W	L	T	Min.	GA	GAA	SA	Sv%	SHO
565	552	237	232	76	32793	1522	2.78	16187	.906	25

PATRICK ROY

Name: Patrick Roy
Born: October 5, 1965, Quebec City, Quebec
Catches: Left
Height: 6-2
Weight: 185

"I can't hear what Jeremy says because my ears are blocked by my two Stanley Cup rings."
- Patrick Roy responding in a war of words with Jeremy Roenick

No one does it better than Patrick Roy. Even when things go bad the way they did in a four-goal first period in the 2002 Stanley Cup playoffs rout at the hands of Detroit's Red Wings, Roy did it with his accustomed drama and flair.

He's the National Hockey League's all-time greatest winner in goal (his 516 regular-season wins are 69 more than runnerup Terry Sawchuk's).

From his rookie season of 1985–86 on, Roy acted like he belonged, leading the Montreal Canadiens to an unbelievable Stanley Cup-winning 15-game run with a 1.92 goals-against average.

All the Quebec City native did in his debut season was win the Conn Smythe Trophy and then he did it again with a 16-4 playoff record and a 2.13 goals-against average in 1992–3 as the Canadiens again won the Stanley Cup.

But like the shelling he received this past season from Detroit, it was a nine-goal barrage that he was forced to endure in 1995 that saw him exit Montreal screaming at his bosses there on his way to the Colorado Avalanche, where he won another pair of Stanley Cups in 1996 and 2001.

Just one game to note there. Roy recorded 63 saves in a triple-overtime 1–0 win in 1996 that could not have been more dramatic or spectacular.

The other numbers in Roy's resume are likewise impressive: three Conn Smythe Trophies, three Jennings Trophies, three Vezina Trophies, nine All-Star Games, five times either first- or second team NHL All-Star, most 30-plus win seasons (10), career playoff record for games played (196), most playoff wins (121), and most playoff wins in a single season (16, twice).

Roy's career highlights take five full pages in the Avalanche's media guide.

But numbers alone don't tell the story of Roy's fierce competitiveness and his daredevil butterfly style that allows shooters nothing easy, no clear angles, not many rebounds.

In *The Hockey News* 100 People of Power and Influence in hockey, Roy ranks No. 13, highest among all active players.

CAREER TOTALS										
GPI	GS	W	L	T	Min.	GA	GAA	SA	Sv%	SHO
966	714*	516	300	118	56467	2409	2.56	26630	.909	61

TERRY SAWCHUK

Name: Terrance Gordon Sawchuk
Born: December 28, 1929, Winnipeg, Manitoba
Died: May 31, 1970
Catches: Left
Height: 5-11
Weight: 195

"He was great. ... Really great."

- American Hockey League President Maurice Podoloff, later NBA commissioner, on Terry Sawchuk

He was special. He was haunted. He was driven. He was a genius. Everything Terry Sawchuk did made that clear. From that deep crouch of a stance that forced his stitched-up face aggressively out onto the ice as a defiant beacon to the way he punished himself off the ice, Sawchuk was in a class by himself.

He was clearly one of the greatest goaltenders of all time. And one of the game's least known people even as he was one of its most famous. He was the counterpoint to Gordie Howe on those great Detroit Red Wing teams of the Fifties. Sawchuk's 103 career shutouts are truly in a class of their own, a record—like Joe Dimaggio's 56 game hitting streak—that will probably never be challenged.

Sawchuk played 21 seasons for five teams—14 for Detroit—and did some amazing things, to his opponents and—tragically—to himself. He'd started as strong as any young goalie ever, with an 11-shutout, 70-game Calder Cup-winning rookie season in 1951-1952 with the Red Wings when he posted a goals-against average of 1.98.

And it just got better. Three Stanley Cups and three Vezina Trophies came quickly over the next four years. He would finish with four Cups. Consider the unbelievable stats in his 1952 Cup run—eight straight wins, four shutouts, and a 0.67 goals-against average. And then he was off, sent away to Boston for reasons that remain unclear. Sawchuk certainly didn't understand it. But it made him wonder. Did he belong? After struggling badly in Boston with depression after being away from his family, he came back to Detroit and picked it up again. But there were always the demons that seemed to torment his spirit.

So what if he won the most games for a National Hockey League goalie ever. It never seemed enough. Sawchuk would never know how good he was. His 1971 induction into the Hockey Hall of Fame came a year after his tragic death after an incident in his home that has been described as everything from a "domestic accident" to a "fight." Whatever, it was the tragic ending that Sawchuk's sad life seemed to almost be foretelling. In the first three Goaltender Surveys conducted from 1994 through 1996, Sawchuk was voted third, then second and finally the top goaltender in NHL history.

CAREER TOTALS										
GPI	GS	W	L	T	Min.	GA	GAA	SA	Sv%	SHO
972	0*	447	331	171	57254	2390	2.50	0*	-*	103

BILLY SMITH

Name: William John Smith
Born: December 12, 1950, Perth, Ontario
Catches: Left
Height: 5-10
Weight: 185

"We're the best. We made one mistake in two nights on the road—one mistake—and you can't say enough about a hockey team like that."
– Billy Smith after 1982 Stanley Cup win

They always talk about his stickwork. True, Billy Smith liked to whack and attack opponents who got to close to the goal with his stick. It seemed to be an extension of the New York Islanders' aggressive personality.

And they were right. Smith didn't earn the "Battling Billy" moniker for nothing. He was a combative son of a gun. It wasn't for nothing that Smith leads all goalies in penalty minutes. This guy loved to mix it up.

No wonder the New York Islanders were able to string those four Stanley Cups together from 1980 through 1983. They took no prisoners, took nothing from anyone. Except their personality. They took that from Smith. Some of it anyway.

It seemed Smith wasn't happy unless he was upset about something, whether it was an opponent, the media or his own teammates.

Smith set the tone for the Islanders, playing well for the regular season but turning it up a couple of notches in the playoffs. He won just one Vezina Trophy for his regular-season play but regularly excelled in postseason play.

And in 1979 he became the first National Hockey League goalie ever to score a goal when he managed that feat against Colorado as the last man to touch the puck before a Colorado player accidentally knocked it into his own net after the goalie had been pulled.

After the four Stanley Cups, Smith would go on to break Ken Dryden's career playoff mark with his 81st win. But there wasn't much more in the tank as the Edmonton's Oilers supplanted the Islanders.

Retiring in 1989, Smith would go on to be inducted into the Hockey Hall of Fame in 1993.

	CAREER TOTALS									
GPI	GS	W	L	T	Min.	GA	GAA	SA	Sv%	SHO
680	0*	305	233	105	38431	2031	3.17	7184*	.885*	22

JOSE THEODORE

Name: Jose Theodore
Born: September 13, 1976, Laval, Quebec
Catches: Right
Height: 5-10
Weight: 182

"Everyone in this dressing room knows what Jose is capable of. We all know how valuable he is to our club."

– Doug Gilmour

He maybe the best young goalie in the game today.

No one seemed to know about him before the 2001–2002 season.

To say that precious few hockey fans outside Montreal had heard of Jose Theodore would hardly be a stretch. Now the 25-year-old Laval, Quebec native is fast becoming a household name.

Along with Colorado Avalanche goalie Patrick Roy and Calgary Flames forward Jarome Iginla, Theodore was a finalist for the Hart Trophy as the National Hockey League's best player. The odds on Theodore being a part of that trio before the season were non-existent.

Theodore also was a finalist for the Vezina Trophy along with Roy and Phoenix Coyote Sean Burke. That he'd be in a contest with the man he idolizes—Roy—is almost too much for Theodore to imagine.

"I remember when I was a kid and he won his first Vezina, I was so impressed," Theodore said of Roy. "Now to be nominated for the Vezina and the Hart with him is really special."

No matter what happens with the individual awards, Theodore had a year that no one can take from him. It was a year that says he's arrived.

"He's the reason we made the playoffs and he's the reason we got this far and that's why he's up for both awards," said Canadien teammate Stephane Quintal as Montreal made it into the playoffs for the first time since 1998.

Theodore finished the year with a 30-24-10 record, a 2.11 goals-against average (fourth best in the NHL), seven shutouts (second-best in the league) and with an NHL-best .931 save percentage.

His great lateral movement, his quick hands and his ability to make a big save after giving up a goal are traits that have made Theodore so special in his first time in the spotlight.

CAREER TOTALS										
GPI	GS	W	L	T	Min.	GA	GAA	SA	Sv%	SHO
191	175	71	84	19	10560	439	2.49	5151	.915	15

VLADISLAV TRETIAK

Name: Vladislav Tretiak
Born: April 26, 1952, Dmitrov, Soviet Union
Catches: Left
Height: 6-1
Weight: 202

"Today's goalies should strive for mastering that profusion of techniques which Tretiak had."

– Anatoly Tarasov, Russian National Hockey Team coach

He may have come along too soon to play in the National Hockey League but Vladislav Tretiak was so special, so talented, such a unique talent that he is included in every list of the game's greatest goalies despite his lack of NHL playing experience.

Tretiak was that good. Big and strong at 6-feet-1 and 202 pounds, he dominated international competition for the Central Red Army team that he joined as a 15-year-old. By then, he had already become his own coach, Russian National Team coach Anatoly Tarasov said.

His Central Red Army team won 13 Soviet League championships in 15 years as Tretiak earned 14 straight Soviet League first-team All-Star selections from 1971 through 1984. But his fame didn't stay overseas.

Tretiak played in two of the most famous hockey games ever—against Montreal's Canadiens in 1975 and in the 1980 Olympics finals against the "Miracle on Ice" USA team.

So maybe it's no surprise he was the first Russian inducted into the Hockey Hall of Fame in 1989. He led the USSR hockey team to three goald medals—in 1972, 1976 and 1984. He played on 11 World Championship hockey teams and nine European champs. Three times he was named Best European Hockey Player (1981, 1982, 1983).

GUMP WORSLEY

Name: Lorne John Worsley
Born: May 14, 1929, Montreal, Quebec
Catches: Left
Height: 5-7
Weight: 180

"Anyone who wears one is a chicken. My face is my mask."

- Gump Worsley

The name seemed perfect for a hockey goalie.

Gump.

Way better than Lorne, which was Gump Worsley's given name.

And just right for the Hockey Hall of Fame plaque the stump-like Worlsey earned in 1980 after 21 seasons in the National Hockey League, four Stanley Cups, and stints with the New York Rangers, Montreal Canadiens and Minnesota North Stars.

Like so many stellar goalies, Worsley was good from the start. He won the Calder Trophy as Rookie of the Year for a bad Rangers team in 1952–1953.

He would then be fortunate enough to move on from New York to Montreal, where he won his four Stanley Cups in just seven years.

Worsley has shared a pair of Vezina Trophies and played in four All-Star Games and was named a first-team All-Star in 1968.

It was a combination of bad teams, advancing age and a fear of flying that got Worsley out of the game after more than two decades at the age of 44.

By then, he was at least wearing a goalie mask, although only for the final six games of his career. Worlsey had disdained the idea of wearing a mask earlier in his career.

CAREER TOTALS										
GPI	GS	W	L	T	Min.	GA	GAA	SA	Sv%	SHO
861	0*	335	352	150	50183	2407	2.88	0*	-*	43

THE PLAYERS

DEFENSEMEN

BRYAN BERARD

Name: Bryan Berard
Born: March 5, 1977, Woonsocket, Rhode Island
Shoots: Left
Height: 6-1
Weight: 210

"I love Toronto, definitely, and the organization has been great to me."
—New York Ranger Bryan Berard

Bryan Berard has been a New York Islander, Toronto Maple Leaf and now New York Ranger since earning the Calder Trophy in 1996–1997 as the National Hockey League rookie of the year.

The Woonsocket, Rhode Island native is actually working for his fourth franchise. He'd originally been drafted by the Ottawa Senators, who took him first overall in the 1995 draft.

So you couldn't blame Berard if some days he had to stand in front of the mirror in his uniform saying: "If it's Monday, I must be in Manhattan," or something like that.

And now next year is up for grabs. Berard, arguably the second biggest comeback guy of the season after being left mostly blind in his right eye after being hit with a stick, might end up back in Toronto.

Berard began playing hockey at the age of six and must have been offensive-mided in his early days, idolizing Mario Lemieux. On his way up, in the Central Hockey League and the Ontario Hockey League, he was the top defender and top rookie. Only in his opening NHL season and this past season has he been able to play every one of the 82 games because of injuries those other seasons. In his rookie year, Berard finished ninth among all defensemen in scoring.

Which tells you what you need to know about this young defender. He can score when it matters. And when he scores a goal, it's often a game-winner.

The well-traveled Berard got off to a very good start. *The Sporting News* Rookie of the Year finished second among rookies in points, assists, power play assists, power play points and was third in power play shots.

A year later he was third on the Islanders in assists, points and goals, and second in power play scoring. Then it was on to the Maple Leafs the next season but not before getting three of his four goals as game-winners for the Isles in 17 games and then getting five of nine game-winning goals as a Leaf.

CAREER TOTALS											
GP	G	A	Pts	+/-	GWG	GTG	S	S%	PPG	SHG	PIM
372	36	145	181	- 20	8	2	729	4.9	16	1	295

RAY BOURQUE

Name: Raymond Jean Bourque
Born: December 28, 1960, Montreal, Quebec
Shoots: Left
Height: 6-0
Weight: 223

"When I got here in Boston, I was told you've got to have pride in that jersey and you've got to go out there and play with pride and recognize what this is all about. If you didn't, you had people telling you about it."
—Ray Bourque on the night Boston retired his jersey

By the numbers, here's a quick look at one of the best defensemen and most popular of players in the history of hockey.

* One is the number of Stanley Cups won by Bourque, a 21-year NHL veteran who did it in his last season and his first with the Colorado Avalanche at the age of 40.

* One is also the number of Calder Trophy awards he earned—and the maximum anyone can earn—as the NHL's rookie of the year in 1979.

* Five is the number of Norris Trophies earned (1987, 1988, 1990, 1991, 1994) as the league's outstanding defenseman

* Six is the number of second-team All-Star awards (1981, 1983, 1989, 1995, 1999)

* 10 is the number of first-team All-Star awards (1980, 1982, 1984, 1985, 1986, 1987, 1988, 1990, 1994, 2001).

* 19 is the number of All-Star Games he's played in.

You could also just describe Bourque without numbers. He's intelligent, using just enough force to get control of the puck rather than to check indiscriminately. At 6-0, 223 pounds, Bourque is a serious scoring threat on the power play with his powerful slap shot from the left side.

And he's basically a good guy. All of Boston seemed to be rooting for him to get his Stanley Cup that final season even if it was for a team other than the Bruins. His No. 77 has been retired by both Boston and Colorado.

Bourque finished up as the leading defenseman ever in games, goals, assists and points after the 2000–2001 season. He'd already joined Denis Potvin and Paul Coffey as the only defensemen to score 300 goals and became only the fifth NHL player to record 1,000 assists joining Wayne Gretzky, Gordie Howe, Marcel Dionne and Coffey.

Not a bad way to go out.

CAREER TOTALS											
GP	G	A	Pts	+/-	GWG	GTG	S	S%	PPG	SHG	PIM
1612	410	1169	1579	528	60	14	6206	6.6	173	16	1141

CHRIS CHELIOS

Name: Chris Chelios
Born: January 25, 1962, Chicago, Illinois
Shoots: Right
Height: 6-1
Weight: 190

"Chris Chelios and Niklas Lidstrom better hope they don't get beaten up during the playoffs this year as they will be heading down the red carpet nominated for the same award when the NHL hosts its own version of the Academy Awards at the National Hockey League Awards Show in Toronto on June 20."

—John Veitch, www.letsgowings.com columnist

A blue-chip player for a trio of storied franchises, Chris Chelios is an 18-year National Hockey League veteran of Montreal's Canadiens (1984–1990), Chicago's Blackhawks (1990–1998) and Detroit's Red Wings (1999–present).

At every stop, the 40-year old Chicago native has been both a leader and a winner. He was the first American-born player ever to captain the Canadiens. He's also the first American-born player to win the James Norris Trophy as the NHL's top defender, something he did in 1989, 1993 and 1996. He was also the NHL Plus-Minus Award winner this past season.

And again this year, Chelios—along with teammate Niklas Lidstrom and Colorado Avalanche Rob Blake—is a Norris finalist.

In 1985–86, having played just 41 games, Chelios managed to score 34 points in the regular season and then 19 more points as the Canadiens won their 22nd—and Chelios' first—Stanley Cup. It was Chelios' first cup.

He's been an NHL first-team All-Star in 1989, 1993, 1995 and 1996. He was second-team in 1991 and 1997.

In Chicago, Chelios drove the Blackhawks to Norris titles twice in his first three years there and at the end of the 1993–1994 season, *The Hockey News* ranked him as the fourth-best player in hockey. When he was traded to Detroit in 1999, Chelios led the Hawks in all-time penalty minutes with 1,495 in 664 games.

A former player for the University of Wisconsin and Chicago's Mt. Carmel High School, Chelios was one of six defensemen named to the Blackhawks' 75th Anniversary All-Time Team.

A big part of Chelios' career has been his international play. He played for three U.S. Olympics teams (1984, 1998, 2002) and for the Team USA Juniors in 1982 and Team USA in 1984 and won a gold medal with the U.S. team in the World Cup of Hockey in 1996.

CAREER TOTALS											
GP	G	A	Pts	+/-	GWG	GTG	S	S%	PPG	SHG	PIM
1260	174	700	874	291	29	5	3187	5.5	68	11	2556

KING CLANCY

Name: Francis Michael Clancy
Born: February 25, 1903, Ottawa, Ontario
Died: November 8, 1986
Shoots: Left
Height: 5-7
Weight: 155

"Probably the best all-around man, as far as morale, ability, and effort for his team is concerned, that ever was."
—Toronto owner Conn Smythe on King Clancy

It was a 65-year love affair between Francis Michael "King" Clancy and the game of hockey. From his rookie season in 1921–1922 till the day he died in 1986, the King was a hockey man. He was also a Hockey Hall of Famer for 28 years while he was still alive and able to enjoy the honor.

He was a little guy, just 5-foot-7 and 155 pounds, and one of the smallest defensemen ever to play the game in the National Hockey League. But when Ottawa sold him—and two other players—to the Toronto Maple Leafs for $35,000 in 1930, it was considered the largest deal in hockey history.

It was said of Clancy, who was one of those personality-plus guys, that he never backed down from a fight—and never won one in his 16-year NHL career.

One of the better stories about him is that one night working as a referee in Boston, Clancy was heckled by a fan he immediately offered to fight. Luckily for Clancy, the fan turned down the offer. The fan was Jack Sharkey, then the world heavyweight boxing champion.

By the time he retired five years later, Clancy had led Ottawa's Senators to a pair of Stanley Cup titles and Toronto to one. He had given the fans their money's worth with his "Charley Hustle" style of throwing his body around on the ice. Never backing down. Never giving in or giving up.

Clancy would go on to positions as coach, referee, assistant general manager and aide to Coach Punch Imlach. He assisted unpopular owner Harold Ballard and was a goodwill ambassador for the Maple Leafs organization until the day he died.

The King Clancy Trophy is awarded annually now to a player for his community service work.

CAREER TOTALS											
GP	G	A	Pts	+/-	GWG	GTG	S	S%	PPG	SHG	PIM
592	137	147	284	0*	0*	0*	0*	- *	0*	0*	914

DIT CLAPPER

Name: Aubrey Victor Clapper
Born: February 9, 1907, Newmarket, Ontario
Died: January 21, 1978
Shoots: Right
Height: 6-2
Weight: 195

"Dit Clapper remains the only Bruin to play on three Cup teams, the only player in NHL history named an All-Star at forward and defense, and he'll forever be the first player to play 20 NHL seasons."

—Boston Bruins media guide

This was one tough—and gentlemanly—guy.

Dit Clapper played right wing and defense for the Boston Bruins at a distinctly modern-day size of 6-feet-2, 200 pounds. In the years from 1927 through 1947, Clapper's size and strength was unusual.

Why the name Dit? Well, his given name was Aubrey and that surely wouldn't fit. And he couldn't pronounce "Vic," so Dit it was for the big, strong guy who would lead the Bruins to three Stanley Cups wearing that familiar No. 5 jersey.

From Newmarket, Ontario, Clapper was more than tough. He was a skilled athlete, a very good lacrosse player who signed a pro hockey contract with Boston at the age of 19. Soon he was on offense and combined with Cooney Weiland and Dutch Gainor to become the "Dynamite Line" that finished an amazing 38-5-1 in 1930. Then it was back to defense for Dit for the back half of his career, where he was a solid, controlling presence on the blue line.

Clapper has the distinction of being one of just two NHL players ever named to a postseason All-Star team at defenseman and wing. He was the first NHL player ever to play 20 seasons with the same team.

He was elected to the Hockey Hall of Fame in 1947 while still an active player. He was so good, they just waived the rules for Clapper to get in.

How good was he? Knowledgeable NHL people say he was this good: That he ranks right up there with other Bruin defensemen Bobby Orr, Raymond Bourque and Eddie Shore.

Not bad company to share.

CAREER TOTALS											
GP	G	A	Pts	+/-	GWG	GTG	S	S%	PPG	SHG	PIM
833	228	246	474	0*	0*	0*	0*	-*	0*	0*	462

PAUL COFFEY

Name: Paul Douglas Coffey
Born: June 1, 1961, Weston, Ontario
Shoots: Left
Height: 6-0
Weight: 205

"I'm at peace with myself. I did what I wanted to do—play in the NHL for 21 seasons."
—Paul Coffey on retiring October 3, 2001

Raymond Bourque's retirement after winning his first Stanley Cup title at the age of 40, overshadowed another retirement.

The similarities are eerie. The other high-scoring defenseman in NHL history, also 40 and a 21-year veteran, retired early in the 2001–2002 season.

Paul Coffey won four Stanley Cups and is the career playoff scoring leader (196 points in 194 games) among defensemen. Only Bourque leads his 1,531 points in regular-season scoring for defensemen.

The pair are 1-2 in all sorts of career scoring stats for blueliners.

Coffey was a 14-time All-Star who played on three Canada Cup winners and won three Norris trophies as the NHL's best defenseman.

"Priorities change," Coffey said. "As a professional athlete, your life has to be dominated by hockey, giving an effort north of 100 percent. My family is where my life is at right now.

"I was able to play on championship teams both in the NHL and at the international level alongside so many players, and I will remember these experiences forever."

Coffey won Stanley Cups at Edmonton in 1984, 1985 and 1987 and in 1991 with Pittsburgh.

He also played for Los Angeles, Detroit, Hartford, Philadelphia, Chicago, Carolina and Boston.

Maybe that was the biggest difference. Bourque was Boston's for 20 years. Coffey, a 6-foot, 190-pounder from Weston, Ontario, was everywhere. That's often how it seemed when his team was on a power play. With his skating and stickhandling skills, he was often just too good for overmatched defensemen at a numbers disadvantage.

Coffey set a number of records for a defenseman including most goals in a season, 48 in 1985-86; most assists, 6, and most points, 8, in a game, March 14, 1986; most goals, 12, most assists, 25, and most points, 37, in the playoffs, 1985; and most points in a single playoff game, 6, May 14, 1985.

CAREER TOTALS											
GP	G	A	Pts	+/-	GWG	GTG	S	S%	PPG	SHG	PIM
1409	396	1135	1531	294	44	4	4385	9.0	135	20	1802

DOUG HARVEY

Name: Douglas Norman Harvey
Born: December 19, 1924, Montreal, Quebec
Died: December 26, 1989
Shoots: Left
Height: 5-11
Weight: 187

"I didn't have a bonus for goals so why not set up the guys that needed them?"

—Doug Harvey

How good a baseball player would Wayne Gretzky have been? What if Gordie Howe had played football, how good would he have been?

We don't have to ask that question about Doug Harvey. We know that one of the greatest defensemen in the history of hockey was a terrific baseball player. The same for football. The hand-eye coordination, toughness and strength he brought to a career on the ice left a legacy that challenges even the greatest blueliners.

Harvey was a halfback-sized Montreal Canadien, powerful and quick, who always seemed in control, especially as his hometown team racked up five straight Stanley Cups beginning in 1955–56.

Harvey owned his opponents, some said, just as much as he owned the 10 straight first-team All-Star spots or the seven Norris Trophies (second only to Bobby Orr's eight).

Harvey was in control of the game when he was on the ice. He could set any tempo—fast or slow—that would benefit his team. And then he could set up his teammates, looking for them more often than trying to score himself.

There were those who criticized him. In his early days, it sometimes looked like he wasn't trying because he was so under control. And of course, when he helped form the players association, that earned him no fans in front offices anywhere.

Jean Beliveau once said of Harvey, "When I joined Montreal, he was the best defenseman I'd ever seen."

Harvey was inducted into the Hockey Hall of Fame in 1973 after a career that saw him play in 13 All-Star Games.

CAREER TOTALS											
GP	G	A	Pts	+/-	GWG	GTG	S	S%	PPG	SHG	PIM
1113	88	452	540	11*	0*	0*	46*	4.3*	1*	0*	1216

TIM HORTON

Name: Miles Gilbert Horton
Born: January 12, 1930, Cochrane, Ontario
Died: February 21, 1974
Shoots: Right
Height: 5-10
Weight: 180

"Few players brought more dedication or honour to the game. He was my idea of a pro."

—Bobby Hull

There was a legendary quality about the late Tim Horton that has all the elements of the Paul Bunyan story. Maybe it was the combination of dying young—he was 44 and still playing—in a tragic single-car accident after 24 years in the National Hockey League.

Maybe it was the belief that during all that time, the 5-foot-10, 180-pound Cochrane, Ontario native was the league's strongest player—and its greatest peacemaker.

Maybe it was the "Horton Bear Hug" that he used to immobilize and separate fighters until they thought better of it.

Tim Horton played in 1,446 regular season games, scoring 115 goals with 403 assists for a total of 518 points. Some say he pretty much invented the slapshot. He played 17 full seasons and three partial seasons for the Toronto Maple Leafs. He then went on to play with the New York Rangers and Pittsburgh Penguins before his final years with the Buffalo Sabres.

Tim Horton was killed in an automobile accident on February 21, 1974, driving back to Buffalo from a game in Toronto.

He played on four Stanley Cup teams, was an All-Star player six times, and won the Bicknell Cup as the Most Valuable Player in 1968–69.

"I know he was the backbone of our team in Buffalo", said Punch Imlach, who had coached him in Toronto. "(His death) was a terrible loss, not only to his family and the team, but to the game of hockey."

There's one other thing that will make Canadians, especially, remember Miles Gilbert "Tim" Horton. His name is on the most popular chain of donut shops in Canada and in some U.S. states. There are more than 2,000 in all now after expanding from the one that Horton and a partner started in 1965. There is also a Tim Horton Childrens Foundation to carry on his concern for children.

CAREER TOTALS											
GP	G	A	Pts	+/-	GWG	GTG	S	S%	PPG	SHG	PIM
1446	115	403	518	81*	16*	2*	845*	2.8*	17*	2*	1611

RED KELLY

Name: Leonard Patrick Kelly
Born: July 9, 1927, Simcoe, Ontario
Shoots: Left
Height: 5-11
Weight: 180

"Red Kelly was more than just a hockey player, he was truly one of the more interesting people in hockey history."

—Hockey Over Time: The History of NHL Hockey

If tough guys are what it takes to make good defensemen, championship boxers should do even better on the blue line.

Leonard Patrick "Red" Kelly may be proof that they do.

But then what explains his later success as a scorer?

This guy was as good with a stick as he was with his hands and feet.

He had to be. In all of hockey history, his eight Stanley Cups (four with Detroit's Red Wings, four with Toronto's Maple Leafs) are more than any other player who did not play for the Montreal Canadiens.

Kelly was a versatile complement to a team of superstars like Gordie Howe, Ted Lindsay and Sid Abel in Detroit.

But when he was traded to New York and threatened to retire, Kelly got another shot—and another position—from Toronto's Punch Imlach, who wanted him to play center next to Frank Mahovlich. Kelly was off to a new life in hockey instead of retiring from it.

From 1950 through 1963, he was an All-Star 13 of 14 seasons. He won the Norris Trophy as the league's best defender in 1954 and the Lady Byng Trophy four times.

Kelly was inducted into the Hockey Hall of Fame in 1969.

He came back to coach and reached varying levels of success with the expansion Los Angeles Kings, the Pittsburgh Penguins and finally back to Toronto and the Maple Leafs, before retiring from the game.

CAREER TOTALS											
GP	G	A	Pts	+/-	GWG	GTG	S	S%	PPG	SHG	PIM
1316	281	542	823	0*	5*	5*	0*	-*	9*	1*	327

NICKLAS LIDSTROM

Name: Nicklas E. Lidstrom
Born: April 28, 1970, Vasteras, Sweden
Shoots: Left
Height: 6-1
Weight: 195

"Chris Chelios and Nicklas Lidstrom better hope they don't get beaten up during the playoffs this year as they will be heading down the red carpet nominated for the same award when the NHL hosts its own version of the Academy Awards at the National Hockey League Awards Show in Toronto on June 20."

—John Veitch, www.letsgowings.com columnist

Nicklas Lidstrom is the first European-born player to win the James Norris Trophy as the National Hockey Legue's top defenseman. He'd been closing in on the Norris for years and finally managed to capture it in 2001.

This year he's done even better. He's nominated with teammate Chris Chelios for the Norris again—with Colorado's Rob Blake—and also nominated for The Lady Byng Trophy for gentlemanly play. He had nine goals and 50 assists this past season, good for second in scoring among defenseman.

You could tell Lidstrom was well on his way as the runner-up for the Calder Trophy as rookie of the year to Pavel Bure. Soon he was the No. 2 defenseman in scoring on the Detroit Red Wings behind the legendary Paul Coffey, whom he would soon succeed.

At 6-feet-2 and 195 pounds, Lidstrom is a neat blend of strength, speed and toughness with the kinds of hand-eye-foot coordination that comes from playing soccer, tennis and golf.

As early as 1999, *The Hockey News* had Lidstrom ranked as its No. 6 player among the league's Top 50 stars and then followed that with a No. 7 ranking for him the next year and a No. 6 ranking this past year. Also this past season, Lidstrom was named by The Sporting News to its All-Star first team as a defenseman.

Lidstrom, with his two early Stanley Cup rings, has also been a consistent second in voting for both the Lady Byng Trophy and for the Norris Trophy.

As far as the Red Wings are concerned, the team has honored Lidstrom in the one way professional athletes understand. His $8 million annual salary is tops on the star-studded Wings, equalled only by the now-retired Dominik Hasek.

Lidstrom, who maintains his home in Sweden, has played for his home country internationally since 1990.

CAREER TOTALS											
GP	G	A	Pts	+/-	GWG	GTG	S	S%	PPG	SHG	PIM
853	145	481	626	218	15	3	2154	6.7	71	8	220

SCOTT NIEDERMAYER

Name: Robert Scott Niedermayer
Born: August 31, 1973, Edmonton, Alberta
Shoots: Left
Height: 6-1
Weight: 200

"Olympian Scott Niedermayer continues to rank among the top two-way blueliners in the NHL."

—Matt Canamucio, NHL Editor, The Sports Network

Scott Niedermayer has displayed defensive mettle—and medals—in better than a decade of top-level, tenacious hockey.

He has a pair of Stanley Cup championships as a New Jersey Devil (1995, 2000). The Edmonton native also earned an Olympic Gold medal in 2002 for Canada. Brother Rob is a center for the Calgary Flames. Their father, Rob, is a physician in their home town of Cranbrook, British Columbia.

In the year he was drafted (1991 as the third selection overall behind No. Eric Lindros), Scott Niedermayer became the youngest player ever to play for the New Jersey Devils at 18 years, 1 month, 13 days. He had been runner-up to Lindros the year before as the top draft prospect.

He's also in the category of "franchise players." Those are players who were drafted first by their franchises and have stayed with the same team their entire career. Only nine players drafted before Niedermayer have that distinction.

But Niedermayer's first real notice came in his first Stanley Cup finals in 1995, when he led the Devils defenders and scored on an end-to-end rush in Game 2 of New Jersey's four-game sweep of Detroit.

Scott has been the key man in the Devils' stingy defenses ever since, reprising that first Stanley Cup with a second in 2000. He has also represented Canada in international play since his junior days in 1990–91 and 1991–92. He played for Team Canada in the 1996 World Cup and the 2002 Olympics.

CAREER TOTALS											
GP	G	A	Pts	+/-	GWG	GTG	S	S%	PPG	SHG	PIM
730	87	296	383	129	20	2	1321	6.6	39	1	372

BOBBY ORR

Name: Robert Gordon Orr
Born: March 20, 1948, Parry Sound, Ontario
Shoots: Left
Height: 6-0
Weight: 197

"Nureyev on ice."
—Boston Globe columnist Ray Fitzgerald of Bobby Orr

The name sounds if it should be on a trophy at St. Andrews—Robert Gordon "Bobby" Orr.

To watch him play was to know he was destined for hockey. He changed the way the game was played. No defenseman before Bobby Orr had ever figured out how to play offense from defense the way the Boston Bruin superstar did. He saw the game in a different way.

And then he acted on it. The first defenseman to score more than 100 points in a season, Orr scored 120, 139, 117, 101, 122 and 135 points for the six seasons beginning in 1969–1970. He was so good he made grown men (in Boston, anyway) cry when they talked about him. The greatest hockey player ever, they would say. Heck, he was the greatest team sport player ever, many Bruin diehards would contend, even if he did take some chances with his body on many of his rushes.

The 6-foot-1, 197-pounder from Parry Sound, Ontario gave Bruin fans somebody to cheer for. He led Boston to Stanley Cups in 1970 and 1972 and only his 11 knee surgeries limited his game that depended on uncanny vision and unparalleled timing. In his final three seasons of a 13-year National Hockey League career, he played just 26 games and retired in 1976. Three years later he was inducted into the Hockey Hall of Fame.

Orr's honors are almost too numerous to mention: Hart Memorial Trophy (1970, 1971, 1972); Conn Smythe Trophy (1970, 1972); Art Ross Trophy (1970, 1975); Calder Memorial Trophy (1967); NHL Plus-Minus Leader (1969, 1970, 1971, 1972, 1974 and 1975); Lester Patrick Trophy (1979) and Lester Pearson Award (1975).

Still considered one of hockey's most important people at the age of 53, Orr is No. 76 on *The Hockey News* Top 100 People of Power and Influence as an agent for Woolf Associates, as a member of the Hockey Hall of Fame selection committee and a spokesperson for NHL-endorsed products.

Orr also generated the most famous action photo in the history of hockey. That's the one where he's just fired a goal past Glenn Hall of St. Louis in the 1970 Stanley Cup finals in overtime and is flipped up by a Blues defenseman as he crosses the face of the goal and then leaps into a body-floating-free, three-feet-in-the-air, parallel-to-the-ice, arms-raised-in-exultation living collectible poster that will last as long as the game does.

CAREER TOTALS											
GP	G	A	Pts	+/-	GWG	GTG	S	S%	PPG	SHG	PIM
657	270	645	915	597*	26	8	2795*	9.2*	76	16	953

SANDIS OZOLINSH

Name: Sandis Ozolinsh
Born: August 3, 1972, Riga, Latvia
Shoots: Left
Height: 6-3
Weight: 205

"Sometimes I don't even want to be on the ice. I'm self-conscious and I just don't want to mess up."

—Sandis Ozolinsh

Sandis Ozolinsh has not only shown the way in San Jose, he's shown it in Colorado, in Carolina and now in Florida. The native of Riga, Latvia has been on a nine-year career path in the National Hockey League that's gone in one direction—southeast.

They remember the 6-foot-3, 205-pounder everywhere he's been. In San Jose, for example, Sandis led the Sharks to their first-ever playoff appearance in 1994.

At Colorado in 1996, he led all defensemen in scoring and got his first—as well as the Avalanche's first—Stanley Cup title. Two years later, he was No. 41 on *The Hockey News* Top 50 players list.

Then it was on to Carolina where he started in the 2001 NHL All-Star Game, his fifth All-Star appearance. That made him Carolina's first All-Star Game starter since the team moved to North Carolina from Hartford.

Now Sandish has finished his 10th NHL season in his fourth NHL city. It's a long way for the former Dynamo Riga and Russian Junior player. So is the $5, million annual salary he's earning.

Ozolinsh finished the 2001–02 season with 29 points for the Panthers in 37 games.

CAREER TOTALS											
GP	G	A	Pts	+/-	GWG	GTG	S	S%	PPG	SHG	PIM
661	141	324	465	-10	19	3	1464	9.6	56	4	498

BRAD PARK

Name: Douglas Bradford Park
Born: July 6, 1948, Toronto, Ontario
Shoots: Left
Height: 6-0
Weight: 200

"Now we'll find out who has ethics. Does University of Toronto have any other law scholarships named for convicted felons or disbarred lawyers?"

—Brad Park after Alan Eagleson admitted defrauding the Players Association of millions of dollars

In the history of the National Hockey League, there may never have been a more dominant defenseman or a more polished power play practicioner, who managed never to win the Norris Trophy than Brad Park.

Not that it was Park's fault. The Toronto native just had the bad timing to finish second on six occasions—four times to Bobby Orr and two more to Denis Potvin.

He also had to endure nine operations during his 17-year career but still managed to play 60 games or more 13 times. He could skate fast and handle the puck while he did. He was smart and poised.

Park was a big part of one of hockey's biggest trades. On November 7, 1975, Park, Jean Ratelle and Joe Zanussi were dealt from the New York Rangers to the Boston Bruins, for Phil Esposito and Carol Vadnais. Bruin Park led Boston to four straight Adams Division titles and two Stanley Cup finals in 1977 and 1978.

Park also played for the Detroit Red Wings, whom he also coached after he left the ice. He was elected to the Hockey Hall of Fame in 1988.

He was a nine-time NHL All-Star and won the Bill Masterson Memorial Trophy in 1984. He scored 213 goals with 683 assists, a total of 896 points in 1,113 regular season games. His playoff totals were 35 goals, 90 assists for 125 points in 161 playoff games.

CAREER TOTALS											
GP	G	A	Pts	+/-	GWG	GTG	S	S%	PPG	SHG	PIM
1113	213	683	896	358	28	9	2820	7.6	93	5	1429

PIERRE PILOTE

Name: Joseph Albert Pierre Paul Pilote
Born: December 11, 1931, Kenogami, Quebec
Shoots: Left
Height: 5-10
Weight: 178

"I had traveled a long road to get to the NHL. I didn't play organized hockey until I was 17."
—Pierre Pilote.

Pierre Pilote was perfect for Chicago. He was one tough guy, even if he carried only 178 pounds on his 5-foot-10 frame.

They liked that toughness in Chicago, where he played 377 consecuative games in one stretch.

But it took more than that to convince the locals of his toughness. And Pilote, the Kenogami, Quebec native who didn't play a game of organized hockey until he was 17, provided it for them.

Call it a 1-2 punch. In the same scuffle during a game against the mighty Canadiens, Pilote knocked out both Richard brothers—Maurice "The Rocket" and Henri "The Pocket Rocket." In Chicago, even for a French Canadian, that's the kind of thing that will earna spot on a float in the St. Patrick's Day Parade.

Pilote could pass the puck and hustle down the ice. He and Elmer Vasko teamed up on defense, and many said the pair was the best in the National Hockey League.

Pilote took over as Blackhawks captain in 1960 and promptly led Chicago to the Stanley Cup. He was the steady hand who allowed stars like Bobby Hull and Stan Mikita to show their stuff.

The rest of the league knew it. Pilote was an All-Star eight straight years from 1960 through 1967 and won the Norris Trophy three seasons in a row from 1963 through 1965. After the 1968-1969 season at Toronto, Pilote retired from the game.

The Hockey Hall of Fame inducted Pilote in 1975.

CAREER TOTALS											
GP	G	A	Pts	+/-	GWG	GTG	S	S%	PPG	SHG	PIM
890	80	418	498	-3*	6*	1*	117*	3.4*	13*	1*	1251

DENIS POTVIN

Name: Denis Charles Potvin
Born: October 29, 1953, Ottawa, Ontario
Shoots: Left
Height: 6-0
Weight: 205

"Denis Potvin has so much to offer. He's a good teacher. It's one thing to have the knowledge, but most star players have the knowledge but can't express it. He can do both."
—Panthers Coach Mike Keenan after a coaching session for his defensemen from Panthers broadcaster Potvin

When the New York Islanders drafted Denis Potvin as the first pick in the Amateur Draft in 1973, they were sure he was the best defenseman to come into the draft since the great Bobby Orr.

They were right.

No wonder they had to resist all sorts of trade offers before the draft. Others knew, too, how good Potvin would be. The 6-foot, 205-pound Ottawa native had the goods. The lefthanded defenseman could pass, shoot and handle the puck as easily as he could bang with his body.

Potvin won the Calder Trophy as the NHL's Rookie of the Year in the 1973-74 season after scoring 17 goals and 54 points in 77 games. Potvin also racked up 175 penalty minutes.

He would go on to win the Stanley Cup four years in a row as an Islander (1980–83) on his way to his selection in the Hockey Hall of Fame in 1991.

With Potvin as the captain, the Islanders would beat the Philadelphia Flyers in six games to start their Stanley streak, then downed Minnesota, Vancouver and Edmonton as they captured three more championships.

He played in nine NHL All-Star Games and won the Norris Trophy three times (1976, 1978, 1979). And at the end of his 13-year NHL career, all with the Islanders, he would become the first defenseman to reach 1,000 career points (310 goals, 742 assists).

He also saw his No. 5 raised to the Nassau Coliseum ceiling in retirement.

CAREER TOTALS											
GP	G	A	Pts	+/-	GWG	GTG	S	S%	PPG	SHG	PIM
1060	310	742	1052	460	44	9	3053	10.2	127	10	1354

CHRIS PRONGER

Name: Chris Pronger
Born: October 10, 1974, Dryden, Ontario
Shoots: Left
Height: 6-6
Weight: 220

"He's one of the top defensemen in the league, and he plays a ton of minutes in every situation. And he's tough to play against. It's a big hole."

—Blues forward Scott Mellanby on the season-ending knee injury to teammate Chris Pronger

Chris Pronger has become the almost-$10 Million Man. Well, $9 million to be exact. Not bad for a 28-year-old defenseman whose first job was as a dishwasher.

At 6-feet-6, the 220-pound Pronger has long been one of the tallest guys to make a living on skates. Now he's one of the highest-paid.

Averaging more than 30 minutes a game on the ice in both 1998–1999 and 1999–2000, Pronger was tops in the league in game action and the only one above the 30-minute mark. Ray Bourque, Chris Chelios, Brian Leetch and Al Macinnis trailed him.

The St. Louis Blues had to think that all of this was a possibility when they gave up All-Star Brendan Shanahan in 1995 for Pronger, Hartford's first choice and the second overall, in the 1993 Entry Draft.

Pronger won the Plus-Minus Award and finished third in the Norris Trophy race. The nest year the Blues named him captain.

By 1998-1999, Pronger was recording 46 points, 132 hits and 119 blocked shots in 67 games. *The Hockey News* had him ranked eighth in their Top 50 Players list that year.

Then the Blues moved up to the Presidents Trophy the following year with a team-record 51 wins. Pronger joined some special company, especially for a defenseman. He doubled up on awards, taking both the Hart Trophy for league MVP and the Norris Trophy for the league's best defender.

The last defenseman who did that, was Bobby Orr in 1972, two years before Pronger was born.

At the end of the 2000 season, Pronger was up to No. 4 on the *The Hockey News'* Top 50 list of players.

CAREER TOTALS											
GP	G	A	Pts	+/-	GWG	GTG	S	S%	PPG	SHG	PIM
637	79	263	342	128	10	3 1	387	5.7	37	2	1000

LARRY ROBINSON

Name: Larry Clark Robinson
Born: June 2, 1951, Winchester, Ontario
Shoots: Left
Height: 6-4
Weight: 225

"Most of the fixing had to be between the ears, not on the ice."

—Larry Robinson on his role as stand-in coach for the New Jersey Devils Stanley Cup run in 2000

They called Larry Robinson "Big Bird," but the 6-foot-4, 225-pound defenseman was more than a cartoon character. The Winchester, Ontario native was the real deal with really big numbers.

When Robinson retired, he had played a then-record 227 playoff games—a number exceeded eventually by Mark Messier—in a record 20 consecutive postseasons. Lots of players' entire careers don't last that many games.

No one else ever went to that many straight playoffs.

Six times Robinson helped Montreal to Stanley Cup titles. And then just for himself, as a late replacement coach for Robbie Ftorek with the New Jersey Devils in 2000, he took home another one. Robinson also won a pair of Norris Trophies (1977, 1980), the Conn Smythe Trophy (1978) and the NHL Plus-Minus Leader (1977).

In addition to the Devils, Robinson was head coach with the Los Angeles Kings for four seasons (1995–1999). During that first year with the Kings, Robinson was inducted into the Hockey Hall of Fame.

A terrific puckhandler, Robinson was much more than a big, strong banger. He was also a tremendous success in international play. The three Team Canada clubs he played on in the Canada Cup—1976, 1981 and 1984—all won championships.

CAREER TOTALS											
GP	G	A	Pts	+/-	GWG	GTG	S	S%	PPG	SHG	PIM
1384	208	750	958	730	29	10	2338	8.9	66	3	793

SERGE SAVARD

Name: Serge A. Savard
Born: January 22, 1946, Montreal, Quebec
Shoots: Right
Height: 5-11
Weight: 172

"It's my greatest souvenir in my life in sports. It's just a great feeling (to return), it's hard to describe. It has been 30 years."

—Serge Savard returning to Moscow arena where Team Canada beat Soviets in Summit Series

Serge Savard took full advantage of being born in Montreal and playing hockey there.

His eight Stanley Cups all came in the white, blue and red colors of his hometown Canadiens.

Not bad for a little guy (172 pounds and just 5-foot-11) who won his first Stanley Cup during his first season in the league (1968).

But look at what he did in Year 2. Savard not only led his Canadiens to a second straight title, he also became the first defenseman to win the Conn Smythe Trophy as the Most Valuable Player in the postseason.

He didn't do it alone on defense, however. Larry Robinson and Guy Lapointe were right beside him those days in Montreal.

Savard would go on to help the Habs to Cup wins in 1971, 1973 and 1976 through 1979. The man they called "The Senator" for his political interests would go on to work in party politics in Quebec. He'd also return to the Canadiens for a period as the team's general manager.

His final two seasons were in Winnipeg where he played for the Jets (1981–1983) after retiring briefly from the game.

Savard overcame a pair of broken legs in the 1971 and 1972 seasons and was eventually named the winner of the Bill Masterson Trophy for perseverance and and dedication to the game.

He was inducted into the Hockey Hall of Fame in 1986.

CAREER TOTALS											
GP	G	A	Pts	+/-	GWG	GTG	S	S%	PPG	SHG	PIM
1040	106	333	439	460*	13	9	1384*	7.7*	23	9	592

EARL SEIBERT

Name: Earl Walter Seibert
Born: December 7, 1911, Berlin, Ontario
Died: May 12, 1990
Height: 6-2
Weight: 198

"Yeah, I killed him."

—Earl Seibert when asked if he'd ever played against Howie Morenz.

Earl Seibert was far ahead of his time in the National Hockey League, although you have to think he'd just as soon not have been.

But because of an injury in his minor league days that would stay with him his entire career, Seibert became the first player in the National Hockey League to wear a helmet every game.

This was back in 1931 when there were some football players not wearing helmets. But Seibert would, the result of a concussion he'd suffered in the Can-Am League.

A big man for those days at 6-foot-2 and 198 pounds, Seibert was a no-nonsense guy. By the end of his second year, he'd led the New York Rangers to a Stanley Cup. But negotiating with him was no picnic, especially when he got his father, Oliver, a Hockey Hall of Fame player from the turn of the century, involved. Soon the Rangers had shipped Seibert off to Chicago.

Ten straight seasons in Chicago Seibert was named an All-Star. That impressive run would be exceeded only by Gordie Howe, Maurice Richard, Bobby Hull and Doug Harvey.

During Seibert's time, the two premier defensemen were Eddie Shore and himself. Shore said Seibert was the only man he wouldn't want to fight. But before leading his Blackhawks to a Stanley Cup in 1938, Seibert was a part of one of hockey's most tragic incidents.

In tying up Howie Morenz of the Canadiens against the boards one night in Chicago, somehow Morenz fell and shattered his leg, ending his career. Six weeks later, Morenz died, unable to handle the fact that his career was over.

Seibert would have to deal with it the rest of his life. It wasn't easy.

Asked if he ever played against Morenz, Seibert's answer was: "Yeah, I killed him."

He was elected to the Hockey Hall of Fame in 1963, two years after his father had been named. Oliver and Earl Seibert are the only father-son Hall of Famers.

CAREER TOTALS											
GP	G	A	Pts	+/-	GWG	GTG	S	S%	PPG	SHG	PIM
1362	658	1004	1662	161	.87	11	4362	15.1	190	50	852

EDDIE SHORE

Name: Edward William Shore
Born: November 25, 1902, Fort Qu'Appele, Saskatchewan
Died: March 16, 1985
Shoots: Right
Height: 5-11
Weight: 190

"The Boston Bruins fielded strong teams, led by fine players before 1926-27, but they never won a championship or had a player the whole town talked about until Eddie Shore arrived that season."
—Boston Bruins media guide

Eddie Shore was more than just a big, strong, tough, determined defenseman. He was a mean one, too.

Not only would he get himself to a place on the ice, with one of his patented end-to-end rushes, he would get there in a very bad mood.

They say it was the result of growing up on a ranch in Saskatchewan where his duties had him breaking in ponies and doing all the sorts of physical chores that made him the big, bad burly dude who terrorized the National Hockey League.

After Boston's Bruins rescued him from the Western Canada Hockey League, Shore would go on to set new records for penalty minutes. He would also be half of one of the early tragedies in hockey history when a Shore hit to the head ended the career of Toronto's Ace Bailey, who became the beneficiary of the game's first-ever major benefit game.

Shore led the Bruins—people said he could control a game from the defensive end—to their first Stanley Cup title in 1929. A decade later, he did it again. Upon retirement, Shore would become player coach-owner of the Springfield Indians in the American Hockey League and become something of a precursor to the Vince Lombardi school of hard knocks coaching.

He was inducted into the Hockey Hall of Fame in 1945 and 52 years later, in 1997, *The Hockey News* listed him as the No. 10 player in all of hockey history.

During his playing days, he won the Hart Trophy four times (1933, 1935, 1936 and 1938). He also was named winner of the Lester Patrick Trophy in 1970 for service to hockey in the United States.

CAREER TOTALS											
GP	G	A	Pts	+/-	GWG	GTG	S	S%	PPG	SHG	PIM
550	105	179	284	0*	0*	0*	0*	-*	0*	0*	1047

SYL APPS

Name: Charles Joseph Sylvanus Apps
Born: January 18, 1915, Paris, Ontario
Died: December 24, 1998
Shoots: Left
Height: 6-0
Weight: 185

"Nobody with a name like that could possibly become a pro hockey player."

—Toronto Maple Leafs owner Conn Smythe on prospect Sylvanus Apps

A man for all seasons?

Without a doubt, Charles Josephus Sylvanus "Syl" Apps was that and much more—great college football player, Olympic pole-vaulter and National Hockey League All-Star.

He was also a man for his country, serving in World War II and missing several seasons during his prime playing days.

Syl Apps was one of those people who seemed almost too good to be true. His upstanding personal qualities were matched by his athletic abilities. A tough, strong hockey player with a sharp shot, it almost seems too simplistic to reduce Apps' personal history to merely sports.

His first notice came as a 185-pound football star at Hamilton's McMaster University. He was good enough in football for his hockey talents to just be assumed. But he also had a date in Berlin with the 1936 Olympics as a pole-vaulter. So hockey would have to wait when Apps would become the Calder Cup-winning rookie of the year in 1937 on his way to NHL first-team All-Star in 1939 and 1942, before missing much of the next year with a serious leg injury and then going away to war for next two seasons after that.

A tough guy who almost never fought on the ice—although he did very well the few times he did, Apps once went an entire season (1942) without a fight to earn the Lady Byng Trophy. That was the year Apps captained the Maple Leafs to a Stanley Cup.

There are many stories about Apps and his too-good-to-be-true attitude. There was his unprecedented offer to give back $1,000—one-sixth of his 1942–1943 salary—to the Maple Leafs because he felt he wasn't earning it, while recovering from a broken leg.

Maybe it shouldn't be a surprise that after his hockey career, Apps went on to government service in both the legislature and as a government minister.

There is one other measure of how people felt about Apps. He is the only person in all three Hockey Halls of Fame as well as the Canadian Sports Hall of Fame and the Canadian Amateur Athletics Hall of Fame.

He also has his Toronto jersey retired in Maple Leaf Gardens.

CAREER TOTALS											
GP	G	A	Pts	+/-	GWG	GTG	S	S%	PPG	SHG	PIM
423	201	231	432	0*	0*	0*	0*	-*	0*	0*	56

JEAN BELIVEAU

Name: Jean Arthur Beliveau
Born: August 31, 1931 Trois Rivieres, Quebec
Shoots: Left
Height: 6-3
Weight: 210

"It was like running into the side of a big oak tree. I bounced right off the guy and landed on the seat of my pants."

—NHL player Bill Ezinicki on hitting Jean Beliveau the first time

He was the first modern hockey player, big, strong, smooth, natural, able to cover the ice in long, sweeping strides, Jean Beliveau used his 6-foot-3, 210-pound body tvery effectively.

And even though his arrival into the National Hockey League was marked by something of a turf war in Quebec, Beliveau's playing days with Montreal didn't seem at all marred by the personal contretemps that so often seemed to intrude on the life of players in the Forum.

Beliveau seemed always somehow above it. "Le Gros Bill" just went out and played hockey in his cool, composed way.

And he did so for a long time at a very high level. and in a very classy way. Some would say the classiest. The Jean Beliveau Fund for underprivileged children seemed perfectly to suit him.

"Any parent could use Jean Beliveau as a pattern or role model. He provides hockey with a magnificent image," said NHL president Clarence Campbell. "I couldn't speak more highly of anyone associated with our game than I do of Jean."

For 19 seasons, Beliveau was a Montreal Canadien. He made the playoffs a record 16 years.

Then there were the trio of tens. Beliveau was Canadien captain for 10 of those years. And a first-team All-Star for 10 as well.

There were those 10 Stanley Cup championships. And twice he won the Hart Trophy (in 1956 and 1964) as the league's MVP.

He also won the Art Ross Trophy, the President's Cup, the Conn Smythe Trophy and was named to the Hockey Hall of fame in 1972.

In a later-day career as successful businessman, Beliveau also became the Canadiens' good will ambassador.

CAREER TOTALS											
GP	G	A	Pts	+/-	GWG	GTG	S	S%	PPG	SHG	PIM
1144	358	852	1210	506	38	23	2587	13.8	99	32	1453

BOBBY CLARKE

Name: Robert Earle Clarke
Born: August 14, 1939, Flin Flon, Manitoba
Shoots: Left
Height: 5-10
Weight: 185

"The greatest player in the game for helping his team."
—Flyer Coach Fred Shero describing Bobby Clarke

When you see Bobby Clarke today in his National Hockey League team executive's role, wearing his pinstripe suit and tie, it's hard to imagine him as the leader of one of the most physically intimidating teams in the history of hockey.

Or to picture the red-haired Clarke with his teeth out, glaring menacingly as he searches for the next opponent to take a shot at.

But that was the essence of the most famous man to come out of Flin Flon, Manitoba.

He may have just been 5-foot-10 and 185 pounds, but this was one tough guy, even if he had to convince teams his diabetes would be no hindrance to him. Not that it didn't take a trip to the Mayo Clinic and a serious daily diet to keep it that way through his career.

But Clarke had to be tough. There was no other way for a man to captain the Philadelphia Flyers to two straight Stanley Cups in 1974 and 1975. In those years, the Flyers proved that an expansion team could thoroughly intimidate the NHL's original six—and anyone else who got in the Broad Street Bullies' way.

Clarke had an instant impact in Philadelphia as the team's second pick in the 1969 draft. He would go on to win three Hart Trophies, two first-team All-Star spots and three times score more than 100 points, including a career-high 119 in 1976.

He was a magnificent leader, a man who inspired his teammates to play hard and and to do all the tough things. He battled on defense and in the corners. He scrambled for the puck on faceoffs and became a master of that skill.

After his hockey days, Clarke has gone on to his second stint as Flyers' general manager after time running both the Minnesota North Stars and Florida Panthers.

Clarke also played in the historic Summit Series between Canada and the Soviet Union in 1972 and has had a number of international leadership roles for Canada teams. He was inducted into the Hockey Hall of Fame in 1987.

He also earned the Bill Masterson Trophy (1972), the Lester B. Pearson Award (1973), the Lester Patrick Trophy (1980), the Selke Trophy (1983) and the NHL Plus/Minus Award (1976).

CAREER TOTALS											
GP	G	A	Pts	+/-	GWG	GTG	S	S%	PPG	SHG	PIM
1362	658	1004	1662	161	.87	11	4362	15.1	190	50	852

ALEX DELVECCHIO

Name: Alex Peter Delvecchio
Born: December 4, 1932, Ft. William, Ontario
Shoots: Left
Height: 6-0
Weight: 195

"It never really bothered me. Gordie was the greatest player of all time. When you played with him, and he gave you the puck, you just knew that some good things were going to happen for the Red Wings."

—Alex Delvecchio on being Gordie Howe's teammate

Ted Lindsay was on one side of him, Gordie Howe was on the other. And in front of Alex Delvecchio in his center slot on the Detroit Red Wings' "Production Line" for a number of years was one Sid Abel.

Not bad company.

The Red Wings were like that. Good company for a solid, slick, quick and classy skater like Alex "Fats" Delvecchio from the very start of his 24 seasons in Detroit. In all that time, he would miss a mere 43 games. And after teammate Howe, he was just the second player to complete 20 seasons with the same team.

By the time the Ft. William, Ontario native had spent four years in Hockeytown, Delvecchio and his mates had already earned three Stanley Cup rings.

The gentlemanly son of Italian immigrants would go on to earn three Lady Byng Trophies, a Lester Patrick Trophy and play in 13 NHL All-Star Games during a distinguished career that saw him move his familiar No. 10 to the left wing with Howe and Norm Ullman for a time and be awarded the captain's "C" in 1962, a designation he held for a dozen years.

Delvecchio was one of just three NHL players to make the All-Star team at two positions—center and left wing.

His career Red Wings totals are impressive, especially considering the talent around him. Delvecchio played in 1,549 games, scored 456 goals, recorded 825 assists. And then he became a Red Wings coach and general manager.

Delvecchio was second in the numbers behind Howe in all scoring statistics. Today he's third, also behind Steve Yzerman. But just take his 456 goals scored. Only five other NHL players had ever scored that many.

In 1977, Delvecchio was inducted into the Hockey Hall of Fame.

CAREER TOTALS											
GP	G	A	Pts	+/-	GWG	GTG	S	S%	PPG	SHG	PIM
1549	456	825	1281	33*	34*	7*	1084*	11.8*	63*	5*	383

MARCEL DIONNE

Name: Marcel Ephege Dionne
Born: August 3, 1951, Drummondville, Quebec
Shoots: Right
Height: 5-9
Weight: 190

Marcel Dionne is the answer to that old question about a tree falling in the forest with no one around. Does anyone hear it?

Well, if you're Marcel Dionne, laboring mostly in the hockey wilderness of Los Angeles in those early expansion days, you can make them hear you if you do your job well for as long as Dionne did.

That was 18 years for Dionne and 731 regular season goals. Only Wayne Gretzky and Gordie Howe scored more. And Dionne's 1,771 total points were likewise behind only the totals of Gretzky and Howe.

Dionne's scoring battles with Gretzky were legendary. In Gretzky's rookie season, Dionne and Gretzky tied with 137 points, but Dionne—with 53 goals to Gretzky's 51—was awarded his lone scoring title.

The next season he finished with 135 points, but lost to Gretzky this time.

From his early years with the Detroit Red Wings, it was obvious the 5-foot-9, 180-pound Drummondville, Quebec native could score. In 1974-1975, he recorded 121 points as a Red Wing. But in 1978, Dionne would become the National Hockey League's first free agent.

As a King for a dozen seasons, Dionne went on to the most memorable years of his career, especially after forming the Triple Crown Line with Dave Taylor and Charlie Simmer. Dionne scored at least 50 goals as a King six times.

Dionne would be traded to the New York Rangers to complete his Hall of Fame career, which culminated in his official induction in 1992.

Honors that came Dionne's way included: the Lady Byng Trophy (1975, 1977), the Art Ross Trophy (1980), the Lester B. Pearson Award (1979, 1980). He would also play in eight All-Star Games.

The Kings retired Dionne's No. 16 on November 8, 1990.

CAREER TOTALS											
GP	G	A	Pts	+/-	GWG	GTG	S	S%	PPG	SHG	PIM
1348	731	1040	1771	44	74	39	5366	13.6	234	19	600

PHIL ESPOSITO

Name: Philip Anthony Esposito
Born: February 20, 1942, Sault Ste. Marie, Ontario
Shoots: Left
Height: 6-1
Weight: 205

"Jesus Saves: Espo scores on the rebound."

—popular bumper sticker in Boston in the mid-1970s

The secret to Phil Esposito's scoring was simple: He could get to the slot on the ice where he could score in every way a player could score.

And there was nothing you could do about it. The 6-foot-1, 210-pounder from Sault Ste.Marie was just too tough and strong and determined.

Some said he was just a garbage scorer, cleaning up the left-overs of others. But that wasn't it. Phil Esposito didn't care how he scored. They all counted, didn't they?

"I'd rather see Bobby Orr with the puck at the right point than Esposito with the puck in the slot," goaltender Rogie Vachon said. "It comes off his stick so fast that you can't see it until it's behind you."

That's the way Esposito racked up 717 goals with 873 assists for 1590 points in only 1282 regular season games.

Espo was also the first National Hockey League player to reach the century mark when he scored 126 points in the 1968-1969 season on 49 goals and 77 assists.

That was two seasons after being traded from the Chicago Blackhawks to the Boston Bruins, where he became an NHL scoring machine. How can anyone forget his 1970-1971 season when he scored 76 goals in 78 games.

One thing they won't forget in Boston is the two Stanley Cups (1970, 1972) Esposito helped take the Bruins to—or his four scoring titles.

His impressive list of honors included 10 All-Star Game appearances, three Art Ross Trophies, two Hart Trophies, two Lester B. Pearson Awards and a Lester Patrick Award.

Esposito was inducted into the Hockey Hall of Fame in 1984 and be the key player in bringing hockey to the Tampa Bay area after serving as coach and general manager of the Rangers for three years.

On retiring in 1981, Esposito had 717 goals, 873 assists and 1,590 points in 1,282 games over 18 seasons, good for fourth on the NHL all-time list in goals and points.

CAREER TOTALS											
GP	G	A	Pts	+/-	GWG	GTG	S	S%	PPG	SHG	PIM
1282	717	873	1590	197*	118	29	4595*	14.0*	249	23	910

PETER FORSBERG

Name: Peter Forsberg
Born: July 20, 1973, Ornskoldsvik, Sweden
Shoots: Left
Height: 6-0
Weight: 205

"I'd pay big money to watch Peter (Forsberg) The Greatest play. And I always get in free."

—Denver Post columnist Woody Paige

When *The Hockey News* was considering recently who should be considered as "franchise players," they came up with just five.

One of them was Peter Forsberg.

Sweden's Magic Boy, the first hockey player to appear on a Swedish postage stamp, the first National Hockey League player to host the Stanley Cup overseas, was the answer. And he continues to be.

The 6-foot, 205-pound son of a hockey coach from Ornskoldsvik, Sweden can do it all. He can skate with speed. he can set up the play, he can protect the puck, he can do pretty much whatever it is a hockey team needs him to do at both ends of the ice.

"He can play everywhere, anywhere and in any situation," said Philadelphia Flyers coach Ken Hitchcock.

And he's one of the many reasons why the Eric Lindros draft deal has made so many people happy in Avalanche Land.

Forsberg, a pick of the Flyers, was sent to Quebec (now Colorado) in that multi-player Lindros deal. What do you want to bet the Flyers would like to have him back?

Forsberg won the Calder Cup as rookie of the year and a Stanley Cup in 1996.

He's also won an Olympic gold medal, that he pretty much accounted for himself by scoring the game-winning goal in the shootout with Canada in 1994.

His father Kent, coached Peter with Team Sweden in the 1996 World Cup, 1998 Olympics and 1998 World Championships.

"Forsberg gets right up and hits you back," says New Jersey Devil Jason Arnott. "That's why he's one of the best."

Jeremy Roenick went even further.

"He has the physical talent with hands that are so electric. His brains make him one of the smartest players on the ice. When you combine all of that, there's no better all-around player in all of the NHL. There's not one."

CAREER TOTALS											
GP	G	A	Pts	+/-	GWG	GTG	S	S%	PPG	SHG	PIM
466	169	411	580	139	31	1	1193	14.2	46	14	444

RON FRANCIS

Name: Ronald Michael Francis
Born: March 1, 1963, Sault Ste. Marie, Ontario
Shoots: Left
Height: 6-3
Weight: 200

"I thought if I could play ten seasons that it would be a successful career and I'd be satisfied. As I got older and went beyond that mark, I saw things in a different light."
—Ron Francis

There may have been more underrated players in the National Hockey League the past two decades than Ron Francis, but it wouldn't be easy to list any.

Or to list even one.

Ron Francis has been laboring pretty much somewhere off in his own world, it seems.

Maybe in leading his Carolina Hurricanes past the Montreal Canadiens in the 2002 playoffs, perhaps, the original Hartord Whaler will finally be recognized for what he is.

And that is simply one of the best, most-consistent and durable all-around talents in National Hockey League history.

He's clearly a Hall of Famer.

For 10 seasons, he was a Whaler, or maybe that should be "The" Whaler. He led them in scoring five times, in assists nine times and was MVP four times. Then he was traded to Pittsburgh and earned his two Stanley Cups (1991, 1992) alongside Mario Lemieux. That's when folks outside New England started to really notice the 6-foot-3, 200-pounder from Sault Ste. Marie.

He then went on to a Selke Trophy (in 1995), when he led the NHL in assists, and a couple of Lady Byngs (1995, 1998) before ending up in 1999 with his old franchise—Hartford, and in a new state—Carolina, and with a new name—Hurricanes.

Quietly he has moved onto this impressive list of all-time career scorers who have totaled 1,600 points: Wayne Gretzky, Gordie Howe, Marcel Dionne, Mark Messier and Steve Yzerman.

Then there's Francis.

It's almost like some sort of multiple-choice question. Which of these does not belong? It would be an easy call. All those glitzy names and Ron Francis.

He's even higher on the all-time career assist list alone in the top three—with only Gretzky and Paul Coffey. Among current players, only Messier has scored more points.

Along with Howe, he is the only other player in National Hockey League history to score 50 points or more in 20 consecutive seasons.

CAREER TOTALS											
GP	G	A	Pts	+/-	GWG	GTG	S	S%	PPG	SHG	PIM
1569	514	1187	1701	21	76	12	3507	14.7	173	11	935

WAYNE GRETZKY

Name: Wayne Doug Gretzky
Born: January 26, 1961, Brantford, Ontario
Shoots: Left
Height: 6-0
Weight: 185

"The fact that the record was broken by someone who's such a great person takes away any sense of loss that I might have."
—Gordie Howe on Wayne Gretzky passing him as the NHL's all-time leading scorer

Where to begin? How to describe the incomparable career of the man they've always called "The Great One"?

He was young and slim and always a star, it seemed, from the time he hit the ice professionally as a 17-year-old in the World Hockey Association.

When he finished, here was the astounding tally: Most career points—2,328; most career assists—1,563; most goals in one season, 92, in 1981–1982; most assists in a season, 163, in 1985–1986; most points in a season, 215, in 1985–1986; most goals, 110, most assists, 236, and most points, 346, in a playoff career; most games with three or more goals, 48; most seasons with 100 or more points, 13; highest average assists per game, 1.497, and points per game, 2.230.

And here's the one number that makes the point as well as any. Gretzky's final total of 2,857 regular season points was 1,007 more—that's right, 1,007—more than that of the No. 2 man, Gordie Howe. Although this might put it into better focus, Wayne Gretzky, with his no-look and wraparound passes, has more assists than any other player in hockey history has points. Oh, and he's the only player to break the 200-point barrier in hockey history with his 212-point total (92 goals, 120 assists) in 1981–1982 and topping it in 1985–86 with 215 (52 goals, 163 assists).

Gretzky won the Hart Trophy as MVP a record nine times and the Ross Trophy as the leading scorer another nine times. But all those impressive numbers were not just individual ones. Gretzky led his Edmonton Oilers to four Stanley Cup titles in nine years.

Then it was on to do some proselytizing. First Gretzky helped establish the game in America's Sunbelt with an eight-year stay in Los Angeles and one unlikely Stanley Cup finals run. Then it was off to the East Coast and the New York Rangers for three seasons, with a short stop in St. Louis on the way.

Waiving the three-year eligibility period, the Hockey Hall Of Fame took The Great One in right away in 1999 and, echoing the year of his induction, decreed that no NHL franchise will ever issue Gretzky's famed No. 99.

CAREER TOTALS											
GP	G	A	Pts	+/-	GWG	GTG	S	S%	PPG	SHG	PIM
1362	658	1004	1662	161	.87	11	4362	15.1	190	50	852

DALE HAWERCHUK

Name: Dale Martin Hawerchuk
Born: April 4, 1963, Toronto, Ontario
Shoots: Left
Height: 5-11
Weight: 190

"He has the same instincts, that puck sense, of Gretzky."
—Mike Doran, director of player personnel, Winnipeg Jets

Always they saw him in the light of Wayne Gretzky. Always that was unfair to Dale Hawerchuk.

But there's nothing much a player can do about when he comes along. And so for a super junior prospect, one who has been good from a very early age, one whose father had said, "He was skating before he could walk," saying he was "like Gretzky" was just the way it went.

Especially when his junior honors seemed almost Gretzky-like. Even now, Hawerchuk's junior days are the stuff of legend. He could skate. He could score.

He was the next Gretzky, for sure.

Except for this. There will not be another Gretzky.

Hawerchuk was what he was. He was the first pick in the 1981 Entry Draft by the Winnipeg Jets.

He was one of only three rookies—Mario Lemieux and Peter Stastny were the others—to score 100 points in his rookie year, when he earned the Calder Trophy as rookie of the year. And that was at the age of 18.

And his team, the Jets, had been turned around in a way that no other ever had—48 points in all. He would go on to record 100-point seasons in five of the next six years.

He also finished as runnerup to the Hart Trophy. But by 1990, despite having written his name all over the Jets record book, he was traded to Buffalo's Sabres. He also showed up during that time for every Canada Cup call, four in all, from 1982 through 1991. And he relished the chance to play on the line behind Gretzky, Mario Lemieux and Mark Messier.

Hawerchuk would go on to the St. Louis Blues and eventually the Philadelphia Flyers with a final All-Star Game for him the 1995–1996 season.

But the next year at 34, he retired, with a splendid record of 15 playoffs in 16 seasons and more than a point-per-game average for 13 straight seasons.

And good enough, it is expected, to earn him a Hockey Hall of Fame selection in the near future.

CAREER TOTALS											
GP	G	A	Pts	+/-	GWG	GTG	S	S%	PPG	SHG	PIM
1188	518	891	1409	-92	49	13	3754	13.8	182	13	730

MARIO LEMIEUX

Name: Mario Lemieux
Born: October 10, 1965, Montreal, Quebec
Shoots: Right
Height: 6-4
Weight: 225

"No one could have done it but Mario Lemieux."

—NHL Commissioner Gary Bettman on the group he put together to save the Penguins

Mario Lemieux was—is—something special.

In 1984, a National Hockey League that already had its Great One had to make room for the Magnificent One. Wayne Gretzky, say hello to Mario Lemieux.

With a flair for the dramatic, Lemieux scored on his very first National Hockey League shift, repaying the Pittsburgh Penguins who had drafted him No. 1 in 1984. Then he went on to become one of just three rookies to reach 100 points.

That was only the start of a career that in many ways has no equal in hockey history. No one has overcome more illness and injury to revive not only his own career, but his own team and his town. It was just what we should have expected.

In effect, Mario has had two careers. There was the first—the standard superstar version—where he posted 168 points, then 199 (second only to Gretzky's 212 in a year), then 160 and 161 even in a comeback year after a season off because of a back injury.

There were also the two Stanley Cups he brought home to Pittsburgh, not to mention the season that saw him take off a month for radiation treatments for his Hodgkin's disease, then return to earn his fourth Ross Trophy and the Hart Trophy.

Lemieux won so many awards it's hard to know how to list them—four Lester Pearson Awards, six Art Ross Trophies, the Conn Smythe in back-to-back seasons of 1991 and 1992 and eight All-Star team selections. He was also named the Dodge Performer of the Year Award (1988, 1989), the Dodge Ram Tough Award (1989), the ProSet/NHL Player of the Year Award (1992), the Bill Masterton Memorial Trophy (1993) and the Alka-Seltzer Plus Award (1993).

And that should have been it as he became an owner at 33 to save the financially strapped Penguins and went right into the Hockey Hall of Fame in 1997.

But then he did something truly worthy of his Magical moniker. He came back. In the entire history of hockey, only two other Hall of Famers—Gordie Howe and Guy Lafleur—have ever managed that.

When he was just 21, Trevor Linden was asked to carry on the captain's "C" on his

CAREER TOTALS											
GP	G	A	Pts	+/-	GWG	GTG	S	S%	PPG	SHG	PIM
812	654	947	1601	158	70	9	3300	19.8	219	48	769

TREVOR LINDEN

Name: Trevor Linden
Born: April 11, 1970, Medicine Hat, Alberta
Shoots: Right
Height: 6-4
Weight: 214

When he was just 21, Trevor Linden was asked to carry on the captain's "C" on his Vancouver Canucks jersey. No player that young had ever been so honored as the 6-foot-4, 214-pounder from Medicine Hat, Alberta.

After eight seasons in Vancouver, Linden was off to New York for two years with the Islanders, then to Montreal for two with the Canadiens, then to D.C. for more than a year as a Washington Capital and then back to Vancouver with a trade in 2001–2002.

Back to where he'd been runner-up for the Calder Cup in his rookie year, where he'd been named Hockey News' rookie of the year and, at the age of 18, was the youngest player on the all-rookie team.

And where he'd led the Canucks to a crazy seven-game Stanley Cup Finals loss to the New York Rangers in the 1993–1994 season as the Canucks went 28–0 in games when he scored a goal. That was the third year in a row that the Canucks won 40 games, something they had never done before.

A year later, Linden won the King Clancy Award for leadership on and off the ice.

He also played in 482 straight games through December 7, 1997.

Linden has also had a busy international career for Canada, playing in the World Juniors in 1987-1988 and then for Canada in the 1991 and 1997 World Championships and the 1996 World Cup and the 1998 Olympics.

CAREER TOTALS											
GP	G	A	Pts	+/-	GWG	GTG	S	S%	PPG	SHG	PIM
1008	316	421	737	-54	37	5	2299	13.7	105	14	775

ERIC LINDROS

Name: Eric B. Lindros
Born: February 28, 1973, London, Ontario
Shoots: Right
Height: 6-4
Weight: 235

"The guy who stepped up to the plate for them was Eric Lindros. That's his job…to step up and make sure his team comes out of here with a win and he was able to do that."
—Florida Panthers Coach Mike Keenan

It's never been easy being Eric Lindros.

But certainly interesting.

After winning the Bobby Clarke Trophy four times as the Philadelphia Flyers most valuable player, Lindros and the above-named Clarke engaged in a game of chicken that saw the 6-foot-4, 235-pound center sit out the entire 2000–2001 National Hockey League season.

And there seemed to be a chance that would be it for the big guy's playing days.

Lindros wasn't going to play for the Flyers and the Flyers weren't going to let him go anywhere else without getting something of value and so there they stood staring at each other until a trade with the New York Rangers sent Lindros to Manhattan for three players and a draft pick.

Maybe no one should be surprised. After all, that's the way Lindros came into the league—in a cloud of controversy and uncertainty. He'd said he wouldn't play in Quebec but the Nordiques picked him No. 1 overall anyway. And then they dickered until June 30 when in an arbitrator's decision, Lindros was awarded to the Flyers for six players—including Peter Forsberg and Ron Hextall—and cash in a dynasty-creating deal.

Unfortunately for Clarke and the Flyers, the dynasty that deal created turned out to be in Colorado, where the Quebec franchise turned into the Avalanche.

Not that Lindros was a bust in Philly. Far from it. By the end of his all-rookie season, Lindros was ranked the No. 2 player in all of hockey on the *Hockey News* Top 25 list.

By 1994-1995, Lindros was named Flyers captain and won both the Lester Pearson and Hart Trophies, *The Hockey News'* Player of the Year Award, and named a first-team All-Star.

There was one problem. The biggest, strongest player in hockey, some would contend, was too big and strong for his own good. His physical style of play exposed Lindros himself to injuries even more than it did his opponents.

And even though it must seem that No. 88 has been around forever, Eric Lindros is just 29. Plenty of time to get where everyone was so sure he would.

CAREER TOTALS											
GP	G	A	Pts	+/-	GWG	GTG	S	S%	PPG	SHG	PIM
558	327	405	732	207	41	9	1840	17.8	94	7	1084

MARK MESSIER

Name: Mark John Douglas Messier
Born: January 18, 1961, Edmonton, Alberta
Shoots: Left
Height: 6-1
Weight: 210

"The only way this would be a career-ending injury is if I didn't come back and there's no way I'm thinking like that."
—Mark Messier of his shoulder surgery in 2002

If it seems like Mark Messier is the guy who's always there, there's a reason for that. He always is where it matters.

Like in the playoffs.

No player in the history of the National Hockey League has ever played in as many Stanley Cup playoff games as Messier. Only two have scored more points than the 1,804 he's tallied on 658 goals and 1,146 assists. And they would be Wayne Gretzky and Gordie Howe.

So the Edmonton native is in the company of the best in the game—ever.

He's won six Stanley Cups in his 23 seasons and the New York Rangers media guide has a full page devoted to his awards and honors.

At 6-feet-1 and 210 pounds, Messier was never the biggest or the fastest of the star centers. But if you could bottle leadership, Messier could sell it.

He helped lead his hometown Oilers—with a little help from Wayne Gretzky in four of the Stanley Cups—to NHL titles five times in seven years from 1983–1984 to 1989–1990. And then he brought a Stanley Cup—the first in 54 years—to Broadway and the New York Rangers.

Messier is the only player in hockey history to captain two different franchises to Stanley Cup championships.

Now in his second stint with the Rangers, Messier just keeps adding to his totals and honors. He already has a pair of Hart Trophies (1990, 1992), a Conn Smythe (1984), two Lester B. Pearsons (1990, 1992), four NHL first-team All-Star selections, one second-team and 14 All-Star appearances. He's even just undergone his first-ever career surgery with season-ending arthroscopic work on his shoulder.

Among active players, he's the leader in goals scored, assists and total points. He has eight career and seven career playoff records where he's in the top six of all time. Which isn't a bad place to be some days. Like the three-day period from March 17 to 19 in 2000.

On March 17, 2000 Messier passed Alex Delvecchio for fourth place on the all-time scoring list. Two days later, he passed Marcel Dionne for third.

CAREER TOTALS											
GP	G	A	Pts	+/-	GWG	GTG	S	S%	PPG	SHG	PIM
1602	658	1146	1804	209	84	16	3998	16.5	170	60	1838

STAN MIKITA

Name: Stanley Guoth Mikita
Born: May 20, 1940, Sokolce, Czechoslavakia
Shoots: Right
Height: 5-9
Weight: 169

"I grew up watching the Hawks; they were my favorite team—Bobby Hull and Stan Mikita."
—Toronto Maple Leafs goalie Ed Belfour

Has anyone ever gotten more out of his opportunities than Stan Mikita?

It's hard to imagine that anyone could have.

Adopted by his aunt and uncle at the age of 8, the Czech-born Stanley Guoth would take their name on his way to a 22-year career with the Chicago Blackhawks.

St. Catharines, Ontario gave him the chance to skate and Mikita took it from there. The fact that he played at 169 pounds never did seem to matter. His heart was always big enough to make up for any physical shortcomings .

And did they ever love him in the only hometown he would have in the National Hockey League. Mikita was Chicago's kind of player. Determined to make it, Mikita wasn't above matching his points with his penalty minutes..

But here's the kind of guy he was. When his daughter asked him about the penalties one time, Mikita decided to do something about it. And do something he did. He would become the first player in hockey history to win the Ross, Hart and Lady Byng trophies in the same season. He led in scoring, gentlemanly play and most valuable player voting.

Not bad for a little guy from Sokolce, Czechoslovakia.

Or anyone else, for that matter.

Mikita was a major part in the Blackhawks run to the Stanley Cup in 1960, the first time they had done it since 1937–1938.

But he was more than just tough. Stan Mikita was one smart guy. He was the first hockey player to use a curved blade on his hockey stick. And he developed the protective helmet he would wear throughout his career.

Mikita is also the last player to lead the league in scoring over a full season with fewer than 100 points. He was named to eight All-Star teams and won the rare trifecta in one season of the Ross, Hart and Lady Byng that he was the first to accomplish. He won the Ross in 1963–1964 and 1964–1965 as well. And in 1976, he was named the Lester Patrick Trophy winner.

In 1983, he was named to the Hockey Hall of Fame.

CAREER TOTALS											
GP	G	A	Pts	+/-	GWG	GTG	S	S%	PPG	SHG	PIM
1394	541	926	1467	159*	67*	19*	2624*	12.4*	128*	12*	1270

MIKE MODANO

Name: Mike Modano
Born: June 7, 1970, Livonia, Michigan
Shoots: Left
Height: 6-3
Weight: 205

"I've changed my style, and it's helped my game a lot. People still look at my points and production, but there's a lot more to this game than scoring goals."

—Mike Modano

He's one of the most recognizable players in the game, certainly in his home town of Dallas. Mike Modano has had the good fortune to be with the Stars franchise his whole career and has built on that opportunity—on and off the ice.

From modeling to TV appearances to his own Web site and charitable foundation, the 6-foot-3, 205-pound Livonia, Michigan native seems to have it all together.

He's ranked fifth on the *The Hockey News* Top 50 players list, up from 16th six years earlier, and is earning $ 8 million this year.

There's not much Mike Modano can't do. He plays both ways with speed, passing ability, a sound feel for the game, good puck control, strong checking, and a sensational shot. At the 2000 Stars Super Skills event, he won the fastest-shot competition with one registering a sizzling 103.4 miles per hour.

In his 13th season with the Stars, he owns the franchise record for goals. He's scored seven hat tricks with a career-high 50 goals in 1993–1994.

Seven times he's been voted winner of the Stars Masterson Trophy by his teammates as the club's MVP. He is just the fourth American-born player (with Joe Mullen, Pat LaFontaine and Tony Amonte) to post eight 30-goal seasons.

And his eighth 30-goal season, his 11th 20-goal season, his ninth 40-assist season, his ninth 70-point season, his eighth 70-point season and his 10th 60-point season are all franchise records.

One indication of Modano's athletic ability came in the 1998 Isuzu Celebrity Golf Classic when he won the long drive contest with a 379-yard drive, 10 yards past runner-up John Elway, the former Denver Broncos quarterback.

CAREER TOTALS											
GP	G	A	Pts	+/-	GWG	GTG	S	S%	PPG	SHG	PIM
946	416	561	977	103	65	15	2989	13.9	112	25	638

HOWIE MORENZ

Name: Howarth William Morenz
Born: June 21, 1902, Mitchell, Ontario
Died: March 8, 1937
Shoots: Left
Height: 5-9
Weight: 165

"He was the greatest of all time."

—Toronto Maple Leafs Coach Dick Irvin

It's not easy to tell National Hockey League fans about Howie Morenz because they'll hear things that simply do not compute.

"He was the greatest of all time," said Toronto Maple Leafs Coach Dick Irvin.

"The Babe Ruth of Hockey," they called him."The Stratford Streak," The Canadien Comet," "The Hurling Habitant" and "The Mitchell Meteor" were others.

But could a 5-foot-9, 165-pound center, no matter how fast, no matter how well he handled the puck, no matter how many nicknames he had, be that good?

Howie Morenz could.

And if he played in all the right places—Montreal, New York and Chicago—the way Morenz did. And if he did all the right things like leading the Canadiens to a Stanley Cup title his first year in the league at the age of 21. He paced the NHL in scoring over the next seven seasons, winning the Hart Trophy three times despite a number of injuries.

Morenz may have earned more respect from his contemporaries than any pro athlete ever. Here's what Rangers Coach Lester Patrick told his team one night before facing Morenz.

"Don't hit Morenz tonight," Patrick said. "The little guy is nursing a leg so sore he shouldn't be playing. He only dressed because he knows the New York fans are anxious to see him perform. So get in his way and go easy on him and his gimpy leg."

And then there's this. No one ever departed the game in so tragic and dramatic a fashion. Even now it's almost too terrible to recall.

Chasing a puck into the boards, Morenz was checked hard by the game's biggest, toughest, meanest defender, 6-foot-3, 220-pound Earl Seibert.

Unfortunately for Morenz, his skate blade got wedged into a crack in the boards as Seibert drove through him legally, breaking Morenz's leg as he fell to the ice.

Morenz died six weeks later of complications, unable, some say, to handle the knowledge that his playing days were over.

He was one of the first 12 players to inducted into the Hockey Hall of Fame in 1945.

CAREER TOTALS											
GP	G	A	Pts	+/-	GWG	GTG	S	S%	PPG	SHG	PIM
550	270	197	467	0*	0*	0*	0*	-*	0*	0*	563

MICHAEL PECA

Name: Michael Anthony Peca
Born: March 26, 1974, Toronto, Ontario
Shoots: Right
Height: 6-0
Weight: 190

"It's an honor and a privilege to represent your country and that's what should come out in your game. You want to prove to the world that you are the best."
—Michael Peca

Not all that big for a center at 6-feet and 190 pounds, Michael Peca tries to be in the right place at the right time, where his teammates need him to be. A fixture at the top of the voting for the Frank J. Selke Trophy annually for the National Hockey League's top defensive forward, Peca won it in 1996–1997 when he led the league with six shorthanded goals.

The assistant captain for the 2002 gold medal-winning Canadian Olympic team, Peca has had an extensive international career beginning with his gold medal in 1993 with the Canadian Junior team in the World Championships and as captain of Team Canada in the 2001 World Championships.

Drafted by the Vancouver Canucks, Peca played 37 games with the Canucks in parts of his first two seasons before moving on to Buffalo where he became the Sabres' captain.

The highlight of Peca's stay in Buffalo had to be his team's run to the Stanley Cup finals in 1999 when he totaled 13 assists in 21 playoff games.

Peca recorded two assists in six games in Team Canada's skate to the gold in February. Peca also has the distinction of scoring both the last goal for Buffalo in Memorial Auditorium and the first goal in the team's new HSBC Center.

Starting in 1998, Peca has been included in *The Hockey News* Top 50 players listing, first at No. 49, then No. 35.

An indication of how Peca is respected in the league is this. After being traded to the New York Islanders in the summer of 2001, the Toronto native was named the Islanders team captain at the start of the season.

CAREER TOTALS											
GP	G	A	Pts	+/-	GWG	GTG	S	S%	PPG	SHG	PIM
480	127	162	289	62	23	4	940	13.5	32	20	446

HENRI RICHARD

Name: Joseph Henri Richard
Born: February 29, 1936, Montreal, Quebec
Shoots: Right
Height: 5-7
Weight: 160

Pocket Rocket indeed.

Henri Richard might have had the most fitting nickname ever conferred on an athlete. The little guy—he was 5-feet-7 and 160 pounds of pure propellant—managed to launch himself on the hockey world right in his hometown of Montreal.

And in doing so, he silenced all those who said he was too small or not as fiery as his older brother Maurice, "The Rocket."

For any doubters, check out Lord Stanley's Cup. See if there's a name on it 11 times—as a player.

There's one. Joseph Henri Richard.

In 20 seasons, the Pocket Rocket helped the Canadiens to 11 Cups in a career that saw him play more games than anyone else who had ever suited up for the Habs. And he didn't waste any time, getting his first five in his first five seasons in the NHL.

When he succeeded the 6-foot-3, 210-pound Jean Beliveau as captain of the Canadiens, the little guy was just as popular, they say, as Le Gros Bill. And that is really saying something. He became just the ninth player in hockey history to score 1,000 points in his career, finishing with 1,046 (358 goals, 688 assists) in 1,256 games.

In an incredible 180 playoff games, Richard added another 129 points (40 goals, 89 assists). They still talk about his Stanley Cup tying and winning goals against the Chicago Blackhawks in Game 7 of the Finals to win his 10th Cup as an aging veteran.

Despite the fact that he didn't play with the almost out-of-control emotion of his brother, Henri Richard showed that he could play, win and survive for two decades at the top of the hockey world.

A tavern owner throughout his career and retirement, Richard was inducted into the Hockey Hall of Fame in 1979.

CAREER TOTALS											
GP	G	A	Pts	+/-	GWG	GTG	S	S%	PPG	SHG	PIM
1256	358	688	1046	126*	28*	9*	1279*	7.3*	19*	0*	928

MILT SCHMIDT

Name: Milton Conrad Schmidt
Born: March 5, 1918, Kitchener, Ontario
Shoots: Left
Height: 6-0
Weight: 185

"The ultimate Bruin."

—The Boston Globe

The Boston Globe was right. Milt Schmidt was "the ultimate Bruin."

What else to call an athlete who spends 37 years with a franchise as a player, a Stanley Cup winner, a captain, an All-Star, a coach and a general manager the way Milt Schmidt did with the Boston Bruins.

For that, Schmidt—No. 15 for the Bruins in his career—earned a spot as the 15th greatest athlete in New England history in the Globe's all-time top 100. He did it with his tough, aggressive play that earned him one broken bone after another, it seemed.

Llike the man who topped the list as the greatest Boston area athlete, Ted Williams, Schmidt lost nearly four of the prime years of his career to World War II. The Kitchener, Ontario native was a member of the Royal Canadian Air Force.

Those were some special times. Schmidt recalled the last game before the famed Bruins Kraut Line—himself, Woody Dumart and Bobby Bauer—left for the service. Fans would recall that in the 1939–1940 season the trio finished 1-2-3 in scoring—led by Schmidt's 52 points.

"It was against the Canadiens, and we beat them badly," he said. "I don't think I'll ever forget what happened after the game. The players on both teams lifted the three of us on their shoulders and carried us off the ice and the crowd gave us an ovation. A man couldn't ever forget a game like that."

Just as Bruin fans couldn't forget Schmidt, or the two Stanley Cups he led the Bruins to. The first, in 1939, was the first-ever for the franchise. Then the Bruins came back and did it again in 1941. They did it in the minimum—in those days—number of games, eight. No other team had ever managed that in NHL history.

After the war, it took Schmidt a good year to get back in the swing of things but by 1947, he was a first-team All-Star again. And at the age of 33, managed to win the Hart Trophy as the league's MVP. At his retirement in 1955, Schmidt had scored 575 points with 229 goals in 778 games. Schmidt would even go on to Washington as general manager and sometime coach for two seasons after Boston before being inducted into the Hockey Hall of Fame in 1961.

CAREER TOTALS											
GP	G	A	Pts	+/-	GWG	GTG	S	S%	PPG	SHG	PIM
776	229	346	575	0*	0*	0*	0*	-*	0*	0*	466

PETER STASTNY

Name: Peter Stastny
Born: September 18, 1956, Bratislava, Czechoslovakia
Shoots: Left
Height: 6-1
Weight: 200

"I used to look up to all the good players, but they [his brothers Marian and Anton] were special. And, of course, Stan Mikita, too."
—Peter Stastny

Peter Stastny may have been the ultimate in international hockey heroes. The Bratislava, Czechoslovakia native defected after the 1980 Olympics in Lake Placid, to play in the National Hockey League for the Quebec Nordiques. He would be joined by brothers Anton and Marian in Quebec.

It didn't take long for Czechoslovakia's best player to show what he could do in the NHL. He scored an amazing 109 points (39 goals, 70 assists) in his Calder Cup-winning rookie season. And he went on to score 100 points six straight years after that including a best of 139. Through the 1980s, only Wayne Gretzky would outscore Peter Stastny.

His 39 rookie goals would remain a record for rookies until Teemu Selanne's rookie season.

After playing for his homeland of Czechoslovakia in that first Olympics, then Canada in the Canada Cup and finally Slovakia in the Lillehammer Olympics, Stastny became the greatest scoring international player ever with 1,239 points when he retired. Only Jari Kurri has passed him.

Peter Stastny would also play for the St. Louis Blues and the New Jersey Devils before he would be elected to the Hockey Hall of Fame in 1998 and the International Ice Hockey Federation's Hall of Fame in 2000.

CAREER TOTALS											
GP	G	A	Pts	+/-	GWG	GTG	S	S%	PPG	SHG	PIM
977	450	789	1239	-12	54	11	2374	19.0	145	7	824

NELS STEWART

Name: Nelson Robert Stewart
Born: December 29, 1902, Montreal, Quebec
Died: August 21, 1957
Shoots: Left
Height: 6-1
Weight: 195

"Nels Stewart wasn't the most graceful skater of his era, but his shot was so deadly accurate, he became known as 'Old Poison'."

—CBS.Sportsline.com

Could Nels Stewart score?

How about two goals in four seconds. No one ever did it faster when Stewart managed that feat in 1931 against Boston. It was finally tied in 1955 by Deron Quint of Winnipeg.

When Stewart retired from the game in 1940, he was the National Hockey League's leading all-time scorer. His mark stood until Maurice Richard passed him in 1952.

Stewart also won a pair of Hart Trophies as MVP in 1926 and 1930. He led his Montreal Maroons to the Stanley Cup in 1926. And he won the Art Ross Trophy in 1926, as well.

Starting in 1929-1930, he began play on the famous S Line with Babe Seibert and Hooley Smith.

A hard-driving 6-foot-1, 195-pounder who was born in Montreal and grew up in Toronto, Nels Stewart was a tough, aggressive player with a knack for scoring.

Stewart also played for the Boston Bruins and the New York Americans in a 15-year NHL career from 1925 through 1940..

He was inducted into the Hockey Hall of Fame in 1962.

CAREER TOTALS											
GP	G	A	Pts	+/-	GWG	GTG	S	S%	PPG	SHG	PIM
650	324	191	515	0*	0*	0*	0*	-*	0*	0*	953

MATS SUNDIN

Name: Mats Johan Sundin
Born: February 13, 1971, Bromma, Sweden
Shoots: Right
Height: 6-4
Weight: 225

"I remember when I got drafted by the Nordiques, I didn't even know what that was."

—Mats Sundin

Mats Sundin was the first European player ever taken No. 1 in the NHL Draft. Hard to believe it now but that was more than a dozen years ago.

Like so many great National Hockey League players, Sundin scored a goal in his first official game, going on to score 23 goals along with 36 assists for a 59-point rookie season.

Now with the Toronto Maple Leafs, Sundin is a big part of their resurgence. The biggest part, many would say, despite a broken wrist that kept him out of much of the Stanley Cup playoff action in 2002.

A natural leader, the Bromma, Sweden native is in his fifth year as Maple Leaf captain. He's led his team in points for seven years and led in assists in six.

At 6-foot-4 and 225 pounds, Sundin is a part of the new-look NHL, bigger, stronger, faster. With Chris Chelios, he is the only player to be named to the first All-Star team in the 1991 Canada Cup and the 1996 World Cup.

In Sweden, where he took up hockey at age 5, Sundin idolized NHL players Kent Nilsson and Borje Salming.

He's been an NHL All-Star in 1996, 1997 and 1998 and a member of the NHL World All-Stars 1999, 2000 and 2001.

CAREER TOTALS											
GP	G	A	Pts	+/-	GWG	GTG	S	S%	PPG	SHG	PIM
930	397	545	942	44	67	10	2682	14.8	96	23	759

BRYAN TROTTIER

Name: Bryan John Trottier
Born: July 17, 1956, Val Marie, Saskatchewan
Shoots: Left
Height: 5-11
Weight: 195

"Bryan John Trottier was among the NHL's elite centremen during the majority of his eighteen NHL seasons."
—from Trottier's Hockey Hall of Fame induction ceremony

Bryan Trottier could do it all. He could outscore anyone of his era, that was a given for the once-underaged draft pick from the plains of Val Marie, Saskatchewan. He could pass, play defense, he could see the game develop on the ice, he could feel the pressure and do just about anything asked of him.

But the 5-foot-11, 195-pounder meant more to a team than just what he could do on his own. He could rack up impressive statistics in a team concept. He could lead the National Hockey League in scoring and lead his New York Islander team to four Stanley Cup titles.

He could anchor the best line in hockey—with Mike Bossy on his right and Clark Gillies on his left—with his pinpoint passing and shooting. And he could lead in the best of all possible ways—with an attitude that the team always comes first. In those pre-Wayne Gretzky days, he was the NHL's best center.

The high-scoring Trottier scored 524 goals for a total of 1,425 career points—sixth all-time when he retired. In the Islanders' first Stanley Cup season in 1980, he led all playoff scorers with 29 points in 24 games. After the four straight Stanley Cups on the Island, Trottier headed off to Pittsburgh where he helped the Penguins to two more in a row in 1991 and 1992.

Trottier hit the ice on the fly, winning the Calder Trophy as the NHL's rookie of the year in 1975–1976. Within five years, he was the league's top scorer and winner of the Art Ross Trophy in 1978–1979 as well as the Hart Trophy as MVP.

He would also win a Conn Smythe Trophy as the top postseason player and a King Clancy Award for community service. He was also the NHL's Man of the Year in 1987–1988 and was inducted into the Hockey Hall of Fame in 1997.

CAREER TOTALS											
GP	G	A	Pts	+/-	GWG	GTG	S	S%	PPG	SHG	PIM
1279	524	901	1425	452	68	15	2841	18.4	161	19	912

ALEXEI YASHIN

Name: Alexei Yashin
Born: November 5, 1973, Sverdlovsk, Russia
Shoots: Right
Height: 6-3
Weight: 225

"He's always been a great player . . . He's hard to contain now."
—Toronto center Darcy Tucker on Alexei Yashin

He's been very good since his draft a decade ago. But now, Alexei Yashin is also very much improved. Listen to what they're saying about him after the 2002 playoffs.

"I thought Alexei was our best player in the playoffs," New York Islanders Coach Peter Laviolette said. "He had a lot of points, triple that in opportunities. He played well at both ends of the ice."

The man playing against him, Maple Leafs center Darcy Tucker, noticed the impact of the 6-foot-3, 225-pound strongman.

"He played great," Tucker said. "They double-shifted him. He played in all situations. He played phenomenally well. Maturity is a thing that maybe he's found in his game. He's always been a great player. The battles on the boards he's winning, he uses his size. He's hard to contain now."

That's pretty much been the thinking on where Yashin would end up since Ottawa picked him second overall in the 1992 NHL Entry Draft. He then went on to lead all rookies in assists and finish second in points as the only rookie to appear in the All-Star Game.

Yashin earned a bronze medal tin 2002 with the Russian team in the Salt Lake City Olympics and played for the European team in the NHL All-Star Game with an assist.

A year ago he finished second in the NHL for game-winning goals with 10. The year before when he led Ottawa with 94 points, Alexei was a finalist for the Hart Trophy and Lester B. Pearson Award as Most Valuable Player and an NHL second-team All-Star as Senators captain while reaching career highs in goals, assists and points.

Internationally, he's represented Russia in World Championships six times and two more times in World Juniors with a gold medal in each. He also earned a silver medal in the 1998 Olympics.

CAREER TOTALS												
GP	G	A	Pts	+/-	GWG	GTG	S	S%	PPG	SHG	PIM
582	250	316	566	-62	36	3	1950	12.8	92	4	247

STEVE YZERMAN

Name: Stephen Gregory Yzerman
Born: May 9, 1965, Cranbrook, British Columbia
Shoots: Right
Height: 5-11
Weight: 185

"I remember seeing (NHL president) Clarence Campbell hand the Stanley Cup to Bobby Clarke in 1974, and I thought how wonderful it would be to be in his shoes."
—Steve Yzerman

It's hard to believe that Steve Yzerman has been around for almost two decades in the National Hockey League.

It seems like only yesterday he was the 18-year-old Detroit rookie playing in his first All-Star Game—or the young Cranbrook, British Columbia native who would be elevated to Red Wings captain three years later, the youngest in franchise history to be so honored.

But maybe it's starting to register now, that he's the longest-serving captain in league history.

Or that after a 42-year Stanley Cup drought in Detroit, Yzerman did get to know what it felt like to lift the Stanley Cup in 1997. And then in 1998. And again in 2002.

"The sheer joy of winning, raising the Cup, that's the only reason you play," Yzerman said later. "When I came here, all we talked about was making the playoffs. The team had only made the playoffs once in something like 13 seasons. It had gotten so bad we couldn't even sell out in the playoffs that year against St. Louis."

Now Detroit can call itself Hockeytown again. And Steve Yzerman, more than anyone else, is the reason. He's done it with his flying feet and quick hands and inspired leadership. And he's done it from day one.

They still talk about his 87-point rookie year almost as much as his 155 points five years later as he was ticking off six straight 100-point-plus seasons between 1987–88 and 1992–93. When Yzerman scored his 1,000th NHL point, he joined Red Wings Gordie Howe and Alex Delvecchio in that special group.

After the second Stanley Cup, Yzerman was named Conn Smythe Trophy winner in 1998. He'd also earned a Lester B. Pearson Award in 1989.

One other award rates a special place. After growing up in the Ottawa suburb of suburb of Nepean, Ontario, he saw the town rename the Nepean Sportsplex's hockey rink the Steve Yzerman Hockey Arena in 1996.

But they better hold up on engraving the plaque for his list of honors because Yzerman shows no signs of slowing down as he moves up the list of all-time NHL scorers. Clearly he's going to be very close to the top by the time his career is over.

CAREER TOTALS											
GP	G	A	Pts	+/-	GWG	GTG	S	S%	PPG	SHG	PIM
1362	658	1004	1662	161	87	11	4362	15.1	190	50	852

MIKE BOSSY

Name: Michael Jean Bossy
Born: January 22, 1957, Montreal, Quebec
Shoots: Right
Height: 6-0
Weight: 186

"We picked the guy we needed."

—Islanders Coach Al Arbour on selecting Mike Bossy in the NHL draft

For some reason, there was always a "but" attached to anything Mike Bossy ever seemed to do. And that label was placed on a young Bossy well before he made it to the National Hockey League as a rookie in the 1977–1978 season. He didn't like to fight, they said, he played little defense, he was timid, yada, yada, yada.

And so it went as Bossy proceeded to do one thing that silenced his critics. He led his New York Islanders to four straight—count 'em, four—Stanley Cups.

Sounds like more than just a sharpshooter looking to his own stats. And of course Mike Bossy was more than that. He was an integral part of one of hockey's best-ever lines with Clark Gillies and Bryan Trottier.

In fact, after the draft in which Bossy hadn't been selected until No. 15 by the Isles, Coach Al Arbour inserted him into that line and watched it work in the exhibition season.

That's when Arbour issued his proclamation: "We picked the guy we needed."

Those four Cups vindicated Arbour's decision. And Bossy vindicated himself with his stick, scoring 53 goals in winning a Calder Cup with a total of 92 points as the NHL's rookie of the year.

And it went from there. Fifty goals the next year and point totals of 118, 149, 136 and 126 in following years. And on it went for Bossy until, well, until all but one of his scoring records would be eclipsed by the game's greatest scorers—Guy Lafleur and Wayne Gretzky. That one remaining record saw Bossy become the only NHL player ever to score 50 or more goals nine straight seasons. And yet oddly Bossy never once won a scoring title.

Bossy was also the first to equal Maurice Richard's 50 goals in 50 games and that was just a pit stop on his way to 1,126 points in a decade of finding the back of the net, including two straight Stanley Cup winners in 1982 and 1983. He won the Conn Smythe Trophy in 1982, the Lady Byng in 1983, 1984 and 1986 and was inducted into the Hockey Hall of Fame in 1991 and by 1998, *The Hockey News* named him as No. 20 on their Top 50 NHL players ever.

CAREER TOTALS											
GP	G	A	Pts	+/-	GWG	GTG	S	S%	PPG	SHG	PIM
752	573	553	1126	380	82	15	2705	21.2	181	8	210

JOHN BUCYK

Name: John Paul Bucyk
Born: May 12, 1935, Edmonton, Alberta
Shoots: Left
Height: 6-0
Weight: 215

"I never knew anyone who could hit harder."

—Bobby Orr

They've had all sorts of names for lines in the National Hockey League. The Kraut Line, the "S" Line, but the Uke Line?

The Ukranian-Canadian Line, of course. That's the Boston Bruins line that featured Hockey Hall of Famer John Bucyk at left wing along with Vic Stasiuk and Bronco Horvath, who it turns out was Yugoslavian, but apparently that was close enough.

Just the place you'd expect a guy nicknamed "The Chief" because of his resemblance to a noble Native-American Indian to be playing.

And play the indestructible John Bucyk did. And play and play. For 23 seasons in all, 21 in Boston, where The Chief set all sorts of records on his way to the Hockey Hall of Fame in 1981.

Bucyk, a strong, durable 215 pounds, used his heft—with surprising speed and skating skills—to both protect himself and do damage to less-athletic opponents well into his forties after being traded to Boston by Detroit for Terry Sawchuk in 1958.

As a Bruin, he would be only the fifth NHL player to reach the 50-goal mark, hitting for 51 with 65 assists in 1970-1971. And that date is right. Bucyk did it a dozen seasons after being traded from Detroit.

Unlike so many, Bucyk seemed to be skating downhill the longer his career went. He just picked up momentum, not to mention a pair of Stanley Cups, a Lester Patrick Trophy and a pair of Lady Byngs for his gentlemanly and unpenalized play.

After his retirement, *The Hockey News* named Bucyk one of the Top 50 NHL players of all time.

CAREER TOTALS											
GP	G	A	Pts	+/-	GWG	GTG	S	S%	PPG	SHG	PIM
1540	556	813	1369	146*	69*	15*	1723*	19.1*	136*	1*	497

PAVEL BURE

Name: Pavel V. Bure
Born: March 31, 1971, Moscow, Russia
Shoots: Left
Height: 5-10
Weight: 189

"Bure has many detractors in the NHL, and they are mostly the players that he plays against and with. He has become a one-dimensional 'cookie monster,' who has conveniently cut the ice in half."

—ESPN's Darren Pang

The evidence can support several positions on the worth of Pavel Bure these days. But the more that comes in, the more it looks like Bure might not be worth the $10 million a year salary that he's getting.

Or should we say "earning?"

And isn't that the point.

What is the deal with Pavel Bure?

What's the deal indeed?

The Moscow native was ranked the 10th-best player in the National Hockey League by *The Hockey News* at the end of the 1998–1999 season but he's now a New York Ranger and the Blueshirts didn't make the playoffs this last season. So what's happened?

Isn't Bure the same player who was second in the league in scoring in 1999–2000 with 94 points and ranked No. 7 that year among hockey's best players?

And isn't he the guy who won the Richard Trophy for the second year in 2000–2001 scoring a league-best 59 goals while playing an NHL-best 26:52 minutes a game while getting off a team-record 384 shots?

And isn't Pavel Bure the player who won a Calder Trophy as Rookie of the Year, and the player who scored 60 goals in back-to-back seasons and led the Canucks to the 1994 Stanley Cup finals? Isn't he?

Maybe he is. And maybe he isn't. That's the question.

The numbers seem to say that Bure can help a mediocre team but not do so much for a team that's really awful. Got that?

And his 161 goals the past three seasons (more than any other player in the NHL) aren't enough to make up for what he doesn't do.

Pang's quote above says it all for the 31-year-old Bure, who may have a few seasons to prove he is the player he was—or the one he's being paid to be.

The NHL is waiting.

						CAREER TOTALS						
GP	G	A	Pts	+/-	GWG	GTG	S	S%	PPG	SHG	PIM
663	418	331	749	38	56	6	2994	14.0	116	33	468

CHARLIE CONACHER

Name: Charles William Conacher
Born: December 20, 1909, Toronto, Ontario
Died: December 30, 1967
Shoots: Right
Height: 6-1
Weight: 200

"It felt like somebody had turned a blow torch on me. I couldn't sit down for a week."

—King Clancy after being hit from behind by a Charlie Conacher shot

They say he had the hardest shot in hockey. And that makes sense. At 6-feet-1 and 200 pounds, Charlie Conacher was about as big as they come during the years from the late 1920s through the early 1940s.

But it was more than his size. It was coming out of one of Canada's most athletic families that saw three Conacher brothers—Charlie, Lionel and Roy—all make it to the Hockey Hall of Fame.

It was coming out of a family of 10 kids, where there was hour after hour of practicing as a youngster growing up in a tough part of Toronto.

It was what Charlie Conacher did in a career that started in Toronto as a Maple Leaf and moved on to the Detroit Red Wings and the New York Americans in the last two of a dozen National Hockey League seasons.

Along the way, Conacher showed he could score any way he needed to score. Five times in six years from 1930 to 1936 he led the NHL in goals scored. No wonder, some would say, Conacher just would not be stopped as he would put himself, any defender who got in his way and the puck, into the net.

See the net. See the puck. Put the puck in the net any way you can.

Charlie Conacher could.

Only he couldn't stay healthy doing it that way. That's the downside of those all-out rushes with little concern for one's own health. Conacher's injuries would fill a virtual Gray's Anatomy starting with a lost kidney and breaks in both of his hands and wrists.

On the famed Kid Line with Harvey Jackson and Joe Primeau, Conacher led his Maple Leafs to a Stanley Cup in 1932. He won the Art Ross Trophy in both 1934 and 1935 as the NHL's leading scorer.

CAREER TOTALS											
GP	G	A	Pts	+/-	GWG	GTG	S	S%	PPG	SHG	PIM
459	225	173	398	0*	0*	0*	0*	-*	0*	0*	523

PATRIK ELIAS

Name: Patrik Elias
Born: April 13, 1976, Trebic, Czech Republic
Shoots: Left
Height: 6-1
Weight: 195

"Elias is the biggest bargain in the NHL . . . he will make $750,000 this year and is scheduled
to earn the same amount the next two years. A lot of agents would make the case he's worth
10 times that amount."
—The Hockey News

How good a bargain Patrik Elias is depends on your point of view.

If you're the New Jersey Devils, having one of the Top 100 People of Power and
Influence in Hockey—and one of just 13 players on the list—and having to pay him just
a bit over $2 million for three years is a heck of a deal.

But from the point of view of Elias, it stinks. Listen to what the 26-year-old native of
Trebic, Czech Republic, has to say about the "bargain" he is.

"I don't think the deal is fair at all. To be honest about it, I signed because I didn't
have any options," Elias said. "I got screwed by the free agency rules because I didn't
have any rights."

Other than that, how do you feel, Patrik?

The Devils certainly feel fine about all of this. The 6-foot-1, 195-pound Elias was
there in 2000 with the Stanley Cup-winning assist on Jason Arnott's Game 6 goal against
the Dallas Stars. No surprise that. Elias led the playoffs that year in assists with 13 and
his 20 points tied for the club lead.

The next season Elias led the Devils from his left wing spot to a franchise-record 48
wins with a team-record 96 points on his way to first-team All-National Hockey
League honors.

CAREER TOTALS											
GP	G	A	Pts	+/-	GWG	GTG	S	S%	PPG	SHG	PIM
395	141	180	321	97	31	3	931	15.1	33	4	209

MIKE GARTNER

Name: Michael Alfred Gartner
Born: October 29, 1959, Ottawa, Ontario
Shoots: Right
Height: 6-0
Weight: 187

"I have a God-given ability to skate. I haven't really worked on my legs at all during my career."
—Mike Gartner

Consistent he was. Mike Gartner was always there. Always where he should be. He just wasn't there for a Stanley Cup.

He got close, however, traded away just three months before the New York Rangers won in 1994.

In 19 seasons, Mike Gartner scored 1,335 points (708 goals, 627 assists) in 1,432 games. Not bad for a guy who started out as a Cincinnati Stinger in the World Hockey Association.

There was a reason for those numbers. Gartner could skate and skate awfully fast, scoring 30 or more goals in 15 of his 19 seasons, an NHL record. No one has ever been more consistent for that long in the league.

How fast was Gartner? Well, at the unbelievable age of 36, he won the "Fastest Skate Competitor" in the NHL for the third year in a row.

But those were the kinds of honors Gartner had to settle for. No player has done more for a longer time in the NHL without winning a single individual award or trophy at the end of the season.

"As a player, obviously, I would have loved to have been a part of a Stanley Cup team," Gartner said once. "But the Rangers traded me right at the deadline that year and it wasn't meant to be. I really would have loved to be a part of that. But my years with the Canada Cup helped make up for it."

In all, Gartner played for Canada eight times in international competitions.

"I was a man playing a boy's game until the age of 38," Gartner said, "and I had a great time doing it."

Mike Gartner was inducted into the Hockey Hall of Fame in 2001.

CAREER TOTALS											
GP	G	A	Pts	+/-	GWG	GTG	S	S%	PPG	SHG	PIM
1432	708	627	1335	67	90	21	5090	13.9	217	23	1159

BERNIE GEOFFRION

Name: Bernard Andre Joseph Geoffrion
Born: February 16, 1931, Montreal, Quebec
Shoots: Right
Height: 5-9
Weight: 166

"Listen fellas, I've got to tell you this. I'm not the greatest coach in the world. But if you look around this room, you'll see that I don't have the greatest players either."

—Bernie Geoffrion before coaching his expansion Atlanta Flames team in its first game

Bernie Geoffrion had something the rest of the men who played the game could only wish they had.

He had the best hockey nickname ever.

It just doesn't get better than "Boom Boom."

The irony of that name has always been that "Boom Boom" was a mere 5-feet-9 and 166 pounds, by almost any standards an itty, bitty guy in a game where hitting—and being hit—was what it was all about.

What Bernie Geoffrion could hit—and hit hard—was the puck with a slap shot well ahead of anyone of his time. He could also play the point on the power play because of that strong shot.

Heck, Bernie Geoffrion might have had a Hall of Fame career even if he couldn't play and shoot and score. But he could. And he played in the place where it mattered the most, in Montreal.

In his first full season with the Canadiens, he led them in goals on the way to a Calder Cup-winning Rookie of the Year start. And he and his Habs just kept getting better, eventually winning a Stanley Cup in his third season and then another five in a row for a career total of six in his 16 seasons.

And "Boom Boom"? All he did was become the second NHL player to score 50 goals in a season on his way to a near-record 95-point season in 1960–1961. That earned him both a Hart and Art Ross Trophy that year.

After retiring in 1964, then coaching, coming back to play a couple of years with the New York Rangers and then moving on to help Atlanta's Flames get started, Geoffrion gave up the game because of his health.

He was inducted into the Hockey Hall of Fame in 1972 on the strength of his 822 total points (339 goals, 429 assists) in 883 games.

CAREER TOTALS											
GP	G	A	Pts	+/-	GWG	GTG	S	S%	PPG	SHG	PIM
883	339	429	822	161	.87	11	4362	15.1	190	50	852

MICHEL GOULET

Name: Michel Goulet
Born: April 21, 1960, Peribonka, Quebec
Shoots: Left
Height: 6-1
Weight: 195

"I'm as proud to be working for the Avalanche as I was to play for two great organizations—the Quebec Nordiques and Chicago Blackhawks."
—Michel Goulet

He's known today as one of the best player personnel guy in the business for stocking his Colorado Avalanche team's roster with so much talent as the team's vice president for player personnel. *The Hockey News* lists Michel Goulet among its 100 People of Power and Influence in Hockey this year.

Here's what they say about Goulet's off-ice work: "The Avalanche has the best talent pool in hockey, thanks to keen scouting and adept trading. Goulet runs the pantry while head scout Jim Hammett and his staff scour for talent. One reason the Avalanche are drawn in to trade rumors is the depth of their organization."

Not a word about Michel Goulet the National Hockey League player, the 16th greatest goal-scorer in NHL history and the third highest among left wingers.

Not a word about his 15 seasons in the league, 14 of them with 20 or more goals. Not a word about how Goulet could score during 11 seasons with the Quebec Nordiques and then another four with the Chicago Blackhawks.

Not a word about his 1,152 total points (548 goals, 604 assists).

And not a word about his career-ending accident on the ice that sent him tumbling headfirst into the boards, severely injuring his head and neck in a 1994 game.

Goulet, a five-time NHL All-Star, was inducted into the Hockey Hall of Fame in 1998 after already joining the Avalanche.

CAREER TOTALS											
GP	G	A	Pts	+/-	GWG	GTG	S	S%	PPG	SHG	PIM
1089	548	604	1152	96	64	16	3143	17.4	178	16	825

BILL GUERIN

Name: Bill Guerin
Born: November 9, 1970, Worcester, Massachusetts
Shoots: Right
Height: 6-2
Weight: 210

"Bill is someone you can always count on."

—Joe Thornton

Born in Massachusetts, Bill Guerin saw his pro hockey career start in his home state at Springfield and years later return—with the Boston's Bruins, the team Guerin rooted for as a kid.

After a decade in the National Hockey League with the New Jersey's Devils and the Edmonton Oilers, the 6-foot-2, 210-pound right wing from Boston College was back home where he led his Eagles to an NCAA Final Four spot as a freshman.

Guerin played for the U.S. team in the 1998 Winter Olympic Games at Nagano and helped the 1996 U.S. team to a World Cup title after playing for the U.S. twice in World Junior play in 1989 and 1990.

His single most glorious day in hockey may have been at his first All-Star Game last year when Guerin recorded a personal trifecta—he scored a hat trick, was named All-Star Game MVP and won the title of the game's fastest skater. Not a bad day.

Other days the photogenic Guerin has shown another side of him.

He's appeared in a role as an actor on the soap opera *All My Children*, although he noted how tough it was to learn the lines. And he's been a model in magazines like *Vanity Fair* and *Marie Claire* with a visage that doesn't look like your classic hockey mug.

Guerin signed for the Dallas Stars in July 2002.

CAREER TOTALS											
GP	G	A	Pts	+/-	GWG	GTG	S	S%	PPG	SHG	PIM
733	256	248	504	58	43	2	2086	12.3	75	2	1036

DANY HEATLEY

Name: Dany Heatley
Born: January 21, 1981, Freibourg, Germany
Shoots: Left
Height: 6-2
Weight: 210

"Dany is a scoring machine. He really has a nose for the net. He's got great size, tremendous hands and vision and is one of those players you classify as a pure goal scorer."

—Wisconsin Coach Jeff Sauer

He's only the second U.S. college player to be the top-ranked prospect heading into Draft Day. And from the looks of his first season in the National Hockey League, the man they call "Heater"—6-foot-2, 210-pound Dany Heatley—was ranked right where he should have been.

Here's what *The Hockey News* said of Heatley and his Atlanta Thrashers rookie teammate Ilya Kovalchuk, who were tabbed as among The Top 100 People of Power and Influence in Hockey their first season in the league. Only 11 other NHL players earned that tag.

"There are two reasons to pay to see the Thrashers this season and they're both rookies," *The Hockey News* said. "Heatley, 20, is a force as he drives to the net. Kovalchuk, 18, is one of the most dynamic scorers to come along in years."

Dany Heatley may have been born in Freibourg, Germany but he grew up playing hockey in Calgary—on the frozen outside ice or on the roads—as a kid, playing wherever he could.

Then he followed his father Murray to the University of Wisconsin where he earned virtually every honor available to a college player.

And now he's finished his first season showing much promise with a 67-point season (26 goals, 41 assists) with all sorts of rookie awards along the way.

The guy can handle the puck, shoot it quickly, and knows where he is on the ice. There's a sense that he's been doing this for a long time and even if that's not the case yet, it will be.

Figure Dany Heatley to be a factor—and a very big factor—in the NHL for a very long time. He'd better be if Atlanta is to have a chance.

CAREER TOTALS											
GP	G	A	Pts	+/-	GWG	GTG	S	S%	PPG	SHG	PIM
82	26	41	67	-19	4	0	202	12.9	7	0	56

GORDIE HOWE

Name: Gordon Howe
Born: March 31, 1928, Floral, Saskatchewan
Shoots: Right
Height: 6-1
Weight: 205

"He was not only the greatest hockey player I've ever seen, but also the greatest athlete."
—Hockey Hall of Famer Bill Gadsby on Gordie Howe

They called him Mr. Hockey. And they were right. He was.

He liked to say that "Hockey is a man's game." It was Gordie Howe's game for sure.

Had the National Hockey League followed the NBA's lead and chosen a player for the league logo the way the NBA did with Jerry West, you don't even have to guess who that would have been the guy.

Gordie Howe would have been the one.

For starters, he played most of his career in the place they call "Hockeytown."

Howe arrived in Detroit early, stayed late and could do the three things a hockey player has to do: He could skate, he could score and he could hit people. He was simply the toughest man ever to play the game.

By the time he was 17, Gordie Howe had earned a place on the Red Wings' Production Line with fellow Hall of Famers-to-be Ted Lindsay and Sid Abel as the trio finished 1-2-3 in NHL scoring for the 1946–1947 season.

That was the beginning of a trend for Howe who would be a top 10 scorer for 21 straight seasons and in the top five for 20 of those. He led the league's scorers six times on his way to a Hockey Hall of Fame induction 1n 1970 as soon as he finally stopped playing.

Only that wasn't it for "Mr. Hockey". One of only three Hall of Fame players to return to the ice, Howe joined sons Mark and Marty in the World Hockey Association for the Houston Aeros and then moved on to play a full season with the NHL's Hartford Whalers as a 51-year-old.

Here is the career worksheet of hockey's greatest workhorse: four Stanley Cups (1950, 1952, 1954, 1955); 1,850 points (801 goals, 1,049 assists) in 1,767 NHL games; six Art Ross Trophies, six Hart Trophies, a Lester Patrick, 21 NHL All-Star selections (12 first-team, nine second) and 23 NHL All-Star Games.

His numbers—2,589 total points in 32 seasons overall (1.071 goals, 1,518 assists) may have been passed by Wayne Gretzky but not his longevity. He simply outlasted everyone.

Gordie Howe was already a star in 1948 when Bobby Orr was born, and he was still playing in 1979 when Orr retired.

CAREER TOTALS											
GP	G	A	Pts	+/-	GWG	GTG	S	S%	PPG	SHG	PIM
1767	801	1049	1850	87*	33*	6*	1141*	13.3*	91*	12*	1685

BOBBY HULL

Name: Robert Marvin Hull
Born: January 3, 1939, Pointe Anne, Ontario
Shoots: Left
Height: 5-10
Weight: 195

"Bobby (Hull) was the dominant one. He was 'Give me the puck and I'll bull through everybody.'"
—Pat Quinn, Toronto Maple Leafs coach

Bobby Hull was Bo Jackson on ice skates. Flying muscles. A solid blur. Power and speed in one package.

It was always hard to know which of Bobby Hull's many hockey skills mattered most. Was he the bull-in-the-china-shop player who could skate like the wind?

Or was he the flashy flyer who could crunch an opponent and his own slap shot with equal 100-plus miles-per-hour devastation?

Or was he like Jackson, an almost superhuman blend of speed and muscle who simply could not be separated from either of his amazing talents?

Bobby Hull was the whole package who led the National Hockey League seven times in goal scoring, three times in points and won a pair of Stanley Cups as the prototypical Chicago Blackhawk.

He was just 5-feet-10 but his 195 pounds allowed him to put his name in the record books four times for 50-goal seasons, a place where only two players before him had ever gone. And he became the second player ever to reach 100 points in a season on his way to a dozen All-Star team selections (10 times first-team) in his 13 NHL seasons.

Then he left, to give the World Hockey Association instant credibility with the Winnipeg Jets as the Hawks refused to take seriously the multi-million dollar offer the new league was waving in front of Hull in 1972.

But they were. And off Hull went for six seasons in the WHA, admitting that unlike so many athletes, it was pretty much about the money. His son Brett would go on to make millions of dollars more in his NHL career.

Together they would become the only father-son MVP winners in hockey history when Brett would earn the Hart Trophy in 1991 to match the two of his father.

After a final NHL season following consolidation of the leagues in 1979–1980, Bobby Hull was inducted into the Hockey Hall of Fame in 1983.

Hull finished with 1,170 total points (610 goals, 560 assists) in 1,063 NHL regular season games; 129 points (62 goals, 67 assists) in 119 NHL playoff games; 639 points (303 goals, 335 assists) in 411 WHA regular season games.

CAREER TOTALS											
GP	G	A	Pts	+/-	GWG	GTG	S	S%	PPG	SHG	PIM
1063	610	560	1170	105*	65*	24*	1819*	13.2*	121*	18*	640

BRETT HULL

Name: Brett A. Hull
Born: August 9, 1964, Belleville, Ontario
Shoots: Right
Height: 5-11
Weight: 203

"Brett (Hull) has always gotten himself into a position where a good playmaker could find him."
—Pat Quinn, Toronto Maple Leafs coach

He's just as blond as his dad but Brett Hull's path to breaking many of his Hall of Fame father Bobby Hull's records has taken him in a different direction.

While Bobby was all brute force and speed, Brett—even though an inch taller and maybe eight pounds heavier than his dad at 5-11 and 203 pounds—has always been more of a slick scorer.

One way Brett Hull has liked to describe his scoring was that he did it in "stealth mode." That's how he was able to pass his dad's National Hockey League career total of 610 goals two years ago. The Hulls are the only father-son combo to ever reach the 500-goal club individually.

While Bobby Hull did all of his first 13 years of NHL scoring in Chicago, Brett has moved around, from Calgary to St. Louis to Dallas to Detroit.

And as strong as Brett's play was in five years at the top of the NHL scoring lists with the Blues where he led the league in goal-scoring three straight years and became just the second player ever to record 50 goals in 50 games in back-to-back seasons, it was his first year in Dallas that saw Hull help the Stars to a Stanley Cup in 1999. He would repeat that acheivement in 2002 as a member of the Detroit Red Wings.

A U.S. citizen, Hull has played for his country in a number of international competitions including the 1991 Canada Cup, the 1996 World Cup and World Championships and the 1998 and 2002 Olympics.

CAREER TOTALS											
GP	G	A	Pts	+/-	GWG	GTG	S	S%	PPG	SHG	PIM
1101	679	567	1246	19	100	10	4406	15.4	243	19	424

JAROME IGINLA

Name: Jarome Iginla
Born: July 1, 1977, Edmonton, Alberta
Shoots: Right
Height: 6-1
Weight: 210

"This is about who's been the best player in 2001-2002. And that's Iggy. He scores goals. He sets up plays. He hits. He'll fight. He's meant everything to us."
—Flames center Craig Conroy

Could a player from a team that didn't even make the playoffs earn an MVP award? That was the question posed so often to Jarome Iginla at the end of the 2001-2002 season.

"It's not up to me," was the standard response from the Calgary Flames right winger. "Other people make those decisions."

Only it was, actually, up to Iginla. What Jarome did on the ice, determined that he was, indeed, the best player in the National Hockey League for the 2001–2002 season and the leading candidate for the Hart Trophy as the league's MVP.

"Should our record be considered when they're voting for the Hart Trophy? Absolutely not. Look at *his* record," said Calgary Coach Greg Gilbert of the fifth-place Flames. "Iggy has done all he could to make this season a success for the Calgary Flames."

Since expansion, only Mario Lemieux and Wayne Gretzky have led the league in scoring for non-playoff teams and only Lemieux went on to win the MVP award.

Iginla got off to a good start in the postseason awards chase when *The Sporting News* named him its Player of the Year. The 24-year-old Iginla, who led the league in goals with 52 and scoring with 96 points, won the player voting with a total of 101, far ahead of second-place Patrick Roy, who received just 22.

Iginla has recorded just about one-quarter of his team's goals and is involved in nearly half of its scoring this past season.

"He's carried this team on his shoulders a lot of nights," Calgary's Denis Gauthier said. "Too many nights."

A strong and swift 6-foot-1, 210-pounder from Edmonton, Iginla resembles a baseball catcher, as well he should. He handled that position well enough as a youngster to earn a spot on the Canadian National Junior Baseball Team in 1992.

But just four years later, Iginla was leading his Canadian Junior National Hockey Team to a World Championship and his sport was set for him. The 2001–2002 season has made it clear how correct a call Iginla made to go with hockey.

CAREER TOTALS											
GP	G	A	Pts	+/-	GWG	GTG	S	S%	PPG	SHG	PIM
470	174	189	363	12	23	6	1330	13.1	53	4	289

JAROMIR JAGR

Name: Jaromir Jagr
Born: February 15, 1972, Kladno, Czech Republic
Shoots: Left
Height: 6-2
Weight: 232

"I think I'm old enough to have short hair now. No more of that girl stuff."

—Jaromir Jagr

He's already won two Stanley Cups, a World Junior Championship, been named a first-team All-Star six times and won the Art Ross Trophy as the leading scorer five times as well, so what is this talk about Jaromir Jagr growing up and getting his hair cut short?

That's just Jagr. He may be a speedy 6-foot-2 and 232 pounds, but there's always been a certain boyishness— both good and bad—about the play of the Czech winger.

The native of Kladno, Czech Republic became the first European-born player to lead the National Hockey League in scoring in the strike-shortened 1994–1995 season. His 70 points equalled the total of Eric Lindros although Jagr won the tiebreaker with more goals.

Jagr earned his first scoring title the year Mario Lemieux was sitting out because of medical problems. But his back-to-back Stanley Cups came with Jagr beside Lemieux with the Pittsburgh Penguins in 1991 and 1992.

By the end of that year, Jagr had skyrocketed to No. 2 on *The Hockey News* list of the top 40 players in the NHL.

Jagr was clearly just getting started, upping his scoring totals to 149, 95, 102 and 127 the next four seasons and shattering marks for scoring by a winger. Only three European-born players have ever scored more points in a career than Jagr and only three players in NHL history have won more than Jagr's five Ross Trophies.

His 127 points for Pittsburgh in the 1998–1999 season earned him his first Hart Trophy as the NHL's MVP. He'd already earned the No. 1 player in the game from The Hockey News the year before.

Now a Washington Capitol with 12 years in the league behind him, Jagr is being counted on the get the Caps over the hump again in the Nation's Capital.

CAREER TOTALS											
GP	G	A	Pts	+/-	GWG	GTG	S	S%	PPG	SHG	PIM
875	470	688	1158	207	81	10	3108	15.1	120	9	623

PAUL KARIYA

Name: Paul Kariya
Born: October 16, 1974, Vancouver, British Columbia
Shoots: Left
Height: 5-10
Weight: 172

"While there's a strong sentiment Kariya's talents are going to waste in Anaheim, he's still a player in many senses of the word."
—The Hockey News

No player makes the point better that hockey is a team game than Paul Kariya, the Anaheim Mighty Duck who has been exiled to Orange County.

Too bad about Kariya, people say. Nice guy. Lots of talent. Wish he played on a team that could help him show it. Now that Teemu Selanne has left for San Jose, Kariya is a lone duck and out of luck it seems.

Sure, he's still at No. 70 in *The Hockey News* 100 People of Power and Influence list—down from No. 27 the year before. That's not bad considering only 13 players made the list at all. But the citation refers to him "as one of the most thoughtful NHLers and his reasoned perspective was heard by the injury-analysis committee. Look for him to assume a greater role with the NHLPA."

And he's only 27. Too bad they're talking about Kariya as if he's an elder statesman.

The Vancouver native of Japanese ancestry has accomplished much in his eight years in the National Hockey League despite his small 5-foot-10, 172-pound stature. He owns three gold medals—from the 2002 Olympics as well as the 1993 Junior World's Championships and 1994 World's Championships.

He even won an NCCA title at Maine. He's a three-time first-team NHL All-Star and winner of the Hobey Baker Award in 1994 in college and a pair of Lady Byng Trophies in 1996 and 1997 when he was embarking on a high-scoring career that saw him annually in the NHL's top five scorers.

Kariya is the all-time leading scorer for the Mighty Ducks and the leading career scorer ever for an expansion team and has held or set 51 Duck team records.

CAREER TOTALS												
GP	G	A	Pts	+/-	GWG	GTG	S	S%	PPG	SHG	PIM	
524	275	313	588	55	42	3	2198	12.5	96	15	165	

ILYA KOVALCHUK

Name: Ilya Kovalchuk
Born: April 15, 1983, Tver, Russia
Shoots: Right
Height: 6-2
Weight: 220

"A player like that comes once in a hundred years!"
—Team Russia assistant GM Igor Kuperman on Ilya Kovalchuk

His first-year Atlanta Thrashers teammate Dany Heatly won the first Rookie of the Year award for the 2001–2002 season given by *The Sporting News*. But the folks who know best say this is the way it's going to be.

Ilya Kovalchuk will be the National Hockey League's next great player.

"One of the most dynamic scorers to come along in years," *The Hockey News* says of the 6-foot-2, 220-pound Russian right wing who just turned 19 April 15.

He'd already earned a spot in *The Hockey News* 100 People of Power and Influence in the game before ever playing an official game. Not bad.

Especially not bad considering only 12 other current players made the cut.

After an abbreviated 65 games his first season cut short because of a shoulder injury that dropped his rookie of the year chances, Kovalchuk—with 29 goals and 22 assists for 51 points—proved the scouts right.

Here's how he was described a year ago: "excellent skater with impressive speed, quickness and acceleration"…"strong player with a mean streak"…"outstanding puck-handling skills and scoring ability"…"very colorful and confident player"…"potential to be a franchise player."

That he is. Here's Kovalchuk after scoring six goals in an All-Star exhibition game: "I didn't take the game seriously. I showed only what I wanted to show."

So maybe that's why in addition to all the praise above, Kovalchuk has also earned descriptions like "cocky" and "arrogant." And he's not all that keen about defense, either,critics say.

But that didn't keep Thrashers general manager Don Waddell from saying that getting the chance to choose Kovalchuk first in the draft was "the most important thing that's happened to our franchise." The pick made Kovalchuk the first Russian player to ever be chosen No. 1.

CAREER TOTALS											
GP	G	A	Pts	+/-	GWG	GTG	S	S%	PPG	SHG	PIM
65	29	22	51	-191	.4	1	184	15.8	7	0	28

JARI KURRI

Name: Jari Kurri
Born: May 18, 1960, Helsinki, Finland
Shoots: Right
Height: 6-1
Weight: 195

"Don't worry, I look after you. I be the policeman."
—Jari Kurri to Wayne Gretzky in the early 1980s in Edmonton

Jari Kurri didn't win many individual awards—actually he won just one, and that was a Lady Byng Trophy—but all that would be is an indictment of individual awards and not of the flying Finn who could do it all.

To some, Kurri will always be one of the National Hockey League's most-underrated players ever. To others, he'll be Scottie Pippen to Wayne Gretzky's Michael Jordan.

As if just being Jari Kurri wasn't enough.

Are five Stanley Cups enough?

Or 601 career goals? Only seven players before Kurri ever managed that many.

Is it enough to be the highest-scoring European-born player ever?

What about his 14 playoff goals on the way to the 1984 Stanley Cup, the first of five for his Edmonton Oilers? Or the 19 playoff goals he got the next year after a regular season 135 points (71 goals, 64 assists)?

After a year off and stints with the Los Angeles Kings, the New York Rangers, the Mighty Ducks of Anaheim and the Colorado Avalanche, Kurri called it quits.

In addition to his 601 goals he had 797 assists for a career scoring total of 1,398 points. Enough for any Hockey Hall of Famer, which Kurri became as soon as he was eligible in 2001. *The Hockey News* also named him one of the Top 50 players of the century.

Of his complementary role with the great Gretzky, Kurri had a simple explanation: "Wayne and I were no secret, really. He was a great passer and I liked to hit the holes and shoot the puck." And shoot it quickly and accurately, earning him his "Master of the One-Timer" moniker.

He was smooth, unselfish, lethal, a tough defender and a great teammate.

CAREER TOTALS											
GP	G	A	Pts	+/-	GWG	GTG	S	S%	PPG	SHG	PIM
1251	601	797	1398	298	72	16	3142	19.1	155	39	545

GUY LAFLEUR

Name: Guy Damien LaFleur
Born: September 20, 1951, Thurso, Quebec
Shoots: Right
Height: 6-0
Weight: 185

"Everybody knew that he represented something special as a maker of excellence on the ice. What not enough people are aware of is his decency off the ice."

—**sportswriter Red Fisher on the retirement of Guy Lafleur's jersey in Montreal**

Guy Lafleur was Jari Kurri—only with trophies.

Both could score. Each played for a dynasty.

Lafleur's 1,353 career points (560 goals, 793 assists) just about equaled Kurri's 1,398 for Edmonton.

His five Stanley Cups for Montreal, the team he'd dreamed of playing for as a youngster growing up in Thurso, Quebec, mirrored Kurri's five for the Oilers.

But where Kurri was virtually unnoticed at award time, the exciting Lafleur took home National Hockey League hardware galore—three Art Ross Trophies, three Lester Pearson Awards, two Hart Trophies, a Conn Smythe and a Plus/Minus leader.

Kurri had to settle for getting to play alongside Wayne Gretzky.

The strong and speedy Lafleur also earned six first-team NHL All-Star selections. There's even an award with his name on it, given to the playoff MVP in the Quebec Major Junior Hockey League.

Lafleur was inducted into the Hockey Hall of Fame in 1988 before becoming one of three Hall of Famers to return to the ice (Gordie Howe and Mario Lemieux were the others) after three years off with the New York Rangers and Quebec Nordiques.

Lafleur did have a flair for the dramatic, becoming the first NHL player ever to score 50 goals in 50 games. That will get you noticed.

And then Lafleur went on to do something else no NHL player had ever done—he scored 50 goals and 100 points for six consecutive seasons.

Again, that's the kind of thing that makes folks pay attention. And "le Demon Blond" could certainly do that.

CAREER TOTALS											
GP	G	A	Pts	+/-	GWG	GTG	S	S%	PPG	SHG	PIM
1126	560	793	1353	453	97	22	3521	15.9	153	3	399

TED LINDSAY

Name: Robert Blake Theodore Lindsay
Born: July 25, 1925, Renfrew, Ontario
Shoots: Left
Height: 5-8
Weight: 163

"I just had the desire to wind up my career with the Red Wings."

—Ted Lindsay on his return to Detroit for a final season in 1964 after having been gone seven years

It was easy alliteration—"Terrible" Ted Lindsay.

It was wrong, of course.

Lindsay was a terror, for sure, even at an undersized 5-feet-8 and 163 pounds. But the little left winger always made the teams he played for and the players he played beside decidedly better for his having been there.

So what if his face took the brunt of his all-out, never-back-down style of play? They stopped counting Lindsay's stitches at 400.

But don't get the wrong idea. Lindsay wasn't just some lightweight boxing champ in pads. He could skate and score and—playing with Gordie Howe and Sid Abel on Detroit's famed Production Line—he could pass the puck. How else could that line have finished 1-2-3 in scoring one season.

And even next to Howe, Lindsay did manage an Art Ross Trophy year when he led the NHL in scoring with 85 points in 1949–1950.

How else could the Red Wings have won four Stanley Cups with little Ted Lindsay in the middle of things as the Detroit captain?

But for all that Lindsay had done for Detroit, the sentiment didn't come back his way from the organization. When Lindsay joined with several other National Hockey League veterans to organize a union of players in 1957, he was promptly shipped out to Chicago despite a dozen productive seasons in Detroit.

After three years in Chicago, Lindsay retired for four seasons, only to return to the Red Wings for one final season, helping the Wings to finish first just like the old days.

But then he did something else off the ice that will always be remembered, like his union work. Inducted into the Hockey Hall of Fame in 1966, Lindsay refused to attend the all-male induction banquet. He said he owed too much to his family to shut some of them out.

By the next year, women were able to attend the dinner, thanks to "Terrible" Ted Lindsay, an out-of-date NHL tradition was undone.

CAREER TOTALS											
GP	G	A	Pts	+/-	GWG	GTG	S	S%	PPG	SHG	PIM
1068	379	472	851	0*	1*	0*	0*	-*	1*	0*	1808

FRANK MAHOVLICH

Name: Francis William Mahovlich
Born: January 10, 1938, Timmins, Ontario
Shoots: Left
Height: 6-0
Weight: 205

"His long powerful strides enable Mahovlich to easily outskate defenders while Frank's shot is one of the most powerful in the NHL."
—1964-1965 Parkhurst Series Hockey Card No. 130

Frank Mahovlich was as big and strong and talented a hockey player as anyone ncknamed "The Big M" had a right to be.

He could make tough plays look easy.

But for the 6-foot, 205-pound left wing from Timmins, Ontario, it didn't always come easy. Sure there were the six Stanley Cups over 17 seasons in Toronto, Detroit and Montreal.

And those 15 All-Star selections are impressive.

And how about beating out Bobby Hull for rookie of the year and the 1958 Calder Trophy. Not a bad start on a 22-season trip through the NHL and the World Hockey Association that would end up in the Hockey Hall of Fame.

But as good as Mahovlich was, as strong as he could be, something always seemed to happen.

He almost broke Maurice Richard's 50-goal record at the age of 23. But didn't.

He always seemed to get those smattering of boos at home in Toronto, for whatever reason, whenever he came up short. Even when his teams won. Depression was the opponent he often couldn't beat, it would turn out. No matter how well he played.

But he didn't give in and would move on to Detroit and Montreal, where he won his final two Stanley Cups, and returned to his first-team NHL All-Star form.

And in the bargain, he got to play for a few seasons with younger brother Pete, "Little M."

He even got the chance to earn some big money in a four-year deal that took him to the WHA and kept him on the ice until he was 40.

From there it was a quick trip to the Hockey Hall of Fame in 1981, where he was destined to go from Day 1.

And where there were no boos this time.

CAREER TOTALS											
GP	G	A	Pts	+/-	GWG	GTG	S	S%	PPG	SHG	PIM
1181	533	570	1103	173*	48*	13*	1662*	15.4*	90*	11*	1056

DICKIE MOORE

Name: Richard Winston Moore
Born: January 6, 1931, Montreal, Quebec
Shoots: Left
Height: 5-10
Weight: 168

"I haven't seen anything like that in a long time. Not since I was in St. Louis and Dickie Moore was icing his knee after every game have I seen anything like Yzerman."
—Scotty Bowman comparing Dickie Moore with Steve Yzerman.

There were reasons why the Montreal Canadiens won six Stanley Cups from 1953 through 1960.

One of them was named Richard Winston "Dickie" Moore. He was a Montreal native and they knew he was coming to help.

All reports said the young man could handle the puck on his stick as well as anyone and had a shot that was as accurate as it was powerful.

They were right. His junior scoring days carried right over into the National Hockey League. He even erased one of the great Gordie Howe's records with his 96 points (41 goals, 55 assists) in 1958–1959, a point better than Howe's previous mark.

By then, after a Stanley Cup in 1953 and in the middle of the five-year run from 1956 through 1960, Moore was on his fifth Cup-winning Canadien team. And winning his second straight scoring title.

But injuries finally got the best of Moore by the end of 1962–1963. And the six-time NHL All-Star was gone for a year before returning for a season in Toronto with the Maple Leafs. Then it was two more years off and a final 27-game stint in St. Louis with the Blues in 1967-1968. And then Moore was gone for good.

He was inducted into the Hockey Hall of Fame in 1974.

CAREER TOTALS											
GP	G	A	Pts	+/-	GWG	GTG	S	S%	PPG	SHG	PIM
719	261	347	608	-8*	1*	1*	37*	13.5*	1*	0*	652

ZIGGY PALFFY

Name: Zigmund Palffy
Born: May 5, 1972, Skalica, Slovakia
Shoots: Left
Height: 5-10
Weight: 183

"He's the most unathletic-looking superstar."
—Chicago's Mark Janssens on Ziggy Palffy

It didn't take Zigmund "Ziggy" Palffy long to show the National Hockey League what he could do.

In his second season with the New York Islander team that drafted him, the 5-foot-10, 182-pound pride of Skalica, Slovakia, Palffy fired a 43-goal, 44-assist, 87-point performance at the league to announce his arrival as a 23-year-old right wing.

A year later he upped the scoring ante to 90 (48 goals, 42 assists) and soon he was ranked at No. 22 in *The Hockey News* Top 50 players listing.

Then it was off to Los Angeles where the Kings had secured him in an eight-player deal in 1999. Palffy would continue his team-pacing ways with an 89-point (38 goals, 51 assists) initial season on the West Coast and a continued stay on the Top 50 list as he led the Kings with a plus–22 plus/minus rating and a team-leading 19:30 minutes a game for the forwards.

Six times he's represented Slovakia in international competition including a pair of Olympics.

Were he not a hockey player, the left-handed shooting Palffy says he'd be a pro tennis player.

CAREER TOTALS											
GP	G	A	Pts	+/-	GWG	GTG	S	S%	PPG	SHG	PIM
531	265	280	545	38	36	4	1638	16.2	77	14	251

MAURICE RICHARD

Name: Joseph Henri Maurice Richard
Born: August 4, 1921, Montreal, Quebec
Died: May 27, 2000
Shoots: Left
Height: 5-10
Weight: 170

"He was an icon in Montreal, in Quebec. People just worshipped him, so did we all."
—teammate Dickie Moore on Maurice Richard

If there had ever been any doubt of where Joseph Henri Maurice "Rocket" Richard stood in the hearts of his Quebec fans, his funeral on May 31, 2000, would have made it clear.

Make that his state funeral, the first ever for an athlete in Canada. At Montreal's Notre Dame Basilica. With flags lowered to half-mast. And Quebec's National Assembly suspended for the day. That was a day after some 115,000 paid their respects in the Molson Center.

He was 78. And a victim of abdominal cancer. And Canadians knew one thing for certain.

There would never be another like him.

Not even close.

And the feeling from the fans for Richard, well it went both ways. Former teammate Dickie Moore said Richard understood his responsibility to his fans: "He said, 'You know Dickie, I play to satisfy the people. They expect me to score and I give it everything to please them.'"

Which is exactly what the 5-foot-10, 170-pounder did despite an injury-plagued youth career that made people wonder if his body was up to it. He lasted 18 years with eight Stanley Cups, 544 goals and 14 straight All-Star teams. Five times he led the league in scoring and he had the first-ever 50 goals in 50 games and was the first player to 500 career goals.

It was always his temper that was the issue. You couldn't count his famous fights on two hands. And his riot, well, that was a two-fisted answer from Canadien fans to the league's strong response and season-ending suspension for a multiple-stick-breaking incident that Richard inflicted on Boston Bruin Hal Laycoe.

An upset Richard could give lessons in anger to Bob Knight. The Montreal fans loved it right to the end, which came in 1960. His Hockey Hall of Fame induction came just a year later.

CAREER TOTALS											
GP	G	A	Pts	+/-	GWG	GTG	S	S%	PPG	SHG	PIM
978	544	421	965	0*	0*	0*	0*	-*	0*	0*	1285

TEEMU SELANNE

Name: Teemu Selanne
Born: July 3, 1970, Helsinki, Finland
Shoots: Right
Height: 6-0
Weight: 201

"There is no evil side to him."

—Paul Kariya on his former teammate Teemu Selanne

Teemu Selanne knows how to make an entrance.

All Selanne did when the Winnipeg Jets finally got him on the ice four years after drafting the Helsinki native was obliterate the previous record for rookie goal scoring of Mike Bossy by 23. And he broke Peter Stastny's rookie points record, also by 23.

That's what happens when you blast off with 76 goals and 132 total points the way the 6-foot, 201-pound part-time race car driver did.

He went from Finnish League All-Star to National Hockey League All-Star in the twinkling of an eye. He also earned the Calder Trophy as Rookie of the Year and a first-team All-Star spot.

Players like Selanne they tab "pure goal-scorers." And to certify that, Selanne was the 1999 winner of the first Maurice Richard Trophy awarded the NHL's goal-scoring leader. And on hand to give it to Selanne was The Rocket himself.

Three times now Selanne has led the league in goal-scoring from his right wing spot. And six times Selanne has participated in All-Star Games.

After four seasons with Winnipeg, Selanne added another four in Anaheim and and then two more in San Jose for the improving Sharks.

With Kariya, Selanne combined for 552 points in Anaheim, the most for a pair of teammates in six seasons.

CAREER TOTALS											
GP	G	A	Pts	+/-	GWG	GTG	S	S%	PPG	SHG	PIM
719	408	447	855	37	61	10	2505	16.3	127	6	273

KEITH TKACHUK

Name: Keith Matthew Tkachuk
Born: March 28, 1972, Melrose, Massachusetts
Shoots: Left
Height: 6-2
Weight: 225

"I'd rather answer dumb questons from the media in Phoenix than answer dumb ones in Philadelphia."

—Keith Tkachuk on possibly being traded for Eric Lindros

Keith Tkachuk always seems to have an answer. He knew he would be leaving Phoenix but wasn't all that keen on Philadelphia in a swap for Eric Lindros.

So he got in a double shot with one answer.

"I'd rather answer dumb questions from the media in Phoenix than answer dumb ones in Philadelphia," Tkachuk said.

Take that Phoenix media. Ditto for you folks in Philadelphia.

And of course, Tkachuk did it all with a smile. The way he always does.

Tkachuk got what he wanted, an $8.3 million dollar a year deal in St. Louis where he didn't downgrade the Blues who gave up five players for him..

A big, strong, 6-foot-2, 225-pound left wing from Melrose, Massachusetts, Tkachuk was the first American-born player to lead the National Hockey League in goal-scoring with his 52 in Phoenix in 1996–1997.

When Tkachuk left Phoenix where he was captain the last six years, he was the franchise leader in game-winning goals and minutes played and second all-time in career goals and power-play goals.

Internationally he's played for Team USA in three Olympics (1992, 1998 and 2002).

CAREER TOTALS											
GP	G	A	Pts	+/-	GWG	GTG	S	S%	PPG	SHG	PIM
725	367	339	706	43	48	9	2301	15.9	129	12	1639

JACK ADAMS

Name: Jack Adams
Born: June 14, 1895, Fort William, Ontario
Died: May 1, 1968
Teams Coached: Detroit Red Wings, 1927-1947
20 Years: 413-390-161
Playoff Record: 52-52-1
Stanley Cups Won: 1936, 1937, 1943

"Mr Adams was like a father to me. When I joined the Red Wings organization I was only 16 years old, and he looked after me as though I was his own son."
—Hall of Fame player Gordie Howe on hearing of Adams' death.

Jack Adams is the National Hockey League's original triple threat. He's the only man in NHL history to have his name on the Stanley Cup as a player, as a coach and as a general manager.

But the Stanley Cup isn't the only hardware with his name on it. The Jack Adams Award has been designated by the NHL to honor the league's top coach each season.

Remember, this was a man inducted into the Hockey Hall of Fame as a player. Not that there's a way for a coach to get inducted just as a coach. They don't do that at the Hockey Hall of Fame. But he was very good, especially during his years in Vancouver in the Pacific Coast Hockey League, where he once scored six goals in a losing Stanley Cup finals game in 1922. And he did get another Cup as a skater for Ottawa.

But a case could easily be made that Adams' contributions to the game were mostly after he left the ice.

After several years with Toronto St. Pat's and the year in Ottawa, Adams took over a struggling Detroit team in the NHL. And take over he did. Some would say he was the ultimate authoritarian, and that would not be a compliment.

He did it all—publicity man, business manager and traveling secretary—as well as coach and GM. Some accused him of tight-fistedly running off talent because he refused to pay. Others say he two-fistedly would go after the officials in their dressing room after a game to dispute a call. This was one tough, loud guy.

And effective. For those who criticize his way with the talent, just look at the players he developed for the Winged Wheels. Start with Gordie Howe, add in Ted Lindsay, Terry Sawchuk, Alex Delvecchio and all the others that helped Detroit to an amazing seven-year run in first place.

But that wasn't all. As general manager, he built a strong farm system and was responsible for a dozen regular-season championships and seven Stanley Cups in his 35 years in Detroit.

AL ARBOUR

Name: Al Arbour
Born: November 1, 1932, Sudbury, Ontario
Teams Coached: St. Louis 1970-1973, New York Islanders, 1973-1994
22 Years: 781-577-248
Playoff Record: 123-86-0
Stanley Cups Won: 1980, 1981, 1982, 1983

"The most important thing I learned was that you've got to handle people. The game is not all Xs and O's."

—former Islander player Butch Goring, who followed Arbour into coaching.

Any way you look at it—athletically, alphabetically or simply as a coach—Al Arbour would always be right at the very top of any list. As he is here.

As a tenacious, not to mention bespectacled, defenseman out of Sudbury, Ontario, Arbour skated for three Stanley Cup teams with Detroit, Chicago and Toronto.

But even before he'd finished playing, Arbour was being asked to coach the expansion St. Louis Blues. After returning to the ice to skate, Arbour stayed with the Blues before being fired in 1973. That led him to his big chance to coach with another expansion team—the New York Islanders. And there he became one of the great National Hockey League coaches of all time.

By the numbers, make it the second-greatest behind only Scotty Bowman, whom he trails for most games and most regular-season and playoff victories His four Stanley Cups won from 1980 to 1983 trail only Toe Blake, Bowman and Hap Day.

It took Arbour just a season on Long Island before the team's improvement could not be missed. Four straight 100-point seasons were just the buildup for the Islanders in the late 1970s and then it happened—Stanley Cups in four straight seasons to start the 1980s. Only Montreal (twice) had ever managed to win four in a row in the league.

And it could have been five had it not been for the next dynasty to come along—the Glen Sather-Wayne Gretzky Edmonton Oilers. The Oilers took the Isles down in the finals in 1984.

As a player in 626 NHL games, Alan "Radar" Arbour won the Eddie Shore Award in 1965 and made the NHL All-Star roster in 1969. As a coach, he was presented the Jack Adams Award as coach of the year in 1979, right before starting his Stanley Cup string. And in 1992, he was awarded the Lester Patrick Trophy for service to hockey in the United States.

Arbour, one of 18 selectors on the NHL Legends Committee, helps decide on future Hall of Famers. The Hockey Hall of Fame has already made that decision on Arbour, inducting him in 1996 as one of the builders of the game.

TOE BLAKE

Name: Toe Blake
Born: August 21, 1912, Victoria Mines, Ontario
Died: May 17, 1995
Teams Coached: Montreal, 1955-68
13 Years: 500-255-159
Playoff Record: 82-37-0
Stanley Cup Won: 1956, 1957, 1958, 1959, 1960, 1965, 1966, 1968

"In the 1960s we had a very good team but we were not head and shoulders above the rest of the league as we had been in the 1950s. The difference was that we had the very best coach {Toe Blake} in hockey and a man who could get the best out of his players at all times."

–Jean Beliveau.

Was he was a better player or coach?

When a major sports figure plays and coaches at the level that Hector "Toe" Blake reached with the Montreal Canadiens, it's usually easy to decide which of those two is correct.

Just check the numbers. Look at the honors. Tally up the trophies.

Some guys can play. Others can coach. It's the rare bird who can do both.

Toe Blake could do both—big-time.

He could skate—with first the Montreal Maroons and then the Canadiens—before he was earning his nickname as either "the Lamplighter" or the "Old Lamplighter" in honor of his scoring ability.

By 1938–1939, Blake was the NHL's leading scorer and MVP. And soon he was paired up with Maurice Richard for some great years in Montreal, helping the Canadiens win their first Stanley Cup in 13 years.. But in 1948, his playing career effectively ended after a broken leg in a game with the New York Rangers.

But another career was starting. The bilingual Blake would get his chance to go home to Montreal after four years as player-coach in the Quebec Senior Hockey League.

Montreal wanted him to take control of his line-mate, the excitable Maurice Richard. All Blake did was win five staright Stanley Cups, a feat never before accomplished. It didn't hurt that he had players like Jacques Plante, Henri and Maurice Richard, Jean Beliveau, Dickie Moore and Bernie Geoffrion. No wonder this team played in 10 straight Stanley Cup finals.

Blake won two more back-to-back Cups in 1965 and 1966 and finished off his coaching career with Stanley Cup No. 8 in 1968.

It hardly mattered for his Hall of Fame status. Blake had been elected to the Hockey Hall of Fame two years earlier as a player.

SCOTTY BOWMAN

Name: Scotty Bowman
Born: September 18, 1933, Montreal, Quebec
Teams Coached: St. Louis, 1967-71; Montreal 1971-79; Buffalo, 1979-1987; Pittsburgh, 1991-1993; 1993-2002.
28 Years: 1244–583–314
Playoff Record 51–21–10
Stanley Cups Won: 1973, 1976, 1977, 1978, 1979, 1992, 1997, 1998, 2002

"Bowman's stature was as much deserved recognition of his accomplishments as it was a sad testament to the state of the professional coaching ranks. Owners and managers had downgraded the job, often with the approval of the players, to a glorified consultant's role."
—Biographer Douglas Hunter in "Scotty Bowman: A Life in Hockey."

His players may not like him but they do respect him.

He can't stand mediocrity or underachievers.

Sports Illustrated called him "the best coach ever in any professional sport."

An *ESPN* fan poll says he was the fourth-greatest coach in the 20th Century.

He's the all-time winningest NHL coach in both regular season and playoffs over 29 seasons including a record nine Stanley Cup wins with Montreal (1973, 1976–1979), Pittsburgh (1992) and Detroit (1997, 1998, 2002).

He is already a member of the Hockey Hall of Fame as the only coach in NHL history to guide a team to 60-win seasons (1977, 1996) and one of only two coaches in the four major sports to win a championship with three different teams.

And yet there's this. We know so much about Scotty Bowman and yet we don't know him. One biographer, Douglas Hunter, calls him "inscrutable."

His players would agree. "Trying to understand Scotty is like trying to explain abstract painting," says Shawn Burr, a left-winger traded by Bowman to Tampa Bay.

In Pittsburgh, they called him "Rain Man" for the way his photographic memory helped him know his statistics.

And then there's this—his work ethic. Goaltender Glenn Hall once said that Bowman was thinking when everyone else was sleeping.

Born in Montreal in 1933, William Scott "Scotty" Bowman has coached all sorts of teams—great ones, not-so-great ones, should-be-good ones and ones on the rise. He's been an old-fashioned disciplinarian with all of them. And it's mostly worked.

Biographer Hunter thinks that coaching hockey is strategy in motion. "Running the bench is Bowman's talent. He is so good at it, he may not have to think about it."

Bowman won five Stanley Cups with the Montreal Canadiens, didn't win much with the Buffalo Sabres, then came back to grab a Stanley Cup with the Pittsburgh Penguins and got three more with the Detroit Red Wings, as talented a team as hockey has seen.

HAP DAY

Name: Hap Day
Born: June 1, 1901, Owen Sound, Ontario
Died: February 17, 1990
Teams Coached: Toronto, 1940-1950
10 Years: 259-206-81
Playoff Record: 49-31-0
Stanley Cups Won: 1942, 1945, 1947, 1948, 1949

"The only man to serve as captain, coach and general manager for the club."

—Selection committee's citation naming Hap Day one of 25 greatest Maple Leafs of all time."

The 1940s were happy days in Toronto, thanks to a man by the name of Hap Day, who happened to be heading up the Maple Leafs.

Five Stanley Cup titles in 10 years, that was the winning tab run up by Day, an NHL player all the way back to his college days with Toronto's St. Pat's team.

In fact, Day's 10 years as a coach weren't even a third of his 33-year National Hockey League career. He'd even been a referee for two seasons before taking over the Maple Leafs.

His chance came when Conn Smythe decided to let Dick Irvin go to Montreal with Major Smythe going overseas for World War II.

And in an era when nicknames mattered, when they called guys "The Rocket" and "Boom-Boom," "Toe" and "King," Day really was a perpetually cheerful guy. Maybe he was just happy they weren't calling him by his proper name, Clarence, anymore. First they called him "Happy" then simply "Hap."

But certainly not hapless. A pharmacy student at the University of Toronto, Day was encouraged to turn pro with the St. Pat's team while still in school. But the Owen Sound, Ontario native didn't want to give up school so he held out for $5,000. And got it.

That started a 33-year career with the Maple Leafs organization for the 5-10, 175-pound Day. He even ran a drug store in Maple Leaf Gardens as a player. Described as a "natural leader," it's no wonder the Leafs named him captain for the years 1926 through 1936. Paired with King Clancy on defense, the Hall of Fame pair was as good as any duo in the league and won a Stanley Cup for Toronto in 1932.

Day was tough and demanding on his players. And even tougher on the officials since he'd been one himself and knew the rule book better than most of them. Even after he left coaching, Day ran the Leafs until 1957 and won another Stanley Cup title.

In the 1941–1942 championship finals, Day led his team to the greatest recovery in Stanley Cup history as the Maple Leafs were the only team ever to come back from a 3–0 deficit to win four straight games and the Cup.

He was inducted into the Hockey Hall of Fame in 1961.

PUNCH IMLACH

Name: George "Punch" Imlach
Born: March 15, 1918, Toronto, Ontario
Died: December 1, 1987
Teams Coached: Toronto, 1958-1969; Buffalo, 1970-1972; Toronto, 1979-1980
14 Years: 402-337-150
Playoff Record: 44-48-0
Stanley Cups Won: 1962, 1963, 1964, 1967

During his tenure with the Leafs, Punch Imlach developed a reputation as a motivator, particularly skilled at utilizing the qualities of veteran players. Imlach's 1967 Cup-winning Leafs were the oldest winners in league history."

—Buffalo Sports Hall of Fame induction statement

The facts are fairly straightforward for George "Punch" Imlach's National Hockey League coaching career. He began his business behind the bench with the Toronto Maple Leafs, where from 1958 through 1969, the Leafs had just one losing season.

But of course that wasn't what was most important. Most important were the four Stanley Cups the club won (1962, 1963, 1964 and 1967). Note the first three came, as they say on *ESPN*, back to back to back.

Only six coaches in NHL history won more games. And only three—Scotty Bowman, Toe Blake and Hap Day—won more Stanley Cups. Numbers like that, you would think, would have stood Imlach in good stead in Toronto, where he'd gone from assistant general manager to NHL icon in 11 seasons. Well, think again. After finishing out of the running in 1969, Imlach was bounced. And Buffalo was thrilled.

The Sabres were an instant success, the folks in Western New York say, on the ice and in the arena seats thanks to Imlach's understanding of how to put a team together.

In three seasons the Sabres were in the playoffs. In five seasons, they reached the Stanley Cup finals. Imlach was getting more praise for his work with the new kids on the block than he ever did with the four Stanley Cups for the Maple Leafs. Imlach accomplished this all with an interesting blend of the new—rookie draft pick Gilbert Perreault could not have been a better choice and the old—ex-Maple Leafs like Dick Duff, Reg Fleming, Don Marshall, Tim Horton and Floyd Smith, from Toronto.

Even with a heart condition forcing him to step down from coaching after the 1972 season, Imlach retained the GM reins and in his authoritarian old school ways, kept the Sabres headed upward in a way they've found hard to match since.

Andy Bathgate said Imlach "worked his players too hard in practice and demanded more of them than they were prepared to give."

Imlach did appear willing to pay the price. Called back to Toronto for two final seasons. Imlach's turbulent tenure was ended by a major heart attack in 1981. In 1984 he was inducted into the Hockey Hall of Fame. He died the next year.

DICK IRVIN

Name: Dick Irvin
Born: July 19, 1892, Hamilton, Ontario
Died: March 16, 1957
Teams Coached: Chicago, 1928-1931; Toronto, 1931-1940; Montreal, 1940-1955; Chicago, 1955-1956
27 Years: 692-527-230
Playoff Record: 100-88-2
Stanley Cups Won: 1932, 1944, 1946, 1953

"To you from failing hands we throw the torch. Be yours to hold it high."
—words from the poem "In Flanders Fields" that Coach Dick Irvin had emblazoned along a wall in the Canadiens dressing room in 1952.

When a coach has helped take the two National Hockey League franchises that mattered the most—Toronto and Montreal—to the top, where else could we expect to find him but also at the pinnacle?

And at the top was exactly where James Dickenson "Dick" Irvin found himself on top when he retired from coaching in 1956. No other NHL coach had ever reached the 692 regular season wins Irvin had earned at Chicago, Toronto and Montreal.

When Ottawa's Roger Neilson was elavated to coach his team in the final two games this season, he joined an exclusive club—men who had coached 1,000 regular-season games. Only eight had reached it before him and Irvin was the first. Following him were Scotty Bowman, Al Arbour, Billy Reay, Mike Keenan, Pat Quinn, Bryan Murray and Jacques Demers.

Among those four Stanley Cup championships was the first ever for the Maple Leafs in 1931.

But building the Canadiens back to where the NHL needed the team playing in The Forum to be may have been Irvin's greatest accomplishment. After leading Toronto to the finals six more times in the decade, Irvin resigned in 1940.

Some would say that what Irvin did in 15 years in Montreal—the longest coaching tenure anyone has ever managed in that pressure-packed job—to save the floundering Habs from financial ruin was his greatest accomplishment by far. One thing that all agree on is that the former great center from hockey's early days inspired his players to skate with the passion he displayed in a career during World War I with teams like the Portland Rosebuds before a short stint with the NHL's Chicago Blackhawks.

A fractured skull soon had Irvin coaching in Chicago, then Toronto and Montreal.

Irvin returned to Chicago for a year with his old team and then he retired in 1956. His 1958 induction to the Hockey Hall of Fame came a year after his death.

TOMMY IVAN

Name: Tommy Ivan
Born: January 31, 1911, Toronto, Ontario
Died: June 24, 1999
Teams Coached: Detroit, 1947-1954; Chicago, 1956-1958
9 Years: 288-174-111
Playoff Record: 36-31-0
Stanley Cups Won: 1950, 1952, 1954

"Break another seat in practice and it's coming out of your paycheck."

—Blackhawks GM Tommy Ivan to Dennis Hull, Bobby's brother who had a heavier, but far less accurate, shot than his brother.

Tommy Ivan, with that jutting jaw, handsome profile and shock of gleaming white hair combed back on his head always looked like the hockey coach from Central Casting.

Knocked out of a chance to play in the National Hockey League after a fractured cheekbone before World War II, Ivan was in the right place after the war. He was in Detroit.

So was Gordie Howe. After working as a referee and then minor league coach for Detroit's Omaha and Indianapolis teams, Ivan was ready when the Red Wings decided to make a change behind the bench. He'd already made the acquaintance of the 17-year-old Howe at Indianapolis.

But according to Howe, that wasn't enough to get him much time on the ice. "I was getting very few shifts until one night I saw one of my teammates getting beat up, so I jumped over the boards and nailed the guy on the other team," Howe said. "Coach Ivan asked me, 'Don't you like that player?' And I replied that I didn't like anyone. At that point, he realized that I had grown up, and I didn't miss many shifts after that."

Ivan clearly understood what it took to win and having Howe banging on people was a good start. Those are the kinds of things you learn in the Central Hockey League where today, the most valuable player is presented the Tommy Ivan Trophy.

Ivan has another distinction. Of the 10 coaches who've been behind the bench in at least four NHL All-Star Games, only Ivan—with his 3–0–1 record—is undefeated. Thanks to his league-leading Wings, Ivan coached in the 1948, 1949, 1950 and 1952 games.

But Ivan's greatest accomplishment in those years was putting together the famous Production Line of Sid Abel, Ted Lindsay and Howe. It took them three seasons after the assembly job by Ivan to get that first Stanley Cup in a season when the line finished 1-2-3 in scoring as Lindsay won the title.

From 1948 through 1955, the Red Wings won seven straight league titles and three Stanley Cups for him with a lineup of seven Hall of Famers including Terry Sawchuk, Alex Delvecchio and Marcel Pronovost.

MIKE KEENAN

Name: Mike Keenan
Born: October 21, 1949, Toronto, Ontario
Teams Coached: Philadelphia, 1984-1988; Chicago, 1988-1992; New York Rangers, 1993-1994; St. Louis, 1994-1997; Vancouver, 1997-2000; Florida, 2001-2002
16 Years: 528-416-127-6
Playoff Record: 91-69-0
Stanley Cups Won: 1994

"He may be hockey's premier example of the new-breed sports coach, still basically hierarchical and conservative but trying to upholster the old authoritarianism with plush and cozy New Age motivational techniques."
—Robert Lipsyte, The New York Times

It's not that Mike Keenan keeps wearing out his welcome, it's just that people keep making him offers. Sometimes they want him to come to their town and coach for them. And other times they want him to leave and go very far away. Sometimes he wears them out. Sometimes they wear him out.

But it's always interesting. In Philadelphia, there were a pair of Stanley Cup finals for the Flyers in 1985 and 1987. Ditto for Chicago and the Blackhawks in 1992. In New York, the Rangers got all their money's worth in 1994 when they made the trip to the finals with Keenan pay off with the franchise's first Stanley Cup in 54 years. Then it was off to St. Louis. And Vancouver. And Boston. And now Florida, where after a half-season, Keenan said he'd gotten feelers from the Rangers to return to New York and try to get something out of their staggering $70 million payroll.

Keenan said he had a job to do in South Florida. And so he stayed.

He's home in Florida.

It's been an interesting run for the 52-year-old Toronto native who took over in Florida in December as the fifth all-time NHL coach in career regular season games coached and games won and fourth in playoff wins.

Keenan has won a Jack Adams Award as the league's top coach for his 1984-1985 Flyers and has been named to coach in three NHL All-Star Games. The year before he got the Flyers' job he'd been a sensation at the University of Toronto where he was 41-5-3 and won the Canadian national championship before getting his first NHL job at the age of 34.

He's coached seven teams and almost never missed the playoffs. He's been called "sometimes irascible," "authoritarian" and even "despotic." Add to that "no-nonsense disciplinarian," "complex," "intelligent," "contradictory," "introspective," and "a master at transforming marginal players into overachievers."

JACQUES LEMAIRE

Name: Jacques Lemaire
Born: September 17, 1945, LaSalle, Quebec
Teams Coached: Montreal, 1983-1985; New Jersey, 1993-1998; Minnesota, 2000-2002
9 Years: 298-233-94-14
Playoff Record: 49-34-0
Stanley Cups Won: 1995

"This man (Jacques Lemaire) is about two things: winning and teaching. Everything else really doesn't matter, so if he's less than cooperative with the press, it's all about priorities."
—Dennis Bernstein, editor, New Jersey Devils Fanzine

Jaques Lemaire has 11 Stanley Cup rings, ten of which he earned as a player and coach at Montreal. But the one he'll always remember is the one he earned in 1995 when he led the New Jersey Devils to that franchise's first-ever title. The Devils did it by going 16–4 in the playoffs including 10–1 on the road.

That championship came a year after Lemaire had earned his only Jack Adams Trophy as the league's best coach. Inducted into the Hockey Hall of Fame as a player in 1984, Lemaire played in a pair of NHL All-Star Games in 1970 and 1973.

A native of LaSalle, Quebec, Lemaire was a 5-10, 180-pound center and left winger who shot from the left side in a playing career from 1967 through 1979.

Lemaire was only the fifth player in NHL history to score a second Stanley Cup-winning goal in 1979. He'd also done it two years earlier for the first time. After a stint as player-coach in Switzerland, Lemaire returned to the NHL as head coach of the Habs.

Lemaire's regular season totals show 366 goals and 469 assists for a total of 835 NHL points in 853 games. In the playoffs, Lemaire's 61–78–139 totals came in 145 games. As a coach, he's 298-233-94-14 in nine regular seasons and 49-34 in the playoffs.

Lemaire's move back into coaching the past two seasons with the expansion Minnesota Wild reunited him with former teammate Doug Risebrough, the Minnesota GM who teamed with Lemaire in Montreal from 1974 through 1979.

He explained his philosophy in a recent interview after a game this past season.

"Every time we got the puck, we'd just give it to them, instead of skating or making a good play. Sometimes we do that because we don't want to make a mistake, so we're just sending the puck. And that IS a mistake. That's why I often tell the players, play with confidence, you have to be able to do it, say 'I'm gonna do it. I'm gonna carry it. I'm gonna skate with it. I'm gonna make a play."

LESTER PATRICK

Name: Lester Patrick
Born: December 30, 1883, Drummondville, Quebec
Died: June 1, 1960
Teams Coached: New York Rangers, 1926 1939
13 Years: 281-216-107
Playoff Record: 32-26-7
Stanley Cups Won: 1928, 1933

"Patrick, Lester B and Frank A: Canadian brothers who as managers, owners and league officials helped establish professional ice hockey in Canada and who aided the expansion of the National Hockey League to the United States."
—Encyclopedia Brittanica

Lester Patrick didn't have to spend a life in hockey. Nor did his brother Frank. The former McGill University players had starred with their father's Renfrew Millionaires and Montreal Wanderers teams and then took those two team names literally, heading West where their wealth lay in the family's timber holdings.

But their hearts were in hockey. And what the Patrick family did would not be matched by anyone else—in Canada or in the United States—in the history of the game for its impact. Frank went to coach Boston and then Montreal while Lester took over New York from 1926 through 1946 and set up hockey's first real farm system.

No wonder the National Hockey League's most prestigious honor is named the Lester Patrick Award. It was presented to the NHL by the New York Rangers in 1966, to honor the memory of Lester Patrick, who spent 50 years as a player, coach, general manager, owner and NHL governor. Eligible recipients include players, coaches, referees and linesmen, as well as team and league executives.

Lester Patrick deserves such attention. No one did more. He took hockey west, founding the Pacific Coast Hockey Association with his brother and using the family fortune to build two hockey palaces with artificial ice in Vancouver and Victoria. In fact, the 10,500-seat Denman Street Arena in Vancouver was—at the cost of $175,000—a hockey building second only to Madison Square Garden. And the 4,000-seat Willow Street Arena in Victoria would cost another $110,000.

In those days from 1911 through 1924, hockey was happening back East. And soon enough, Lester Patrick would be running the Rangers, getting the New York franchise off to a flying start as coach and general manager by leading it to the playoffs in all but one of his first 16 years with the club with Stanley Cups in 1928 and 1933.

Ever the activist, however, Lester Patrick wasn't content to remain behind the bench. In 1928, for example, with no backup goaltender, the 44-year-old Patrick stepped out of his street clothes and into his hockey gear to replace injured goalie Lorne Chabot and beat the Montreal Maroons in Game 2 of the Stanley Cup Finals.

PAT QUINN

Name: Pat Quinn
Born: January 29, 1943, Hamilton, Ontario
Teams Coached: Philadelphia, 1978-1982; Los Angeles, 1984-1987; Vancouver, 1990-1996; Toronto, 1998-2002
16 Years: 527-399-137-12
Playoff Record: 68-64-0 (2002 results not included)

"Under the guidance of Pat Quinn, the Leafs have gained the reputation as hockey's most unrelenting whiners, a group that starts bellyaching as soon as they get to the rink if their cafe lattes aren't quite hot enough."
—Toronto Star hockey columnist Damien Cox

The Hockey News has Pat Quinn at No. 22 in its current rankings of hockey's 100 People of Power and influence. And they say it's easy to understand why Quinn, 58, trails only Scotty Bowman among active coaches on the list. He led Team Canada to an Olympic Gold in Salt Lake City with the team Wayne Gretzky provided him.

He's also has the Maple Leafs organization surging a bit these days in his role as the lone combination coach and general manager in the league today.

Here's *The Globe* and *Mail*'s Stephen Brunt: "Pat Quinn, the coach of the Toronto Maple Leafs, seems perpetually aggrieved. In the games of the regular season that don't matter all that much, in the games of the playoffs that matter a lot, he sees conspiracies all around. 'The ref got us here,' he'll say, and then the ref didn't get them there. For expressing those kind of dangerous thoughts in public earlier in this postseason, his wallet was made considerably lighter by the people at the National Hockey League's head office."

At $1.5 million a year, the league's highest-paid coach can afford the hits on his wallet, at least. And he has Gretzky in his corner. In the run-up to the Olympics, Gretzky was asked whether he was keeping an eye on Quinn to see how Quinn was handling his team. Gretzky was quick to show his support.

"No, we're not watching Pat," Gretzky said. "How Pat coaches is up to him, and he'll communicate with Ken (Hitchcock) and Jacques (Martin), as well as Wayne Flemming (another assistant) on how to handle the players and coach the team."

Quinn is remembered as a 6-foot-3, 220-pound 21-year-old defenseman nick-named "Cheyenne" for his resemblance to that TV cowboy and his liking for cowboy boots and hats from his Tulsa Oiler days in the minors. After four seasons in the CHL, mostly in Tulsa where he had a home, Quinn went on to play nine seasons in the NHL with the Toronto Maple Leafs, Atlanta Flames and Vancouver Canucks.

Twice Quinn has been named the NHL's coach of the year and with this year's gold medal in hockey, he's done it all except capture the Stanley Cup.

ART ROSS

Name: Arthur Howie Ross
Born: January 13, 1886, Naughton, Ontario
Died: August 5, 1964
Teams Coached: Montreal Wanderers, 1917-1918; Hamilton Tigers, 1922-1923; Boston Bruins, 1924-1945
18 Years: 368-300-90
Playoff Record: 27-33-5
Stanley Cups Won: 1929, 1939

"He knows the game and everybody in it. He's got courage, too. He's just the man to manage the Bruins."

—Boston Bruins owner Charles Adams

Art Ross was many things. One of 13 children who grew up in a family in Whitefish Bay. One of the Hockey Hall of Fame's first class of inductees in 1945.

One great defenseman, a tough 5-foot-11, 190-pounder who won Stanley Cups in back-to-back years on different teams in 1907 and 1908 and developed the accursed "trap" defense so many hockey fans love to hate. He was described by opponents as "the greatest stickhandler of his day and a man who could stop on a dime."

Ross was one smart guy, too. The synthetic rubber puck he developed was still in use into the late 1990s and the B-shaped goal net he designed lasted through the 1980s.

And he'll always be remembered since his name is on the trophy annually awarded to the National Hockey League's top scorer. Ross first presented it himself in 1941 and it's been presented annually since 1948 to the NHL's top points scorer.

Ross himself had played for a succession of teams until reaching the Ottawa Senators for the 1914–15 and 1915–16 seasons, when he came up with his "trap" system to defend against a fast Montreal club by having three defensemen positioned 30 feet in front of his team's net as Ross's Ottawa club beat Montreal with it.

A players-rights advocate, Ross wanted a league owned by the players back in those early days of the game. And he did things like develop a protective helmet as well as a protective pad for the Achilles tendon.

But after a short stint as an NHL referee, Ross was offered the Boston Bruins coaching job by owner Charles Adams and ran the Boston franchise for the next 30 years, bringing three Stanley Cup titles to Boston, two as coach and three overall. The teams Ross built finished first 10 times, second six more and won 724 games, losing only 582.

Ross was also awarded the Lester Patrick Trophy for his service to hockey in the United States in 1984.

GLEN SATHER

Name: Glen Cameron Sather
Born: September 2, 1943, High River, Alberta
Teams Coached: Edmonton, 1979-1989; Edmonton, 1994
11 Years: 464-268-110
Playoff Record: 89-37-1
Stanley Cups Won: 1984, 1985, 1987, 1988

"Glen Sather has been one of hockey's most successful executives for nearly two decades. His administrative and coaching talents enabled the Edmonton Oilers to become one of the most successful clubs in NHL history."

—Hockey Hall of Fame Induction citation in 1997

Glen Sather played 660 National Hockey League games with the Boston Bruins, Pittsburgh Penguins, New York Rangers, St. Louis Blues, Montreal Canadiens, Minnesota North Stars and Edmonton Oilers.

And that was just his warmup act.

The important part of Sather's career was still to come, as coach—and general manager—of the Oilers, where his talented teams skated off with Stanley Cups in 1984, 1985, 1987 and 1988 when he was coach and again in 1990 when he was General Manager.

Hard to top that. Only now Sather has moved on to try to do just that. And to top it on the brightest stage in hockey, New York's Madison Square Garden where the Rangers are trying to discover the magic once again and spending some $70 million in annual payroll to do so.

It's doubtful, however, even Sather can reprise the trade-and-sign deal he managed back at the end of his World Hockey Association days when he got 17-year-old Wayne Gretzky, then with Indianapolis, to become an Oiler. Gretzky wasn't alone. Those Oiler teams would have the likes of goalie Grant Fuhr to go with Mark Messier, who was already there. Following them would be Paul Coffey, Andy Moog and Jari Kurri.

Sather, 58, and known as "Slats" to his friends, was inducted into the Hockey Hall of Fame in 1997 as the first-ever Edmonton Oiler to be so honored. It came 11 years after he'd won the Jack Adams Award as the league's top coach. Under Sather, the Oilers organization produced a 791-660-215 record in 1,666 games over 22 years. In doing so, Sather became the second-longest-tenured general manager in the NHL.

FRED SHERO

Name: Fred Shero
Born: October 23, 1925, Winnipeg, Manitoba
Died: November 24, 1990
Teams Coached: Philadelphia, 1971-1978; New York Rangers, 1978-1981
10 Years: 390-225-119
Playoff Record: 63-47-0
Stanley Cups Won: 1974, 1975

"Win together and we walk forever together."

—Fred Shero on the lockerrom chalkboard before Game 6 in the 1974 Stanley Cup finals

Here's all you need to know of how they feel about Fred Shero, the two-time Stanley Cup winning former Flyers coach, in the City of Brotherly Love.

In a 1999 *Philadelphia Daily News* poll, Shero was selected as the city's greatest professional coach or manager, beating out the likes of Connie Mack, Dick Vermeil, Greasy Neale, Billy Cunningham, Dallas Green and Alex Hannum.

Not bad for a former New York Rangers defenseman from Winnipeg who played just three seasons in the National Hockey League. After winning his first of two straight Stanley Cups in 1974 with The Broad Street Bullies, Shero earned the Jack Adams Award as the NHL's top coach.

But it appears he'll never have to walk away from the admiration of Philly fans.

In a way, that sentiment only evokes one of Shero's famous coaching touches. He would deliver to his players a simple saying before the game on the lockerroom blackboard. The one that will remain forever in Philly sports lore came before Game 6 in the 1974 finals.

"Win together and we walk together forever," Shero wrote.

Apparently he will. As will most of the Flyers from that era who remain in the Philadelphia area today. It is indeed a group that seems to have stayed together forever

Even if Shero has passed on. A battle with cancer took his life in 1990 at the age of 65.

They called Shero "The Fog" for the way he drifted off and yet he was a major coaching innovator. Hiring an assistant coach, installing playing systems, studying game and practice films, conducting morning skates, were all Shero ideas. Maybe when he was drifting off, he was thinking about things like that.

But Shero was hardly an intellectual. The son of Russian immigrants, Shero could have been a professional boxer but turned the chance down in order to be a NHL player. Those who saw them say his practices could be more like football practices—tough, hard-hitting and full of pads and punches and all sorts of wild drills concocted by Shero to teach one lesson or another.

APRIL 13, 1927 (Game 4, Stanley Cup Finals)

Ottawa Senators   **3**
Bostons Bruins   **1**

At the Ottawa Auditorium

Modern era of Stanley Cup begins

It was the first of what can be called the modern era of the Stanley Cup. The winner of the National Hockey League would have exclusive rights to the legendary hardware thanks to the disbanding of the Pacific Coast Hockey Association and the West Coast Hockey League.

But "modern" here goes only so far. Artificial ice had come to the Ottawa Auditorium just four years before. In April, that technology went only so far. Two of the first three games in the five-game series (one each in Boston and Ottawa) ended in ties that could not be continued after the first 20-minute overtime because of bad ice. There were no Zambonis then, either.

So that left Game 4 in Ottawa's 6,500-seat Auditorium where the Senators showcased the best talent in the early NHL in front of the fewest fans in the smallest market. Boston was a different story. The fast-improving franchise under coach Art Ross had received 29,000 applications for Stanley Cup tickets.

While the Senators had the talent—King Clancy, Cy Denneny, Alex Connell, Hec Kilrea and Frank Nighbor— the Bruins had the Bad Boys, as they would prove in a tough 3 1 final game loss to the Senators. Eddie Shore, one of the toughest defenders ever to play in any era, set the tone for the Bruins.

In the final game Boston's Billy Couture was thrown out of the NHL for attacking two referees during the game and other players were fined $350 for what were termed "wild acts of intimidation." With a 2–0 edge because of the two ties, Ottawa was declared the winner since Boston could not catch up.

And the Stanley Cup?

Word is that the Cup spent most of the offseason in King Clancy's apartment where it was used to hold letters, bills, chewing gum and cigar butts.

Ottawa Senators: Alex Connell, King Clancy, George (Buck) Boucher, Ed Gorman, Frank Finnigan, Alex Smith, Hec Kilrea, Hooley Smith, Cy Denneny, Frank Nighbor, Jack Adams, Milt Halliday

Boston Bruins: Frank Frederickson, Harry Oliver, Jimmy Herberts, Eddie Shore, Percy "Perk" Galbraith, Lionel Hitchman, Sprague Cleghorn, Bill Boucher, Bill "Red" Stuart, Billy Coutu, Harry Meeking, Hal Winkler

APRIL 7, 1928 (Game 2, Stanley Cup Finals)

New York Rangers   **2**
Montreal Maroons   **1**

At the Montreal Forum

Coach Patrick plays in goal for 43 minutes

The new Montreal Forum hosted its first Stanley Cup in 1928 and it was a series for the ages with one of the most dramatic moments in Cup history.

That happened in Game 2, after an opening win by the favored Maroons, clearly the best team in the National Hockey League coming into the Finals. And they would get all five games in Montreal since the Ringling Brothers, Barnum and Bailey Circus had been booked for the Rangers Madison Square Garden home ice.

And then the Rangers took another blow—literally—as goalie Lorne Chabot was hit in the eye with a slap shot in Game 2 and knocked out for the series. And there was no backup goalie. The Maroons refused to let the Rangers use Ottawa goalie Alex Connell, who was in the stands.

So Rangers coach Lester Patrick, hired for the incredible salary of $18,000 a year, had 10 minutes to find a goalie. He did. He found himself, a former defenseman, at age 44 and never having been a goalie in his playing days, going between the pipes. He stopped 18 of 19 shots as he led his Rangers to a most-improbable 2–1 win to even the series.

After signing a backup goalie from the New York Americans, Joe Miller, the Rangers went on to win the series 3–2 for the first gigantic upset in Stanley Cup history.

New York Rangers: Lorne Chabot, Taffy Abel, Leon Bourgault, Ching Johnson, Bill Cook, Bun Cook, Frank Boucher, Billy Boyd, Murray Murdoch, Paul Thompson, Alex Gray, Joe Miller, Patsy Callighen, Lester Patrick

Montreal Maroons: Nels Stewart, Reginald "Hooley" Smith, Albert "Babe" Siebert, Joe Lamb, Mervyn "Red" Dutton, Jimmy Ward, Merlyn "Bill" Phillips, Russell Oatman, Dunc Munro, Bill Touhey, Fred Brown, Leighton "Happy" Emms, Frank Carson, James "Flat" Walsh, Clint Benedict

MARCH 29, 1929 (Game 2, Stanley Cup Finals)

Boston Bruins   **2**
New York Rangers   **1**

At Madison Square Garden

First All-American Stanley Cup Finals

It was the first-ever All-American Stanley Cup in 1929 as the American finalists from the previous two years—the Boston Bruins and the New York Rangers—hooked up in a best-of-three series.

But after the surging Bruins of Art Ross won Game 1, Game 2 would be all there was if the Bruins prevailed. And they did, thanks to the sensational work in goal of 23-year-old rookie Cecil "Tiny" Thompson, who came into the finals with a 1.18 goals-against average and 26 wins, both NHL bests.

That's pretty much the way the decisive game went as the Boston defense, led by the menacing macho man Eddie Shore, went 7–0 in the playoffs, allowing just three goals.

The Bruins won the game they had to win as Bill Carson fired in a third-period goal to break a 1–1 tie and Thompson (and his 0.60 goals-against playoff average) was unbeatable the rest of the way for a 2–1 victory and Beantown's first Stanley Cup.

And it wasn't like they were playing nobodies. The Rangers had a Hall of Fame front line of center Frank Boucher and wings— as well as brothers — Bill and Frederick "Bun" Cook.

Boston Bruins: Cecil (Tiny) Thompson, Eddie Shore, Lionel Hitchman, Perk Galbraith, Eric Pettinger, Frank Fredrickson, Mickey Mackay, Red Green, Dutch Gainor, Harry Oliver, Eddie Rodden, Dit Clapper, Cooney Weiland, Lloyd Klein, Cy Denneny, Bill Carson, George Owen, Myles Lane

New York Rangers: Frank Boucher, Bill Cook, Frederick "Bun" Cook, Paul Thompson, Murray Murdoch, Melville "Butch" Keeling, Leo Bourgeault, Clarence "Taffy" Abel, Melville "Sparky" Vail, Russell Oatman, Ivan "Ching" Johnson, Billy Boyd, Gerald Carson, John Roach

APRIL 3, 1930 (Game 2, Stanley Cup Finals)

Montreal Canadiens   **4**
Boston Bruins   **3**

At the Montreal Forum

Montreal surprise champion Bruins

It was one of the great collapses of all time. One ranking has it the fourth-greatest "choke" in all of hockey history.

The defending Stanley Cup champion Boston Bruins were building one of the great dynasties in early National Hockey League history.

And the Bruins had the record to prove it in 1930. Boston came into the series with a 38–5–1 record, the best winning percentage in NHL history at .875.

The Bruins had the best defensemen (Eddie Shore), the best goalie (Tiny Thompson) and the Dynamite Line of Cooney Weiland, Dit Clapper and Dutch Gainor.

The Canadiens hadn't even won their division. But after prevailing 3–0 at Boston in Game 1, the Canadiens were home in the Forum needing just one win for the Stanley Cup in the best-of-three series.

And even better for Boston, the Bruins had not lost two straight games all year.

Until April 3, that is. That's when Howie Morenz led the Habs into the place where they would be for most of the rest of the 20th Century, at the top of the hockey world in North America, as well as into the hearts of their fans.

And into the hearts of Montreal and all of Quebec.

It all started with a 4–3 win over a Boston team that couldn't contain Morenz' length-of-the-rink rushes. That was one more goal than Boston had allowed in the entire Stanley Cup playoffs a year before.

Montreal Canadiens: George Hainsworth, Marty Burke, Sylvio Mantha, Howie Morenz, Bert McCaffrey, Aurel Joliat, Albert Leduc, Pit Lepine, Wildor Larochelle, Nick Wasnie, Gerald Carson, Armand Mondou, Georges Mantha, Gus Rivers

Boston Bruins: Ralph "Cooney" Weiland, Aubrey "Dit" Clapper, Norman "Dutch" Gainor, Marty Barry, Eddie Shore, Harry Oliver, Percy "Perk" Galbraith, George Owen, Bill Carson, Duncan "Mickey" MacKay, Lionel Hitchman, Harry Connor, Myles Lane, Bob Taylor, Cecil "Tiny" Thompson

APRIL 9, 1931 (Game 3, Stanley Cup Finals)

Chicago Black Hawks   3   (3OT)
Montreal Canadiens   2

At the Montreal Forum

Gardiner keeps Canadiens at bay

A year later and Montreal's "Flying Frenchmen" were back to defend their Stanley Cup title and to make a statement—in both French and English—that Montreal was the place for the best hockey—anywhere.

The Chicago Black Hawks were the challengers this time. After splitting two games in Chicago, the teams were off to the Forum, where they would play a dramatic Game 3 into three overtimes.

And what happened there was a 3–2 Chicago win for a 2–1 series lead that the Black Hawks could not hold. Montreal, behind Howie Morenz—the game's first legitimate superstar—and a host of speedy cohorts, came back to win the final two games for their second Stanley Cup in a row.

But that Game 3 was special.

And like almost everything that went well for the Blackhawks in those days, it all went back to the work of a young goalkeeper—26-year-old Chuck Gardiner—who would become one of the best of all time in a tragically short career.

Gardiner's first appearance in the Stanley Cup—and his ability to shut down the speedy Canadiens for nearly six periods and earn a second straight win for the offensively challenged Blackhawks—made Game 3 a special moment in hockey history. The winning goal came from Marvin Wentworth, 13 minutes, 50 seconds into the third period of overtime.

Montreal Canadiens: George Hainsworth, Wildor Larochelle, Marty Burke, Sylvio Mantha, Howie Morenz, Johnny Gagnon, Aurel Joliat, Armand Mondou, Pit Lepine, Albert Leduc, Georges Mantha, Art Lesieur, Nick Wasnie, Bert McCaffrey, Gus Rivers, Jean Pusie

Chicago Blackhawks: Johnny Gottselig, Tom Cook, Frank Ingram, Rosario "Lolo" Couture, Stewart Adams, Harold "Mush" March, Victor Desjardins, Vic Ripley, Elwyn "Doc" Romnes, Art Somers, Marvin "Cyclone" Wentworth, Earl Miller, Teddy Graham, Ernest "Ty" Arbour, Helge "Bulge" Bostrom, Roger Jenkins, Clarence "Taffy" Abel, Ed Vokes, Chuck Gardiner

APRIL 13, 1933 (Game 4, Stanley Cup Finals)

New York Rangers   **1**   **(OT)**
Toronto Maple Leafs   **0**

At Maple Leaf Gardens

Rangers win in overtime

The new $1.5 million Maple Leaf Gardens was the scene but the New York Rangers were the team. Especially after the Leafs had to survive a grueling series against Boston's Bruins in the Stanley Cup semifinals. Their 1–0 win took 10 minutes, 24 seconds to be decided.

The Rangers used that early edge to their advantage in wins in Game 1 at Madison Square Garden and Game 2 in Toronto, where the annual arrival of the circus in New York sent the Stanley Cup finals north for the rest of the best-of-five series.

But after Toronto finally got to the new Rangers' goalie Andy Aitkenhead for a 3–2 win in Game 3. The Rangers still needed one more win to claim their second Stanley Cup in five years.

After three periods in Game 4, there was no decision. And no score. And against a Rangers lineup featuring the Hall of Fame trio of Frank Boucher with brothers Bill and "Bun" Cook on the same line, that was some accomplishment for the Maple Leafs defenders led by King Clancy and Hap Day.

But it wasn't enough. Aitkenhead was brilliant again for the Rangers and then Bill Cook came through at 7:33 in overtime with a goal for a 1–0 win that sent the Stanley Cup back to Broadway.

New York Rangers: Ching Johnson, Butch Keeling, Frank Boucher, Art Somers, Babe Siebert, Bun Cook, Andy Aitkenhead, Ott Heller, Ozzie Asmundson, Gord Pettinger, Doug Brennan, Cecil Dillon, Bill Cook (Captain), Murray Murdoch, Earl Seibert

Toronto Maple Leafs: Harvey "Busher" Jackson, Charlie Conacher, Joe Primeau, Francis "King" Clancy Bob Gracie, Harold "Baldy" Cotton, Clarence "Happy" Day, Ace Bailey, Ken Doraty, Andrew Blair, Bill Thoms, George "Red" Horner, Alex Levinsky, Harold Darragh, Stewart Adams, Dave Downie Lorne Chabot

APRIL 10, 1934 (Game 4, Stanley Cup Finals)

Chicago Black Hawks   **1**   **(2OT)**
Detroit Red Wings   **0**

At Chicago Stadium

Gardiner's shutout wins Cup for Black Hawks

Sports does not get any more dramatic, any more tragic or triumphant, than the deciding game of the 1934 Stanley Cup finals.

That's because it wasn't about a team—the Black Hawks, or a town—Chicago, or even a first-ever title.

It wasn't even so much about the game.

It was about a man, Chuck Gardiner. He was just 29 and about to play the final game of one of the greatest careers ever for a goaltender.

Some say it was the greatest. Gardiner, a native of Scotland who grew up in Winnipeg, had resurrected the Black Hawks. A below-.500 team a year before, the Hawks turned into a playoff prospect thanks to Gardiner's 1.73-goals-against average and 10 shutouts in a season that saw him play every minute of every game for the sixth straight year despite suffering from serious headaches that would not go away through the entire season.

In the Finals against the Detroit Red Wings, Gardiner opened by holding Detroit to one goal in a 2–1 double-overtime Chicago win. He held the Wings to a single goal in Game 2, a 4–1 Chicago win. After a 5–2 loss to Detroit, Chicago was still one win away from its first Stanley Cup. But Gardiner was feeling worse. He would be in so much pain from his headaches, that he would slump across the crossbar of the net when play went to the other end.

And yet in the decisive Game 4, Gardiner stopped all 40 shots Detroit sent his way in the double-overtime game before Mush March managed the game's lone score.

Chicago had its Stanley Cup. Which Gardiner had given it to them. Sadly, in two months he would be gone. The only goalie whose name is engraved on the Stanley Cup as his team's captain collapsed at his Winnipeg home with a brain hemorrhage and died on June 13.

Chicago Black Hawks: Taffy Abel, Lolo Couture, Lou Trudel, Lionel Conacher, Paul Thompson, Leroy Goldworthy, Art Coulter, Roger Jenkins, Don McFayden, Tommy Cook, Doc Romnes, Johnny Gottselig, Mush March, Johnny Sheppard, Chuck Gardiner (Captain), Bill Kendell

Detroit Red Wings: Larry Aurie, Ralph "Cooney" Weiland, John Sorrell, Herbie Lewis, Ebbie Goodfellow, Frank Carson, Gordon Pettinger, Leighton "Happy" Emms, Eddie Wiseman, Lloyd Gross, Doug Young, Teddy Graham, Wilfie Starr, Walter Buswell, Gus Marker, Fred Robertson, Burr Williams, John Gallagher, Ron Moffatt, Harry "Yip" Foster, John Roach

MARCH 24, 1936 (Game 1, Stanley Cup semifinals)

Detroit Red Wings   1   **(6OT)**
Montreal Maroons   0

At the Montreal Forum

Hockey's longest ever game

No one knew it at the time but the more than 10,000 fans who showed up at the Forum for the first postseason playoff game in 1936 between the Detroit Red Wings and the Montreal Maroons were in for a long night. A very long night.

It was a night like no other in hockey history.

It was a game started on March 24 that did not finish until well into March 25 and the crowd of 9,500 was treated to six overtimes before sending them home at 2:25 a.m.

This single game required almost three games worth of play and two hours and 51 minutes to produce just one goal.

A night that would send the Red Wings, 1–0 winners over the defending Stanley Cup Maroons, off to a Stanley Cup of their own.

But it wasn't easy. Hobbled Red Wing goalie Norm Smith had hung tough as the pre-Zamboni ice got rougher and rougher. Smith made an incredible 92 saves but he needed help. Finally, he got it. But not until the Wings had used up gallons of rubbing alcohol between periods.

For the first time in the game, Detroit inserted a player with the unlikely name of Modere "Mud" Bruneteau in the sixth overtime and it paid off. The seldom-used rookie, who had scored just two goals in the season, soared past the defense, took a pass and fired the Wings' 66th shot of the night.

This one found the net. Just like that. "Mud" beat Montreal goalie Lorne Chabot and at the improbable time of 176:30, hockey's longest game was over.

Detroit Red Wings Johnny Sorrell, Syd Howe, Marty Barry, Herbie Lewis, Mud Bruneteau, Wally Kilrea, Hec Kilrea, Gordon Pettinger, Bucko McDonald, Scotty Bowman, Pete Kelly, Doug Young, Ebbie Goodfellow, Normie Smith

Montreal Maroons: Reginald "Hooley" Smith, Lawrence "Baldy" Northcott, Jimmy Ward, Bob Gracie, Russ Blinco, Dave Trottier, Earl Robinson, Gus Marker, Herbert Cain, Lionel Conacher, Marvin "Cyclone" Wentworth, Allan Shields, Stewart Evans, Joe Lamb, Lorne Chabot, Bill Beveridge

APRIL 2, 1939 (Game 7, Stanley Cup Finals)

Boston Bruins	**2**	**(3OT)**
New York Rangers	**1**	

At Boston Garden

"Sudden Death" Hill clinches victory

This was the year the National Hockey League decided to go back to a best-of-seven playoff format. But you have to think the Boston Bruins and New York Rangers carried the best-of-seven theme to the limit.

And then some.

Of course the teams were tied at three games apiece with a 12–11 goal differential in favor of the Bruins.

In the previous six games, there were five overtime periods. Three games went past regulation with Game 1 going 35 seconds short of a fourth overtime.

So what do you think happened when the teams hit the Boston Garden ice for the deciding game? Maybe an overtime? Or two?

How about three. When it was over, the best-of-seven format had been expanded to more than nine regulation games.

Game 7 was memorable, as was expected. It was the first Game 7 in the NHL playoffs since 1919. And a new hero was born for the homestanding Bruins who would go on to win the Stanley Cup easily in the finals against Toronto.

Mel Hill would be the man for Boston. Just say Hill was accustomed to working overtime when he fired in the sudden-death goal eight minutes into the third overtime to send the Bruins into the playoffs with a 2-1 win. That was Hill's third sudden-death goal in the series.

And it earned him a nickname of—what else?—"Sudden Death" Hill that he surely deserved.

Boston Bruins: Bobby Bauer, Mel Hill, Flash Hollett, Roy Conacher, Gord Pettinger, Milt Schmidt, Woody Dumart, Jack Crawford, Ray Getliffe, Frank Brimsek, Eddie Shore, Dit Clapper, Bill Cowley, Jack Portland, Red Hamill, Cooney Weiland

New York Rangers: Clint Smith, Neil Colville, Phil Watson, Bryan Hextall, Alex Shibicky, Wilbert "Dutch" Hiller, Lynn Patrick, Mac Colville, Cecil Dillon, Ott Heller, Walter "Babe" Pratt, George Allen, Arthur Coulter, Murray "Muzz" Patrick, Joe Krol, Bill Carse, Larry Molyneaux, Dave Kerr, Bert Gardiner

APRIL 13, 1940 (Game 6, Stanley Cup Finals)

New York Rangers   3   (OT)
Toronto Maple Leafs   2

At Maple Leaf Gardens

Hextall scores sudden-death winner for New York

After their seven-game, eight-overtime Stanley Cup semifinals loss a year earlier to the champion Boston Bruins, the powerful New York Rangers were back again in 1940. General manager Lester Patrick would have sons Lynne and Murray (Muzz) to help his Rangers get the job done.

And this time the Rangers survived regular-season winner Boston in the semis to face the Toronto Maple Leafs for the Cup. The Leafs were in their sixth Finals in eight years—and they had lsot the previous five.

Under first-year coach Frank Boucher, the Rangers took Games 1 and 2 at home, then said goodbye for the duration as the circus took over Madison Square Garden again.

Home ice was good for the Maple Leafs as they won two of their own before the Rangers rallied for an overtime win in Game 5 on Muzz Patrick's goal.

The Stanley Cup would be theirs for the first time in seven years if the Rangers could win Game 6 against Conn Smythe's Maple Leafs.

It took an overtime again, but not a seventh game, to get the job done. This time it was the Rangers' Bryan Hextall, who led the National Hockey League in goals, whose sudden death goal gave the Rangers a 3–2 win—and the Cup.

It also provided a one-of-a-kind picture after the trophy presentation. For the first time in Stanley Cup history, a father and two sons would be joined on the same Stanley Cup-winning team.

New York Rangers: Dave Kerr, Art Coulter, Ott Heller, Alex Shibicky, Mac Colville, Neil Colville, Phil Watson, Lynn Patrick, Clint Smith, Muzz Patrick, Babe Pratt, Bryan Hextall, Kilby Macdonald, Dutch Hiller, Alf Pike, Sanford Smith

Toronto Maple Leafs: Gordie Drillon, Syl Apps, David "Sweeney" Schriner, Bob Davidson, Robert "Red" Heron, Erwin "Murph" Chamberlain, Pete Langelle, Regis "Pep" Kelly, Gus Marker, Rudolph "Bingo" Kampman, Lex Chisholm, Nick Metz, Hank Goldup, Billy Taylor, George "Red" Horner, Wally Stanowski, Wilfred "Bucko" McDonald, Jack Church, Reg Hamilton, Don Metz, Phil Stein, Walter "Turk" Broda

APRIL 18, 1942 (Game 7, Stanley Cup Finals)

Toronto Maple Leafs   3
Detroit Red Wings   1

At Maple Leaf Gardens

Toronto reverse 0–3 deficit

No team had ever been down 3–0 in a best-of-seven Stanley Cup finals and come back to win four straight to capture the cup.

And yet here they were, Toronto's Maple Leafs, having been smoked 4–3, 9–3 and 3–0 by the underdog Detroit Red Wings in the first three games of the 1942 finals now just one win away from the Cup. The Leafs were on home ice as well.

There was one problem. Six times the Leafs had reached the Finals since 1932 and all six times they had fallen short. Heavily favored this year, after dropping three in a row, winning the next three games wouldn't mean much if they lost the one that mattered.

And they were well on their way to doing just that, trailing 1–0 into the third period. Detroit was trying to make Syd Howe's goal early in the second period stand up.

It looked like maybe they would. Less than 13 minutes remained and the Red Wings still held on. But then Toronto's Sweeney Schriner scored to tie it before two more Maple Leaf goals—the game-winner from Pete Langelle and an insurance goal from Schriner sealed it.

The 3-1 Toronto win and the 4–0 sweep after trailing 0–3 was officially the greatest comeback—and the only time a team would ever reverse an 0–3 deficit—in Stanley Cup history.

Toronto Maple Leafs: Wally Stanowski, Syl Apps, Bob Goldham, Gord Drillon, Hank Goldup, Ernie Dickens, Dave "Sweeney" Schriner, Bucko McDonald, Bob Davidson, Nick Metz, Bingo Kampman, Don Metz, Gaye Stewart, Turk Broda, Johnny McCreedy, Lorne Carr, Pete Langelle, Billy Taylor

Detroit Red Wings: Don Grosso, Sid Abel, Eddie Wares, Syd Howe, Modere "Mud" Bruneteau, Carl Liscombe, Roy "Gus" Giesebrecht, Joe Carveth, Adam Brown , Ken Kilrea, Pat McReavy, Jack Stewart, Eddie Bush, Gerry Brown, Jimmy Orlando, Alex Motter, Ebbie Goodfellow, Bill Jennings, Alvin "Buck" Jones, Connie Brown, Doug McCaig, Johnny Mowers, Joe Turner, Joe Fisher, Bob Whitelaw

APRIL 10, 1947 (Game 2, Stanley Cup Finals)

Toronto Maple Leafs   4
Montreal Canadiens   0

At the Montreal Forum

Toronto surprise Canadiens

It's the thing that gives coaches nightmares.

It's why your mother always told you that if you don't have anything good to say about someone, better not to say anything at all.

Unfortunately for the Montreal Canadiens, the best team in the NHL through the first full post-World War II regular season, someone didn't tell the Canadiens' star goalie Bill Durnan how— in the lingo of the day—"Loose lips sink ships."

And so, after Montreal's dominating 6–0 Game 1 win to open the Stanley Cup, Durnan wondered: "How did these guys get in the playoffs anyway?"

Bad idea, Bill.

Because the Maple Leafs weren't all that bad. They had been the league's top scorers and finished second in the standings. Some thought that with Ted Kennedy, Howie Meeker and Syl Apps, they had the best offensive talent in the NHL. So that Game 1 humiliation—and Durnan's barb—became just the motivation the Maple Leafs needed.

With four power play goals, they showed Durnan how they did it. And into the bargain, Toronto replied with a shutout to match Montreal's in the opener. And then Toronto got a bonus in what would become a decisive Game 2.

Montreal's tempestuous star Maurice "Rocket" Richard, the leading scorer in the NHL, was ejected from Game 2 and suspended for Game 3 because of high-sticking.

That was all it took for Toronto to breeze to four wins in the five games after Durnan's crack for a 4–2 Cup win that answered the question for all time just how the Maple Leafs had gotten there.

Toronto Maple Leafs: Turk Broda, Garth Boesch, Gus Mortson, Jim Thomson, Wally Stanowski, Bill Barilko, Harry Watson, Bud Poile, Ted Kennedy, Syl Apps, Don Metz, Nick Metz, Bill Ezinicki, Vic Lynn, Howie Meeker, Gaye Stewart, Joe Klukay, Gus Bodnar, Bob Goldham

Montreal Canadiens: Maurice "Rocket" Richard, Hector "Toe" Blake, Billy Reay, Leo Gravelle, Elmer Lach, Buddy O'Connor, Jim Peters, Ken Reardon, Roger Leger, George Allen, Erwin "Murph" Chamberlain, Ken Mosdell, Glen Harmon, Leo Lamoreaux, Emile "Butch" Bouchard, Bob Fillion, John Quilty, Hubert Macey, Doug Lewis, George Pargeter, Frank Eddolls, Joe Benoit, Bill Durnan, Murdo MacKay

APRIL 23, 1950 (Game 7, Stanley Cup Finals)

Detroit Red Wings   4
New York Rangers   3

At Olympia Stadium, Detroit

Detroit outlast New York

Between them they'd knocked out Montreal and three-time Stanley Cup winner Toronto to create an All-American Finals featuring Detroit's Red Wings, the regular-season champions and the New York Rangers, back for the first time in a decade.

But each team had a significant problem. Detroit would not have superstar Gordie Howe, who suffered a fractured skull in the Toronto series.

New York would not have a place to play again as the circus was in town again, making Madison Square Garden unavailable. The Rangers decided to play two of their home games—Games 2 and 3—in Toronto, of all places. But the other five would be in Detroit where Olympia Stadium was always a comfortable place for the Red Wings.

Somehow the underdog Rangers managed to take a 3–2 lead thanks to a pair of overtime game-winning goals by center Don Raleigh.

And if a series tied 3–3 in the seventh game weren't close enough, the dramatic Game 7 itself was tied at 3–3 as the game moved into a second overtime, only for Detroit to snatch Game 6, 5–4.

How great a tribute that was to the underdog Rangers, who were playing their seventh straight game on the road and fifth in the series in Detroit.

As strong as Sid Abel and Ted Lindsay played in the series without Howe in Detroit's Production Line, the man who stepped into the starring role when he was really needed was Red Wing Pete Babando. One of the few Americans in the National Hockey League, Babando fired in the game-winner for Detroit.

Detroit Red Wings: Harry Lumley, Jack Stewart, Leo Reise, Clare Martin, Al Dewsbury, Lee Fogolin, Marcel Pronovost, Red Kelly, Ted Lindsay, Sid Abel, Gordie Howe, George Gee, Jimmy Peters, Marty Pavelich, Jim McFadden, Pete Babando, Max McNab, Gerry Couture, Joe Carveth, Steve Black, John Wilson, Larry Wilson

New York Rangers: Edgar Laprade, Tony Leswick, Ed Slowinski, Don Raleigh, Dunc Fisher, Buddy O'Connor, Alex Kaleta, Pentti Lund, Nick Mickoski , Pat Egan, Jack McLeod, Fred Shero, Allan Stanley, Walter "Gus" Kyle, Frank Eddolls, Jean Lamirande, Jack Lancien, Winston "Bing" Juckes, Norman "Odie" Lowe, Don Smith, Wally Stanowski, Sherman White, Doug Adam, Jean Denis, Jack Gordon, Fern Perreault, Emile Francis, Bill Kyle, Jack Evans, Bill McDonagh, John "Chick" Webster, Chuck Rayner

APRIL 21, 1951 (Game 5, Stanley Cup Finals)

Toronto Maple Leafs   3   **(OT)**
Montreal Canadiens   2

At Maple Leaf Gardens

The overtime series

From an All-American finals the year before, it was back to an All-Canadian Stanley Cup in 1951.

It was the Toronto Maple Leafs against the unlikely Montreal Canadiens, who had just dispatched the Detroit Red Wings and their record-breaking 101 regular season points, 36 more than Montreal had earned.

After seven overtimes produced two losses in the first two games, Detroit was dusted in six. Montreal would then face a Toronto team that had blasted Boston.

Between them they would produce a dramatic Finals unlike any other in hockey history. Every game would go into overtime. Parity anyone?

The teams split overtime wins to start in Toronto, with the Maple Leafs getting Game 1, Montreal Game 2. Improbably Toronto would sweep both overtimes at the Forum and return needing just a win at home to earn the Cup.

But the pattern had been set. This would not be easy, especially not at home.

And of course, it wasn't. Montreal led 2–1 late in the game, forcing the Maple Leafs to do something desperate. So they pulled their goalie and put in an extra offensive player—and it worked.

It worked in time. With a mere 32 seconds left in regulation, Maple Leaf Tod Sloan scored to send the game once again into overtime. And once again, the pattern held. For the third straight game, Toronto would do what it took. This time it was a defenseman—Bill Barilko—who would get the game-winner at 2:53 in OT.

Tragically, it would be Barilko's last goal. Just 24, he would die in an airplane crash soon after the season.

Toronto Maple Leafs: Turk Broda, Al Rollins, Jim Thompson, Gus Mortson, Bill Barilko, Bill Juzda, Fern Fleman, Hugh Boltom, Ted Kennedy, Sid Smith, Tod Sloan, Cal Gardner, Howie Meeker, Harry Watson, Max Bentley, Joe Klukay, Danny Lewicki, Ray Timgren, Flaming Mackell, Johnny McCormack, Bob Hassard

Montreal Canadiens: Maurice "Rocket" Richard, Elmer Lach, Bert Olmstead, Ken Mosdell, Doug Harvey, Calum MacKay, Floyd Curry, Billy Reay, Norm Dussault, Jim "Bud" MacPherson, Bernie "Boom-Boom" Geoffrion, Glen Harmon, Emile "Butch" Boucher, Vern Kaiser, Tom Johnson, Paul Meger, Paul Masnick, Bob Dawes, Jean Beliveau, Bert Hirschfeld, Frank King, Claude Robert, Gerry Desaulniers, Louis Denis, Gerry Plamondon, Hugh Currie, Dick Gamble, Fred "Skippy" Burchell, Dollard St. Laurent, Ernie Roche, Tom Manastersky, Gerry McNeil, Sid McNabney, Eddie Mazur, Ross Lowe

MARCH 27, 1952 (Game 7, Stanley Cup semifinals)

Detroit Red Wings   1
Toronto Maple Leafs   0

At Olympia Stadium, Detroit

The "octopus" incident

Two for the price of one was what the 1952 postseason would bring. Two one-of-a-kind hockey moments in games tied together by the same Stanley Cup playoffs.

Both are well remembered forever, even if only one of them involved a great play and a great player.

The other involved an octopus, which makes it obvious the Detroit Red Wings were involved. And indeed they were.

It was a brainstorm of the Brothers Cusimano. If their beloved Red Wings could sweep to the Stanley Cup in the minimum eight games, something that had never been done before, it called for recognition. So to illustrate that point, what better show-and-tell item than the aforementioned octopus. Jerry Cusimano noted to brother Pete that its eight arms represented the eight games it would take the Red Wings to sweep.

"Why don't we throw it on the ice," Jerry is reported to have told Pete. Pete agreed if Jerry would boil it first. And so he did, hiding it under his seat until Gordie Howe scored to put the Red Wings up for good on the visiting Maple Leafs and then the octopus toss was introduced into the Olympia.

The players didn't know what to do. One linesman did, getting as far away from it as possible. One Red Wing started to hit it with his stick. The crowd went wild and Detroit went on to sweep in the minimum eight games against Toronto and Montreal.

That was it until the next time Detroit made the playoffs and a sportswriter wondered if the octopus would reappear. So the Brothers Cusimano obliged. And a tradition was born. And now the octopi fly whenever the Wings do well.

Detroit Red Wings: Terry Sawchuk, Bob Goldham, Ben Woit, Red Kelly, Leo Reise, Marcel Pronovost, Ted Lindsay, Tony Leswick, Gordie Howe, Metro Prystai, Marty Pavelich, Sid Abel, Glen Skov, Alex Delvecchio, John Wilson, Vic Stasiuk, Larry Zeidel

Toronto Maple Leafs: Ted Kennedy, Tod Sloan, Max Bentley, Cal Gardner, Harry Watson, Jim Thomson, Howie Meeker, Hugh Bolton, Danny Lewicki, Joe Klukay, Gus Mortson, Bob Solinger, Fern Flaman, George Armstrong, Ray Timgren, Bill Juzda, Rudy Migay, Jim Morrison, Leo Boivin, Walter "Turk" Broda, Eric Nesterenko, Bob Sabour, Frank Mathers, John McLellan, Earl Balfour, Tim Horton, Al Rollins

APRIL 8, 1952 (Game 7, Stanley Cup semifinals)

Montreal Canadiens   3
Boston Bruins   1

At the Montreal Forum

Richard's amazing goal clinches win

It's not easy to up stage an octopus. But if one player in the National Hockey League could, well, it would be the one they called The Rocket.

Maurice Richard was his name and the dramatic, the impossible, the can't-take-your-eyes-off-him, I-can't-believe-he-did-that, was his game.

So now you know. In a seven-game series as close as two teams could play it, the Bruins and Canadiens were all even in the first six games and fired up for what Game 7 would bring. For Canadiens fans watching in horror at the Forum, what would come their way wasn't encouraging.

Not when Richard was knocked unconscious in a vicious collision. So when The Rocket returned from unconsciousness to the ice after missing 16 minutes of the third period, it was more than encouraging for the Habs partisans.

But when The Rocket skated through the entire Boston Bruin team to score the go-ahead goal in the final period, it would become one of the most famous—and legendary—goals in NHL playoff history. But that 3–1 win was the end of it for the Canadiens.

The octopus mojo would prove too much as inspired Red Wing goalie Terry Sawchuk would allow Montreal just two goals in four games as the Wings won in the minimum eight. The Rocket was shut out.

Montreal Canadiens: Elmer Lach, Bernie "Boom-Boom" Geoffrion, Maurice "Rocket" Richard, Paul Meger, Billy Reay, Dick Gamble, Floyd Curry, Bert Olmstead, Dickie Moore, Doug Harvey, Ken Mosdell, Dollard St. Laurent, Emile "Butch" Bouchard, John McCormack, Tom Johnson, Ross Lowe, Jim "Bud" MacPherson, Paul Masnick, Lorne Davis, Gerry Couture, Calum MacKay, Gene Achtymich, Don Marshall, Gary "Duke" Edmundson, Bob Fryday, Cliff Malone, Gerry McNeil, Eddie Mazur, Stan Long

Boston Bruins: Milt Schmidt, Johnny Peirson, Dave Creighton, Jack McIntyre, Dunc Fisher, Ed Sandford, Real Chevrefils, George "Red" Sullivan, Fleming Mackell, Bill Quackenbush, Adam Brown, Woody Dumart, Walter "Gus" Kyle, Hal Laycoe, Bill Ezinicki, Ed Kryzanowski, Lorne Ferguson, Leo Labine, Murray Henderson, Pentti Lun, Vic Lynn, Ray Barry, Bobby Bauer, Jim Henry, Bob Armstrong

APRIL 16, 1954 (Game 7, Stanley Cup Finals)

Detroit Red Wings   2
Montreal Canadiens   1

At Olympia Stadium, Detroit

Harney hands Red Wings the Cup

When these teams played, it was like a Hall of Fame All-Star Game.

For the Detroit Red Wings, the stalwarts who skated on to the ice were Gordie Howe, Terry Sawchuk, Ted Lindsay, Alex Delvecchio, Red Kelly and on and on.

The Montreal Canadiens could match the Wings and raise them one or two with Maurice "The Rocket" Richard, Jean Beliveau, Bernie "Boom Boom" Geoffrion, Doug Harvey, Dickie Moore and Jacques Plante and a strong supporting cast.

So when they went head-to-head for the Stanley Cup in the 1950s, it was usually special. But the 1954 finals was more than that. And as it did so often, it came down to one last game.

After alternating wins with Detroit's production line of Howe, Lindsay and Delvecchio getting the upper hand one game and Richard and Moore coming back the next, it was all tied up at three games apiece with one to go.

Just the way it was four years before. Pete Babando was the Red Wing hero then. This time it would be Tony Leswick who would get the credit for the overtime goal that was deflected off Montreal defender Harvey's skate and into the Canadiens' net for a 2–1 Detroit win.

Detroit Red Wings: Terry Sawchuk, Red Kelly, Bob Goldham, Ben Woit, Marcel Pronovost, Al Arbour, Keith Allen, Ted Lindsay, Tony Leswick, Gordie Howe, Marty Pavelich, Alex Delvecchio, Metro Prystai, Glen Skov, John Wilson, Bill Dineen, Jim Peters, Earl Reibel, Vic Stasiuk

Montreal Canadiens: Maurice "Rocket" Richard, Bernie "Boom-Boom" Geoffrion, Bert Olmstead, Ken Mosdell, Doug Harvey, Jean Beliveau, Paul Masnick, Elmer Lach, Calum MacKay, Floyd Curry, Eddie Mazur, Tom Johnson, John McCormack, Dollard St. Laurent, Paul Meger, Dick Gamble, Emile "Butch" Bouchard, Lorne Davis, Dickie Moore, Jim "Bud" MacPherson, Andre Corriveau, Fred "Skippy" Burchell, Ed Litzenberger, Gerry Desaulniers, Jacques Plante, Gerry McNeil, Gaye Stewart

MARCH 17, 1955 (Regular season game)

Detroit Red Wings win by forfeit over the Montreal Canadiens

At the Montreal Forum

The Richard riot

Hockey would never have another night like this one in Montreal. Good thing, too.

One was more than enough. It was St. Patrick's Day but all March 17, 1955 will ever be known for in Montreal is the Richard Riot.

Because that's exactly what it was for the outraged Canadien fans who went on a rampage that shut down the Forum, turned downtown Montreal into a war zone that saw one hundred arrests made as more than 10,000 Montreal fans inside the Forum and at least 800 protestors outside rioted until 3 a.m. They were unhappy over the season-long suspension meted out to Montreal's Maurice "The Rocket" Richard for a fight four days earlier in Boston that saw him slug a linesman after being scalped by a high-sticking Hal Lycoe.

Unfortunately for the prospect of peace, the man who meted out the suspension—NHL president Clarence Campbell—came to the Forum and took his regular seat for the Montreal-Detroit game the very day that he had penalized Richard. Canadien fans were not pleased. They threw everything they could get their hands on. Finally after a period of play with Detroit leading 4–1, one fan broke through heavy security to get to Campbell, slapping and then punching him. The riot was on.

The game, however, was off. A preview of the next month's Stanley Cup Finals, this one went to the Red Wings by forfeit. Just as the Cup would be won when Montreal found out it didn't have enough without the Rocket, although the Canadiens did extend Detroit to seven games.

Maybe that should have been a tipoff. Montreal would come back the next year to begin a run of five straight Stanley Cup titles. And Detroit with Gordie Howe would not win another.

Detroit Red Wings: Terry Sawchuk, Red Kelly, Bob Goldham, Marcel Pronovost, Ben Woit, Jim Hay, Larry Hillman, Ted Lindsay, Tony Leswick, Gordie Howe, Alex Delvecchio, Marty Pavelich, Glen Skov, Earl Reibel, John Wilson, Bill Dineen, Vic Stasiuk, Marcel Bonin

Montreal Canadiens: Bernie "Boom-Boom" Geoffrion, Maurice "Rocket" Richard, Jean Beliveau, Bert Olmstead, Ken Mosdell, Doug Harvey, Dickie Moore, Calum MacKay, Jack LeClair, Tom Johnson, Floyd Curry, Emile "Butch" Bouchard, Dollard St. Laurent, Paul Ronty, Jim "Bud" MacPherson, Don Marshall, Eddie Mazur, Paul Meger, Guy Rousseau, Jean-Guy Talbot, Jean Lamirande, Andre Binette, Garry Blaine, Jim Bartlett, Claude Evans, Orval Tessier, Charlie Hodge, Jacques Plante, Dick Gamble

APRIL 22, 1962 (Game 6, Stanley Cup Finals)

Toronto Maple Leafs   2
Chicago Blackhawks   1

At the Chicago Stadium

Toronto surprise Chicago

The defending Stanley Cup champion Chicago Blackhawks had just beaten the Montreal Canadiens for a second straight year—this time in the semifinals—and it looked like another title for Chicago.

But then Toronto's Maple Leafs jumped out two games to zip on the strength of a suffocating defense that shut down the Hawks' Bobby Hull and Stan Mikita.

But Chicago came back on defense with Glenn Hall holding Toronto to one goal in the next two games to tie it 2–2. Then the dam burst. Eight Toronto goals swamped Hall in Game 5 but he came back to construct what looked like a series-tying shutout in Game 6.

Especially after Hull busted in the game's first goal midway through the third period. That was all it took to set off a wild Chicago Stadium ruckus that stopped the game to clear the ice of all the debris that had been tossed down by Hawk fans prematurely celebrating. They insisted on counting their chickens before they were hatched.

And they would pay for it.

All it took were two Toronto goals and the Maple Leafs had almost 11 minutes to get them. It didn't take that long. Bob Nevin scored the equalizer in two minutes and then Dick Duff nailed the Cup winner.

And all Chicago fans could do was wonder why. Their 1961 champions had just lost on home ice to a team that hadn't won the Stanley Cup since 1951.

Toronto Maple Leafs: Johnny Bower, Don Simmons, Carl Brewer, Tim Horton, Bob Baun, Allan Stanley, Al Arbour, Larry Hillman, Red Kelly, Dick Duff, George Armstrong, Frank Mahovlich, Bob Nevin, Ron Stewart, Bill Harris, Bert Olmstead, Bob Pulford, Eddie Shack, Dave Keon, Ed Litzenburger, John MacMillan

Chicago Blackhawks: Bobby Hull, Stan Mikita, Bill Hay, Bronco Horvath, Pierre Pilote, Ab McDonald,Ken Wharram, Murray Balfour, Eric Nesterenko, Ron Murphy, Elmer Vasko, Gerry Melnyk, Jack Evans, Reg Fleming, Dollard St. Laurent, Bob Turner, Chico Maki, Wayne Hillman, Murray Hall, Glenn Hall, Merve Kuryluk

APRIL 23, 1964 (Game 6, Stanley Cup Finals)

Toronto Maple Leafs 4 **(OT)**
Detroit Red Wings 3

At Olympia Stadium, Detroit

Baun wins game on broken ankle

You just knew something good was going to happen here. Both semifinal series had gone the full seven games for the first time since 1943. Toronto was back for the fifth time in six years and the two-time defending champs were facing a hungry Detroit team that hadn't won the Stanley Cup since 1955. Gentlemen, start your Zambonis.

But as much as the heroics of Detroit's Gordie Howe, Terry Sawchuk and Alex Delvecchio were countered by Toronto's Andy Bathgate and and Larry Jeffrey in a series of one-goal decisions, this one came down to a Maple Leaf player without the name recognition of that group.

And his heroics would turn the decisive Game 6 into one for the ages. To make it even more memorable, Toronto's Bobby Baun dropped his offensive dynamite on Detroit even though he was noted much more for his muscle than his stickhandling. But there was more. More than the early goals of Howe and Eddie Joyal that gave Detroit a 2–1 lead.

There was Baun on a stretcher being carried off the ice after getting whacked in the ankle by a shot in the third period. He was finished, the Olympia fans must have thought. Somehow though, Baun was back on the ice in overtime.

And there he was scoring the winning goal just 2:43 into overtime.

Baun later discovered he'd been playing on a fractured ankle.

Detroit had its heart cut out in Game 6 and had little fight left in a 4–0 Game 7 loss.

Toronto Maple Leafs: Johnny Bower, Carl Brewer, Tim Horton, Bob Baun, Allan Stanley, Larry Hillman, Al Arbour, Red Kelly, Gerry Ehman, Andy Bathgate, George Armstrong, Ron Stewart, Dave Keon, Billy Harris, Don McKenny, Jim Pappin, Bob Pulford, Eddie Shack, Frank Mahovlich, Eddie Litzenberger

Detroit Red Wings: Gordie Howe, Alex Delvecchio, Norm Ullman, Parker MacDonald, Bruce MacGregor, Doug Barkley, Floyd Smith, Larry Jeffrey, Andre Pronovost, Pit Martin, Marcel Pronovost, Bill Gadsby, Eddie Joyal, Albert Langlois, Ron Ingram, Alex Faulkner, Paul Henderson, Claude LaForge, Lowell MacDonald, Irv Spencer, Art Stratton, John MacMillan, Billy McNeill, John Miszuk, Wayne Muloin, Ted Hampson, Hank Bassen, Harrison Gray, Jim Watson, Pat Rupp, Bill Mitchell, Howie Menard, Ron Harris, Warren Godfrey, Pete Goegan, Roger Crozier, Terry Sawchuk, Bob Dillabough, Bob Champoux

MAY 10, 1970 (Game 4, Stanley Cup Finals)

Boston Bruins   **4**   **(OT)**
St. Louis Blues   **3**

At Boston Garden

Orr flies in to win Cup

It had been 29 years. Twenty-nine long years since the Stanley Cup had come Boston's way. So this was a big deal. The Bruins had won nine straight playoff games and needed just one more on the Boston Garden ice against the visitng St. Louis Blues for a four-game Stanley sweep.

The Bobby Orr-led Bruins were just so much better than the third-year expansion Blues. And they'd shown it in winning 6–1, 6–2 and 4–1. What hope the Blues had was in their Hall of Fame duo of aging, alternating goalies—Jacques Plante and Glenn Hall. But Plante got plunked in the mask and was sent to the hospital with a concussion leaving Hall all alone.

Coach Scotty Bowman's Blues ignored all talk of a sweep and played like they belonged. The West champs even took a 2–1 lead and forced the Bruins to tie it late in the third period at 3–3 on a score from veteran Hall of Famer John Bucyk just to get it into overtime.

And then it happened, the play that is frozen in hockey action photos— and Bruins fans—forever.

Orr grabbed the puck a half-minute into overtime and sped toward the Blues' goal, dishing off to Sanderson to his right. It came back to Orr perfectly timed. Orr flipped into the air by a Blues defenseman as he crossed the face of the goal, leaping into a free-floating figure, parallel to the ice with his arms raised in exultation

For 32 years that photo has said it all. In one instant, one of the game's greatest players of all time scores to win a Stanley Cup in overtime and literally leaves the ice in celebration.

Boston Bruins: Gerry Cheevers, Ed Johnston, Bobby Orr, Rick Smith, Dallas Smith, Bill Speer, Gary Doak, Don Awrey, Phil Esposito, Ken Hosge, John Bucyk, Wayne Carleton, Wayne Cashman, Derek Sanderson, Fred Stanfield, Ed Westfall, John McKenzie, Jim Lorentz, Don Marrcotte, Bill Lesuk, Dan Schock

St. Louis Blues: Phil Goyette, Gordon "Red" Berenson, Frank St. Marseille,Ab McDonald, Gary Sabourin, Tim Ecclestone, Larry Keenan, Bill McCreary, Barclay Plager, Jim Roberts, Ron Anderson, Andre Boudrias, Jean-Guy Talbot, Bob Plager, Terry Crisp, Terry Gray, Bill Plager, Noel Picard, Ray Fortin, Norm Dennis, Wayne Maki, Camille Henry, Al Arbour, Jacques Plante, Gary Edwards, Ron Buchanan, Jaroslav Jirik, Glenn Hall, Ernie Wakely

MAY 11, 1971 (Game 7, Stanley Cup Finals)

Montreal Canadiens 3
Chicago Blackhawks 2

At Chicago Stadium

Rookie Dryden and veteran Richard win Cup

One of the teams hadn't even made the playoffs the year before. The other hadn't won a Stanley Cup in a decade. Yet here they were—the Montreal Canadiens, full of fight, tradition and all sorts of unrest and unhappiness, trying to outlast the Chicago Blackhawks in a steamy arena where one report indicated some 20,000 fans filled a building designed to hold 17,317 for hockey.

Both teams had a big-name cast. Chicago lined up Bobby and Dennis Hull, Stan Mikita and goalie Tony Esposito.

The Canadiens could call on Jean Beliveau, Henri "Pocket Rocket" Richard, Pete Mahovlich, Jaques Lemaire and rookie goalie Ken Dryden.

Neither team had lost at home, however. Considering the dissension caused by Al MacNeil's coaching in Game 7, it appeared Chicago would have the edge in Game 7.

Except for this.

The Canadiens—out of the playoffs a year earlier—had won Stanley Cups the two seasons before that. They may not have known how to keep quiet but somehow the Canadiens knew how to win.

The Blackhawks didn't. That's always been the perception. But they were winning, 2-0, in the second period. And on home ice. The Canadiens didn't score until just 26 minutes were left.

But then Richard, the center of so much of the unrest and public second-guessing of MacNeil, used all of his 16 years' experience to fire in a pair of goals and Dryden— with almost no experience—stopped everything the Hawks could throw at him.

And the Canadiens won. Again.

Montreal Canadiens: Ken Dryden, Rogatien Vachon, Jacques Laperriére, Jean-Claude Tremblay, Guy Lapointe, Terry Harper, Pierre Bouchard, Jean Béliveau, Marc Tardiff, Yvan Cournoyer, Réjean Houle, Claude Larose, Henri Richard, Phil Roberto, Pete Mahovlich, Leon Rochefort, John Ferguson, Bobby Sheehan, Jacques Lemaire, Frank Mahovlich, Bob Murdoch, Chuck Lefley

Chicago Blackhawks: Bobby Hull, Stan Mikita, Dennis Hull, Pit Martin, Bryan Campbell, Pat Stapleton, Cliff Koroll, Chico Maki, Jim Pappin, Danny O'Shea, Gerry Pinder, Dan Maloney, Lou Angotti, Bill White, Eric Nesterenko, Keith Magnuson, Jerry Korab, Doug Jarrett, Paul Shmyr, Doug Mohns, Larry Romanchych, Rick Foley, Tony Esposito, Ken Brown, Gilles Meloche, Ray McKay, Gerry Desjardins

SEPTEMBER 28, 1972 (Game 8, Summit Series)

Team Canada	**6**
USSR	**5**

At Luzhniki Ice Palace, Moscow

Summit Series thriller

Thirty years later, Canadians consider it the greatest moment in their hockey heritage. Middle-aged men can recall listening to the game in school on that fall afternoon. On this day Canada's place in ice hockey was established in a Cold War battle on the ice that the Canadians seemed almost certain to lose. In an eight-game series against the Soviets, the slow-starting National Hockey League stars playing for Canada would have to win three straight games in Moscow to do it.

How unlikely was that after losing two and tying one in four games against the Soviets in Canada? But on two game-winning goals by Paul Henderson, they had given themselves a chance. The Canadians had to win this final game even though the series was tied 3–3–1. A tie would allow the Soviets to claim a one-goal advantage in the series—and the overall win. Then Henderson did it again. With 34 seconds left in the final period, he fired in his third straight game-winner for a 6–5 victory for Canada. The voice of hockey in Canada, Foster Hewitt, called it for his country. "Henderson scores for Canada."

This wasn't pretty business. The Soviets switched officials the night before. One of the two originally designated had mysteriously come down with food poisoning. But the Canadians would have none of it, even threatening to go home without playing the game. Each team would eventually get to pick one for the game.

After two periods, the USSR led 5–3. Canada was in trouble, although the players felt confident. Phil Esposito scored right away to make it 5–4. And then he fired a shot that Yvan Cournoyer rebounded for a 5–5 tie although the goal judge didn't turn on the light, setting off a melee between Soviet soldiers and upset Canadian officials and players. Finally, on a play that saw him twice fire rebound shots at Soviet goalie Vladislav Tretiak, Henderson got the winning score at the 19:26 mark.

Team Canada: Ken Dryden, Tony Esposito, Ed Johnston, Pat Stapleton, Bill White, Don Awrey, Rod Seiling, Dale Tallon, Jocelyn Gueremont, Serge Savard, Vic Hadfield, Richard Martin, Gilbert Perreault, Red Berenson, Peter Mahovlich, Frank Mahovlich, Wayne Cashman, Mickey Redmond, Stan Mikita, Bobby Clarke, Jean Ratelle, Bill Goldsworthy, Ron Ellis, Rod Gilbert, Dennis Hall, Brian Glennie, Yvan Cournoyer, Brad Park, L J P Parise, Marcel Dionne, Guy Lapointe, Paul Henderson, Gary Bergman, Phil Esposito

USSR National Team: Vladislov Tretiak, Vladimir Shepavolov, Igor Romishevsky, Vladimir Lutchenko, Gennady Tsygankov, Alexander Ragulin, Vitali Davydov, Viktor Kuzkin, Alexander Gusev, Boris Mikhailov, Vladimir Petrov, Valeri Kharlamov, Alexander Maltsev, Alexander Yakushev, Yuri Binov, Vyacheslav Anisin, Yevgeny Mishakov, Vyacheslav Soldukhin, Vladimir Shadrin, Vladimir Nikulov

MAY 19, 1974 (Game 6, Stanley Cup Finals)

Philadelphia Flyers   **1**
Boston Bruins   **0**

At the Spectrum, Philadelphia

Broad Street Bullies are first expansion champions

They didn't look, sound, act, think or play like an expansion team. They were the "Broad Street Bullies" and no apologies were needed for their arrival into the Stanley Cup finals in 1974.

Sure, they were underdogs to the establishment Boston Bruins and a star-studded cast led by Bobby Orr and Phil Esposito. But the Flyers had a Bobby of their own—Bobby Clarke.

They had something else. Two somethings, actually. Goalkeeper Bernie Parent was one of them. The 29-year-old, like six Flyer teammates, was a Boston castoff.He made it his series, earning the Conn Smythe Trophy as the Most Valuable Player.

Then there was Kate Smith, the famed singer whose recorded rendition of "God Bless America" had helped the Flyers to 36 home-ice wins, was there in person.

The Bruins didn't have a chance. Actually any team with Orr would, although the rugged Flyers used four centers starting with Clarke to keep him away from the play as much as possible. Clarke did more than that, specializing in faceoffs and power plays.

Flyer Coach Fred Shero had figured out how all this would work and he was right. It did. And to his 12 regular-season shutouts, Parent added one more in the biggest game of the year and the biggest of his career. Rick MacLeish scored on a power play in the opening period of Game 6 and Parent made it stand all the way)

Kate Smith—and every Flyer fan—could not have been happier.

Philadelphia Flyers: Bernie Parent, Ed Van Impe, Tom Bladon, André Dupont, Joe Watson, Jim Watson, Barry Ashbee, Bill Barber, Dave Schultz, Don Saleski, Gary Dornhoefer, Terry Crisp, Bobby Clarke, Simon Nolet, Ross Lonsberry, Rick MacLeish, Bill Flett, Orest Kindrachuk, Bill Clement, Bob Kelly, Bruce Cowick, Al MacAdam, Bobby Taylor

Boston Bruins: Phil Esposito, Bobby Orr, Ken Hodge, Wayne Cashman, Johnny Bucyk, Bobby Schmautz, Carol Vadnais, Don Marcotte, Gregg Sheppard, Terry O'Reilly, Andre Savard, Dallas Smith, Dave Forbes, Derek Sanderson, Fred O'Donnell, Al Sims, Darryl Edestrand, Rich Leduc, Gary Doak, Ken Broderick, Gilles Gilbert, Bob Gryp, Doug Gibson, Dave Hynes, Al Simmons, Ross Brooks

MAY 10, 1979 (Game 7, Stanley Cup semifinals)

Montreal Canadiens   **5**   **(OT)**
Boston Bruins   **4**

At the Montreal Forum

Too many men on the ice

It wasn't the Finals but it was realistically the series that determined the 1979 Stanley Cup winner.

If the Montreal Canadiens were to win their fourth straight Stanley Cup, they would have to beat the Boston Bruins. As usual, that wasn't going to be easy.

The Canadiens actually fell behind 3–1 on their own ice in Game 7.

Montreal tied the game in the third period but Boston's "Lunch Pail Gang" hit back as Rick Middleton silenced the Forum faithful with a goal 3 minutes 59 seconds from the end of regulation.

In their haste to keep Montreal out Boston went with a defensive formation of six men plus a netminder. Play continued for a few seconds before linesman John D'Amico noticed. He signaled the penalty and on the ensuing power play Guy Lafleur scored the equaliser.

Midway through the first overtime period, an Yvon Lambert goal sent Montreal into the Finals with a 5–4 win.

The Canadiens would keep the magic going as they erased the surprising New York Rangers 4–1. They did so after giving the Rangers a 1-0 start in a first-game 4–1 upset in Montreal.

The Canadiens weren't going to lose to the Rangers. Only the Bruins had had a chance to beat them in a series that saw three games decided by one goal.

But when the Stanley Cup was presented, it was the Canadiens accepting it for the fourth consecutive year and 22nd time overall.

Montreal Canadiens: Ken Dryden, Larry Robinson, Serge Savard, Guy Lapointe, Brain Engblom, Gillies Lupien, Rick Chartraw, Guy Lafleur, Steve Shutt, Jacques Lemaire, Yvan Cournoyer, Réjean Houle, Pierre Mondou, Bob Gainey, Doug Jarvis, Yvon Lambert, Doug Risebrough, Pierre Larouche, Mario Tremblay, Cam Connor, Pat Hughes, Rod Langway, Mark Napier, Michel Larocque, Richard Sévigny

Boston Bruins: Rick Middleton, Peter McNab, Terry O'Reilly, Jean Ratelle, Wayne Cashman, Bob Miller, Don Marcotte, John Wensink, Bobby Schmautz, Brad Park, Mike Milbury, Dick Redmond, Al Sims, Rick Smith, Dwight Foster, Al Secord, Gary Doak, Stan Jonathan, Dennis O'Brien, Bill Bennett, Tom Songin, Gerry Cheevers, Graeme Nicolson, Ab DeMarco, Jim Pettie, Gilles Gilbert

FEBRUARY 22, 1980 (Olympics semifinal)

United States	**4**
USSR	**3**

Lake Placid Ice Arena

Miracle on ice

It always sounded so right. "Miracle on Ice." Because that's what it was. They were kids. Average age 22. Completed untested. And they were playing the best hockey team in the world. That's what the Soviets were. They hadn't lost a game in 12 years. They were better than the best NHL all-stars and they had proved it. They'd beaten these same U.S. kids 10–3 a week before the 1980 Winter Olympics at Madison Square Garden and despite the strong performance of the U.S. team in the games and the home ice and the 8,500 fans at the Lake Placid Arena, it was time to get real.

Sure, the U.S. had beaten West Germany, the Czech Republic, Norway and others but this was another level altogether. The Soviets were something special. And they started to show it right away, scoring first. But the U.S. kids countered with a score of their own. The U.S. tied it twice. It was 3–3 early in the final period. Was it possible? Could it happen?

The game wasn't even telecast live so throughout the host nation, no one was thinking the unthinkable. Not yet. But in the arena, and on the ice, amazingly, they were. Then it happened. Mike Eruzione of Boston University scored the go-ahead goal midway through the final period. After 10 minutes, it was official. U.S.A. 4, USSR 3.

"Do you believe in miracles?" Al Michaels asked on the telecast. But this wasn't the end of it. A win over Finland would be needed to get the gold. But a team that could beat the USSR could do that and they did. The game has been selected by ESPN as the greatest game played in the 20th Century.

When the Winter Olympics returned to the United States this year, they brought the Miracle Makers back, asking the 1980 hockey team of Coach Herb Brooks to light the torch in Salt Lake City.

U.S. Olympic team: Mark Johnson, Rob McClanahan, Steve Christoff, Neal Broten, Mark Pavelich, Dave Silk, Mike Eruzione, Phil Verchota, William "Buzz" Schneider, Eric Strobel, Dave Christian, John Harrington, Jack O'Callahan, Mike Ramsey, Bill Baker, Ralph Cox, Ken Morrow, Bob Suter, Jack Hughes, Mark Wells, Les Auge, Gary Ross, Dave Delich, Tim Harrer, Jim Craig, Steve Janaszak, Bruce Horsch

USSR Olympic team: Vladislav Tretiak, Vladimr Myshkin, Valeri Vasilov, Vasili Perushkin, Zinetula Bilyatedinov, Sergei Starikov, Aleksei Kasatanov, Vyacheslav Fetisov, Boris Mikhailov, Vladimir Petrov, Valeri Kharlamov, Helmut Balderis, Alexander Maltkev, Viktor Schlutkov, Sergei Makarov, Vladimir Golikov, Alexander Golikov, Yuri Lebedev, Alexander Skvortsov, Sergei Kapustin, Viktor Shalinov, Vladimir Krutov

MAY 24, 1980 (Game 6, Stanley Cup Finals)

New York Islanders   **5**   **(OT)**
Philadelphia Flyers   **4**

At Nassau Veterans Memorial Coliseum, Uniondale, L.I.

The Islanders win their first Cup

No New York Islander had ever scored a bigger goal than the one Bobby Nystrom fired in at 7:11 in overtime on May 24. This one gave the Islanders, so often the poor relation in New York area professional sports, the franchise's first Stanley Cup.

And it made them legit. After eight seasons. Not a long wait, actually, considering that it was the first Stanley Cup in New York in 40 years.

Nystrom's goal gave the Isles a 5–4 win in the deciding sixth game and a title they could celebrate on Long Island for a very long time.

Bryan Trottier's 29 playoff points, a Stanley Cup record, would earn him the Conn Smythe Trophy as playoff MVP.

For the Islanders, it was their second one-goal win over the Flyers. The opening game had been a 4–3 win for Coach Al Arbour's team.

Game 6 was tied at 2–2 entering the second period. Then goals from Mike Bossy and Nystrom put the Islanders in charge, just 20 minutes away from becoming the second expansion team to win the Stanley Cup—the Flyers were the first—but Philadelphia weren't ready to laydown. First Bob Dailey made it 4–3, then John Paddock scored to tie things up. Then it was sudden death. With seven minutes gone, Arbour sent in his third line—Lorne Henning, John Tonelli and Nystrom—who quickly combined for two passes and to set up the backhanded goal by Nystrom.

New York Islanders: Gord Lane, Jean Potvin, Bob Lorimer, Denis Potvin, Stefan Persson, Ken Morrow, Dave Langevin, Duane Sutter, Garry Howatt, Clark Gillies, Lorne Henning, Wayne Merrick, Bob Bourne, Steve Tambellini, Bryan Trottier, Mike Bossy, Bob Nystrom, John Tonelli, Anders Kallur, Butch Goring, Alex McKendry, Glenn Resch, Billy Smith

Philadelphia Flyers: Ken Linseman, Reggie Leach, Brian Propp, Bill Barber, Bobby Clarke, Rick MacLeish, Paul Holmgren, Mel Bridgman, Bob Dailey, Bob Kelly, Behn Wilson, Dennis Ververgaert, Al Hill, Norm Barnes, Jim Watson, Tom Gorence, Mike Busniuk, John Paddock, Andre Dupont, Frank Bathe, Jack McIlhargey, Dave Gardner, Gary Morrison, Don Gillen, Blake Wesley, Dennis Patterson, Rick St. Croix, Pete Peeters, Phil Myre

MAY 24, 1986 (Game 5, Stanley Cup Finals)

Montreal Canadiens   **4**
Calgary Flames   **3**

At the Calgary Saddledome

Rookie Roy is Montreal's Stanley Cup king

This was not the way it was supposed to go. Usually when the Montreal Canadiens won a Stanley Cup—as they had done 22 times, more than any franchise in hockey history —you would just nod and say how the Canadiens sure knew how to get it done.

Even when they had an off year and finished, oh, say second or third in the regular season.

But seventh? With enough rookies on the club to field a baseball team? And with a first-year coach? Not even the Canadiens could pull that off, could they?

Turns out in 1986 they could.

But it took some doing. The Edmonton's Oilers, going for their third straight Cup, had to go down in flames. And they did, to the Flames, to boot. It set up the first all-Canadian Finals for 19 years.

That gigantic upset of Edmonton opened things up for everyone. And the man who stepped up was barely out of his boyhood, 20-year-old Montreal goalie Patrick Roy.

Roy became the youngest ever to win the Conn Smythe Trophy on his way to winning 15 playoff games as a rookie. In Game 5 he recorded his first shutout of the finals with a 1–0 win.

And it was Roy's save against the Flames' Jamie Macoun with 14 seconds left that finally gave the Canadiens their deciding 4–3 fifth-game win. The game, and cup-winning goal had come from Bobby Smith midway through the third period. It was the Canadiens' third one-goal win in the four needed to capture the Cup that became a battle of longshots.

Montreal Canadiens: Bob Gainey, Doug Soetaert, Patrick Roy, Rick Green, David Maley, Ryan Walter, Serge Boisvert, Mario Tremblay, Bobby Smith, Craig Ludwig, Tom Kurvers, Kjell Dahlin, Larry Robinson, Guy Carbonneau, Chris Chelios, Petr Svoboda, Mats Naslund, Lucien DeBlois, Steve Rooney, Gaston Gingras, Mike Lalor, Chris Nilan, John Kordic, Claude Lemieux, Mike McPhee, Brain Skrudland, Stephane Richer

Calgary Flames: Joe Mullen, Dan Quinn, Lanny McDonald, John Tonelli, Gary Suter, Hakan Loob, Joel Otto, Jim Peplinski, Carey Wilson, Steve Bozek, Doug Risebrough, Perry Berezan, Paul Reinhart, Jamie Macoun, Colin Patterson, Neil Sheehy, Tim Hunter, Terry Johnson, Paul Baxter, Rik Wilson, Reggie Lemelin, Yves Courteau, Brian Bradley, Nick Fotiu, Mike Vernon, Robin Bartell, Mark Lamb, Dale DeGray, Marc D'Amour, Mike Eaves, Brett Hull

MAY 31, 1987 (Game 7, Stanley Cup Finals)

Edmonton Oilers   **3**
Philadelphia Flyers   **1**

At Northlands Coliseum, Edmonton

Gretzky and Oilers win third Cup

The Edmonton Oilers came back with a vengeance. They came back to win the third Stanley Cup they thought should have won in 1986.

That's when the Oilers discovered nothing is ever owed or given to you.Success must be earned.

This time that's just what the Oilers did. In Game 7 against the Philadelphia Flyers and with everything on the line, it was the Oilers who stepped up to a decisive 3–1 win.

They had jumped out to 2–0 and 3–1 leads in games in the Finals only to see the Flyers knock them off twice in a row taking Games 5 and 6 on 4–3 and 3–2 decisions, respectively and turn the best-of-seven series into one game.

Even for Wayne Gretzky, this one was big—"the biggest game I've ever played," The Great One said.

The Oilers of Coach Glen Sather played like it, especially after falling behind 1–0, early in the first period then firing off 43 shots for the game and limiting the Flyers to just two in the final period. Mark Messier set much of the tone for this one. And Jari Kurri and Glenn Anderson scored the final two goals that put the Oilers over the top for the third time in four years.

Edmonton Oilers: Glenn Anderson, Jeff Beukeboom, Kelly Buchberger, Paul Coffey, Grant Fuhr, Randy Gregg, Wayne Gretzky, Charlie Huddy, Dave Hunter, Mike Krushelnyski, Jari Kurri, Moe Lemay, Kevin Lowe, Craig MacTavish, Kevin McClelland, Marty McSorley, Mark Messier, Andy Moog, Craig Muni, Kent Nilsson, Jaroslav Pouzar, Reijo Ruotsalainen, Steve Smith, Esa Tikkanen

Philadelphia Flyers: Tim Kerr Peter Zezel Dave Poulin Brian Propp Mark Howe Pelle Eklund Rick Tocchet Murray Craven Doug Crossman Brad McCrimmon Derrick Smith Scott Mellanby Ilkka Sinisalo Ron Sutter Lindsay Carson J.J. Daigneault Kjell Samuelsson Brad Marsh Dave Brown Ron Hextall Glen Seabrooke Ed Hospodar Brian Dobbin Daryl Stanley John Stevens Al Hill Don Nachbaur Mark Freer Greg Smyth Jere Gillis Jeff Chychrun Ray Allison Kevin McCarthy Tim Tookey, Mike Stothers, Steve Smith Craig Berube, Kerry Huffman, Glenn "Chico" Resch

MAY 25, 1989 (Game 6, Stanley Cup Finals)

Calgary Flames   4
Montreal Canadiens   2

At the Montreal Forum

Flames shock Canadiens

This time it went the Flames' way. No matter how unlikely that would seem.

No matter how great the odds.

One team had won a record 23 Stanley Cups. The other had won none.

One team—the storied Montreal Canadiens—had never lost a deciding Stanley Cup Finals game on its Forum ice in 61 years.

And the other team hadn't won one anywhere. And to make things worse, the Calgary Flames found themselves on the Forum ice, where no visiting team had ever skated off with the Stanley Cup.

Even though they were leading three games to two as they skated onto the ice that May 25, the trends did not look good for the Flames.

They were battling two opponents—the Canadiens and history.

As hard as it may be to believe, history lost. The Flames won 4–2 in the game and the series. Behind veteran Lanny McDonald and Conn Smythe winner Al MacInnis, the first defenseman to lead the Stanley Cup playoffs in scoring, they put the Canadiens away in six.

And they did it on Forum ice by winning three straight after an overtime loss.

Doug Gilmour did more than anyone in Game 6 with two goals, the final one an empty-netter with just over a minute left to seal the championship.

Calgary Flames: Mike Vernon, Rick Wamsley, Al MacInnis, Brad McCrimmon, Dana Murzyn, Ric Nattress, Joe Mullen, Lanny McDonald (Co-Captain), Gary Roberts, Colin Patterson, Hakan Loob, Theoren Fleury, Jiri Hrdina, Tim Hunter (Assistant Captain), Gary Suter, Mark Hunter, Jim Peplinski (Co-Captain), Joe Nieuwendyk, Brain MacLellan, Joel Otto, Jamie Macoun, Doug Gilmour, Rob Ramage, Norman Green

Montreal Canadiens: Mats Naslund, Bobby Smith, Chris Chelios, Stephane Richer, Guy Carbonneau, Claude Lemieux, Shayne Corson, Petr Svoboda, Russ Courtnall, Mike McPhee, Brian Skrudland, Mike Keane, Ryan Walter, Larry Robinson, Brent Gilchrist, Bob Gainey, Craig Ludwig, Rick Green, Eric Desjardins, Gilles Thibaudeau, Patrick Roy, Jyrki Lumme, Steve Martinson, Jocelyn Lemieux, Stephan Lebeau, Benoit Brunet, Donald Dufresne, Randy Exelby, Brian Hayward

JUNE 2, 1993 (Game 2, Stanley Cup Finals)

Montreal Canadiens   3
Los Angeles Kings   2

At the Montreal Forum

McSorley curved stick incident

Things did not look good for the home team. The Montreal Canadiens had already lost Game 1 of the 1993 Stanley Cup playoffs on their home ice to the Los Angeles Kings. And they trailed 2–1 in Game 2 with less than two minutes to go.

Oh well, despite those 23 Stanley Cup titles, this Montreal team wasn't supposed to win anyway.

And if they lost this one—going 0 for 2 at home to start—they weren't very likely to have any kind of a shot. Only two NHL teams had ever lost the first two Stanley Cup games at home and won the Cup. No one had done it in 27 years.

So what to do? Here's what Canadiens coach Jaques Demers decided to do: Measure the curve on the stick of the Kings' Marty McSorley. Hey, it looked pretty curvy.

It was maybe a full quarter-inch more than the allowed half-inch curve. So McSorley was penalized and the Canadiens had their chance.

Netminder Patrick Roy was pulled out of goal and the Canadiens assaulted the Kings 6–on–4 and made their poor power play work for once. It took just 32 seconds. Defenseman Eric Desjardins got the game-tying goal — his second.

And then the Canadiens won it in overtime as Desjardins became the first defender ever to get a hat-trick in the Stanley Cup Finals. It took just 51 extra seconds to do it.

The Forum ghosts had struck again, everyone agreed. No one gets caught with a curved stick at the end of a Stanley Cup game. And no defensemen gets a hat-trick.

Only they did. It's the only way Montreal could have won this one. And then they won three more. Somehow. Some way.

Montreal Canadiens: Guy Carbonneau (Captain), Patrick Roy, Mike Keane, Eric Desjardins, Stephen Lebeau, Mathieu Schneider, Jean-Jacques Daigneault, Denis Savard, Lyle Odelein, Todd Ewen, Kirk Muller, John LeClair, Gilbert Dionne, Benoit Brunet, Patrice Brisebois, Paul Di Pietro, Andre Racicot, Donald Dufresne, Mario Roberge, Sean Hill, Ed Ronan, Kevin Maller, Vincent Damphousse, Brian Bellows, Gary Leeman, Rob Ramage

Los Angeles Kings: Luc Robitaille, Jari Kurri, Tony Granato, Jimmy Carson, Mike Donnelly, Wayne Gretzky, Rob Blake, Tomas Sandstrom, Alexei Zhitnik, Marty McSorley, Corey Millen, Darryl Sydor, Charlie Huddy, Lonnie Loach, Pat Conacher, Dave Taylor, Mark Hardy, Warren Rychel, Gary Shuchuk, Robert Lang, Brent Thompson, Kelly Hrudey, Guy Leveque, Sean Whyte, Tim Watters, Robb Stauber, Marc Fortier, Jeff Chychrun, Marc Potvin, Jim Thomson, Brandy Semchuk, David Goverde, Darryl Williams, Frank Breault, Rick Knickle, Rene Chapdelaine

JUNE 14, 1994 (Game 7, Stanley Cup Finals)

New York Rangers   **3**
Vancouver Canucks   **2**

At Madison Square Garden

New York win first Cup in 54 years

The last time the New York Rangers won the Stanley Cup, the game wasn't on television. There was a good reason for that. In 1940, there were almost no television sets anywhere, no cameras and no TV stations. Heck, Howard Cosell was still in short pants.

But by 1994, anyone could watch the Rangers try to end their 54 years of futility. The Rangers would have to wait, however, until Game 7 to see if they could finally pull it off.

They could, as it turned out, but it wasn't easy. It was dramatic and stressful, the Rangers reported later, just trying to get through the final 3–2 win. They'd been embarrassed long enough. Five expansion teams had already won Stanley Cups since the Rangers last won one.

One numbers cruncher noted that they'd gone through six team presidents, 24 coaches and 4,150 games without winning the Cup.

And then it happened. The talent had been getting better and Mark Messier and his cast of ex-Edmonton Oilers were proven winners. There was solid goalkeeper Mike Richter and abrasive coach Mike Keenan to keep everybody in line.

Finally there was this: The Rangers' power play returned to life to get the New York team a pair of home-ice goals that lifted them to the 3–2 win over Vancouver's Canucks in the seven-game series. The decisive goal came from Messier in the second period.

It wasn't the best hockey anyone has ever seen on the Garden ice but who cared?. The Rangers had finally won the Cup and silenced the taunting chants of "1940...1940."

New York Rangers: Mark Messier (Captain), Brian Leetch, Kevin Lowe, Adam Graves, Steve Larmer, Glenn Anderson, Jeff Beukeboom, Greg Gilbert, Mike Hartman, Glenn Healy, Mike Hudson, Alexander Karpovtsev, Joe Kocur, Alexei Kovalev, Nick Kypreos, Doug Lidster, Stephane Matteau, Craig MacTavish, Sergei Nemchinov, Brian Noonan, Ed Olczyk, Mike Richter, Esa Tikkanen, Jay Wells, Sergei Zubov

Vancouver Canucks: Pavel Bure, Geoff Courtnall, Cliff Ronning, Jeff Brown, Trevor Linden, Murray Craven, Jyrki Lumme, Jiri Slegr, Greg Adams, Dave Babych, Gino Odjick, Martin Gelinas, Jimmy Carson, Sergio Momesso, Dana Murzyn, Brian Glynn, Jose Charbonneau, Bret Hedican, Gerald Diduck, Adrien Plavsic, John McIntyre, Nathan LaFayette, Tim Hunter, Dane Jackson, Dan Kesa, Evgeny Namestnikov, Neil Eisenhut, Kirk McLean, Shawn Antoski, Stephane Morin, Michael Peca, Kay Whitmore

JUNE 24, 1995 (Game 4, Stanley Cup Finals)

New Jersey Devils   **5**
Detroit Red Wings   **2**

At Byrne Arena, The Meadowlands

Detroit are be-deviled by New Jersey

Defense apparently does win championships. Just the way they say it does.

It certainly did in 1995.

All the New Jersey Devils had to do was break out their neutral-zone trap defense in all its confounding glory and Detroit's offensive-minded Red Wings might as well have mailed their game in.

Get out the broom, the Wings were gone in four.

They entered the final series boasting per-game averages of 36 shots on goal and 3.4 goals. Against the Devils, the revised numbers were a miniscule 19 shots and 1.8 goals. And the team that had scored 19 first-period playoff goals managed just two in the entire Devils series. Those two came in the final—and fourth—game.

But they didn't matter at all.

Maybe they were the result of Game 3 when the Devils jumped on the Red Wings 5–0 on the way to a 5–2 win. So this time the Wings got those two early goals.

And that was it. It didn't matter when they scored. The Devils went from scoring the first five goals in one game to the last five goals in the next.

The result was the same. A 5–2 New Jersey win, only this one meant so much more for coach Jacques Lemaire's team. It meant the first Stanley Cup for a franchise that had tailed in Kansas City and Denver before finding success in New Jersey. Neil Broten scored the game-winning goal just seven minutes into the second quarter. The Conn Smythe Trophy went to another of the "blue-collar" Devils, right-winger Claude Lemieux.

New Jersey Devils: Scott Stevens (Captain), Tommy Albelin, Martin Brodeur, Neil Broten, Sergei Brylin, Robert E. Carpenter, Jr., Shawn Chambers, Tom Chorske, Danton Cole, Ken Daneyko, Kevin Dean, Jim Dowd, Bruce Driver (Alternate Captain), Bill Guerin, Bobby Holik, Claude Lemieux, John MacLean (Alternate Captain), Chris McAlpine, Randy McKay, Scott Niedermayer, Mike Peluso, Stephane J.J. Richer, Brian Rolston, Chris Terreri, Valeri Zelepukin

Detroit Red Wings: Paul Coffey, Sergei Fedorov, Dino Ciccarelli, Keith Primeau, Ray Sheppard, Steve Yzerman, Slava Kozlov, Nicklas Lidstrom, Doug Brown, Bob Errey, Slava Fetisov, Shawn Burr, Vladimir Konstantinov, Darren McCarty, Martin Lapointe, Greg Johnson, Kris Draper, Bob Rouse, Mark Howe, Mike Krushelnyski, Tim Taylor, Terry Carkner, Mike Ramsey, Aaron Ward, Mark Ferner, Stu Grimson, Andrew McKim, Chris Osgood, Mike Vernon

JUNE 10, 1996 (Game 4, Stanley Cup Finals)

Colorado Avalanche   **1**
Florida Panthers   **0**

At the Miami Arena

Changing of the guard

Who the heck are these guys? Where was Montreal? Philadelphia? Toronto? Boston? Detroit? Somebody who'd been here before?

But Colorado and Florida in the Stanley Cup Finals?

Sounds like two college football teams meeting in the Orange Bowl.

There's a hockey team in Florida?

It had been hard enough to accept the fact that Colorado took the Nordiques team that had tried so hard but finally had to give up in Quebec because of economic issues. Now the franchise that had been adding all of the pieces since the day Eric Lindros forced a trade that brought in seven new players found itself in the Finals in its first year in the Rockies.

But Florida?

OK, so it doesn't matter who got to the finals opposite Colorado and new goalie Patrick Roy. Florida somehow did. But the Panthers had to wonder why. In four games they got a grand total of four goals off Roy in four games.

And in the fourth and deciding game, they got none. Roy was just too good, as he was so often when he played with Montreal.

So it was just a matter of time. That time came in the first period of overtime in Game 4, when one of the survivors from that Lindros deal five years earlier, defenseman Uwe Krupp, scored the game's lone goal to clinch the Cup for Colorado in the Avalanche's first try.

Colorado Avalanche: Joe Sakic (Captain), Rene Corbet, Adam Deadmarsh, Stephane Fiset, Adam Foote, Peter Forsberg, Alexei Gusarov, Dave Hannan, Valeri Kamensky, Mike Keane, Jon Klemm, Uwe Krupp, Sylvain Lefebvre, Claude Lemieux, Curtis Leschyshyn, Troy Murray, Sandis Ozolinsh, Mike Ricci, Patrick Roy, Warren Rychel, Chris Simon, Craig Wolanin, Stephane Yelle, Scott Young

Florida Panthers: Scott Mellanby, Rob Niedermayer, Ray Sheppard, Robert Svehla, Johan Garpenlov, Stu Barnes, Martin Straka, Jody Hull, Tom Fitzgerald, Bill Lindsay, Jason Woolley, Gord Murphy, Radek Dvorak, Brian Skrudland, Dave Lowry, Mike Hough, Ed Jovanovski, Terry Carkner, Magnus Svensson, Geoff Smith, Paul Laus, Gilbert Dionne, Brett Harkins, Rhett Warrener, Brad Smyth, David Nemirovsky, John Vanbiesbrouck, Steve Washburn, Bob Kudelski, Mike Casselman, Mark Fitzpatrick

JUNE 7, 1997 (Game 4, Stanley Cup Finals)

Detroit Red Wings   2
Philadelphia Flyers   1

At Joe Louis Arena, Detroit

Red Wings end 42-year Cup drought

Now that the New York Rangers had ended a long championship drought, could Detroit?

Could the Red Wings put the "Hockey" back in Hockeytown?

If the New York team could wipe out 54 years of Stanley Cup frustration, why couldn't Detroit erase the National Hockey League's next-longest futility streak.

They did it with a broom, in the NHL's third straight Stanley Cup sweep. And just two years after the Red Wings had been swept themselves.

For a team that's missed out on more than four decades of finals fun, the game that matters the most is the last one. And it matters as much for the new guy on the block—Captain Steve Yzerman — as for the Red Wings already in the Hockey Hall of Fame.

It mattered for captain Steve Yzerman and coach Scotty Bowman, too. The word was out that he would be gone after the final game but he wasn't.

With a 2–1 final-game win over the Flyers, the team of general manager Bobby Clarke, the player Yzerman idolized when he was a kid, the Red Wings would not be ridding themselves of Bowman. That's not what a team does with the a man winning his seventh Stanley Cup.

The Flyers had scored 61 goals in 15 games before running into the Red Wings. But on the big stage they scored just six in four games. Detroit goalie Mike Vernon allowed just one goal in the clincher and was awarded the Conn Smythe Trophy.

Detroit Red Wings: Steve Yzerman (Captain), Doug Brown, Mathieu Dandenault, Kris Draper, Sergei Fedorov, Viacheslav Fetisov, Kevin Hodson, Tomas Holmstrom, Joe Kocur, Vladimir Konstantinov, Vyacheslav Kozlov, Martin Lapointe, Igor Larionov, Nicklas Lidstrom, Kirk Maltby, Darren McCarty, Larry Murphy, Chris Osgood, Jamie Pushor, Bob Rouse, Tomas Sandstrom, Brendan Shanahan, Tim Taylor, Mike Vernon, Aaron Ward

Philadelphia Flyers: John LeClair, Eric Lindros, Rod Brind'Amour, Mikael Renberg, Eric Desjardins, Trent Klatt, Janne Niinimaa, Dale Hawerchuk, Paul Coffey, Shjon Podein, Joel Otto, Chris Therien, Pat Falloon, Dainius Zubrus, Karl Dykhuis, John Druce, Vaclav Prospal, Petr Svoboda, Michel Petit, Daniel Lacroix, Scott Daniels, Kjell Samuelsson, Craig Darby, Dan Kordic, Colin Forbes, Aris Brimanis, Jason Bowen, Garth Snow, Paul Healey, Frantisek Kucera, Darren Rumble, Ron Hextall

JUNE 19, 1999 (Game 6, Stanley Cup Finals)

Dallas Stars	2	(3OT)
Buffalo Sabres	1	

At the HSBC Center, Buffalo

Hull scores dubious goal in overtime

This is why you sign a Brett Hull. Even if it costs you $17 million for three years.

Because when it counts, when you absolutely have to have somebody, players like Brett Hull will be there.

When the Dallas Stars needed Hull, in the sixth and final game of their first Stanley Cup Finals, it didn't matter that Hull was playing with a pulled groin and one bad knee.

Nor did it matter that he'd been limited to every other shift because of his injuries in Games 3 and 4.

Hull was the one they'd wanted to be in there and as Game 6 moved into triple overtime, Hull was. On every shift.

Hull was also there where he needed to be in front of the Buffalo goal when the rebound presented itself when he was all alone staring at Sabre goalie Dominik Hasek. And then Hull buried the puck into the net. And the Dallas Stars had their first Stanley Cup in a 2–1 triple overtime triumph.

And Hull had shown them how with his second game-winner in the Stars' four victories. Just the way they thought he would.

But how the controversy raged. The NHL had strictly enforced the rule that prevented players entering the goalie's crease to shoot. Except, when Hull scored the winning goal, his left skate was clearly in forbidden territory. Buffalo seethed and demanded an official replay, but none was forthcoming, so the goal stood.

Dallas Stars: Derian Hatcher (Captain), Ed Belfour, Guy Carbonneau, Shawn Chambers, Benoit Hogue, Tony Hrkac, Brett Hull, Mike Keane, Jamie Langenbrunner, Jere Lehtinen, Craig Ludwig, Grant Marshall, Richard Matvichuk, Mike Modano, Joe Nieuwendyk, Derek Plante, Dave Reid, Jon Reid, Jon Sim, Brain Skrudland, Blake Sloan, Darryl Sydor, Roman Turek, Pat Verbeek, Sergei Zubov

Buffalo Sabres: Miroslav Satan, Michael Peca, Michal Grosek, Curtis Brown, Dixon Ward, Joe Juneau, Jason Woolley, Stu Barnes, Brian Holzinger, Alexei Zhitnik, Vaclav Varada, Geoff Sanderson, Darryl Shannon, Richard Smehlik, Wayne Primeau, Erik Rasmussen, James Patrick, Rhett Warrener, Jay McKee, Randy Cunneyworth, Rob Ray, Paul Kruse, Jean-Luc Grand-Pierre, Dean Sylvester, Mike Hurlbut, Dominic Pittis, Jason Holland, Cory Sarich, Martin Biron, Dwayne Roloson, Dominik Hasek

JUNE 10, 2000 (Game 6, Stanley Cup Finals)

New Jersey Devils   2   **(2OT)**
Dallas Stars   1

At Reunion Arena, Dallas

Arnott scores sudden death winner

Each team had shown it belonged here. Each had won a Stanley Cup in the previous five years.

And each knew what it had to do. But only the New Jersey Devils could do it.

They shut the Dallas Stars down. The offensive-minded Stars managed a mere four goals in the final four games of the six-game series. After the teams had combined for 10 goals in Game 1, the next four brought 11 in total and two goals was enough to win every game.

It wasn't nearly enough. Not the way New Jersey plays. There were no rebounds. Nothing easy in front. Turn the slot into the Bermuda Triangle. Make it the place where pucks go to die, particulary in Game 6.

The Devils smothered the Stars just the way they did the Red Wings five years earlier. They did all the little things right and hustled relentlessly. The Devils were clearly quicker to the puck.

Both teams scored in the second period then held on through a scoreless third as Stars goalie Ed Belfour and the Devils Martin Brodeur matched saves. Belfour had the tougher challenge in overtime as the Devils fired 11 shots his way. Dallas had just one shot.

And then it happened. For the third time in five years, a Stanley Cup was won in sudden death as Jason Arnott scored for New Jersey at 8:20 of the second overtime.

New Jersey Devils: Scott Stevens (Captain), Jason Arnott, Brad Bombardir, Martin Brodeur, Steve Brule, Sergei Brylin, Ken Daneyko, Patrik Elias, Scott Gomez, Bobby Holik, Steve Kelly, Claude Lemieux, John Madden, Vladmir Malakhov, Randy McKay, Alexander Mogilny, Sergei Nemchinov, Scott Niedermayer, Krzysztof Oliwa, Jay Pandolfo, Brian Rafalski, Ken Sutton, Petr Sykora, Chris Terreri, Colin White.

Dallas Stars: Mike Modano, Brett Hull, Sergei Zubov, Jamie Langenbrunner, Joe Nieuwendyk, Mike Keane, Darryl Sydor, Brenden Morrow, Richard Matvichuk, Derian Hatcher, Kirk Muller, Blake Sloan, Guy Carbonneau, Aaron Gavey, Roman Lyashenko, Dave Manson, Jonathan Sim, Jere Lehtinen, Grant Marshall, Jamie Pushor, Pavel Patera, Jamie Wright, Joel Bouchard, Brad Lukowich, Derek Plante, Chris Murray, Richard Jackman, Brian Skrudland, Ed Belfour, Manny Fernandez, Warren Luhning, Keith Aldridge, Shawn Chambers, Ryan Christie, Alan Letang.

JUNE 9, 2001 (Game 7, Stanley Cup Finals)

Colorado Avalanche   **3**
New Jersey Devils   **1**

At Pepsi Center, Denver

Bourque gets Cup as NHL leaving gift

It's a team sport, of course. But only one story seemed to matter in the 2001 Stanley Cup Finals.

And it wasn't whether the New Jersey Devils could repeat.

It was whether Ray Borque would leave the game with a championship after 22 seasons. Bourque had labored for more than two decades as one of the National Hockey League's greatest defensemen.

But he'd never gotten closer than a pair of five-game losses in the finals to this moment back in Boston. So after 21 years as a Bruin, he headed out for a last shot in the Rockies.In the Finals Colorado split the first two at home then shared the next pair in New Jersey. It got stranger and stranger as the road team won the next two as well.

But at least Bourque got all the way to Game 7 in the Stanley Cup Finals.

Would he get the Cup? Or would the Devils do it to him?

Which way would the final 60 minutes of Bourque's NHL career go?

Twice he'd been to the finals with the Bruins but never got close to a Cup.

So that's why he spoke up before Games 6 and 7, both games the Avalanche had to win. He told them what it would mean to him if they did.

The game was tied at 1 and the Avalanche players were talking about who would score the next one. "I got it," is all Bourque said simply. And so he did, putting Colorado up 2–1 and getting the game-winner in the deciding game.

Colorado Avalanche: Joe Sakic (Captain), David Aebischer, Rob Blake, Ray Bourque, Greg De Vries, Chris Dingman, Chris Drury, Adam Foote, Peter Forsberg, Milan Hejduk, Dan Hinote, Jon Klemm, Eric Messier, Bryan Muir, Ville Nieminen, Shjon Podein, Scott Parker, Steven Reinprecht, Patrick Roy, Martin Skoula, Dave Reid, Alex Tanguay, Stephane Yelle

New Jersey Devils: Patrik Elias, Alexander Mogilny, Petr Sykora, Scott Gomez, Jason Arnott, Sergei Brylin, Brian Rafalski, Bobby Holik, Randy McKay, John Madden, Scott Niedermayer, Scott Stevens, Sergei Nemchinov, Turner Stevenson, Colin White, Sean O'Donnell, Jay Pandolfo, Bob Corkum, Ken Sutton, Pierre Dagenais, Mike Commodore, Jim McKenzie, Ken Daneyko, Jiri Bicek, Ed Ward, Martin Brodeur, Stanislav Gron, Mike Jefferson, Sascha Goc, John Vanbiesbrouck

JUNE 13, 2002 (Game 5, Stanley Cup Finals)

Detroit Red Wings   3
Carolina Hurricanes   1

At Joe Louis Arena, Detroit

Hasek finally acheives dream

The Detroit Red Wings have become the gold standard—with the silver Stanley Cup. Three times in the last six years the Cup has ended up in Hockeytown, where the Red Wings have been dominant.

They won't have the best coach in hockey history any more. Scotty Bowman, 68, has decided that nine was enough. No coach has won more than nine championships before in any pro sport.

And for Dominik Hasek, it was the superstar goaltender's first and last championship as he joined Bowman in retirement.

The Red Wings ended the feel-good story of the team from Tobacco Road, the Carolina Hurricanes, who unexpectedly were giving respected veteran Ron Francis another turn in the spotlight.

For in this one, the Red Wings left nothing to chance. One first-year Red Wing—Hasek—stopped 16 shots and another—veteran Brendan Shanahan—scored twice in the Red Wings' 3–1 win in Game 5. Tomas Holstrom opened the scoring four minutes into the second period and Shanahan doubled the lead on the power play 10 minutes later. A power play goal from Jeff O'Neill gave Carolina hope going into the last period. The win was confirmed 45 seconds from the end of regulation when Shanahan scored an empty-net goal.

Some might argue that the Wings had set up this win in an earlier Game 3 in Raleigh. After Carolina had earned a surprising split in the first two games in Detroit, the Red Wings came back to devastate the Hurricanes' hearts out with a triple-overtime win.

Detroit Red Wings: Brendan Shanahan, Sergei Fedorov, Brett Hull, Nicklas Lidstrom, Luc Robitaille, Steve Yzerman, Igor Larionov, Chris Chelios, Pavel Datsyuk, Kris Draper, Tomas Holstrom, Darren McCarty, Jason Williams, Jiri Fischer, Jiri Slegr, Sean Avery, Maxim Kuznetsov, Uwe Krupp, Jesse Wallin, Manny Legace, Dominik Hasek, Ladislav Kohn

Carolina Hurricanes: Craig Adams, Kevyn Adams, Bates Battaglia, Jesse Boulerice, Rod Brind'Amour, Erik Cole, Jeff Daniels, Ron Francis, Martin Gelinas, Bret Hedican, Jeff Heerema, Sean Hill, Arturs Irbe, Sami Kapanen, Darren Langdon, Craig MacDonald, Tomas Malec, Marek Malik, Jeff O'Neill, Jean-Marc Pelletier, Randy Petruk, Jaroslav Svoboda, David Tanabe, Nick Tselios, Josef Vasicek, Niclas Wallin, Aaron Ward, Kevin Weekes, Glen Wesley, Tommy Westlund

THE STATS
_____

CAREER REGULAR
SEASON

CAREER REGULAR SEASON

Career Games

Player	Games
Gordie Howe	1767
Larry Murphy	1615
Ray Bourque	1612
Mark Messier	1602
Ron Francis	1569
Alex Delvecchio	1549
John Bucyk	1540
Scott Stevens	1516
Wayne Gretzky	1487
Tim Horton	1446
Dave Andreychuk	1443
Phil Housley	1437
Mike Gartner	1432
Pat Verbeek	1424
Doug Gilmour	1412
Harry Howell	1411
Norm Ullman	1410
Paul Coffey	1409
Dale Hunter	1407
Stan Mikita	1394
Doug Mohns	1390
Larry Robinson	1384
Dean Prentice	1378
Steve Yzerman	1362
Ron Stewart	1353
Marcel Dionne	1348
Al MacInnis	1333
Guy Carbonneau	1318
Red Kelly	1316
Dave Keon	1296

Career Goals

Player	Goals
Wayne Gretzky	894
Gordie Howe	801
Marcel Dionne	731
Phil Esposito	717
Mike Gartner	708
Brett Hull	679
Mark Messier	658
Steve Yzerman	658
Mario Lemieux	654
Luc Robitaille	620
Bobby Hull	610
Dino Ciccarelli	608
Jari Kurri	601
Dave Andreychuk	593
Mike Bossy	573
Guy Lafleur	560
John Bucyk	556
Michel Goulet	548
Maurice Richard	544
Stan Mikita	541
Frank Mahovlich	533
Bryan Trottier	524
Pat Verbeek	522
Dale Hawerchuk	518
Ron Francis	514
Gil Perreault	512
Jean Beliveau	507
Brendan Shanahan	503
Joe Mullen	502
Lanny McDonald	500

Career Assists

Player	Assists
Wayne Gretzky	1963
Ron Francis	1187
Ray Bourque	1169
Mark Messier	1146
Paul Coffey	1135
Gordie Howe	1049
Marcel Dionne	1040
Adam Oates	1027
Steve Yzerman	1004
Mario Lemieux	947
Doug Gilmour	945
Larry Murphy	929
Stan Mikita	926
Bryan Trottier	901
Dale Hawerchuk	891
Al MacInnis	880
Phil Esposito	873
Phil Housley	871
Denis Savard	865
Bobby Clarke	852
Alex Delvecchio	825
Gil Perreault	814
John Bucyk	813
Jari Kurri	797
Guy Lafleur	793
Peter Stastny	789
Jean Ratelle	776
Joe Sakic	774
Bernie Federko	761
Larry Robinson	750

Career Points

Player	Points
Wayne Gretzky	2857
Gordie Howe	1850
Mark Messier	1804
Marcel Dionne	1771
Ron Francis	1701
Steve Yzerman	1662
Mario Lemieux	1601
Phil Esposito	1590
Ray Bourque	1579

Paul Coffey	1531
Stan Mikita	1467
Bryan Trottier	1425
Dale Hawerchuk	1409
Jari Kurri	1398
Doug Gilmour	1384
John Bucyk	1369
Adam Oates	1357
Guy Lafleur	1353
Denis Savard	1338
Mike Gartner	1335
Gil Perreault	1326
Luc Robitaille	1288
Alex Delvecchio	1281
Jean Ratelle	1267
Joe Sakic	1257
Dave Andreychuk	1247
Brett Hull	1246
Peter Stastny	1239
Norm Ullman	1229
Jean Beliveau	1219

Career Plus/Minus

Player	+/-
Larry Robinson	730
Bobby Orr	597
Ray Bourque	528
Wayne Gretzky	518
Bobby Clarke	506
Denis Potvin	460
Serge Savard	460
Guy Lafleur	453
Bryan Trottier	452
Brad McCrimmon	444
Mark Howe	400
Steve Shutt	393
Mike Bossy	381
Scott Stevens	372
Brad Park	358
Dallas Smith	355
Al MacInnis	351
Jacques Lemaire	349
Guy Lapointe	329
Craig Ramsay	323
Bill Hajt	321
Bill Barber	316
Brian Propp	310
Andre Dupont	299
Jean Ratelle	299
Jari Kurri	298
Jimmy Watson	295
Paul Coffey	294
Chris Chelios	291
Wayne Cashman	281

Career Power Play Goals

Player	PPG
Phil Esposito	249
Dave Andreychuk	245
Brett Hull	243
Marcel Dionne	234
Dino Ciccarelli	233
Luc Robitaille	229
Mario Lemieux	219
Mike Gartner	217
Wayne Gretzky	204
Brian Bellows	198
Joe Nieuwendyk	193
Steve Yzerman	190
Pat Verbeek	186
Dale Hawerchuk	182
Mike Bossy	181
Michel Goulet	178
Brendan Shanahan	175
Ray Bourque	173
Ron Francis	173
Pierre Turgeon	173
Mark Messier	170
Steve Larmer	162
Bryan Trottier	161
Al MacInnis	157
Pat LaFontaine	156
Jari Kurri	155
Yvan Cournoyer	153
Guy Lafleur	153
Joe Sakic	153
Bernie Nicholls	152
Jeremy Roenick	152

Career Power Play Assists
(since 1989-90)

Player	PPA
Brian Leetch	352
Ray Bourque	345
Adam Oates	341
Al MacInnis	332
Wayne Gretzky	330
Ron Francis	325
Phil Housley	315
Joe Sakic	299
Paul Coffey	281
Gary Suter	267
Mark Recchi	249
Mark Messier	248
Doug Gilmour	245
Nicklas Lidstrom	242
Larry Murphy	238
Steve Yzerman	238
Pierre Turgeon	236

CAREER REGULAR SEASON

Doug Weight	236
Vincent Damphousse	230
Chris Chelios	228
Jaromir Jagr	228
Mario Lemieux	223
Theo Fleury	220
Mike Modano	220
Sergei Zubov	208
Brett Hull	207
Jeremy Roenick	206
Craig Janney	205
Fredrik Olausson	202
Teemu Selanne	197

Career Short-handed Goals

Player	SHG
Wayne Gretzky	73
Mark Messier	60
Steve Yzerman	50
Mario Lemieux	48
Butch Goring	40
Jari Kurri	39
Dave Poulin	39
Theo Fleury	35
Dirk Graham	35
Derek Sanderson	34
Pavel Bure	33
Guy Carbonneau	32
Bobby Clarke	32
Bill Barber	31
Joe Sakic	31
Peter Bondra	30
Russ Courtnall	29
Sergei Fedorov	29
Craig MacLavish	29
Esa Tikkanen	29
Mark Howe	28
Bernie Nicholls	28
Dave Reid	28
Doug Smail	28
Craig Ramsay	27
Dave Keon	26
Don Luce	26
Jeremy Roenick	26
Eddie Westfall	26
Neal Broten	25
Tom Fitzgerald	25
Rick Middleton	25
Mike Modano	25
Larry Patey	25

Career Short-handed Assists (since 1989-90)

Player	SHA
Mark Messier	40
Chris Chelios	28
Steve Yzerman	25
Andrew Cassels	24
Sergei Fedorov	23
Adam Oates	22
Kelly Miller	20
Rod Brind'Amour	19
Dave Hannan	19
Vincent Damphousse	18
Nicklas Lidstrom	18
Al MacInnis	18
Mats Sundin	18
Kelly Buchberger	17
Shawn Burr	17
Ron Francis	17
Bret Hedican	17
Jeremy Roenick	17
Peter Forsberg	16
Doug Gilmour	16
Jari Kurri	16
Michael Peca	16
Dave Reid	16
Ray Bourque	15
Neal Broten	15
Pavel Bure	15
Theo Fleury	15
Steve Larmer	15
Jyrki Lumme	15
Joe Sakic	15
Ron Wilson	15

Career Game-Winning Goals

Player	GWG
Phil Esposito	118
Brett Hull	100
Guy Lafleur	97
Wayne Gretzky	91
Mike Gartner	90
Steve Yzerman	87
Glenn Anderson	85
Mark Messier	84
Luc Robitaille	83
Brendan Shanahan	83
Mike Bossy	82
Jaromir Jagr	81
Gil Perreault	81
Joe Nieuwendyk	79
Pierre Turgeon	79
Ron Francis	76
Marcel Dionne	74

Dino Ciccarelli	73
Joe Mullen	73
Jeremy Roenick	73
Jari Kurri	72
Stephane Richer	72
Joe Sakic	71
Steve Thomas	71
Mario Lemieux	70
John Bucyk	69
Dave Andreychuk	68
Yvan Cournoyer	68
Vincent Damphousse	68
Sergei Fedorov	68
Bryan Trottier	68

Career Game-Tying Goals

Player	GTG
Marcel Dionne	39
Phil Esposito	29
Wayne Gretzky	26
Bobby Hull	24
Lanny McDonald	24
Garry Unger	24
Bobby Clarke	23
Danny Gare	23
Reggie Leach	23
Pit Martin	23
Guy Lafleur	22
Rick Martin	22
Jean Pronovost	22
Darryl Sittler	22
Mike Gartner	21
Ken Hodge	21
Jean-Paul Parise	21
Dino Ciccarelli	20
Yvan Cournoyer	20
Vic Hadfield	20
Don Lever	20
Nick Libett	20
Jean Ratelle	20
Charlie Simmer	20
Bill Barber	19
Red Berenson	19
Ivan Boldirev	19
Pete Mahovlich	19
Stan Mikita	19
Paul Henderson	18
Rick Kehoe	18
Blaine Stoughton	18

Career Penalty Minutes

Player	PIM
Dave "Tiger" Williams	3966
Dale Hunter	3565
Marty McSorley	3381
Bob Probert	3300
Tim Hunter	3146
Rob Ray	3097
Craig Berube	3049
Chris Nilan	3043
Tie Domi	3027
Rick Tocchet	2974
Pat Verbeek	2905
Dave Manson	2792
Scott Stevens	2722
Willi Plett	2572
Gino Odjick	2567
Chris Chelios	2556
Joey Kocur	2519
Ken Daneyko	2486
Basil McRae	2457
Ulf Samuelsson	2453
Jay Wells	2359
Garth Butcher	2302
Shane Churla	2301
Dave Schultz	2294
Shayne Corson	2279
Laurie Boschman	2265
Gary Roberts	2251
Ken Baumgartner	2244
Rob Ramage	2226
Kevin Dineen	2217

Career Wins

Player	Wins
Patrick Roy	516
Terry Sawchuk	447
Jacques Plante	435
Tony Esposito	423
Glenn Hall	407
Grant Fuhr	403
Mike Vernon	385
John Vanbiesbrouck	374
Andy Moog	372
Tom Barrasso	368
Ed Belfour	364
Rogie Vachon	355
Curtis Joseph	346
Gump Worsley	335
Harry Lumley	330
Martin Brodeur	324
Billy Smith	305
Turk Broda	302
Ron Hextall	296

CAREER REGULAR SEASON

Mike Richter	296	Rogie Vachon	127
Mike Liut	293	Bernie Parent	121
Ed Giacomin	289	John Vanbiesbrouck	119
Dominik Hasek	288	Patrick Roy	118
Dan Bouchard	286	Grant Fuhr	114
Tiny Thompson	284	Dan Bouchard	113
Sean Burke	276	Billy Smith	105
Kelly Hrudey	271	Turk Broda	101
Bernie Parent	271	Ed Belfour	100
Gilles Meloche	270	Ed Giacomin	97
Don Beaupre	268	Cesare Maniago	96
		Sean Burke	92

Career Losses

Player	Losses	Mike Vernon	92
Gump Worsley	352	Johnny Bower	90
Gilles Meloche	351	Greg Millen	89
John Vanbiesbrouck	346	Kelly Hrudey	88
Terry Sawchuk	331	Andy Moog	88
Harry Lumley	329	Tom Barrasso	86
Glenn Hall	326	Martin Brodeur	85
Tony Esposito	306	Al Rollins	83
Patrick Roy	300	Roy Worters	83
Sean Burke	295	Chico Resch	82
Grant Fuhr	295	Curtis Joseph	81
Rogie Vachon	291		

Career Shots Against

Greg Millen	284	Player	SA
Bill Ranford	279	Patrick Roy	26630
Don Beaupre	277	John Vanbiesbrouck	24708
Tom Barrasso	273	Grant Fuhr	24379
Mike Vernon	273	Tom Barrasso	21958
Mike Liut	271	Curtis Joseph	20640
Kelly Hrudey	265	Kelly Hrudey	20328
Kirk McLean	262	Mike Vernon	19967
Gary Smith	261	Sean Burke	19914
Curtis Joseph	260	Andy Moog	19328
Cesare Maniago	259	Mike Richter	18890
Eddie Johnston	257	Don Beaupre	18689
Mike Richter	252	Ed Belfour	18426
Ken Wregget	248	Bill Ranford	18269
Jacques Plante	247	Kirk McLean	16882
Ed Belfour	242	Ken Wregget	16675
Billy Smith	233	Dominik Hasek	16530
Dan Bouchard	232	Ron Hextall	16366
Felix Potvin	232	Felix Potvin	16187
		Guy Hebert	14400

Career Ties

Player	Ties	Martin Brodeur	14329
Terry Sawchuk	171	Arturs Irbe	13989
Glenn Hall	163	Ron Tugnutt	13313
Tony Esposito	151	Mike Liut	13179
Gump Worsley	150	Jocelyn Thibault	12296
Jacques Plante	145	Greg Millen	12246
Harry Lumley	142	Bob Essensa	12105
Gilles Meloche	131	Jeff Hackett	12083
		Glenn Healy	12058

Daren Puppa	11680
Chris Osgood	11505

Career Goals Against

Player	GA
Grant Fuhr	2756
Gilles Meloche	2756
Tony Esposito	2563
John Vanbiesbrouck	2503
Patrick Roy	2409
Gump Worsley	2407
Terry Sawchuk	2390
Tom Barrasso	2369
Rogie Vachon	2310
Greg Millen	2281
Glenn Hall	2222
Mike Liut	2219
Harry Lumley	2206
Mike Vernon	2206
Kelly Hrudey	2174
Don Beaupre	2151
Andy Moog	2097
Dan Bouchard	2063
Bill Ranford	2042
Billy Smith	2031
Sean Burke	1979
Jacques Plante	1964
Ken Wregget	1917
Curtis Joseph	1908
Kirk McLean	1904
Eddie Johnston	1852
Mike Richter	1806
Cesare Maniago	1773
Chico Resch	1761
Ed Belfour	1743

Career Goals Against Average (minimum 100 GPI)

Player	GAA
Alex Connell	1.91
George Hainsworth	1.93
Chuck Gardiner	2.02
Roman Cechmanek	2.03
Lorne Chabot	2.04
Tiny Thompson	2.08
Dave Kerr	2.15
Martin Brodeur	2.21
Dominik Hasek	2.23
Roman Turek	2.23
Ken Dryden	2.24
Evgeni Nabokov	2.24
Roy Worters	2.27

Flat Walsh	2.31
Clint Benedict	2.32
Norman Smith	2.33
Andy Aitkenhead	2.35
Gerry McNeil	2.36
Bill Durnan	2.36
Martin Biron	2.36
Jacques Plante	2.38
Chris Osgood	2.42
Hap Holmes	2.43
Brian Boucher	2.45
John Roach	2.46
Ed Belfour	2.47
Glenn Hall	2.49
Patrick Lalime	2.49
Jose Theodore	2.49
Terry Sawchuk	2.50

Career Shutouts

Player	ShO
Terry Sawchuk	103
George Hainsworth	94
Glenn Hall	84
Jacques Plante	82
Alex Connell	81
Tiny Thompson	81
Tony Esposito	76
Lorne Chabot	73
Harry Lumley	71
Roy Worters	67
Turk Broda	62
Dominik Hasek	61
Patrick Roy	61
Ed Belfour	58
Clint Benedict	58
John Roach	58
Martin Brodeur	55
Ed Giacomin	54
Bernie Parent	54
Dave Kerr	51
Rogie Vachon	51
Ken Dryden	46
Gump Worsley	43
Chuck Gardiner	42
Francis Brimsek	40
John Vanbiesbrouck	40
Tom Barrasso	37
Johnny Bower	37
Curtis Joseph	36
Bill Durnan	34
Chris Osgood	34

CAREER REGULAR SEASON

Career Saves

Player	Saves
Patrick Roy	24208
John Vanbiesbrouck	22185
Grant Fuhr	21603
Tom Barrasso	19566
Curtis Joseph	18732
Kelly Hrudey	18135
Sean Burke	17928
Mike Vernon	17756
Andy Moog	17220
Mike Richter	17084
Ed Belfour	16682
Don Beaupre	16512
Bill Ranford	16220
Dominik Hasek	15276
Kirk McLean	14963
Ken Wregget	14741
Felix Potvin	14665
Ron Hextall	14633
Guy Hebert	13093
Martin Brodeur	13057
Arturs Irbe	12599
Ron Tugnutt	11903
Mike Liut	11573
Jocelyn Thibault	11111
Jeff Hackett	10885
Bob Essensa	10828
Glenn Healy	10680
Greg Millen	10666
Daren Puppa	10472
Chris Osgood	10449

Player	SvPct
Manny Fernandez	.907
Tommy Salo	.906
Felix Potvin	.906
Byron Dafoe	.906
Tomas Vokoun	.906
Ed Belfour	.905
Mike Richter	.904
Jocelyn Thibault	904
Fred Brathwaite	.903
Trevor Kidd	.902
Jeff Hackett	901
Arturs Irbe	.901

Career Save Percentage (minimum 3000 SA)

Player	SvPct
Dominik Hasek	.924
Evgeni Nabokov	.916
Jose Theodore	.915
Roberto Luongo	.915
Steve Shields	.912
Martin Biron	.911
Martin Brodeur	.911
Jean-Sebastien Giguere	.911
Jamie Storr	.911
Mike Dunham	.911
Nikolai Khabibulin	.910
Guy Hebert	.909
Patrick Lalime	.909
Patrick Roy	.909
Chris Osgood	.908
Roman Turek	.908
Curtis Joseph	.908
Olaf Kolzig	.907

THE STATS

CAREER PLAYOFFS

CAREER PLAYOFFS

Career Playoff Games

Player	Games
Patrick Roy	240
Mark Messier	236
Guy Carbonneau	231
Larry Robinson	227
Claude Lemieux	226
Glenn Anderson	225
Bryan Trottier	221
Larry Murphy	215
Ray Bourque	214
Kevin Lowe	214
Chris Chelios	210
Scott Stevens	209
Wayne Gretzky	208
Mike Keane	207
Jari Kurri	200
Paul Coffey	194
Craig MacTavish	193
Brett Hull	186
Dale Hunter	186
Esa Tikkanen	186
Denis Potvin	185
Bobby Smith	184
Charlie Huddy	183
Bob Gainey	182
Doug Gilmour	182
Henri Richard	180
Craig Ludwig	177
Steve Yzerman	177
Al MacInnis	174
John Tonelli	172

Career Playoff Goals

Player	Goals
Wayne Gretzky	122
Mark Messier	109
Jari Kurri	106
Brett Hull	100
Glenn Anderson	93
Mike Bossy	85
Maurice Richard	82
Claude Lemieux	80
Jean Beliveau	79
Mario Lemieux	76
Dino Ciccarelli	73
Esa Tikkanen	72
Bryan Trottier	71
Gordie Howe	68
Steve Yzerman	67
Denis Savard	66
Jaromir Jagr	65
Joe Sakic	65
Yvan Cournoyer	64

Player	
Brian Propp	64
Bobby Smith	64
Bobby Hull	62
Phil Esposito	61
Jacques Lemaire	61
Doug Gilmour	60
Joe Mullen	60
Paul Coffey	59
Stan Mikita	59
Bernie Geoffrion	58
Guy Lafleur	58

Career Playoff Assists

Player	Assists
Wayne Gretzky	260
Mark Messier	186
Ray Bourque	139
Paul Coffey	137
Doug Gilmour	128
Jari Kurri	127
Glenn Anderson	121
Al MacInnis	120
Larry Robinson	116
Larry Murphy	115
Bryan Trottier	113
Sergei Fedorov	111
Denis Savard	109
Denis Potvin	108
Steve Yzerman	108
Chris Chelios	106
Adam Oates	106
Jean Beliveau	97
Mario Lemieux	96
Bobby Smith	96
Ron Francis	93
Gordie Howe	92
Stan Mikita	91
Brad Park	90
Craig Janney	86
Scott Stevens	86
Peter Forsberg	84
Brett Hull	84
Brian Propp	84
Joe Sakic	83

Career Playoff Points

Player	Points
Wayne Gretzky	382
Mark Messier	295
Jari Kurri	233
Glenn Anderson	214
Paul Coffey	196
Doug Gilmour	188
Brett Hull	184

CAREER PLAYOFFS

Bryan Trottier	184	Steve Larmer	26
Ray Bourque	180	Larry Robinson	26
Jean Beliveau	176		
Denis Savard	175		
Steve Yzerman	175		

Career Playoff Power Play Goals

		Player	PPG
Mario Lemieux	172	Brett Hull	37
Denis Potvin	164	Mike Bossy	35
Mike Bossy	160	Dino Ciccarelli	34
Sergei Fedorov	160	Wayne Gretzky	34
Gordie Howe	160	Mario Lemieux	29
Bobby Smith	160	Brian Propp	27
Al MacInnis	159	Al MacInnis	26
Claude Lemieux	157	Steve Yzerman	26
Larry Murphy	152	Jari Kurri	25
Stan Mikita	150	Cam Neely	25
Brian Propp	148	Mark Messier	24
Joe Sakic	148	Denis Savard	24
Jaromir Jagr	147	Bobby Smith	24
Larry Robinson	144	Brian Bellows	23
Adam Oates	143	Denis Potvin	23
Ron Francis	139	Joe Sakic	23
Jacques Lemaire	139	Glenn Anderson	22
Phil Esposito	137	Paul Coffey	21
		Tim Kerr	21

Career Playoff Plus/Minus

Player	+/-	Steve Larmer	21
Charlie Huddy	93	Claude Lemieux	21
Jari Kurri	88	Joe Nieuwendyk	21
Wayne Gretzky	86	Doug Gilmour	20
Randy Gregg	84	Larry Murphy	20
Glenn Anderson	67	Kevin Stevens	20
Paul Coffey	57	Jaromir Jagr	19
Mark Messier	52	Esa Tikkanen	19
Mark Howe	51	Bryan Trottier	18
Steve Smith	49	John LeClair	17
Kevin Lowe	46	Dave Andreychuk	16
Claude Lemieux	43	Mike Gartner	16
Chris Chelios	39	Mats Naslund	16
Sergei Fedorov	39	Bernie Nicholls	16
Peter Forsberg	38	Rick Tocchet	16
Brian Skrudland	35	Rick Vaive	16

Career Playoff Power Play Assists (since 1989-90)

Brendan Shanahan	34	Player	PPA
Sergei Zubov	33	Ray Bourque	51
Dave Hunter	32	Sergei Fedorov	48
Scott Stevens	32	Nicklas Lidstrom	48
Craig Ludwig	31	Mario Lemieux	46
Lee Fogolin	29	Joe Sakic	41
Larry Murphy	29	Paul Coffey	37
Ron Francis	28	Al MacInnis	37
Nicklas Lidstrom	28	Larry Murphy	37
Doug Gilmour	27	Doug Gilmour	36
Jaromir Jagr	27	Steve Yzerman	36
Mike Keane	27		
Kjell Samuelsson	27		

CAREER PLAYOFFS

Sergei Zubov	36	Steve Kasper	3
Ron Francis	35	Steve Konroyd	3
Adam Oates	33	Steve Larmer	3
Peter Forsberg	32	Todd Marchant	3
Brian Leetch	32	Rick Middleton	3
Mark Messier	32	Larry Murphy	3
Wayne Gretzky	30	Rick Paterson	3
Sandis Ozolinsh	30	Brian Propp	3
Steve Duchesne	29	Joe Sakic	3
Jeff Brown	26	Esa Tikkanen	3
Eric Desjardins	26	Dixon Ward	3
Brett Hull	26	Steve Yzerman	3
Brendan Shanahan	26	Peter Zezel	3
Brian Bellows	25		
Kevin Stevens	24		
Craig Janney	23		
Trevor Linden	23		
Joe Juneau	22		
Jason Woolley	22		
Scott Young	22		

Career Playoff Short-handed Goals

Player	SHG
Mark Messier	14
Wayne Gretzky	11
Jari Kurri	10
Hakan Loob	8
Mario Lemieux	7
Guy Carbonneau	6
Paul Coffey	6
Dave Poulin	6
Wayne Presley	6
Bill Barber	5
Bob Bourne	5
Sergei Fedorov	5
Anders Kallur	5
Kelly Miller	5
Brian Rolston	5
Rod Brind'Amour	4
Doug Brown	4
Shayne Corson	4
Russ Courtnall	4
Vincent Damphousse	4
Kris Draper	4
Lorne Henning	4
Brett Hull	4
Kirk Maltby	4
Ed Olczyk	4
Mark Osborne	4
Bryan Trottier	4
Scott Young	4
Brent Ashton	3
Billy Carroll	3

Career Playoff Short-handed Assists (since 1989-90)

Player	SHA
Steve Yzerman	7
Sergei Fedorov	6
Doug Gilmour	6
Eric Desjardins	5
Kris Draper	4
Ron Francis	4
Jari Kurri	4
Igor Larionov	4
Mike Ridley	4
Martin Brodeur	3
Shawn Burr	3
Chris Chelios	3
Wayne Gretzky	3
Calle Johansson	3
Claude Lemieux	3
Al MacInnis	3
Mark Messier	3
Mike Modano	3
Larry Murphy	3
Sergei Nemchinov	3
Dave Poulin	3
Brendan Shanahan	3
Scott Stevens	3
Mikael Andersson	2
Rod Brind'Amour	2
Doug Brown	2
Keith Brown	2
Pavel Bure	2
Guy Carbonneau	2
Pat Conacher	2
Russ Courtnall	2
Ken Daneyko	2
Tom Fitzgerald	2
Dirk Graham	2
Joe Juneau	2
Darius Kasparaitis	2

Jyrki Lumme	2
Craig MacTavish	2
Darren McCarty	2
Marty McSorley	2
Boris Mironov	2
Rem Murray	2
Dana Murzyn	2
Adam Oates	2
Chris Osgood	2
Chris Pronger	2
Marcus Ragnarsson	2
Bob Rouse	2
Mike Sullivan	2
Don Sweeney	2
Chris Tamer	2
Dixon Ward	2

Career Playoff Game Winning Goals

Player	GWG
Wayne Gretzky	24
Brett Hull	23
Claude Lemieux	19
Glenn Anderson	17
Mike Bossy	17
Jaromir Jagr	14
Jari Kurri	14
Joe Sakic	14
Dino Ciccarelli	13
Doug Gilmour	13
Stephane Richer	13
Bobby Smith	13
Vyacheslav Kozlov	12
Mark Messier	12
Joe Nieuwendyk	12
Brian Propp	12
Luc Robitaille	12
Bryan Trottier	12
Chris Drury	11
Sergei Fedorov	11
Peter Forsberg	11
Ron Francis	11
John LeClair	11
Mario Lemieux	11
Ken Linseman	11
Cam Neely	11
Esa Tikkanen	11
Steve Yzerman	11
Geoff Courtnall	10
Joe Murphy	10
Jeremy Roenick	10
Brendan Shanahan	10

Career Playoff Penalty Minutes

Player	PIM
Dale Hunter	727
Chris Nilan	531
Claude Lemieux	519
Rick Tocchet	471
Willi Plett	466
Dave "Tiger" Williams	455
Glenn Anderson	442
Tim Hunter	426
Dave Schultz	412
Duane Sutter	405
Scott Stevens	388
Chris Chelios	387
Jim Peplinski	382
Al Secord	382
Marty McSorley	374
Andre Dupont	352
Basil McRae	349
Dave Manson	343
Terry O'Reilly	335
Ken Linseman	325
Brian Skrudland	323
Sergio Momesso	311
Geoff Courtnall	306
Mel Bridgman	298
Ken Daneyko	294
Garry Howatt	289
Ulf Samuelsson	288
Steve Smith	288
Clark Gillies	287
Shane Churla	282

Career Playoff Wins

Player	Wins
Patrick Roy	148
Grant Fuhr	92
Billy Smith	88
Ken Dryden	80
Ed Belfour	79
Mike Vernon	77
Jacques Plante	71
Andy Moog	68
Martin Brodeur	67
Tom Barrasso	61
Turk Broda	60
Curtis Joseph	58
Terry Sawchuk	54
Gerry Cheevers	53
Dominik Hasek	53
Glenn Hall	49
Ron Hextall	47
Tony Esposito	45

Chris Osgood	41
Mike Richter	41
Gump Worsley	40
Bernie Parent	38
Kelly Hrudey	36
Johnny Bower	35
Pete Peeters	35
Felix Potvin	35
Kirk McLean	34
Don Beaupre	33
Francis Brimsek	32
Jon Casey	32

Career Playoff Losses

Player	Losses
Patrick Roy	90
Glenn Hall	65
Curtis Joseph	58
Ed Belfour	57
Andy Moog	57
Mike Vernon	56
Tom Barrasso	54
Tony Esposito	53
Grant Fuhr	50
Martin Brodeur	48
Terry Sawchuk	48
Harry Lumley	47
Kelly Hrudey	46
Ron Hextall	43
Turk Broda	39
Dominik Hasek	39
John Vanbiesbrouck	38
Felix Potvin	37
Francis Brimsek	36
Jacques Plante	36
Billy Smith	36
Ed Giacomin	35
Pete Peeters	35
Johnny Bower	34
Gerry Cheevers	34
Kirk McLean	34
Bernie Parent	33
Mike Richter	33
Ken Dryden	32
Mike Liut	32

Career Playoff Shots Against

Player	SA
Patrick Roy	6972
Grant Fuhr	4029
Ed Belfour	3815
Curtis Joseph	3577
Tom Barrasso	3569

Mike Vernon	3525
Martin Brodeur	2769
Dominik Hasek	2750
Andy Moog	2694
Ron Hextall	2668
Kelly Hrudey	2607
Mike Richter	2228
Felix Potvin	2169
Kirk McLean	2134
John Vanbiesbrouck	2073
Jon Casey	1832
Chris Osgood	1826
Ken Wregget	1796
Don Beaupre	1580
Bill Ranford	1550
Arturs Irbe	1449
Greg Millen	1347
Olaf Kolzig	1184
Reggie Lemelin	1153
Mike Liut	1082
Sean Burke	993
Pete Peeters	913
Glenn Healy	905
Mario Gosselin	844
Billy Smith	805

Career Playoff Goals Against

Player	GA
Patrick Roy	568
Grant Fuhr	430
Andy Moog	377
Mike Vernon	367
Tom Barrasso	349
Billy Smith	348
Glenn Hall	320
Ed Belfour	308
Tony Esposito	308
Curtis Joseph	304
Kelly Hrudey	283
Ron Hextall	276
Ken Dryden	274
Terry Sawchuk	266
Gerry Cheevers	242
Jacques Plante	237
Pete Peeters	232
Martin Brodeur	226
Don Beaupre	220
Mike Liut	215
Turk Broda	211
Dominik Hasek	202
Mike Richter	202
Harry Lumley	198
Kirk McLean	198

Felix Potvin	195
Greg Millen	193
Jon Casey	192
Gump Worsley	189
Francis Brimsek	186
Reggie Lemelin	186

Career Playoff Goals Against Average (minimum 30 GPI)

Player	GAA
Lorne Chabot	1.54
Dave Kerr	1.74
Tiny Thompson	1.88
Martin Brodeur	1.88
Gerry McNeil	1.89
George Hainsworth	1.93
Turk Broda	1.98
Dominik Hasek	2.03
Bill Durnan	2.07
Jacques Plante	2.14
Ed Belfour	2.14
Olaf Kolzig	2.15
Chris Osgood	2.21
Patrick Roy	2.30
Ken Dryden	2.40
Bernie Parent	2.43
Johnny Bower	2.47
John Davidson	2.48
Harry Lumley	2.49
Chico Resch	2.50
Curtis Joseph	2.53
Terry Sawchuk	2.54
Francis Brimsek	2.54
Johnny Mowers	2.55
Felix Potvin	2.64
Cesare Maniago	2.67
John Vanbiesbrouck	2.68
Mike Vernon	2.68
Mike Richter	2.68
Gerry Cheevers	2.69

Career Playoff Shutouts

Player	ShO
Patrick Roy	22
Curtis Joseph	15
Jacques Plante	14
Turk Broda	13
Martin Brodeur	13
Dominik Hasek	12
Terry Sawchuk	12
Ed Belfour	11
Ken Dryden	10
Clint Benedict	9

Chris Osgood	9
Mike Richter	9
Gerry Cheevers	8
George Hainsworth	8
Dave Kerr	8
Felix Potvin	8
Harry Lumley	7
John Roach	7
Tiny Thompson	7
Tom Barrasso	6
Tony Esposito	6
Grant Fuhr	6
Glenn Hall	6
Kirk McLean	6
Bernie Parent	6
Mike Vernon	6
Johnny Bower	5
Lorne Chabot	5
Chuck Gardiner	5
Olaf Kolzig	5
Gerry McNeil	5
Billy Smith	5
John Vanbiesbrouck	5
Gump Worsley	5

Career Playoff Saves

Player	Saves
Patrick Roy	6398
Grant Fuhr	3618
Ed Belfour	3507
Curtis Joseph	3272
Tom Barrasso	3218
Mike Vernon	3154
Dominik Hasek	2548
Martin Brodeur	2543
Andy Moog	2395
Ron Hextall	2391
Kelly Hrudey	2319
Mike Richter	2025
Felix Potvin	1974
Kirk McLean	1936
John Vanbiesbrouck	1895
Chris Osgood	1665
Jon Casey	1640
Ken Wregget	1632
Don Beaupre	1407
Bill Ranford	1390
Arturs Irbe	1307
Greg Millen	1191
Olaf Kolzig	1098
Reggie Lemelin	1013
Mike Liut	968
Sean Burke	881
Pete Peeters	805

CAREER PLAYOFFS

Glenn Healy	796
Mario Gosselin	742
Billy Smith	725

Career Playoff Save Percentage (minimum 1000 SA)

Player	SvPct
Olaf Kolzig	.927
Dominik Hasek	.927
Ed Belfour	.919
Martin Brodeur	.918
Patrick Roy	.918
Curtis Joseph	.915
John Vanbiesbrouck	.914
Chris Osgood	.912
Felix Potvin	.910
Mike Richter	.909
Ken Wregget	.909
Kirk McLean	.907
Arturs Irbe	.902
Tom Barrasso	.902
Grant Fuhr	.898
Bill Ranford	.897
Ron Hextall	.896
Jon Casey	.895
Mike Vernon	.895
Mike Liut	.895
Don Beaupre	.891
Kelly Hrudey	.890
Andy Moog	.889
Greg Millen	.884
Reggie Lemelin	.879

THE STATS

INDIVIDUAL SINGLE
SEASON

INDIVIDUAL SINGLE SEASON

Individual Single Season Top 30 Lists (Regular Season)

Games Played

Season	Player	GP
1992-93	Jimmy Carson	86
1993-94	Bob Kudelski	86
1993-94	Glenn Anderson	85
1993-94	Mark Lamb	85
1993-94	Joe Reekie	85
2000-01	Bill Guerin	85
1992-93	Jeremy Roenick	84
1992-93	Steve Yzerman	84
1992-93	Pat LaFontaine	84
1992-93	Luc Robitaille	84
1992-93	Mark Recchi	84
1992-93	Adam Oates	84
1992-93	Craig Janney	84
1992-93	Steve Larmer	84
1992-93	Vincent Damphousse	84
1992-93	Mike Gartner	84
1992-93	Trevor Linden	84
1992-93	Dale Hunter	84
1992-93	Dave Gagner	84
1992-93	Russ Courtnall	84
1992-93	Joe Juneau	84
1992-93	Nicklas Lidstrom	84
1992-93	Chris Chelios	84
1992-93	Garth Butcher	84
1992-93	Andrew Cassels	84
1992-93	Geoff Courtnall	84
1992-93	Ken Daneyko	84
1992-93	Mike Donnelly	84
1992-93	Gaetan Duchesne	84
1992-93	Mike Eagles	84
1992-93	Ron Francis	84
1992-93	Dirk Graham	84
1992-93	Adam Graves	84
1992-93	Mike Krushelnyski	84
1992-93	Shawn McEachern	84
1992-93	Mike McPhee	84
1992-93	Kelly Miller	84
1992-93	Sergio Momesso	84
1992-93	Petr Nedved	84
1992-93	Dave Poulin	84
1992-93	Mike Ridley	84
1992-93	Christian Ruuttu	84
1992-93	Rich Sutter	84
1992-93	Don Sweeney	84
1992-93	Pat Verbeek	84
1992-93	Teemu Selanne	84
1992-93	Dean Evason	84
1992-93	Darrin Shannon	84
1992-93	Rob Zamuner	84
1992-93	Doug Zmolek	84
1993-94	Jeremy Roenick	84
1993-94	Joe Sakic	84
1993-94	Mark Recchi	84
1993-94	Brian Leetch	84
1993-94	Larry Murphy	84
1993-94	Vincent Damphousse	84
1993-94	Mats Sundin	84
1993-94	Rod Brind'Amour	84
1993-94	Trevor Linden	84
1993-94	Russ Courtnall	84
1993-94	Nicklas Lidstrom	84
1993-94	Eric Desjardins	84
1993-94	Craig Berube	84
1993-94	Rob Blake	84
1993-94	Kelly Buchberger	84
1993-94	Sylvain Cote	84
1993-94	Gaetan Duchesne	84
1993-94	Adam Graves	84
1993-94	Mark Janssens	84
1993-94	Calle Johansson	84
1993-94	Grant Ledyard	84
1993-94	Sylvain Lefebvre	84
1993-94	Craig Ludwig	84
1993-94	Kelly Miller	84
1993-94	Joe Mullen	84
1993-94	Gord Murphy	84
1993-94	Robert Reichel	84
1993-94	Pat Verbeek	84
1993-94	Randy Wood	84
1993-94	Ted Donato	84
1993-94	Martin Straka	84
1993-94	Keith Tkachuk	84
1993-94	Chris Gratton	84
1993-94	Rob Gaudreau	84
1993-94	Alexandre Daigle	84
1993-94	Darryl Sydor	84
1993-94	Brad May	84
1993-94	Richard Smehlik	84
1993-94	Doug Weight	84
1993-94	Zdeno Ciger	84
1993-94	Joe Sacco	84
1993-94	Bill Lindsay	84
1995-96	Craig Janney	84
1995-96	Darryl Sydor	84

Goals

Season	Player	G
1981-82	Wayne Gretzky	92
1983-84	Wayne Gretzky	87
1990-91	Brett Hull	86
1988-89	Mario Lemieux	85
1970-71	Phil Esposito	76
1992-93	Alexander Mogilny	76

INDIVIDUAL SINGLE SEASON

1992-93 Teemu Selanne	76		1990-91 Adam Oates	90
1984-85 Wayne Gretzky	73		1991-92 Wayne Gretzky	90
1989-90 Brett Hull	72		1974-75 Bobby Orr	89
1982-83 Wayne Gretzky	71		1974-75 Bobby Clarke	89
1984-85 Jari Kurri	71		1975-76 Bobby Clarke	89
1987-88 Mario Lemieux	70			
1988-89 Bernie Nicholls	70		**Points**	
1991-92 Brett Hull	70		*Season Player*	*Pts*
1978-79 Mike Bossy	69		1985-86 Wayne Gretzky	215
1992-93 Mario Lemieux	69		1981-82 Wayne Gretzky	212
1995-96 Mario Lemieux	69		1984-85 Wayne Gretzky	208
1973-74 Phil Esposito	68		1983-84 Wayne Gretzky	205
1980-81 Mike Bossy	68		1988-89 Mario Lemieux	199
1985-86 Jari Kurri	68		1982-83 Wayne Gretzky	196
1971-72 Phil Esposito	66		1986-87 Wayne Gretzky	183
1982-83 Lanny McDonald	66		1987-88 Mario Lemieux	168
1988-89 Steve Yzerman	65		1988-89 Wayne Gretzky	168
1981-82 Mike Bossy	64		1980-81 Wayne Gretzky	164
1992-93 Luc Robitaille	63		1990-91 Wayne Gretzky	163
1986-87 Wayne Gretzky	62		1995-96 Mario Lemieux	161
1989-90 Steve Yzerman	62		1992-93 Mario Lemieux	160
1995-96 Jaromir Jagr	62		1988-89 Steve Yzerman	155
1974-75 Phil Esposito	61		1970-71 Phil Esposito	152
1975-76 Reggie Leach	61		1988-89 Bernie Nicholls	150
1985-86 Mike Bossy	61		1987-88 Wayne Gretzky	149
			1995-96 Jaromir Jagr	149
Assists			1992-93 Pat LaFontaine	148
Season Player	*A*		1981-82 Mike Bossy	147
1985-86 Wayne Gretzky	163		1973-74 Phil Esposito	145
1984-85 Wayne Gretzky	135		1989-90 Wayne Gretzky	142
1982-83 Wayne Gretzky	125		1992-93 Adam Oates	142
1990-91 Wayne Gretzky	122		1985-86 Mario Lemieux	141
1986-87 Wayne Gretzky	121		1970-71 Bobby Orr	139
1981-82 Wayne Gretzky	120		1981-82 Peter Stastny	139
1983-84 Wayne Gretzky	118		1985-86 Paul Coffey	138
1988-89 Wayne Gretzky	114		1979-80 Wayne Gretzky	137
1988-89 Mario Lemieux	114		1979-80 Marcel Dionne	137
1980-81 Wayne Gretzky	109		1992-93 Steve Yzerman	137
1987-88 Wayne Gretzky	109			
1970-71 Bobby Orr	102		**Plus/Minus**	
1989-90 Wayne Gretzky	102		*Season Player*	*+/-*
1987-88 Mario Lemieux	98		1970-71 Bobby Orr	124
1992-93 Adam Oates	97		1976-77 Larry Robinson	120
1992-93 Pat LaFontaine	95		1984-85 Wayne Gretzky	98
1992-93 Doug Gilmour	95		1970-71 Dallas Smith	94
1981-82 Peter Stastny	93		1976-77 Guy Lafleur	89
1985-86 Mario Lemieux	93		1976-77 Steve Shutt	88
1993-94 Wayne Gretzky	92		1971-72 Bobby Orr	86
1995-96 Mario Lemieux	92		1985-86 Mark Howe	85
1995-96 Ron Francis	92		1973-74 Bobby Orr	84
1992-93 Mario Lemieux	91		1975-76 Bobby Clarke	83
1973-74 Bobby Orr	90		1985-86 Brad McCrimmon	83
1985-86 Paul Coffey	90		1981-82 Wayne Gretzky	81
1988-89 Steve Yzerman	90		1974-75 Bobby Orr	80

INDIVIDUAL SINGLE SEASON

1974-75 Bobby Clarke	79	
1976-77 Serge Savard	79	
1972-73 Jacques Laperriere	78	
1981-82 Brian Engblom	78	
1978-79 Bryan Trottier	76	
1983-84 Wayne Gretzky	76	
1984-85 Jari Kurri	76	
1975 76 Bill Barber	74	
1975-76 Steve Shutt	73	
1975-76 Reggie Leach	73	
1977-78 Guy Lafleur	73	
1970-71 Phil Esposito	71	
1970-71 Ken Hodge	71	
1974-75 Serge Savard	71	
1975-76 Pete Mahovlich	71	
1977-78 Larry Robinson	71	
1978-79 Denis Potvin	71	
1985-86 Wayne Gretzky	71	

Power Play Goals

Season Player	PPG
1985-86 Tim Kerr	34
1992-93 Dave Andreychuk	32
1987-88 Joe Nieuwendyk	31
1988-89 Mario Lemieux	31
1995-96 Mario Lemieux	31
1987-88 Michel Goulet	29
1990-91 Brett Hull	29
1992-93 Brett Hull	29
1971-72 Phil Esposito	28
1980-81 Mike Bossy	28
1985-86 Michel Goulet	28
1991-92 Dave Andreychuk	28
1974-75 Phil Esposito	27
1978-79 Mike Bossy	27
1989-90 Brett Hull	27
1992-93 Alexander Mogilny	27
1986-87 Tim Kerr	26
1991-92 Luc Robitaille	26
1992-93 Kevin Stevens	26
1970-71 Phil Esposito	25
1977-78 Mike Bossy	25
1988-89 Tim Kerr	25
1989-90 Cam Neely	25
1993-94 Brett Hull	25
1993-94 Pavel Bure	25
1998-99 Teemu Selanne	25
1988-89 Rob Brown	24
1992-93 Luc Robitaille	24
1992-93 Pierre Turgeon	24
1992-93 Adam Oates	24
1992-93 Teemu Selanne	24
1993-94 Jeremy Roenick	24
1993-94 Luc Robitaille	24

Power Play Assists

Season Player	PPA
1987-88 Mario Lemieux	58
1988-89 Paul Coffey	53
1990-91 Wayne Gretzky	51
1992-93 Phil Housley	50
1988-89 Mario Lemieux	49
1995-96 Mario Lemieux	48
1990-91 Al MacInnis	47
1993-94 Wayne Gretzky	47
1991-92 Phil Housley	46
1992-93 Paul Coffey	46
1985-86 Mario Lemieux	45
1990-91 Brian Leetch	45
1992-93 Dale Hawerchuk	44
1992-93 Doug Gilmour	44
1991-92 Dale Hawerchuk	43
1992-93 Pat LaFontaine	43
1991-92 Wayne Gretzky	42
1993-94 Ray Bourque	42
1995-96 Ron Francis	42
1992-93 Ron Francis	41
1995-96 Wayne Gretzky	41
1989-90 Al MacInnis	40
1993-94 Sergei Zubov	40
1989-90 Ray Bourque	39
1992-93 Mario Lemieux	39
1992-93 Chris Chelios	39
1995-96 Teemu Selanne	39
1989-90 Paul Coffey	38
1989-90 Gary Suter	38
1990-91 Adam Oates	38
1990-91 Ray Bourque	38
1992-93 Adam Oates	38

Short-handed Goals

Season Player	SHG
1988-89 Mario Lemieux	13
1983-84 Wayne Gretzky	12
1984-85 Wayne Gretzky	11
1974-75 Marcel Dionne	10
1987-88 Mario Lemieux	10
1988-89 Dirk Graham	10
1983-84 Kent Nilsson	9
1985-86 Paul Coffey	9
2001-02 Brian Rolston	9
1970-71 Dave Keon	8
1974-75 Don Luce	8
1975-76 Chuck Lefley	8
1980-81 Larry Patey	8
1987-88 Hakan Loob	8
1988-89 Bernie Nicholls	8
1988-89 Esa Tikkanen	8
1990-91 Dave Reid	8

INDIVIDUAL SINGLE SEASON

1991-92 Steve Yzerman	8	
1995-96 Mario Lemieux	8	
2000-01 Steve Sullivan	8	
1970-71 Eddie Westfall	7	
1971-72 Derek Sanderson	7	
1974-75 Craig Ramsay	7	
1974-75 Gregg Sheppard	7	
1980-81 Bob Bourne	7	
1983-84 Guy Carbonneau	7	
1984-85 Brian Propp	7	
1985-86 Mark Howe	7	
1986-87 Wayne Gretzky	7	
1987-88 Steve Larmer	7	
1987-88 Denis Savard	7	
1987-88 Bernie Nicholls	7	
1989-90 Steve Yzerman	7	
1989-90 Dave McLlwain	7	
1990-91 Theo Fleury	7	
1992-93 Steve Yzerman	7	
1992-93 Pavel Bure	7	
1993-94 Brendan Shanahan	7	
2000-01 Theo Fleury	7	
2000-01 Wes Walz	7	

Short-handed Assists

Season Player	SHA
1989-90 Jari Kurri	8
1992-93 Ron Francis	7
1993-94 Mark Messier	7
1993-94 Sergei Fedorov	7
1997-98 Bret Hedican	7
1988-89 Mark Messier	6
1988-89 Jari Kurri	6
1988-89 Craig MacTavish	6
1990-91 Steve Larmer	6
1990-91 Dave Hannan	6
1991-92 Mario Lemieux	6
1992-93 Shawn Burr	6
1995-96 Chris Chelios	6
1996-97 Mark Messier	6
1989-90 Mark Messier	5
1989-90 Mark Osborne	5
1990-91 Kirk Muller	5
1990-91 Chris Chelios	5
1990-91 Kelly Miller	5
1991-92 Mark Messier	5
1991-92 Dirk Graham	5
1992-93 Ray Bourque	5
1992-93 Sergei Fedorov	5
1992-93 Mats Sundin	5
1992-93 Kelly Buchberger	5
1993-94 Dave Hannan	5
1995-96 Steve Yzerman	5
1995-96 Russ Courtnall	5

1996-97 Ray Bourque	5	
1997-98 Theo Fleury	5	
1998-99 Mark Messier	5	
1999-00 Vincent Damphousse	5	
2000-01 Mike Eastwood	5	

Game-Winning Goals

Season Player	GWG
1970-71 Phil Esposito	16
1971-72 Phil Esposito	16
1983-84 Michel Goulet	16
1999-00 Pavel Bure	14
1984-85 Jari Kurri	13
1991-92 Jeremy Roenick	13
1993-94 Cam Neely	13
1997-98 Peter Bondra	13
1975-76 Guy Lafleur	12
1975-76 Yvan Cournoyer	12
1977-78 Guy Lafleur	12
1978-79 Guy Lafleur	12
1981-82 Wayne Gretzky	12
1982-83 Brian Propp	12
1986-87 Joe Mullen	12
1989-90 Brett Hull	12
1989-90 Cam Neely	12
1995-96 Jaromir Jagr	12
1999-00 Jeremy Roenick	12
2000-01 Joe Sakic	12
1968-69 Bobby Hull	11
1970-71 Bobby Hull	11
1972-73 Phil Esposito	11
1973-74 Ken Hodge	11
1974-75 Guy Lafleur	11
1975-76 Reggie Leach	11
1979-80 Danny Gare	11
1983-84 Wayne Gretzky	11
1983-84 Glenn Anderson	11
1983-84 Mike Bossy	11
1984-85 Mike Gartner	11
1987-88 Stephane Richer	11
1988-89 Joe Nieuwendyk	11
1989-90 John MacLean	11
1990-91 Brett Hull	11
1992-93 Adam Oates	11
1992-93 Alexander Mogilny	11
1992-93 Geoff Courtnall	11
1995-96 Sergei Fedorov	11
1997-98 Joe Nieuwendyk	11
1998-99 Brett Hull	11

Game Tying Goals

Season Player	GTG
1988-89 Mike Ridley	9
1981-82 Blaine Stoughton	7

INDIVIDUAL SINGLE SEASON

1971-72 Vic Hadfield	6	
1972-73 Yvan Cournoyer	6	
1973-74 Pit Martin	6	
1976-77 Phil Esposito	6	
1977-78 Danny Gare	6	
1982-83 Marcel Dionne	6	
1968-69 Bobby Hull	5	
1968-69 Andre Lacroix	5	
1968-69 Mike Walton	5	
1969-70 Bill Goldsworthy	5	
1970-71 Ken Hodge	5	
1971-72 Paul Henderson	5	
1973-74 Stan Mikita	5	
1974-75 Reggie Leach	5	
1974-75 J.Bob Kelly	5	
1975-76 Guy Lafleur	5	
1975-76 Reggie Leach	5	
1975-76 Garry Unger	5	
1977-78 Bill Barber	5	
1978-79 Marcel Dionne	5	
1979-80 Lanny McDonald	5	
1979-80 Real Cloutier	5	
1980-81 Wayne Babych	5	
1980-81 Mike Rogers	5	
1981-82 Dino Ciccarelli	5	
1981-82 Michel Goulet	5	
1981-82 Mark Napier	5	
1982-83 Mark Messier	5	
1996-97 Adam Graves	5	

Penalty Minutes

Season	Player	PIM
1974-75	Dave Schultz	472
1981-82	Paul Baxter	409
1991-92	Mike Peluso	408
1977-78	Dave Schultz	405
1992-93	Marty McSorley	399
1987-88	Bob Probert	398
1987-88	Basil McRae	382
1985-86	Joey Kocur	377
1988-89	Tim Hunter	375
1997-98	Donald Brashear	372
1996-97	Gino Odjick	371
1975-76	Steve Durbano	370
1992-93	Gino Odjick	370
1988-89	Basil McRae	365
1997-98	Tie Domi	365
1986-87	Tim Hunter	361
1984-85	Chris Nilan	358
1985-86	Torrie Robertson	358
1986-87	Dave "Tiger" Williams	358
1986-87	Brian Curran	356
1991-92	Rob Ray	354
2001-02	Peter Worrell	354

1988-89 Dave Manson	352	
1977-78 Dave "Tiger" Williams	351	
1989-90 Basil McRae	351	
1988-89 Marty McSorley	350	
1990-91 Rob Ray	350	
1973-74 Dave Schultz	348	
1991-92 Gino Odjick	348	
1993-94 Tie Domi	347	

Wins

Season	Player	W
1973-74	Bernie Parent	47
1950-51	Terry Sawchuk	44
1951-52	Terry Sawchuk	44
1974-75	Bernie Parent	44
1990-91	Ed Belfour	43
1992-93	Tom Barrasso	43
1997-98	Martin Brodeur	43
1999-00	Martin Brodeur	43
1955-56	Jacques Plante	42
1961-62	Jacques Plante	42
1975-76	Ken Dryden	42
1993-94	Mike Richter	42
1999-00	Roman Turek	42
2000-01	Martin Brodeur	42
1976-77	Ken Dryden	41
1992-93	Ed Belfour	41
1999-00	Olaf Kolzig	41
2001-02	Dominik Hasek	41
1954-55	Terry Sawchuk	40
1959-60	Jacques Plante	40
1964-65	Roger Crozier	40
1975-76	Wayne Stephenson	40
1982-83	Pete Peeters	40
1984-85	Pelle Lindbergh	40
1987-88	Grant Fuhr	40
2000-01	Patrick Roy	40
1971-72	Ken Dryden	39
1987-88	Mike Vernon	39
1995-96	Chris Osgood	39
1998-99	Martin Brodeur	39

Losses

Season	Player	L
1970-71	Gary Smith	48
1953-54	Al Rollins	47
1992-93	Peter Sidorkiewicz	46
1951-52	Harry Lumley	44
1950-51	Harry Lumley	41
1993-94	Craig Billington	41
1963-64	Eddie Johnston	40
1943-44	Tubby McAuley	39
1956-57	Al Rollins	39
1957-58	Glenn Hall	39

INDIVIDUAL SINGLE SEASON

1975-76 Denis Herron	39
1949-50 Francis Brimsek	38
1957-58 Ed Chadwick	38
1982-83 Greg Millen	38
1992-93 Bill Ranford	38
1993-94 Bob Essensa	37
1958-59 Terry Sawchuk	36
1963-64 Jacques Plante	36
1974-75 Ron Low	36
1976-77 Tony Esposito	36
1996-97 Felix Potvin	36
1929-30 Joe Miller	35
1972-73 Gerry Desjardins	35
1977-78 Pete LoPresti	35
1982-83 Chico Resch	35
1987-88 Ken Wregget	35
1956-57 Ed Chadwick	34
1962-63 Gump Worsley	34
1968-69 Gerry Desjardins	34
1969-70 Gary Smith	34
1971-72 Roger Crozier	34
1976-77 Jim Rutherford	34
1993-94 Bill Ranford	34
2001-02 Johan Hedberg	34

Ties

Season Player	T
1954-55 Harry Lumley	22
1973-74 Tony Esposito	21
1969-70 Bernie Parent	20
1950-51 Chuck Rayner	19
1962-63 Jacques Plante	19
1977-78 Dan Bouchard	19
1950-51 Jack Gelineau	18
1952-53 Gerry McNeil	18
1949-50 Bill Durnan	17
1954-55 Gump Worsley	17
1960-61 Glenn Hall	17
1974-75 Billy Smith	17
1977-78 Don Edwards	17
1951-52 Jim Henry	16
1951-52 Al Rollins	16
1952-53 Terry Sawchuk	16
1955-56 Glenn Hall	16
1968-69 Bernie Parent	16
1969-70 Cesare Maniago	16
1974-75 Ken Dryden	16
1979-80 Tony Esposito	16
1980-81 Richard Brodeur	16
1993-94 Arturs Irbe	16
1995-96 Grant Fuhr	16
1928-29 George Hainsworth	15
1942-43 Bert Gardiner	15
1949-50 Jack Gelineau	15

1950-51 Gerry McNeil	15
1952-53 Al Rollins	15
1954-55 John Henderson	15
1956-57 Ed Chadwick	15
1956-57 Al Rollins	15
1962-63 Glenn Hall	15
1971-72 Ken Dryden	15
1977-78 Denis Herron	15
1979-80 Phil Myre	15
1997-98 Mike Richter	15
1998-99 John Vanbiesbrouck	15

Shots Against

Season Player	SA
1996-97 Felix Potvin	2438
1993-94 Curtis Joseph	2382
1993-94 Bill Ranford	2325
1993-94 Kelly Hrudey	2219
1992-93 Curtis Joseph	2202
1996-97 Dominik Hasek	2177
1995-96 Grant Fuhr	2157
1997-98 Dominik Hasek	2149
1996-97 Curtis Joseph	2144
1995-96 Felix Potvin	2135
1996-97 Guy Hebert	2133
1992-93 Bob Essensa	2119
1998-99 Guy Hebert	2114
1996-97 Nikolai Khabibulin	2094
1987-88 Grant Fuhr	2066
1992-93 Bill Ranford	2065
1993-94 Arturs Irbe	2064
1982-83 Greg Millen	2056
1995-96 Bill Ranford	2054
1993-94 Bob Essensa	2051
1995-96 Sean Burke	2034
1995-96 Dominik Hasek	2011
1993-94 Felix Potvin	2010
1991-92 Tim Cheveldae	1978
2001-02 Olaf Kolzig	1977
2001-02 Jose Theodore	1972
1991-92 Bill Ranford	1971
1999-00 Olaf Kolzig	1957
1993-94 Patrick Roy	1956
2001-02 Milan Hnilicka	1956

Goals Against

Season Player	GA
1943-44 Tubby McAuley	310
1982-83 Greg Millen	282
1980-81 Greg Millen	258
1970-71 Gary Smith	256
1993-94 Craig Billington	254
1981-82 Mike Liut	250
1992-93 Peter Sidorkiewicz	250

INDIVIDUAL SINGLE SEASON

1950-51 Harry Lumley	246	
1980-81 Tony Esposito	246	
1987-88 Grant Fuhr	246	
1949-50 Francis Brimsek	244	
1975-76 Denis Herron	243	
1982-83 Chico Resch	242	
1951-52 Harry Lumley	241	
1980-81 John Garrett	241	
1985-86 Richard Brodeur	240	
1992-93 Bill Ranford	240	
1995-96 Bill Ranford	237	
1993-94 Bill Ranford	236	
1972-73 Gilles Melocho	235	
1974-75 Ron Low	235	
1982-83 Mike Liut	235	
1993-94 Bob Essensa	235	
1976-77 Tony Esposito	234	
1981-82 Tony Esposito	231	
1981-82 Dan Bouchard	230	
1981-82 Chico Resch	230	
1988-89 Sean Burke	230	
1988-89 Kelly Hrudey	230	
1991-92 Grant Fuhr	230	

Goals Against Average (minimum 20 GPI)

Season Player	GAA
1928-29 George Hainsworth	0.92
1927-28 George Hainsworth	1.05
1925-26 Alex Connell	1.12
1928-29 Tiny Thompson	1.15
1928-29 Roy Worters	1.15
1927-28 Alex Connell	1.24
1928-29 Dolly Dolson	1.37
1928-29 John Roach	1.41
1926-27 Clint Benedict	1.42
1928-29 Alex Connell	1.43
1926-27 Lorne Chabot	1.46
1933-34 Wilf Cude	1.47
1926-27 George Hainsworth	1.47
1928-29 Clint Benedict	1.49
1926-27 Alex Connell	1.49
1927-28 Hal Winkler	1.51
1939-40 Dave Kerr	1.54
1938-39 Francis Brimsek	1.56
1930-31 Roy Worters	1.61
1928-29 Lorne Chabot	1.61
1933-34 Chuck Gardiner	1.63
1927-28 Roy Worters	1.66
1935-36 Tiny Thompson	1.68
1927-28 Clint Benedict	1.70
1926-27 Hal Winkler	1.72
1928-29 Joe Miller	1.73
1930-31 Chuck Gardiner	1.73

1927-28 Hap Holmes	1.73
1927-28 Lorne Chabot	1.74
1932-33 Tiny Thompson	1.76

Shutouts

Season Player	ShO
1928-29 George Hainsworth	22
1925-26 Alex Connell	15
1927-28 Alex Connell	15
1927-28 Hal Winkler	15
1969-70 Tony Esposito	15
1926-27 George Hainsworth	14
1926-27 Clint Benedict	13
1926-27 Alex Connell	13
1927-28 George Hainsworth	13
1928-29 John Roach	13
1928-29 Roy Worters	13
1953-54 Harry Lumley	13
1997-98 Dominik Hasek	13
1928-29 Lorne Chabot	12
1928-29 Tiny Thompson	12
1930-31 Chuck Gardiner	12
1951-52 Terry Sawchuk	12
1953-54 Terry Sawchuk	12
1954-55 Terry Sawchuk	12
1955-56 Glenn Hall	12
1973-74 Bernie Parent	12
1974-75 Bernie Parent	12
1927-28 Lorne Chabot	11
1927-28 Hap Holmes	11
1927-28 Roy Worters	11
1928-29 Clint Benedict	11
1928-29 Joe Miller	11
1932-33 Tiny Thompson	11
1950-51 Terry Sawchuk	11
2000-01 Dominik Hasek	11

Saves

Season Player	Sv
1996-97 Felix Potvin	2214
1993-94 Curtis Joseph	2169
1993-94 Bill Ranford	2089
1996-97 Dominik Hasek	2024
1992-93 Curtis Joseph	2006
1997-98 Dominik Hasek	2002
1993-94 Kelly Hrudey	1991
1996-97 Guy Hebert	1961
1998-99 Guy Hebert	1949
1995-96 Grant Fuhr	1948
1996-97 Curtis Joseph	1944
1995-96 Felix Potvin	1943
1996-97 Nikolai Khabibulin	1901
1992-93 Bob Essensa	1892
1993-94 Arturs Irbe	1855

INDIVIDUAL SINGLE SEASON

1995-96	Dominik Hasek	1850
1995-96	Sean Burke	1844
2001-02	Jose Theodore	1836
1992-93	Bill Ranford	1825
1993-94	Felix Potvin	1823
1995-96	Bill Ranford	1817
1993-94	Bob Essensa	1816
1987-88	Grant Fuhr	1815
1993-94	Patrick Roy	1795
1999-00	Olaf Kolzig	1794
2001-02	Olaf Kolzig	1785
1996-97	Mike Richter	1784
1995-96	Martin Brodeur	1781
1991-92	Curtis Joseph	1778
2001-02	Milan Hnilicka	1777

Save Percentage
(minimum 750 SA)

Season	Player	SvPct
1998-99	Dominik Hasek	.937
1997-98	Dominik Hasek	.932
2001-02	Jose Theodore	.931
1994-95	Dominik Hasek	.930
1993-94	Dominik Hasek	.930
1996-97	Dominik Hasek	.930
1996-97	Jeff Hackett	.927
1996-97	Martin Brodeur	.927
1998-99	Byron Dafoe	.926
1998-99	Ron Tugnutt	.925
2001-02	Patrick Roy	.925
1993-94	John Vanbiesbrouck	.924
1996-97	Patrick Roy	.923
1998-99	Arturs Irbe	.923
1998-99	Nikolai Khabibulin	.923
2000-01	Mike Dunham	.923
1998-99	Guy Hebert	.922
2000-01	Sean Burke	.922
1997-98	Tom Barrasso	.922
1997-98	Trevor Kidd	.922
2000-01	Roman Cechmanek	.921
2001-02	Roman Cechmanek	.921
1998-99	Steve Shields	.921
2000-01	Dominik Hasek	.921
2001-02	Nikolai Khabibulin	.920
1995-96	Dominik Hasek	.920
2001-02	Sean Burke	.920
2001-02	Jean-Sebastien Giguere	920
2000-01	Manny Fernandez	920
2000-01	Roberto Luongo	.920

THE
STANDINGS

FINAL STANDINGS

1917-1918 NHL

Team	W	L	T	Pts
Montreal Canadiens	13	9	0	26
Toronto Arenas	13	9	0	26
Ottawa Senators	9	13	0	18
Montreal Wanderers	1	5	0	2

1918-1919 NHL

Team	W	L	T	Pts
Ottawa Senators	12	6	0	24
Montreal Canadiens	10	8	0	20
Toronto Arenas	5	13	0	10

1919-1920 NHL

Team	W	L	T	Pts
Ottawa Senators	19	5	0	38
Montreal Canadiens	13	11	0	26
Toronto St. Patricks	12	12	0	24
Quebec Bulldogs	4	20	0	8

1920-1921 NHL

Team	W	L	T	Pts
Toronto St. Patricks	15	9	0	30
Ottawa Senators	14	10	0	28
Montreal Canadiens	13	11	0	26
Hamilton Tigers	6	18	0	12

1921-1922 NHL

Team	W	L	T	Pts
Ottawa Senators	14	8	2	30
Toronto St. Patricks	13	10	1	27
Montreal Canadiens	12	11	1	25
Hamilton Tigers	7	17	0	14

1922-1923 NHL

Team	W	L	T	Pts
Ottawa Senators	14	9	1	29
Montreal Canadiens	13	9	2	28
Toronto St. Patricks	13	10	1	27
Hamilton Tigers	6	18	0	12

1923-1924 NHL

Team	W	L	T	Pts
Ottawa Senators	16	8	0	32
Montreal Canadiens	13	11	0	26
Toronto St. Patricks	10	14	0	20
Hamilton Tigers	9	15	0	18

1924-1925 NHL

Team	W	L	T	Pts
Hamilton Tigers	19	10	1	39
Toronto St. Patricks	19	11	0	38
Montreal Canadiens	17	11	2	36
Ottawa Senators	17	12	1	35
Montreal Maroons	9	19	2	20
Boston Bruins	6	24	0	12

1925-1926 NHL

Team	W	L	T	Pts
Ottawa Senators	24	8	4	52
Montreal Maroons	20	11	5	45
Pittsburgh Pirates	19	16	1	39
Boston Bruins	17	15	4	38
New York Americans	12	20	4	28
Toronto St. Patricks	12	21	3	27
Montreal Canadiens	11	24	1	23

1926-1927 Canadian

Team	W	L	T	Pts
Ottawa Senators	30	10	4	64
Montreal Canadiens	28	14	2	58
Montreal Maroons	20	20	4	44
New York Americans	17	25	2	36
Toronto Maple Leafs	15	24	5	35

1926-1927 American

Team	W	L	T	Pts
New York Rangers	25	13	6	56
Boston Bruins	21	20	3	45
Chicago Black Hawks	19	22	3	41
Pittsburgh Pirates	15	26	3	33
Detroit Cougers	12	28	4	28

1927-1928 Canadian

Team	W	L	T	Pts
Montreal Canadiens	26	11	7	59
Montreal Maroons	24	14	6	54
Ottawa Senators	20	14	10	50
Toronto Maple Leafs	18	18	8	44
New York Americans	11	27	6	28

1927-1928 American

Team	W	L	T	Pts
Boston Bruins	20	13	11	51
New York Rangers	19	16	9	47
Pittsburgh Pirates	19	17	8	46
Detroit Cougers	19	19	6	44
Chicago Black Hawks	7	34	3	17

1928-1929 Canadian

Team	W	L	T	Pts
Montreal Canadiens	22	7	15	59
New York Americans	19	13	12	50
Toronto Maple Leafs	21	18	5	47
Ottawa Senators	14	17	13	41
Montreal Maroons	15	20	9	39

1928-1929 American

Team	W	L	T	Pts
Boston Bruins	26	13	5	57
New York Rangers	21	13	10	52
Detroit Cougers	19	16	9	47
Pittsburgh Pirates	9	27	8	26
Chicago Black Hawks	7	29	8	22

1929-1930 Canadian

Team	W	L	T	Pts
Montreal Canadiens	21	14	9	51
Montreal Maroons	23	16	5	51
Ottawa Senators	21	15	8	50
Toronto Maple Leafs	17	21	6	40
New York Americans	14	25	5	33

1929-1930 American

Team	W	L	T	Pts
Boston Bruins	38	5	1	77
Chicago Black Hawks	21	18	5	47
New York Rangers	17	17	10	44
Detroit Falcons	14	24	6	34
Pittsburgh Pirates	5	36	3	13

FINAL STANDINGS

1930-1931 Canadian

Team	W	L	T	Pts
Montreal Canadiens	26	10	8	60
Toronto Maple Leafs	22	13	9	53
Montreal Maroons	20	18	6	46
New York Americans	18	16	10	46
Ottawa Senators	10	30	4	24

1930-1931 American

Team	W	L	T	Pts
Boston Bruins	28	10	6	62
Chicago Black Hawks	24	17	3	51
New York Rangers	19	16	9	47
Detroit Falcons	16	21	7	39
Philadelphia Quakers	4	36	4	12

1931-1932 Canadian

Team	W	L	T	Pts
Montreal Canadiens	25	16	7	57
Toronto Maple Leafs	23	18	7	53
Montreal Maroons	19	22	7	45
New York Americans	16	24	8	40

1931-1932 American

Team	W	L	T	Pts
New York Rangers	23	17	8	54
Chicago Black Hawks	18	19	11	47
Detroit Falcons	18	20	10	46
Boston Bruins	15	21	12	42

1932-1933 Canadian

Team	W	L	T	Pts
Toronto Maple Leafs	24	18	6	54
Montreal Maroons	22	20	6	50
Montreal Canadiens	18	25	5	41
New York Americans	15	22	11	41
Ottawa Senators	11	27	10	32

1932-1933 American

Team	W	L	T	Pts
Boston Bruins	25	15	8	58
Detroit Red Wings	25	15	8	58
New York Rangers	23	17	8	54
Chicago Black Hawks	16	20	12	44

1933-1934 Canadian

Team	W	L	T	Pts
Toronto Maple Leafs	26	13	9	61
Montreal Canadiens	22	20	6	50
Montreal Maroons	19	18	11	49
New York Americans	15	23	10	40
Ottawa Senators	13	29	6	32

1933-1934 American

Team	W	L	T	Pts
Detroit Red Wings	24	14	10	58
Chicago Black Hawks	20	17	11	51
New York Rangers	21	19	8	50
Boston Bruins	18	25	5	41

1934-1935 Canadian

Team	W	L	T	Pts
Toronto Maple Leafs	30	14	4	64
Montreal Maroons	24	19	5	53
Montreal Canadiens	19	23	6	44
New York Americans	12	27	9	33
St. Louis Eagles	11	31	6	28

1934-1935 American

Team	W	L	T	Pts
Boston Bruins	26	16	6	58
Chicago Black Hawks	26	17	5	57
New York Rangers	22	20	6	50
Detroit Red Wings	19	22	7	45

1935-1936 Canadian

Team	W	L	T	Pts
Montreal Maroons	22	16	10	54
Toronto Maple Leafs	23	19	6	52
New York Americans	16	25	7	39
Montreal Canadiens	11	26	11	33

1935-1936 American

Team	W	L	T	Pts
Detroit Red Wings	24	16	8	56
Boston Bruins	22	20	6	50
Chicago Black Hawks	21	19	8	50
New York Rangers	19	17	12	50

1936-1937 Canadian

Team	W	L	T	Pts
Montreal Canadiens	24	18	6	54
Montreal Maroons	22	17	9	53
Toronto Maple Leafs	22	21	5	49
New York Americans	15	29	4	34

1936-1937 American

Team	W	L	T	Pts
Detroit Red Wings	25	14	9	59
Boston Bruins	23	18	7	53
New York Rangers	19	20	9	47
Chicago Black Hawks	14	27	7	35

1937-1938 Canadian

Team	W	L	T	Pts
Toronto Maple Leafs	24	15	9	57
Montreal Canadiens	18	17	13	49
New York Americans	19	18	11	49
Montreal Maroons	12	30	6	30

1937-1938 American

Team	W	L	T	Pts
Boston Bruins	30	11	7	67
New York Rangers	27	15	6	60
Chicago Black Hawks	14	25	9	37
Detroit Red Wings	12	25	11	35

1938-1939 NHL

Team	W	L	T	Pts
Boston Bruins	36	10	2	74
New York Rangers	26	16	6	58
Toronto Maple Leafs	19	20	9	47
New York Americans	17	21	10	44
Detroit Red Wings	18	24	6	42
Montreal Canadiens	15	24	9	39
Chicago Black Hawks	12	28	8	32

FINAL STANDINGS

1939-1940 NHL
Team	W	L	T	Pts
Boston Bruins	31	12	5	67
New York Rangers	27	11	10	64
Toronto Maple Leafs	25	17	6	56
Chicago Black Hawks	23	19	6	52
Detroit Red Wings	16	26	6	38
New York Americans	15	29	4	34
Montreal Canadiens	10	33	5	25

1940-1941 NHL
Team	W	L	T	Pts
Boston Bruins	27	8	13	67
Toronto Maple Leafs	28	14	6	62
Detroit Red Wings	21	16	11	53
New York Rangers	21	19	8	50
Chicago Black Hawks	16	25	7	39
Montreal Canadiens	16	26	6	38
New York Americans	8	29	11	27

1941-1942 NHL
Team	W	L	T	Pts
New York Rangers	29	17	2	60
Toronto Maple Leafs	27	18	3	57
Boston Bruins	25	17	6	56
Chicago Black Hawks	22	23	3	47
Detroit Red Wings	19	25	4	42
Montreal Canadiens	18	27	3	39
Brooklyn Americans	16	29	3	35

1942-1943 NHL
Team	W	L	T	Pts
Detroit Red Wings	25	14	11	61
Boston Bruins	24	17	9	57
Toronto Maple Leafs	22	19	9	53
Montreal Canadiens	19	19	12	50
Chicago Black Hawks	17	18	15	49
New York Rangers	11	31	8	30

1943-1944 NHL
Team	W	L	T	Pts
Montreal Canadiens	38	5	7	83
Detroit Red Wings	26	18	6	58
Toronto Maple Leafs	23	23	4	50
Chicago Black Hawks	22	23	5	49
Boston Bruins	19	26	5	43
New York Rangers	6	39	5	17

1944-1945 NHL
Team	W	L	T	Pts
Montreal Canadiens	38	8	4	80
Detroit Red Wings	31	14	5	67
Toronto Maple Leafs	24	22	4	52
Boston Bruins	16	30	4	36
Chicago Black Hawks	13	30	7	33
New York Rangers	11	29	10	32

1945-1946 NHL
Team	W	L	T	Pts
Montreal Canadiens	28	17	5	61
Boston Bruins	24	18	8	56
Chicago Black Hawks	23	20	7	53
Detroit Red Wings	20	20	10	50
Toronto Maple Leafs	19	24	7	45
New York Rangers	13	28	9	35

1946-1947 NHL
Team	W	L	T	Pts
Montreal Canadiens	34	16	10	78
Toronto Maple Leafs	31	19	10	72
Boston Bruins	26	23	11	63
Detroit Red Wings	22	27	11	55
New York Rangers	22	32	6	50
Chicago Black Hawks	19	37	4	42

1947-1948 NHL
Team	W	L	T	Pts
Toronto Maple Leafs	32	15	13	77
Detroit Red Wings	30	18	12	72
Boston Bruins	23	24	13	59
New York Rangers	21	26	13	55
Montreal Canadiens	20	29	11	51
Chicago Black Hawks	20	34	6	46

1948-1949 NHL
Team	W	L	T	Pts
Detroit Red Wings	34	19	7	75
Boston Bruins	29	23	8	66
Montreal Canadiens	28	23	9	65
Toronto Maple Leafs	22	25	13	57
Chicago Black Hawks	21	31	8	50
New York Rangers	18	31	11	47

1949-1950 NHL
Team	W	L	T	Pts
Detroit Red Wings	37	19	14	88
Montreal Canadiens	29	22	19	77
Toronto Maple Leafs	31	27	12	74
New York Rangers	28	31	11	67
Boston Bruins	22	32	16	60
Chicago Black Hawks	22	38	10	54

1950-1951 NHL
Team	W	L	T	Pts
Detroit Red Wings	44	13	13	101
Toronto Maple Leafs	41	16	13	95
Montreal Canadiens	25	30	15	65
Boston Bruins	22	30	18	62
New York Rangers	20	29	21	61
Chicago Black Hawks	13	47	10	36

1951-1952 NHL
Team	W	L	T	Pts
Detroit Red Wings	44	14	12	100
Montreal Canadiens	34	26	10	78
Toronto Maple Leafs	29	25	16	74
Boston Bruins	25	29	16	66
New York Rangers	23	34	13	59
Chicago Black Hawks	17	44	9	43

1952-1953 NHL
Team	W	L	T	Pts
Detroit Red Wings	36	16	18	90
Montreal Canadiens	28	23	19	75
Boston Bruins	28	29	13	69
Chicago Black Hawks	27	28	15	69
Toronto Maple Leafs	27	30	13	67
New York Rangers	17	37	16	50

FINAL STANDINGS

1953-1954 NHL

Team	W	L	T	Pts
Detroit Red Wings	37	19	14	88
Montreal Canadiens	35	24	11	81
Toronto Maple Leafs	32	24	14	78
Boston Bruins	32	28	10	74
New York Rangers	29	31	10	68
Chicago Black Hawks	12	51	7	31

1954-1955 NHL

Team	W	L	T	Pts
Detroit Red Wings	42	17	11	95
Montreal Canadiens	41	18	11	93
Toronto Maple Leafs	24	24	22	70
Boston Bruins	23	26	21	67
New York Rangers	17	35	18	52
Chicago Black Hawks	13	40	17	43

1955-1956 NHL

Team	W	L	T	Pts
Montreal Canadiens	45	15	10	100
Detroit Red Wings	30	24	16	76
New York Rangers	32	28	10	74
Toronto Maple Leafs	24	33	13	61
Boston Bruins	23	34	13	59
Chicago Black Hawks	19	39	12	50

1956-1957 NHL

Team	W	L	T	Pts
Detroit Red Wings	38	20	12	88
Montreal Canadiens	35	23	12	82
Boston Bruins	34	24	12	80
New York Rangers	26	30	14	66
Toronto Maple Leafs	21	34	15	57
Chicago Black Hawks	16	39	15	47

1957-1958 NHL

Team	W	L	T	Pts
Montreal Canadiens	43	17	10	96
New York Rangers	32	25	13	77
Detroit Red Wings	29	29	12	70
Boston Bruins	27	28	15	69
Chicago Black Hawks	24	39	7	55
Toronto Maple Leafs	21	38	11	53

1958-1959 NHL

Team	W	L	T	Pts
Montreal Canadiens	39	18	13	91
Boston Bruins	32	29	9	73
Chicago Black Hawks	28	29	13	69
Toronto Maple Leafs	27	32	11	65
New York Rangers	26	32	12	64
Detroit Red Wings	25	37	8	58

1959-1960 NHL

Team	W	L	T	Pts
Montreal Canadiens	40	18	12	92
Toronto Maple Leafs	35	26	9	79
Chicago Black Hawks	28	29	13	69
Detroit Red Wings	26	29	15	67
Boston Bruins	28	34	8	64
New York Rangers	17	38	15	49

1960-1961 NHL

Team	W	L	T	Pts
Montreal Canadiens	41	19	10	92
Toronto Maple Leafs	39	19	12	90
Chicago Black Hawks	29	24	17	75
Detroit Red Wings	25	29	16	66
New York Rangers	22	38	10	54
Boston Bruins	15	42	13	43

1961-1962 NHL

Team	W	L	T	Pts
Montreal Canadiens	42	14	14	98
Toronto Maple Leafs	37	22	11	85
Chicago Black Hawks	31	26	13	75
New York Rangers	26	32	12	64
Detroit Red Wings	23	33	14	60
Boston Bruins	15	47	8	38

1962-1963 NHL

Team	W	L	T	Pts
Toronto Maple Leafs	35	23	12	82
Chicago Black Hawks	32	21	17	81
Montreal Canadiens	28	19	23	79
Detroit Red Wings	32	25	13	77
New York Rangers	22	36	12	56
Boston Bruins	14	39	17	45

1963-1964 NHL

Team	W	L	T	Pts
Montreal Canadiens	36	21	13	85
Chicago Black Hawks	36	22	12	84
Toronto Maple Leafs	33	25	12	78
Detroit Red Wings	30	29	11	71
New York Rangers	22	38	10	54
Boston Bruins	18	40	12	48

1964-1965 NHL

Team	W	L	T	Pts
Detroit Red Wings	40	23	7	87
Montreal Canadiens	36	23	11	83
Chicago Black Hawks	34	28	8	76
Toronto Maple Leafs	30	26	14	74
New York Rangers	20	38	12	52
Boston Bruins	21	43	6	48

1965-1966 NHL

Team	W	L	T	Pts
Montreal Canadiens	41	21	8	90
Chicago Black Hawks	37	25	8	82
Toronto Maple Leafs	34	25	11	79
Detroit Red Wings	31	27	12	74
Boston Bruins	21	43	6	48
New York Rangers	18	41	11	47

1966-1967 NHL

Team	W	L	T	Pts
Chicago Black Hawks	41	17	12	94
Montreal Canadiens	32	25	13	77
Toronto Maple Leafs	32	27	11	75
New York Rangers	30	28	12	72
Detroit Red Wings	27	39	4	58
Boston Bruins	17	43	10	44

FINAL STANDINGS

1967-1968 East

Team	W	L	T	Pts
Montreal Canadiens	42	22	10	94
New York Rangers	39	23	12	90
Boston Bruins	37	27	10	84
Chicago Black Hawks	32	26	16	80
Toronto Maple Leafs	33	31	10	76
Detroit Red Wings	27	35	12	66

1967-1968 West

Team	W	L	T	Pts
Philadelphia Flyers	31	32	11	73
Los Angeles Kings	31	33	10	72
St. Louis Blues	27	31	16	70
Minnesota North Stars	27	32	15	69
Pittsburgh Penguins	27	34	13	67
Oakland Seals	15	42	17	47

1968-1969 East

Team	W	L	T	Pts
Montreal Canadiens	46	19	11	103
Boston Bruins	42	18	16	100
New York Rangers	41	26	9	91
Toronto Maple Leafs	35	26	15	85
Detroit Red Wings	33	31	12	78
Chicago Black Hawks	34	33	9	77

1968-1969 West

Team	W	L	T	Pts
St. Louis Blues	37	25	14	88
Oakland Seals	29	36	11	69
Philadelphia Flyers	20	35	21	61
Los Angeles Kings	24	42	10	58
Minnesota North Stars	18	43	15	51
Pittsburgh Penguins	20	45	11	51

1969-1970 East

Team	W	L	T	Pts
Boston Bruins	40	17	19	99
Chicago Black Hawks	45	22	9	99
Detroit Red Wings	40	21	15	95
Montreal Canadiens	38	22	16	92
New York Rangers	38	22	16	92
Toronto Maple Leafs	29	34	13	71

1969-1970 West

Team	W	L	T	Pts
St. Louis Blues	37	27	12	86
Pittsburgh Penguins	26	38	12	64
Minnesota North Stars	19	35	22	60
Oakland Seals	22	40	14	58
Philadelphia Flyers	17	35	24	58
Los Angeles Kings	14	52	10	38

1970-1971 East

Team	W	L	T	Pts
Boston Bruins	57	14	7	121
New York Rangers	49	18	11	109
Montreal Canadiens	42	23	13	97
Toronto Maple Leafs	37	33	8	82
Buffalo Sabres	24	39	15	63
Vancouver Canucks	24	46	8	56
Detroit Red Wings	22	45	11	55

1970-1971 West

Team	W	L	T	Pts
Chicago Black Hawks	49	20	9	107
St. Louis Blues	34	25	19	87
Philadelphia Flyers	28	33	17	73
Minnesota North Stars	28	34	16	72
Los Angeles Kings	25	40	13	63
Pittsburgh Penguins	21	37	20	62
California Seals	20	53	5	45

1971-1972 East

Team	W	L	T	Pts
Boston Bruins	54	13	11	119
New York Rangers	48	17	13	109
Montreal Canadiens	46	16	16	108
Toronto Maple Leafs	33	31	14	80
Detroit Red Wings	33	35	10	76
Buffalo Sabres	16	43	19	51
Vancouver Canucks	20	50	8	48

1971-1972 West

Team	W	L	T	Pts
Chicago Black Hawks	46	17	15	107
Minnesota North Stars	37	29	12	86
St. Louis Blues	28	39	11	67
Philadelphia Flyers	26	38	14	66
Pittsburgh Penguins	26	38	14	66
California Seals	21	39	18	60
Los Angeles Kings	20	49	9	49

1972-1973 East

Team	W	L	T	Pts
Montreal Canadiens	52	10	16	120
Boston Bruins	51	22	5	107
New York Rangers	47	23	8	102
Buffalo Sabres	37	27	14	88
Detroit Red Wings	37	29	12	86
Toronto Maple Leafs	27	41	10	64
Vancouver Canucks	22	47	9	53
New York Islanders	12	60	6	30

1972-1973 West

Team	W	L	T	Pts
Chicago Black Hawks	42	27	9	93
Minnesota North Stars	37	30	11	85
Philadelphia Flyers	37	30	11	85
St. Louis Blues	32	34	12	76
Los Angeles Kings	31	36	11	73
Pittsburgh Penguins	32	37	9	73
Atlanta Flames	25	38	15	65
California Seals	16	46	16	48

1973-1974 East

Team	W	L	T	Pts
Boston Bruins	52	17	9	113
Montreal Canadiens	45	24	9	99
New York Rangers	40	24	14	94
Toronto Maple Leafs	35	27	16	86
Buffalo Sabres	32	34	12	76
Detroit Red Wings	29	39	10	68
Vancouver Canucks	24	43	11	59
New York Islanders	19	41	18	56

FINAL STANDINGS

1973-1974 West

Team	W	L	T	Pts
Philadelphia Flyers	50	16	12	112
Chicago Black Hawks	41	14	23	105
Los Angeles Kings	33	33	12	78
Atlanta Flames	30	34	14	74
Pittsburgh Penguins	28	41	9	65
St. Louis Blues	26	40	12	64
Minnesota North Stars	23	38	17	63
California Seals	13	55	10	36

1974-1975 Adams

Team	W	L	T	Pts
Buffalo Sabres	49	16	15	113
Boston Bruins	40	26	14	94
Toronto Maple Leafs	31	33	16	78
California Seals	19	48	13	51

1974-1975 Smythe

Team	W	L	T	Pts
Vancouver Canucks	38	32	10	86
St. Louis Blues	35	31	14	84
Chicago Black Hawks	37	35	8	82
Minnesota North Stars	23	50	7	53
Kansas City Scouts	15	54	11	41

1974-1975 Patrick

Team	W	L	T	Pts
Philadelphia Flyers	51	18	11	113
New York Islanders	33	25	22	88
New York Rangers	37	29	14	88
Atlanta Flames	34	31	15	83

1974-1975 Norris

Team	W	L	T	Pts
Montreal Canadiens	47	14	19	113
Los Angeles Kings	42	17	21	105
Pittsburgh Penguins	37	28	15	89
Detroit Red Wings	23	45	12	58
Washington Capitals	8	67	5	21

1975-1976 Adams

Team	W	L	T	Pts
Boston Bruins	48	15	17	113
Buffalo Sabres	46	21	13	105
Toronto Maple Leafs	34	31	15	83
California Seals	27	42	11	65

1975-1976 Smythe

Team	W	L	T	Pts
Chicago Black Hawks	32	30	18	82
Vancouver Canucks	33	32	15	81
St. Louis Blues	29	37	14	72
Minnesota North Stars	20	53	7	47
Kansas City Scouts	12	56	12	36

1975-1976 Patrick

Team	W	L	T	Pts
Philadelphia Flyers	51	13	16	118
New York Islanders	42	21	17	101
Atlanta Flames	35	33	12	82
New York Rangers	29	42	9	67

1975-1976 Norris

Team	W	L	T	Pts
Montreal Canadiens	58	11	11	127
Los Angeles Kings	38	33	9	85
Pittsburgh Penguins	35	33	12	82
Detroit Red Wings	26	44	10	62
Washington Capitals	11	59	10	32

1976-1977 Adams

Team	W	L	T	Pts
Boston Bruins	49	23	8	106
Buffalo Sabres	48	24	8	104
Toronto Maple Leafs	33	32	15	81
Cleveland Barons	25	42	13	63

1976-1977 Smythe

Team	W	L	T	Pts
St. Louis Blues	32	39	9	73
Minnesota North Stars	23	39	18	64
Chicago Black Hawks	26	43	11	63
Vancouver Canucks	25	42	13	63
Colorado Rockies	20	46	14	54

1976-1977 Patrick

Team	W	L	T	Pts
Philadelphia Flyers	48	16	16	112
New York Islanders	47	21	12	106
Atlanta Flames	34	34	12	80
New York Rangers	29	37	14	72

1976-1977 Norris

Team	W	L	T	Pts
Montreal Canadiens	60	8	12	132
Los Angeles Kings	34	31	15	83
Pittsburgh Penguins	34	33	13	81
Washington Capitals	24	42	14	62
Detroit Red Wings	16	55	9	41

1977-1978 Adams

Team	W	L	T	Pts
Boston Bruins	51	18	11	113
Buffalo Sabres	44	19	17	105
Toronto Maple Leafs	41	29	10	92
Cleveland Barons	22	45	13	57

1977-1978 Smythe

Team	W	L	T	Pts
Chicago Black Hawks	32	29	19	83
Colorado Rockies	19	40	21	59
Vancouver Canucks	20	43	17	57
St. Louis Blues	20	47	13	53
Minnesota North Stars	18	53	9	45

1977-1978 Patrick

Team	W	L	T	Pts
New York Islanders	48	17	15	111
Philadelphia Flyers	45	20	15	105
Atlanta Flames	34	27	19	87
New York Rangers	30	37	13	73

FINAL STANDINGS

1977-1978 Norris

Team	W	L	T	Pts
Montreal Canadiens	59	10	11	129
Detroit Red Wings	32	34	14	78
Los Angeles Kings	31	34	15	77
Pittsburgh Penguins	25	37	18	68
Washington Capitals	17	49	14	48

1978-1979 Adams

Team	W	L	T	Pts
Boston Bruins	43	23	14	100
Buffalo Sabres	36	28	16	88
Toronto Maple Leafs	34	33	13	81
Minnesota North Stars	28	40	12	68

1978-1979 Smythe

Team	W	L	T	Pts
Chicago Black Hawks	29	36	15	73
Vancouver Canucks	25	42	13	63
St. Louis Blues	18	50	12	48
Colorado Rockies	15	53	12	42

1978-1979 Patrick

Team	W	L	T	Pts
New York Islanders	51	15	14	116
Philadelphia Flyers	40	25	15	95
New York Rangers	40	29	11	91
Atlanta Flames	41	31	8	90

1978-1979 Norris

Team	W	L	T	Pts
Montreal Canadiens	52	17	11	115
Pittsburgh Penguins	36	31	13	85
Los Angeles Kings	34	34	12	80
Washington Capitals	24	41	15	63
Detroit Red Wings	23	41	16	62

1979-1980 Adams

Team	W	L	T	Pts
Buffalo Sabres	47	17	16	110
Boston Bruins	46	21	13	105
Minnesota North Stars	36	28	16	88
Toronto Maple Leafs	35	40	5	75
Quebec Nordiques	25	44	11	61

1979-1980 Smythe

Team	W	L	T	Pts
Chicago Black Hawks	34	27	19	87
St. Louis Blues	34	34	12	80
Vancouver Canucks	27	37	16	70
Edmonton Oilers	28	39	13	69
Colorado Rockies	19	48	13	51
Winnipeg Jets	20	49	11	51

1979-1980 Patrick

Team	W	L	T	Pts
Philadelphia Flyers	48	12	20	116
New York Islanders	39	28	13	91
New York Rangers	38	32	10	86
Atlanta Flames	35	32	13	83
Washington Capitals	27	40	13	67

1979-1980 Norris

Team	W	L	T	Pts
Montreal Canadiens	47	20	13	107
Los Angeles Kings	30	36	14	74
Hartford Whalers	27	34	19	73
Pittsburgh Penguins	30	37	13	73
Detroit Red Wings	26	43	11	63

1980-1981 Adams

Team	W	L	T	Pts
Buffalo Sabres	39	20	21	99
Boston Bruins	37	30	13	87
Minnesota North Stars	35	28	17	87
Quebec Nordiques	30	32	18	78
Toronto Maple Leafs	28	37	15	71

1980-1981 Smythe

Team	W	L	T	Pts
St. Louis Blues	45	18	17	107
Chicago Black Hawks	31	33	16	78
Vancouver Canucks	28	32	20	76
Edmonton Oilers	29	35	16	74
Colorado Rockies	22	45	13	57
Winnipeg Jets	9	57	14	32

1980-1981 Patrick

Team	W	L	T	Pts
New York Islanders	48	18	14	110
Philadelphia Flyers	41	24	15	97
Calgary Flames	39	27	14	92
New York Rangers	30	36	14	74
Washington Capitals	26	36	18	70

1980-1981 Norris

Team	W	L	T	Pts
Montreal Canadiens	45	22	13	103
Los Angeles Kings	43	24	13	99
Pittsburgh Penguins	30	37	13	73
Hartford Whalers	21	41	18	60
Detroit Red Wings	19	43	18	56

1981-1982 Adams

Team	W	L	T	Pts
Montreal Canadiens	46	17	17	109
Boston Bruins	43	27	10	96
Buffalo Sabres	39	26	15	93
Quebec Nordiques	33	31	16	82
Hartford Whalers	21	41	18	60

1981-1982 Patrick

Team	W	L	T	Pts
New York Islanders	54	16	10	118
New York Rangers	39	27	14	92
Philadelphia Flyers	38	31	11	87
Pittsburgh Penguins	31	36	13	75
Washington Capitals	26	41	13	65

1981-1982 Norris

Team	W	L	T	Pts
Minnesota North Stars	37	23	20	94
Winnipeg Jets	33	33	14	80
Chicago Black Hawks	30	38	12	72
St. Louis Blues	32	40	8	72
Toronto Maple Leafs	20	44	16	56
Detroit Red Wings	21	47	12	54

FINAL STANDINGS

1981-1982 Smythe

Team	W	L	T	Pts
Edmonton Oilers	48	17	15	111
Vancouver Canucks	30	33	17	77
Calgary Flames	29	34	17	75
Los Angeles Kings	24	41	15	63
Colorado Rockies	18	49	13	49

1982-1983 Adams

Team	W	L	T	Pts
Boston Bruins	50	20	10	110
Montreal Canadiens	42	24	14	98
Buffalo Sabres	38	29	13	89
Quebec Nordiques	34	34	12	80
Hartford Whalers	19	54	7	45

1982-1983 Patrick

Team	W	L	T	Pts
Philadelphia Flyers	49	23	8	106
New York Islanders	42	26	12	96
Washington Capitals	39	25	16	94
New York Rangers	35	35	10	80
New Jersey Devils	17	49	14	48
Pittsburgh Penguins	18	53	9	45

1982-1983 Norris

Team	W	L	T	Pts
Chicago Black Hawks	47	23	10	104
Minnesota North Stars	40	24	16	96
Toronto Maple Leafs	28	40	12	68
St. Louis Blues	25	40	15	65
Detroit Red Wings	21	44	15	57

1982-1983 Smythe

Team	W	L	T	Pts
Edmonton Oilers	47	21	12	106
Calgary Flames	32	34	14	78
Vancouver Canucks	30	35	15	75
Winnipeg Jets	33	39	8	74
Los Angeles Kings	27	41	12	66

1983-1984 Adams

Team	W	L	T	Pts
Boston Bruins	49	25	6	104
Buffalo Sabres	48	25	7	103
Quebec Nordiques	42	28	10	94
Montreal Canadiens	35	40	5	75
Hartford Whalers	28	42	10	66

1983-1984 Patrick

Team	W	L	T	Pts
New York Islanders	50	26	4	104
Washington Capitals	48	27	5	101
Philadelphia Flyers	44	26	10	98
New York Rangers	42	29	9	93
New Jersey Devils	17	56	7	41
Pittsburgh Penguins	16	58	6	38

1983-1984 Norris

Team	W	L	T	Pts
Minnesota North Stars	39	31	10	88
St. Louis Blues	32	41	7	71
Detroit Red Wings	31	42	7	69
Chicago Black Hawks	30	42	8	68
Toronto Maple Leafs	26	45	9	61

1983-1984 Smythe

Team	W	L	T	Pts
Edmonton Oilers	57	18	5	119
Calgary Flames	34	32	14	82
Vancouver Canucks	32	39	9	73
Winnipeg Jets	31	38	11	73
Los Angeles Kings	23	44	13	59

1984-1985 Adams

Team	W	L	T	Pts
Montreal Canadiens	41	27	12	94
Quebec Nordiques	41	30	9	91
Buffalo Sabres	38	28	14	90
Boston Bruins	36	34	10	82
Hartford Whalers	30	41	9	69

1984-1985 Patrick

Team	W	L	T	Pts
Philadelphia Flyers	53	20	7	113
Washington Capitals	46	25	9	101
New York Islanders	40	34	6	86
New York Rangers	26	44	10	62
New Jersey Devils	22	48	10	54
Pittsburgh Penguins	24	51	5	53

1984-1985 Norris

Team	W	L	T	Pts
St. Louis Blues	37	31	12	86
Chicago Black Hawks	38	35	7	83
Detroit Red Wings	27	41	12	66
Minnesota North Stars	25	43	12	62
Toronto Maple Leafs	20	52	8	48

1984-1985 Smythe

Team	W	L	T	Pts
Edmonton Oilers	49	20	11	109
Winnipeg Jets	43	27	10	96
Calgary Flames	41	27	12	94
Los Angeles Kings	34	32	14	82
Vancouver Canucks	25	46	9	59

1985-1986 Adams

Team	W	L	T	Pts
Quebec Nordiques	43	31	6	92
Montreal Canadiens	40	33	7	87
Boston Bruins	37	31	12	86
Hartford Whalers	40	36	4	84
Buffalo Sabres	37	37	6	80

1985-1986 Patrick

Team	W	L	T	Pts
Philadelphia Flyers	53	23	4	110
Washington Capitals	50	23	7	107
New York Islanders	39	29	12	90
New York Rangers	36	38	6	78
Pittsburgh Penguins	34	38	8	76
New Jersey Devils	28	49	3	59

1985-1986 Norris

Team	W	L	T	Pts
Chicago Black Hawks	39	33	8	86
Minnesota North Stars	38	33	9	85
St. Louis Blues	37	34	9	83
Toronto Maple Leafs	25	48	7	57
Detroit Red Wings	17	57	6	40

FINAL STANDINGS

1985-1986 Smythe

Team	W	L	T	Pts
Edmonton Oilers	56	17	7	119
Calgary Flames	40	31	9	89
Vancouver Canucks	23	44	13	59
Winnipeg Jets	26	47	7	59
Los Angeles Kings	23	49	8	54

1986-1987 Adams

Team	W	L	T	Pts
Hartford Whalers	43	30	7	93
Montreal Canadiens	41	29	10	92
Boston Bruins	39	34	7	85
Quebec Nordiques	31	39	10	72
Buffalo Sabres	28	44	8	64

1986-1987 Patrick

Team	W	L	T	Pts
Philadelphia Flyers	46	26	8	100
Washington Capitals	38	32	10	86
New York Islanders	35	33	12	82
New York Rangers	34	38	8	76
Pittsburgh Penguins	30	38	12	72
New Jersey Devils	29	45	6	64

1986-1987 Norris

Team	W	L	T	Pts
St. Louis Blues	32	33	15	79
Detroit Red Wings	34	36	10	78
Chicago Blackhawks	29	37	14	72
Minnesota North Stars	30	40	10	70
Toronto Maple Leafs	32	42	6	70

1986-1987 Smythe

Team	W	L	T	Pts
Edmonton Oilers	50	24	6	106
Calgary Flames	46	31	3	95
Winnipeg Jets	40	32	8	88
Los Angeles Kings	31	41	8	70
Vancouver Canucks	29	43	8	66

1987-1988 Adams

Team	W	L	T	Pts
Montreal Canadiens	45	22	13	103
Boston Bruins	44	30	6	94
Buffalo Sabres	37	32	11	85
Hartford Whalers	35	38	7	77
Quebec Nordiques	32	43	5	69

1987-1988 Patrick

Team	W	L	T	Pts
New York Islanders	39	31	10	88
Philadelphia Flyers	38	33	9	85
Washington Capitals	38	33	9	85
New Jersey Devils	38	36	6	82
New York Rangers	36	34	10	82
Pittsburgh Penguins	36	35	9	81

1987-1988 Norris

Team	W	L	T	Pts
Detroit Red Wings	41	28	11	93
St. Louis Blues	34	38	8	76
Chicago Blackhawks	30	41	9	69
Toronto Maple Leafs	21	49	10	52
Minnesota North Stars	19	48	13	51

1987-1988 Smythe

Team	W	L	T	Pts
Calgary Flames	48	23	9	105
Edmonton Oilers	44	25	11	99
Winnipeg Jets	33	36	11	77
Los Angeles Kings	30	42	8	68
Vancouver Canucks	25	46	9	59

1988-1989 Adams

Team	W	L	T	Pts
Montreal Canadiens	53	18	9	115
Boston Bruins	37	29	14	88
Buffalo Sabres	38	35	7	83
Hartford Whalers	37	38	5	79
Quebec Nordiques	27	46	7	61

1988-1989 Patrick

Team	W	L	T	Pts
Washington Capitals	41	29	10	92
Pittsburgh Penguins	40	33	7	87
New York Rangers	37	35	8	82
Philadelphia Flyers	36	36	8	80
New Jersey Devils	27	41	12	66
New York Islanders	28	47	5	61

1988-1989 Norris

Team	W	L	T	Pts
Detroit Red Wings	34	34	12	80
St. Louis Blues	33	35	12	78
Minnesota North Stars	27	37	16	70
Chicago Blackhawks	27	41	12	66
Toronto Maple Leafs	28	46	6	62

1988-1989 Smythe

Team	W	L	T	Pts
Calgary Flames	54	17	9	117
Los Angeles Kings	42	31	7	91
Edmonton Oilers	38	34	8	84
Vancouver Canucks	33	39	8	74
Winnipeg Jets	26	42	12	64

1989-1990 Adams

Team	W	L	T	Pts
Boston Bruins	46	25	9	101
Buffalo Sabres	45	27	8	98
Montreal Canadiens	41	28	11	93
Hartford Whalers	38	33	9	85
Quebec Nordiques	12	61	7	31

1989-1990 Patrick

Team	W	L	T	Pts
New York Rangers	36	31	13	85
New Jersey Devils	37	34	9	83
Washington Capitals	36	38	6	78
New York Islanders	31	38	11	73
Pittsburgh Penguins	32	40	8	72
Philadelphia Flyers	30	39	11	71

1989-1990 Norris

Team	W	L	T	Pts
Chicago Blackhawks	41	33	6	88
St. Louis Blues	37	34	9	83
Toronto Maple Leafs	38	38	4	80
Minnesota North Stars	36	40	4	76
Detroit Red Wings	28	38	14	70

FINAL STANDINGS

1989-1990 Smythe

Team	W	L	T	Pts
Calgary Flames	42	23	15	99
Edmonton Oilers	38	28	14	90
Winnipeg Jets	37	32	11	85
Los Angeles Kings	34	39	7	75
Vancouver Canucks	25	41	14	64

1990-1991 Adams

Team	W	L	T	Pts
Boston Bruins	44	24	12	100
Montreal Canadiens	39	30	11	89
Buffalo Sabres	31	30	19	81
Hartford Whalers	31	38	11	73
Quebec Nordiques	16	50	14	46

1990-1991 Patrick

Team	W	L	T	Pts
Pittsburgh Penguins	41	33	6	88
New York Rangers	36	31	13	85
Washington Capitals	37	36	7	81
New Jersey Devils	32	33	15	79
Philadelphia Flyers	33	37	10	76
New York Islanders	25	45	10	60

1990-1991 Norris

Team	W	L	T	Pts
Chicago Blackhawks	49	23	8	106
St. Louis Blues	47	22	11	105
Detroit Red Wings	34	38	8	76
Minnesota North Stars	27	39	14	68
Toronto Maple Leafs	23	46	11	57

1990-1991 Smythe

Team	W	L	T	Pts
Los Angeles Kings	46	24	10	102
Calgary Flames	46	26	8	100
Edmonton Oilers	37	37	6	80
Vancouver Canucks	28	43	9	65
Winnipeg Jets	26	43	11	63

1991-1992 Adams

Team	W	L	T	Pts
Montreal Canadiens	41	28	11	93
Boston Bruins	36	32	12	84
Buffalo Sabres	31	37	12	74
Hartford Whalers	26	41	13	65
Quebec Nordiques	20	48	12	52

1991-1992 Patrick

Team	W	L	T	Pts
New York Rangers	50	25	5	105
Washington Capitals	45	27	8	98
New Jersey Devils	38	31	11	87
Pittsburgh Penguins	39	32	9	87
New York Islanders	34	35	11	79
Philadelphia Flyers	32	37	11	75

1991-1992 Norris

Team	W	L	T	Pts
Detroit Red Wings	43	25	12	98
Chicago Blackhawks	36	29	15	87
St. Louis Blues	36	33	11	83
Minnesota North Stars	32	42	6	70
Toronto Maple Leafs	30	43	7	67

1991-1992 Smythe

Team	W	L	T	Pts
Vancouver Canucks	42	26	12	96
Los Angeles Kings	35	31	14	84
Edmonton Oilers	36	34	10	82
Winnipeg Jets	33	32	15	81
Calgary Flames	31	37	12	74
San Jose Sharks	17	58	5	39

1992-1993 Adams

Team	W	L	T	Pts
Boston Bruins	51	26	7	109
Quebec Nordiques	47	27	10	104
Montreal Canadiens	48	30	6	102
Buffalo Sabres	38	36	10	86
Hartford Whalers	26	52	6	58
Ottawa Senators	10	70	4	24

1992-1993 Patrick

Team	W	L	T	Pts
Pittsburgh Penguins	56	21	7	119
Washington Capitals	43	34	7	93
New Jersey Devils	40	37	7	87
New York Islanders	40	37	7	87
Philadelphia Flyers	36	37	11	83
New York Rangers	34	39	11	79

1992-1993 Norris

Team	W	L	T	Pts
Chicago Blackhawks	47	25	12	106
Detroit Red Wings	47	28	9	103
Toronto Maple Leafs	44	29	11	99
St. Louis Blues	37	36	11	85
Minnesota North Stars	36	38	10	82
Tampa Bay Lightning	23	54	7	53

1992-1993 Smythe

Team	W	L	T	Pts
Vancouver Canucks	46	29	9	101
Calgary Flames	43	30	11	97
Los Angeles Kings	39	35	10	88
Winnipeg Jets	40	37	7	87
Edmonton Oilers	26	50	8	60
San Jose Sharks	11	71	2	24

1993-1994 Northeast

Team	W	L	T	Pts
Pittsburgh Penguins	44	27	13	101
Boston Bruins	42	29	13	97
Montreal Canadiens	41	29	14	96
Buffalo Sabres	43	32	9	95
Quebec Nordiques	34	42	8	76
Hartford Whalers	27	48	9	63
Ottawa Senators	14	61	9	37

1993-1994 Atlantic

Team	W	L	T	Pts
New York Rangers	52	24	8	112
New Jersey Devils	47	25	12	106
Washington Capitals	39	35	10	88
New York Islanders	36	36	12	84
Florida Panthers	33	34	17	83
Philadelphia Flyers	35	39	10	80
Tampa Bay Lightning	30	43	11	71

FINAL STANDINGS

1993-1994 Central

Team	W	L	T	Pts
Detroit Red Wings	46	30	8	100
Toronto Maple Leafs	43	29	12	98
Dallas Stars	42	29	13	97
St. Louis Blues	40	33	11	91
Chicago Blackhawks	39	36	9	87
Winnipeg Jets	24	51	9	57

1993-1994 Pacific

Team	W	L	T	Pts
Calgary Flames	42	29	13	97
Vancouver Canucks	41	40	3	85
San Jose Sharks	33	35	16	82
Anaheim Mighty Ducks	33	46	5	71
Los Angeles Kings	27	45	12	66
Edmonton Oilers	25	45	14	64

1994-1995 Northeast

Team	W	L	T	Pts
Quebec Nordiques	30	13	5	65
Pittsburgh Penguins	29	16	3	61
Boston Bruins	27	18	3	57
Buffalo Sabres	22	19	7	51
Hartford Whalers	19	24	5	43
Montreal Canadiens	18	23	7	43
Ottawa Senators	9	34	5	23

1994-1995 Atlantic

Team	W	L	T	Pts
Philadelphia Flyers	28	16	4	60
New Jersey Devils	22	18	8	52
Washington Capitals	22	18	8	52
New York Rangers	22	23	3	47
Florida Panthers	20	22	6	46
Tampa Bay Lightning	17	28	3	37
New York Islanders	15	28	5	35

1994-1995 Central

Team	W	L	T	Pts
Detroit Red Wings	33	11	4	70
St. Louis Blues	28	15	5	61
Chicago Blackhawks	24	19	5	53
Toronto Maple Leafs	21	19	8	50
Dallas Stars	17	23	8	42
Winnipeg Jets	16	25	7	39

1994-1995 Pacific

Team	W	L	T	Pts
Calgary Flames	24	17	7	55
Vancouver Canucks	18	18	12	48
San Jose Sharks	19	25	4	42
Los Angeles Kings	16	23	9	41
Edmonton Oilers	17	27	4	38
Anaheim Mighty Ducks	16	27	5	37

1995-1996 Northeast

Team	W	L	T	Pts
Pittsburgh Penguins	49	29	4	102
Boston Bruins	40	31	11	91
Montreal Canadiens	40	32	10	90
Hartford Whalers	34	39	9	77
Buffalo Sabres	33	42	7	73
Ottawa Senators	18	59	5	41

1995-1996 Atlantic

Team	W	L	T	Pts
Philadelphia Flyers	45	24	13	103
New York Rangers	41	27	14	96
Florida Panthers	41	31	10	92
Washington Capitals	39	32	11	89
Tampa Bay Lightning	38	32	12	88
New Jersey Devils	37	33	12	86
New York Islanders	22	50	10	54

1995-1996 Central

Team	W	L	T	Pts
Detroit Red Wings	62	13	7	131
Chicago Blackhawks	40	28	14	94
St. Louis Blues	32	34	16	80
Toronto Maple Leafs	34	36	12	80
Winnipeg Jets	36	40	6	78
Dallas Stars	26	42	14	66

1995-1996 Pacific

Team	W	L	T	Pts
Colorado Avalanche	47	25	10	104
Calgary Flames	34	37	11	79
Vancouver Canucks	32	35	15	79
Anaheim Mighty Ducks	35	39	8	78
Edmonton Oilers	30	44	8	68
Los Angeles Kings	24	40	18	66
San Jose Sharks	20	55	7	47

1996-1997 Northeast

Team	W	L	T	Pts
Buffalo Sabres	40	30	12	92
Pittsburgh Penguins	38	36	8	84
Montreal Canadiens	31	36	15	77
Ottawa Senators	31	36	15	77
Hartford Whalers	32	39	11	75
Boston Bruins	26	47	9	61

1996-1997 Atlantic

Team	W	L	T	Pts
New Jersey Devils	45	23	14	104
Philadelphia Flyers	45	24	13	103
Florida Panthers	35	28	19	89
New York Rangers	38	34	10	86
Washington Capitals	33	40	9	75
Tampa Bay Lightning	32	40	10	74
New York Islanders	29	41	12	70

1996-1997 Central

Team	W	L	T	Pts
Dallas Stars	48	26	8	104
Detroit Red Wings	38	26	18	94
Phoenix Coyotes	38	37	7	83
St. Louis Blues	36	35	11	83
Chicago Blackhawks	34	35	13	81
Toronto Maple Leafs	30	44	8	68

FINAL STANDINGS

1996-1997 Pacific

Team	W	L	T	Pts
Colorado Avalanche	49	24	9	107
Anaheim Mighty Ducks	36	33	13	85
Edmonton Oilers	36	37	9	81
Vancouver Canucks	35	40	7	77
Calgary Flames	32	41	9	73
Los Angeles Kings	28	43	11	67
San Jose Sharks	27	47	8	62

1997-1998 Northeast

Team	W	L	T	Pts
Pittsburgh Penguins	40	24	18	98
Boston Bruins	39	30	13	91
Buffalo Sabres	36	29	17	89
Montreal Canadiens	37	32	13	87
Ottawa Senators	34	33	15	83
Carolina Hurricanes	33	41	8	74

1997-1998 Atlantic

Team	W	L	T	Pts
New Jersey Devils	48	23	11	107
Philadelphia Flyers	42	29	11	95
Washington Capitals	40	30	12	92
New York Islanders	30	41	11	71
New York Rangers	25	39	18	68
Florida Panthers	24	43	15	63
Tampa Bay Lightning	17	55	10	44

1997-1998 Central

Team	W	L	T	Pts
Dallas Stars	49	22	11	109
Detroit Red Wings	44	23	15	103
St. Louis Blues	45	29	8	98
Phoenix Coyotes	35	35	12	82
Chicago Blackhawks	30	39	13	73
Toronto Maple Leafs	30	43	9	69

1997-1998 Pacific

Team	W	L	T	Pts
Colorado Avalanche	39	26	17	95
Los Angeles Kings	38	33	11	87
Edmonton Oilers	35	37	10	80
San Jose Sharks	34	38	10	78
Calgary Flames	26	41	15	67
Anaheim Mighty Ducks	26	43	13	65
Vancouver Canucks	25	43	14	64

1998-1999 Northeast

Team	W	L	T	Pts
Ottawa Senators	44	23	15	103
Toronto Maple Leafs	45	30	7	97
Boston Bruins	39	30	13	91
Buffalo Sabres	37	28	17	91
Montreal Canadiens	32	39	11	75

1998-1999 Atlantic

Team	W	L	T	Pts
New Jersey Devils	47	24	11	105
Philadelphia Flyers	37	26	19	93
Pittsburgh Penguins	38	30	14	90
New York Rangers	33	38	11	77
New York Islanders	24	48	10	58

1998-1999 Central

Team	W	L	T	Pts
Detroit Red Wings	43	32	7	93
St. Louis Blues	37	32	13	87
Chicago Blackhawks	29	41	12	70
Nashville Predators	28	47	7	63

1998-1999 Pacific

Team	W	L	T	Pts
Dallas Stars	51	19	12	114
Phoenix Coyotes	39	31	12	90
Anaheim Mighty Ducks	35	34	13	83
San Jose Sharks	31	33	18	80
Los Angeles Kings	32	45	5	69

1998-1999 Southeast

Team	W	L	T	Pts
Carolina Hurricanes	34	30	18	86
Florida Panthers	30	34	18	78
Washington Capitals	31	45	6	68
Tampa Bay Lightning	19	54	9	47

1998-1999 Northwest

Team	W	L	T	Pts
Colorado Avalanche	44	28	10	98
Edmonton Oilers	33	37	12	78
Calgary Flames	30	40	12	72
Vancouver Canucks	23	47	12	58

1999-2000 Northeast

Team	W	L	T	OL	Pts
Toronto Maple Leafs	45	27	7	3	100
Ottawa Senators	41	28	11	2	95
Buffalo Sabres	35	32	11	4	85
Montreal Canadiens	35	34	9	4	83
Boston Bruins	24	33	19	6	73

1999-2000 Atlantic

Team	W	L	T	OL	Pts
Philadelphia Flyers	45	22	12	3	105
New Jersey Devils	45	24	8	5	103
Pittsburgh Penguins	37	31	8	6	88
New York Rangers	29	38	12	3	73
New York Islanders	24	48	9	1	58

1999-2000 Central

Team	W	L	T	OL	Pts
St. Louis Blues	51	19	11	1	114
Detroit Red Wings	48	22	10	2	108
Chicago Blackhawks	33	37	10	2	78
Nashville Predators	28	40	7	7	70

1999-2000 Pacific

Team	W	L	T	OL	Pts
Dallas Stars	43	23	10	6	102
Los Angeles Kings	39	27	12	4	94
Phoenix Coyotes	39	31	8	4	90
San Jose Sharks	35	30	10	7	87
Anaheim Mighty Ducks	34	33	12	3	83

FINAL STANDINGS

1999-2000 Southeast

Team	W	L	T	OL	Pts
Washington Capitals	44	24	12	2	102
Florida Panthers	43	27	6	6	98
Carolina Hurricanes	37	35	10	0	84
Tampa Bay Lightning	19	47	9	7	54
Atlanta Thrashers	14	57	7	4	39

1999-2000 Northwest

Team	W	L	T	OL	Pts
Colorado Avalanche	42	28	11	1	96
Edmonton Oilers	32	26	16	8	88
Vancouver Canucks	30	29	15	8	83
Calgary Flames	31	36	10	5	77

2000-2001 Northeast

Team	W	L	T	OL	Pts
Ottawa Senators	48	21	9	4	109
Buffalo Sabres	46	30	5	1	98
Toronto Maple Leafs	37	29	11	5	90
Boston Bruins	36	30	8	8	88
Montreal Canadiens	28	40	8	6	70

2000-2001 Atlantic

Team	W	L	T	OL	Pts
New Jersey Devils	48	19	12	3	111
Philadelphia Flyers	43	25	11	3	100
Pittsburgh Penguins	42	28	9	3	96
New York Rangers	33	43	5	1	72
New York Islanders	21	51	7	3	52

2000-2001 Central

Team	W	L	T	OL	Pts
Detroit Red Wings	49	20	9	4	111
St. Louis Blues	43	22	12	5	103
Nashville Predators	34	36	9	3	80
Chicago Blackhawks	29	40	8	5	71
Columbus Blue Jackets	28	39	9	6	71

2000-2001 Pacific

Team	W	L	T	OL	Pts
Dallas Stars	48	24	8	2	106
San Jose Sharks	40	27	12	3	95
Los Angeles Kings	38	28	13	3	92
Phoenix Coyotes	35	27	17	3	90
Anaheim Mighty Ducks	25	41	11	5	66

2000-2001 Southeast

Team	W	L	T	OL	Pts
Washington Capitals	41	27	10	4	96
Carolina Hurricanes	38	32	9	3	88
Florida Panthers	22	38	13	9	66
Atlanta Thrashers	23	45	12	2	60
Tampa Bay Lightning	24	47	6	5	59

2000-2001 Northwest

Team	W	L	T	OL	Pts
Colorado Avalanche	52	16	10	4	118
Edmonton Oilers	39	28	12	3	93
Vancouver Canucks	36	28	11	7	90
Calgary Flames	27	36	15	4	73
Minnesota Wild	25	39	13	5	68

2001-2002 Northeast

Team	W	L	T	OL	Pts
Boston Bruins	43	24	6	9	101
Toronto Maple Leafs	43	25	10	4	100
Ottawa Senators	39	27	9	7	94
Montreal Canadiens	36	31	12	3	87
Buffalo Sabres	35	35	11	1	82

2001-2002 Atlantic

Team	W	L	T	OL	Pts
Philadelphia Flyers	42	27	10	3	97
New York Islanders	42	28	8	4	96
New Jersey Devils	41	28	9	4	95
New York Rangers	36	38	4	4	80
Pittsburgh Penguins	28	41	8	5	69

2001-2002 Central

Team	W	L	T	OL	Pts
Detroit Red Wings	51	17	10	4	116
St. Louis Blues	43	27	8	4	98
Chicago Blackhawks	41	27	13	1	96
Nashville Predators	28	41	13	0	69
Columbus Blue Jackets	22	47	8	5	57

2001-2002 Pacific

Team	W	L	T	OL	Pts
San Jose Sharks	44	27	8	3	99
Los Angeles Kings	40	27	11	4	95
Phoenix Coyotes	40	27	9	6	95
Dallas Stars	36	28	13	5	90
Anaheim Mighty Ducks	29	42	8	3	69

2001-2002 Southeast

Team	W	L	T	OL	Pts
Carolina Hurricanes	35	26	16	5	91
Washington Capitals	36	33	11	2	85
Tampa Bay Lightning	27	40	11	4	69
Florida Panthers	22	44	10	6	60
Atlanta Thrashers	19	47	11	5	54

2001-2002 Northwest

Team	W	L	T	OL	Pts
Colorado Avalanche	45	28	8	1	99
Vancouver Canucks	42	30	7	3	94
Edmonton Oilers	38	28	12	4	92
Calgary Flames	32	35	12	3	79
Minnesota Wild	26	35	12	9	73

STANLEY CUP RESULTS

STANLEY CUP RESULTS

Year	Winner	Loser	Games
1927	Ottawa Senators	Boston Bruins	4
1928	New York Rangers	Montreal Maroons	5
1929	Boston Bruins	New York Rangers	2
1930	Montreal Canadiens	Boston Bruins	2
1931	Montreal Canadiens	Chicago Black Hawks	5
1932	Toronto Maple Leafs	New York Rangers	3
1933	New York Rangers	Toronto Maple Leafs	4
1934	Chicago Black Hawks	Detroit Red Wings	4
1935	Montreal Maroons	Toronto Maple Leafs	3
1936	Detroit Red Wings	Toronto Maple Leafs	4
1937	Detroit Red Wings	New York Rangers	5
1938	Chicago Black Hawks	Toronto Maple Leafs	4
1939	Boston Bruins	Toronto Maple Leafs	5
1940	New York Rangers	Toronto Maple Leafs	6
1941	Boston Bruins	Detroit Red Wings	4
1942	Toronto Maple Leafs	Detroit Red Wings	7
1943	Detroit Red Wings	Boston Bruins	4
1944	Montreal Canadiens	Chicago Black Hawks	4
1945	Toronto Maple Leafs	Detroit Red Wings	7
1946	Montreal Canadiens	Boston Bruins	5
1947	Toronto Maple Leafs	Montreal Canadiens	6
1948	Toronto Maple Leafs	Detroit Red Wings	4
1949	Toronto Maple Leafs	Detroit Red Wings	4
1950	Detroit Red Wings	New York Rangers	7
1951	Toronto Maple Leafs	Montreal Canadiens	5
1952	Detroit Red Wings	Montreal Canadiens	4
1953	Montreal Canadiens	Boston Bruins	5
1954	Detroit Red Wings	Montreal Canadiens	7
1955	Detroit Red Wings	Montreal Canadiens	7
1956	Montreal Canadiens	Detroit Red Wings	5
1957	Montreal Canadiens	Boston Bruins	5
1958	Montreal Canadiens	Boston Bruins	6
1959	Montreal Canadiens	Toronto Maple Leafs	5
1960	Montreal Canadiens	Toronto Maple Leafs	7
1961	Chicago Black Hawks	Detroit Red Wings	6
1962	Toronto Maple Leafs	Chicago Black Hawks	6
1963	Toronto Maple Leafs	Detroit Red Wings	5
1964	Toronto Maple Leafs	Detroit Red Wings	7
1965	Montreal Canadiens	Chicago Black Hawks	7
1966	Montreal Canadiens	Detroit Red Wings	6
1967	Toronto Maple Leafs	Montreal Canadiens	6

STANLEY CUP RESULTS

1968	Montreal Canadiens	St. Louis Blues	4
1969	Montreal Canadiens	St. Louis Blues	4
1970	Boston Bruins	St. Louis Blues	4
1971	Montreal Canadiens	Chicago Black Hawks	7
1972	Boston Bruins	New York Rangers	6
1973	Montreal Canadiens	Chicago Black Hawks	6
1974	Philadelphia Flyers	Boston Bruins	6
1975	Philadelphia Flyers	Buffalo Sabres	6
1976	Montreal Canadiens	Philadelphia Flyers	4
1977	Montreal Canadiens	Boston Bruins	4
1978	Montreal Canadiens	Boston Bruins	6
1979	Montreal Canadiens	New York Rangers	5
1980	New York Islanders	Philadelphia Flyers	6
1981	New York Islanders	Minnesota North Stars	5
1982	New York Islanders	Vancouver Canucks	4
1983	New York Islanders	Edmonton Oilers	4
1984	Edmonton Oilers	New York Islanders	5
1985	Edmonton Oilers	Philadelphia Flyers	5
1986	Montreal Canadiens	Calgary Flames	5
1987	Edmonton Oilers	Philadelphia Flyers	7
1988	Edmonton Oilers	Boston Bruins	4
1989	Calgary Flames	Montreal Canadiens	6
1990	Edmonton Oilers	Boston Bruins	5
1991	Pittsburgh Penguins	Minnesota North Stars	6
1992	Pittsburgh Penguins	Chicago Blackhawks	4
1993	Montreal Canadiens	Los Angeles Kings	5
1994	New York Rangers	Vancouver Canucks	7
1995	New Jersey Devils	Detroit Red Wings	4
1996	Colorado Avalanche	Florida Panthers	4
1997	Detroit Red Wings	Philadelphia Flyers	4
1998	Detroit Red Wings	Washington Capitals	4
1999	Dallas Stars	Buffalo Sabres	6
2000	New Jersey Devils	Dallas Stars	6
2001	Colorado Avalanche	New Jersey Devils	7
2002	Detroit Red Wings	Carolina Hurricanes	5

ALL STAR RESULTS

ALL STAR RESULTS

Year	Score	Site
1947	All-Stars 4, Toronto 3	Toronto
1948	All-Stars 3, Toronto 1	Chicago
1949	All-Stars 3, Toronto 1	Toronto
1950	Detroit 7, All-Stars 1	Detroit
1951	1st Team 2, 2nd Team 2	Toronto
1952	1st Team 1, 2nd Team 1	Detroit
1953	All-Stars 3, Montreal 1	Montreal
1954	All-Stars 2, Detroit 2	Detroit
1955	Detroit 3, All-Stars 1	Detroit
1956	All-Stars 1, Montreal 1	Montreal
1957	All-Stars 5, Montreal 3	Montreal
1958	Montreal 6, All-Stars 3	Montreal
1959	Montreal 6, All-Stars 1	Montreal
1960	All-Stars 2, Montreal 1	Montreal
1961	All-Stars 3, Chicago 1	Chicago
1962	Toronto 4, All-Stars 1	Toronto
1963	All-Stars 3, Toronto 3	Toronto
1964	All-Stars 3, Toronto 2	Toronto
1965	All-Stars 5, Montreal 2	Montreal
1966	No Game	
1967	Montreal 3, All-Stars 0	Montreal
1968	Toronto 4, All-Stars 3	Toronto
1969	East 3, West 3	Montreal
1970	East 4, West 1	St. Louis
1971	West 2, East 1	Boston
1972	East 3, West 2	Minnesota
1973	East 5, West 4	NY Rangers
1974	West 6, East 4	Chicago
1975	Wales 7, Campbell 1	Montreal
1976	Wales 7, Campbell 5	Philadelphia
1977	Wales 4, Campbell 3	Vancouver
1978	Wales 3, Campbell 2 (OT)	Buffalo
1979	No Game	
1980	Wales 6, Campbell 3	Detroit
1981	Campbell 4, Wales 1	Los Angeles
1982	Wales 4, Campbell 2	Washington
1983	Campbell 9, Wales 3	NY Islanders
1984	Wales 7, Campbell 6	New Jersey
1985	Wales 6, Campbell 4	Calgary
1986	Wales 4, Campbell 3 (OT)	Hartford
1987	No Game	

ALL STAR RESULTS

1988	Wales 6, Campbell 5 (OT)	St. Louis
1989	Campbell 9, Wales 5	Edmonton
1990	Wales 12, Campbell 7	Pittsburgh
1991	Campbell 11, Wales 5	Chicago
1992	Campbell 10, Wales 6	Philadelphia
1993	Wales 16, Campbell 6	Montreal
1994	East 9, West 8	NY Rangers
1995	No Game	
1996	East 5, West 4	Boston
1997	East 11, West 7	San Jose
1998	North America 8, World 7	Vancouver
1999	North America 8, World 6	Tampa Bay
2000	World 9, North America 4	Toronto
2001	North America 14, World 12	Colorado
2002	World 8, North America 5	Los Angeles

HALL OF FAME

1945
Montagu Allan
Dan Bain
Hobey Baker
Russell Bowie
Chuck Gardiner
Eddie Gerard
Frank McGee
Howie Morenz
Tommy Phillips
Harvey Pulford
Art Ross
Lord Stanley of
Preston
Hod Stuart
Georges Vezina

1946
None

1947
Frank Calder
Dit Clapper
William Hewitt
Aurel Joliat
Francis Nelson
Frank Nighbor
William Northey
Lester Patrick
John Robertson
Claude Robinson
Eddie Shore
James Sutherland
Cyclone Taylor

1948
None

1949
None

1950
Scotty Davidson
Charles Drinkwater
Mike Grant
Si Griffis
Newsy Lalonde
Joe Malone
George
Richardson
Harry Trihey

1951
None

1952
Dickie Boon
Bill Cook
Moose Goheen
Moose Johnson
Mickey MacKay

1953
None

1954
None

1955
None

1956
None

1957
None

1958
Frank Boucher
King Clancy
Sprague Cleghorn
Alex Connell
George Dudley
Red Dutton
Frank Foyston
Frank
Frederickson
Herb Gardiner
George Hay
Dick Irvin
Ching Johnson
Duke Keats
Hugh Lehman
George
McNamara
Paddy Moran
James Norris Sr.
Frank Patrick
Allan Pickard
Donat Raymond
Conn Smythe
Lloyd Turner

1959
Jack Adams
Cy Denneny
Tiny Thompson

1960
Charles Adams
George Boucher
John Kilpatrick
Sylvio Mantha
Frank Selke
Jack Walker

1961
Syl Apps
George Brown
Charlie Conacher
Hap Day
Chaucer Elliott
George
Hainsworth
Bad Joe Hall
Mickey Ion
Percy LeSueur
Paul Loicq
Frank Rankin
Maurice Richard
Milt Schmidt
Oliver Seibert
Cooper Smeaton
Bruce Stuart
Fred Waghorn

1962
Frank Aheam
Punch Broadbent
Walter Brown
Harry Cameron
Rusty Crawford
Jack Darragh
Jimmy Gardner
Billy Gilmour
Wilf Green
Riley Hern
Tom Hooper
Fred Hume
Bouse Hutton
Harry Hyland
Jack Laviolette
Steamer Maxwell
Billy McGimsie

Reg Noble
James Norris
John O'Brien
Didier Pitre
Mike Rodden
Jack Ruttan
Sweeney Schriner
Bullet Joe
Simpson
Alfred Smith
Frank Smith
Barney Stanley
Nels Stewart
Gordon Wilson
Marty Walsh
Harry Watson
Harry Westwick
Fred Whitcroft

1963
Leo Dandurand
Ebbie Goodfellow
Tommy Gorman
Robert Hewitson
Major McLaughlin
Joe Primeau
Earl Seibert

1964
Doug Bentley
Angus Campbell
William Chadwick
Francis Dilio
Bill Durnan
Babe Siebert
Black Jack Stewart

1965
Marty Barry
Clint Benedict
Arthur Farrell
Foster Hewitt
Red Horner
Syd Howe
Thomas Lockhart
Jack Marshall
Bill Mosienko
Blair Russel
Ernest Russell
Fred Scanlan

HALL OF FAME

1966
Max Bentley
Toe Blake
Butch Bouchard
Francis Brimsek
Clarence
Campbell
Ted Kennedy
Elmer Lach
Ted Lindsay
Babe Pratt
Ken Reardon

1967
Turk Broda
Neil Colville
Harry Oliver
Red Storey

1968
Bill Cowley
James Dunn
James Hendy

1969
Sid Abel
Bryan Hextall
Red Kelly
George Leader
Bruce Norris
Roy Worters

1970
Babe Dye
Bill Gadsby
Tom Johnson
Robert LeBel

1971
Harvey Jackson
Gordie Roberts
Terry Sawchuk
Cooney Weiland
Arthur Wirtz

1972
Weston Adams
Jean Beliveau
Bernie Geoffrion
Hap Holmes
Gordie Howe

Hooley Smith

1973
Doug Harvey
Hartland Molson
Chuck Rayner
Tommy Smith
Frank Udvari

1974
Billy Burch
Art Coulter
Thomas
Dunderdale
Charles Hay
Thomas Ivan
Dick Moore
Anatoli Tarasov
Carl Voss

1975
George Armstrong
Ace Bailey
Frank Buckland
Gordie Drillon
Glenn Hall
William Jennings
Pierre Pilote

1976
Johnny Bower
Jack Gibson
Bill Quackenbush
Philip Ross
Bill Wirtz

1977
Bunny Ahearne
Harold Ballard
Joseph Cattarinich
Alex Delvecchio
Tim Horton

1978
Andy Bathgate
John Bickell
Jacques Plante
Samuel Pollock
Marcel Pronovost
William Tutt

1979
Harry Howell
Gordon Juckes
Bobby Orr
Henri Richard

1980
Jack Butterfield
Harry Lumley
Lynn Patrick
Gump Worsley

1981
John Ashley
John Bucyk
Frank Mahovlich
Allan Stanley

1982
Yvan Cournoyer
Emile Francis
Rod Gilbert
Norm Ullman

1983
Ken Dryden
Bobby Hull
Stan Mikita
Harry Sinden

1984
Jacques
Beauchamp
Jim Burchard
Red Burnett
Dink Carroll
Jim Coleman
Fred Cusick
Ted Damata
Marcel Desjardins
Jack Dulmage
Milt Dunnell
Phil Esposito
Elmer Ferguson
Tom Fitzgerald
Trent Frayne
Danny Gallivan
Foster Hewitt
Punch Imlach
Al Laney
Rene Lecavalier

Jacques Lemaire
Jake Milford
Joe Nichols
Basil O'Meara
Bernie Parent
Jim Vipond
Lewis Walter

1985
Charlie Barton
Gerry Cheevers
Red Fisher
George Gross
Zotique
L'Esperance
Budd Lynch
John Mariucci
Charles Mayer
Andy O'Brien
Bert Olmstead
Rudy Pilous
Jean Ratelle
Doug Smith

1986
Leo Boivin
William Hanley
Dick Johnston
Dave Keon
Wes McKnight
Leo Monahan
Tim Moriarty
Lloyd Pettit
Serge Savard

1987
Bill Brennan
Bobby Clarke
Ed Giacomin
Jacques
Laperriere
Rex MacLeod
Ben Olan
Matt Pavelich
Fran Rosa
Bob Wilson
John Ziegler

1988
Tony Esposito
George Hayes

289

HALL OF FAME

Dick Irvin
Guy Lafleur
Buddy O'Connor
Brad Park
Jim Proudfoot
Ed Snider
Scott Young

1989
David Bauer
Dan Kelly
Claude Larochelle
Herbie Lewis
Frank Orr
Darryl Sittler
Vladislav Tretiak

1990
Bill Barber
Fernie Flaman
Jiggs McDonald
Gil Perreault
Bud Poile
Bertrand Raymond

1991
Neil Armstrong
Mike Bossy
Scotty Bowman
Hugh Delano
Bruce Martyn
Denis Potvin
Bob Pulford
Clint Smith

1992
Keith Allen
Marcel Dionne
Woody Dumart
Bob Gainey
Bob Johnson
Frank Mathers
Lanny McDonald
Jim Robson

1993
John D'Amico
Frank Griffiths
Seymour Knox
Guy Lapointe
Edgar Laprade

Fred Page
Al Shaver
Steve Shutt
Billy Smith
Al Strachan

1994
Lionel Conacher
Ted Darling
Brian O'Neill
Harry Watson

1995
Bun Cook
Jack Gatecliff
Brian McFarlane
Larry Robinson
Gunther Sabetzki
Bill Torrey

1996
Al Arbour
Bobby Bauer
Bob Cole
Borje Salming

1997
Gene Hart
Mario Lemieux
Ken McKenzie
Glen Sather
Bryan Trottier

1998
Roy Conacher
Michel Goulet
Howie Meeker
Athol Murray
Yvon Pedneault
Peter Stastny

1999
Russ Conway
Richard Garneau
Wayne Gretzky
Scotty Morrison
Andy Van
Hellemond

2000
Walter Bush

Jim Matheson
Bob Miller
Joe Mullen
Denis Savard

2001
Eric Duhatschek
Slava Fetisov
Mike Gartner
Dale Hawerchuk
Jari Kurri
Mike Lange
Craig Patrick

THE
AWARDS

ART ROSS TROPHY

Awarded to the player who leads the
league in points scored.

1918	Joe Malone
1919	Newsy Lalonde
1920	Joe Malone
1921	Newsy Lalonde
1922	Punch Broadbent
1923	Babe Dye
1924	Cy Denneny
1925	Babe Dye
1926	Nels Stewart
1927	Bill Cook
1928	Howie Morenz
1929	Ace Bailey
1930	Cooney Weiland
1931	Howie Morenz
1932	Harvey Jackson
1933	Bill Cook
1934	Charlie Conacher
1935	Charlie Conacher
1936	Sweeney Schriner
1937	Sweeney Schriner
1938	Gordie Drillon
1939	Toe Blake
1940	Milt Schmidt
1941	Bill Cowley
1942	Bryan Hextall
1943	Doug Bentley
1944	Herb Cain
1945	Elmer Lach
1946	Max Bentley
1947	Max Bentley
1948	Elmer Lach
1949	Roy Conacher
1950	Ted Lindsay
1951	Gordie Howe
1952	Gordie Howe
1953	Gordie Howe
1954	Gordie Howe
1955	Bernie Geoffrion
1956	Jean Beliveau
1957	Gordie Howe
1958	Dick Moore
1959	Dick Moore
1960	Bobby Hull
1961	Bernie Geoffrion
1962	Bobby Hull
1963	Gordie Howe
1964	Stan Mikita

1965	Stan Mikita
1966	Bobby Hull
1967	Stan Mikita
1968	Stan Mikita
1969	Phil Esposito
1970	Bobby Orr
1971	Phil Esposito
1972	Phil Esposito
1973	Phil Esposito
1974	Phil Esposito
1975	Bobby Orr
1976	Guy Lafleur
1977	Guy Lafleur
1978	Guy Lafleur
1979	Bryan Trottier
1980	Marcel Dionne
1981	Wayne Gretzky
1982	Wayne Gretzky
1983	Wayne Gretzky
1984	Wayne Gretzky
1985	Wayne Gretzky
1986	Wayne Gretzky
1987	Wayne Gretzky
1988	Mario Lemieux
1989	Mario Lemieux
1990	Wayne Gretzky
1991	Wayne Gretzky
1992	Mario Lemieux
1993	Mario Lemieux
1994	Wayne Gretzky
1995	Jaromir Jagr
1996	Mario Lemieux
1997	Mario Lemieux
1998	Jaromir Jagr
1999	Jaromir Jagr
2000	Jaromir Jagr
2001	Jaromir Jagr
2002	Jarome Iginla

CALDER TROPHY

Awarded to the most outstanding rookie of the year.

Year	Player
1933	Carl Voss
1934	Russ Blinco
1935	Sweeney Schriner
1936	Mike Karakas
1937	Syl Apps
1938	Cully Dahlstrom
1939	Francis Brimsek
1940	Kilby MacDonald
1941	John Quilty
1942	Grant Warwick
1943	Gaye Stewart
1944	Gus Bodnar
1945	Frank McCool
1946	Edgar Laprade
1947	Howie Meeker
1948	Jim McFadden
1949	Pentti Lund
1950	Jack Gelineau
1951	Terry Sawchuk
1952	Bernie Geoffrion
1953	Gump Worsley
1954	Camille Henry
1955	Ed Litzenberger
1956	Glenn Hall
1957	Larry Regan
1958	Frank Mahovlich
1959	Ralph Backstrom
1960	Bill Hay
1961	Dave Keon
1962	Bobby Rousseau
1963	Kent Douglas
1964	Jacques Laperriere
1965	Roger Crozier
1966	Brit Selby
1967	Bobby Orr
1968	Derek Sanderson
1969	Danny Grant
1970	Tony Esposito
1971	Gil Perreault
1972	Ken Dryden
1973	Steve Vickers
1974	Denis Potvin
1975	Eric Vail
1976	Bryan Trottier
1977	Willi Plett
1978	Mike Bossy
1979	Bobby Smith
1980	Ray Bourque
1981	Peter Stastny
1982	Dale Hawerchuk
1983	Steve Larmer
1984	Tom Barrasso
1985	Mario Lemieux
1986	Gary Suter
1987	Luc Robitaille
1988	Joe Nieuwendyk
1989	Brian Leetch
1990	Sergei Makarov
1991	Ed Belfour
1992	Pavel Bure
1993	Teemu Selanne
1994	Martin Brodeur
1995	Peter Forsberg
1996	Daniel Alfredsson
1997	Bryan Berard
1998	Sergei Samsonov
1999	Chris Drury
2000	Scott Gomez
2001	Evgeni Nabokov
2002	Dany Heatley

CONN SMYTHE TROPHY

Awarded to the most valuable player in
each season's playoff competition.

1965	Jean Beliveau
1966	Roger Crozier
1967	Dave Keon
1968	Glenn Hall
1969	Serge Savard
1970	Bobby Orr
1971	Ken Dryden
1972	Bobby Orr
1973	Yvan Cournoyer
1974	Bernie Parent
1975	Bernie Parent
1976	Reggie Leach
1977	Guy Lafleur
1978	Larry Robinson
1979	Bob Gainey
1980	Bryan Trottier
1981	Butch Goring
1982	Mike Bossy
1983	Billy Smith
1984	Mark Messier
1985	Wayne Gretzky
1986	Patrick Roy
1987	Ron Hextall
1988	Wayne Gretzky
1989	Al MacInnis
1990	Bill Ranford
1991	Mario Lemieux
1992	Mario Lemieux
1993	Patrick Roy
1994	Brian Leetch
1995	Claude Lemieux
1996	Joe Sakic
1997	Mike Vernon
1998	Steve Yzerman
1999	Joe Nieuwendyk
2000	Scott Stevens
2001	Patrick Roy
2002	Nicklas Lidstrom

HART MEMORIAL TROPHY

Awarded to the player "adjudged to be the most valuable to his team."

Year	Player
1924	Frank Nighbor
1925	Billy Burch
1926	Nels Stewart
1927	Herb Gardiner
1928	Howie Morenz
1929	Roy Worters
1930	Nels Stewart
1931	Howie Morenz
1932	Howie Morenz
1933	Eddie Shore
1934	Aurel Joliat
1935	Eddie Shore
1936	Eddie Shore
1937	Babe Siebert
1938	Eddie Shore
1939	Toe Blake
1940	Ebbie Goodfellow
1941	Bill Cowley
1942	Tom Anderson
1943	Bill Cowley
1944	Babe Pratt
1945	Elmer Lach
1946	Max Bentley
1947	Maurice Richard
1948	Buddy O'Connor
1949	Sid Abel
1950	Chuck Rayner
1951	Milt Schmidt
1952	Gordie Howe
1953	Gordie Howe
1954	Al Rollins
1955	Ted Kennedy
1956	Jean Beliveau
1957	Gordie Howe
1958	Gordie Howe
1959	Andy Bathgate
1960	Gordie Howe
1961	Bernie Geoffrion
1962	Jacques Plante
1963	Gordie Howe
1964	Jean Beliveau
1965	Bobby Hull
1966	Bobby Hull
1967	Stan Mikita
1968	Stan Mikita
1969	Phil Esposito
1970	Bobby Orr
1971	Bobby Orr
1972	Bobby Orr
1973	Bobby Clarke
1974	Phil Esposito
1975	Bobby Clarke
1976	Bobby Clarke
1977	Guy Lafleur
1978	Guy Lafleur
1979	Bryan Trottier
1980	Wayne Gretzky
1981	Wayne Gretzky
1982	Wayne Gretzky
1983	Wayne Gretzky
1984	Wayne Gretzky
1985	Wayne Gretzky
1986	Wayne Gretzky
1987	Wayne Gretzky
1988	Mario Lemieux
1989	Wayne Gretzky
1990	Mark Messier
1991	Brett Hull
1992	Mark Messier
1993	Mario Lemieux
1994	Sergei Fedorov
1995	Eric Lindros
1996	Mario Lemieux
1997	Dominik Hasek
1998	Dominik Hasek
1999	Jaromir Jagr
2000	Chris Pronger
2001	Joe Sakic
2002	Jose Theodore

JAMES NORRIS TROPHY

Awarded to defenseman who
demonstrates the greatest all-around
ability in his position.

2000	Chris Pronger		
2001	Nicklas Lidstrom		
2002	Nicklas Lidstrom		

1954	Red Kelly
1955	Doug Harvey
1956	Doug Harvey
1957	Doug Harvey
1958	Doug Harvey
1959	Tom Johnson
1960	Doug Harvey
1961	Doug Harvey
1962	Doug Harvey
1963	Pierre Pilote
1964	Pierre Pilote
1965	Pierre Pilote
1966	Jacques Laperriere
1967	Harry Howell
1968	Bobby Orr
1969	Bobby Orr
1970	Bobby Orr
1971	Bobby Orr
1972	Bobby Orr
1973	Bobby Orr
1974	Bobby Orr
1975	Bobby Orr
1976	Denis Potvin
1977	Larry Robinson
1978	Denis Potvin
1979	Denis Potvin
1980	Larry Robinson
1981	Randy Carlyle
1982	Doug Wilson
1983	Rod Langway
1984	Rod Langway
1985	Paul Coffey
1986	Paul Coffey
1987	Ray Bourque
1988	Ray Bourque
1989	Chris Chelios
1990	Ray Bourque
1991	Ray Bourque
1992	Brian Leetch
1993	Chris Chelios
1994	Ray Bourque
1995	Paul Coffey
1996	Chris Chelios
1997	Brian Leetch
1998	Rob Blake
1999	Al MacInnis

KING CLANCY TROPHY

Awarded to the player who "best
exemplifies leadership on and off the
ice."

1988	Lanny McDonald
1989	Bryan Trottier
1990	Kevin Lowe
1991	Dave Taylor
1992	Ray Bourque
1993	Dave Poulin
1994	Adam Graves
1995	Joe Nieuwendyk
1996	Kris King
1997	Trevor Linden
1998	Kelly Chase
1999	Rob Ray
2000	Curtis Joseph
2001	Shjon Podein
2002	Ron Francis

LADY BYNG TROPHY

Awarded to the player "adjudged to have exhibited the best type of sportsmanship combined with a high standard of playing ability."

1925	Frank Nighbor
1926	Frank Nighbor
1927	Billy Burch
1928	Frank Boucher
1929	Frank Boucher
1930	Frank Boucher
1931	Frank Boucher
1932	Joe Primeau
1933	Frank Boucher
1934	Frank Boucher
1935	Frank Boucher
1936	Doc Romnes
1937	Marty Barry
1938	Gordie Drillon
1939	Clint Smith
1940	Bobby Bauer
1941	Bobby Bauer
1942	Syl Apps
1943	Max Bentley
1944	Clint Smith
1945	Bill Mosienko
1946	Toe Blake
1947	Bobby Bauer
1948	Buddy O'Connor
1949	Bill Quackenbush
1950	Edgar Laprade
1951	Red Kelly
1952	Sid Smith
1953	Red Kelly
1954	Red Kelly
1955	Sid Smith
1956	Earl Reibel
1957	Andy Hebenton
1958	Camille Henry
1959	Alex Delvecchio
1960	Donald McKenney
1961	Red Kelly
1962	Dave Keon
1963	Dave Keon
1964	Ken Wharram
1965	Bobby Hull
1966	Alex Delvecchio
1967	Stan Mikita
1968	Stan Mikita
1969	Alex Delvecchio
1970	Phil Goyette
1971	John Bucyk
1972	Jean Ratelle
1973	Gil Perreault
1974	John Bucyk
1975	Marcel Dionne
1976	Jean Ratelle
1977	Marcel Dionne
1978	Butch Goring
1979	Bob MacMillan
1980	Wayne Gretzky
1981	Rick Kehoe
1982	Rick Middleton
1983	Mike Bossy
1984	Mike Bossy
1985	Jari Kurri
1986	Mike Bossy
1987	Joe Mullen
1988	Mats Naslund
1989	Joe Mullen
1990	Brett Hull
1991	Wayne Gretzky
1992	Wayne Gretzky
1993	Pierre Turgeon
1994	Wayne Gretzky
1995	Ron Francis
1996	Paul Kariya
1997	Paul Kariya
1998	Ron Francis
1999	Wayne Gretzky
2000	Pavol Demitra
2001	Joe Sakic
2002	Ron Francis

LESTER B. PEARSON AWARD

Awarded to the season's most outstanding player.

1971	Phil Esposito
1972	Jean Ratelle
1973	Bobby Clarke
1974	Phil Esposito
1975	Bobby Orr
1976	Guy Lafleur
1977	Guy Lafleur
1978	Guy Lafleur
1979	Marcel Dionne
1980	Marcel Dionne
1981	Mike Liut
1982	Wayne Gretzky
1983	Wayne Gretzky
1984	Wayne Gretzky
1985	Wayne Gretzky
1986	Mario Lemieux
1987	Wayne Gretzky
1988	Mario Lemieux
1989	Steve Yzerman
1990	Mark Messier
1991	Brett Hull
1992	Mark Messier
1993	Mario Lemieux
1994	Sergei Fedorov
1995	Eric Lindros
1996	Mario Lemieux
1997	Dominik Hasek
1998	Dominik Hasek
1999	Jaromir Jagr
2000	Jaromir Jagr
2001	Joe Sakic
2002	Jarome Iginla

MAURICE RICHARD TROPHY

Awarded to the player who leads the league in goals scored.

1999	Teemu Selanne
2000	Pavel Bure
2001	Pavel Bure
2002	Jarome Iginla

VEZINA TROPHY

Until 1981 it was awarded to the goaltender(s) of the team allowing the fewest number of goals during the regular season. Since 1982, it was awarded to the goaltender judged to be the best at his position in the opinion of the general managers.

Year	Winner
1927	George Hainsworth
1928	George Hainsworth
1929	George Hainsworth
1930	Tiny Thompson
1931	Roy Worters
1932	Chuck Gardiner
1933	Tiny Thompson
1934	Chuck Gardiner
1935	Lorne Chabot
1936	Tiny Thompson
1937	Norman Smith
1938	Tiny Thompson
1939	Francis Brimsek
1940	Dave Kerr
1941	Turk Broda
1942	Francis Brimsek
1943	Johnny Mowers
1944	Bill Durnan
1945	Bill Durnan
1946	Bill Durnan
1947	Bill Durnan
1948	Turk Broda
1949	Bill Durnan
1950	Bill Durnan
1951	Al Rollins
1952	Terry Sawchuk
1953	Terry Sawchuk
1954	Harry Lumley
1955	Terry Sawchuk
1956	Jacques Plante
1957	Jacques Plante
1958	Jacques Plante
1959	Jacques Plante
1960	Jacques Plante
1961	Johnny Bower
1962	Jacques Plante
1963	Glenn Hall
1964	Charlie Hodge
1965	Terry Sawchuk
1965	Johnny Bower
1966	Gump Worsley
1966	Charlie Hodge
1967	Glenn Hall
1967	Denis DeJordy
1968	Gump Worsley
1968	Rogie Vachon
1969	Jacques Plante
1969	Glenn Hall
1970	Tony Esposito
1971	Ed Giacomin
1971	Gilles Villemure
1972	Tony Esposito
1972	Gary Smith
1973	Ken Dryden
1974	Bernie Parent
1974	Tony Esposito
1975	Bernie Parent
1976	Ken Dryden
1977	Ken Dryden
1977	Michel Larocque
1978	Ken Dryden
1978	Michel Larocque
1979	Ken Dryden
1979	Michel Larocque
1980	Bob Sauve
1980	Don Edwards
1981	Richard Sevigny
1981	Denis Herron
1981	Michel Larocque
1982	Billy Smith
1983	Pete Peeters
1984	Tom Barrasso
1985	Pelle Lindbergh
1986	John Vanbiesbrouck
1987	Ron Hextall
1988	Grant Fuhr
1989	Patrick Roy
1990	Patrick Roy
1991	Ed Belfour
1992	Patrick Roy
1993	Ed Belfour
1994	Dominik Hasek
1995	Dominik Hasek
1996	Jim Carey
1997	Dominik Hasek
1998	Dominik Hasek
1999	Dominik Hasek
2000	Olaf Kolzig
2001	Dominik Hasek
2002	Jose Theodore

WILLIAM M. JENNINGS TROPHY

Awarded to the goaltender(s) having played a minimum of 25 games for the team with the fewest goals scored against.

1982	Rick Wamsley
1982	Denis Herron
1983	Rollie Melanson
1983	Billy Smith
1984	Al Jensen
1984	Pat Riggin
1985	Tom Barrasso
1985	Bob Sauve
1986	Bob Froese
1986	Darren Jensen
1987	Patrick Roy
1987	Brian Hayward
1988	Patrick Roy
1988	Brian Hayward
1989	Patrick Roy
1989	Brian Hayward
1990	Andy Moog
1990	Reggie Lemelin
1991	Ed Belfour
1992	Patrick Roy
1993	Ed Belfour
1994	Dominik Hasek
1994	Grant Fuhr
1995	Ed Belfour
1996	Chris Osgood
1996	Mike Vernon
1997	Martin Brodeur
1997	Mike Dunham
1998	Martin Brodeur
1999	Ed Belfour
1999	Roman Turek
2000	Roman Turek
2001	Dominik Hasek
2002	Patrick Roy

GLOSSARY

Art Ross Trophy: Awarded to the player who wins the scoring championship during the regular season.

Assist: A pass that leads to a goal being scored. One or two, or none, may be awarded on any goal.

Backchecking: Skating with an opponent through the neutral and defensive zones to try to break up an attack.

Backhand: A pass or shot, in which the player cradles the puck on the off- or backside of the stick blade and propels it with a shoveling motion..

Back pass: A pass left or slid backwards for a trailing teammate to recover.

Blocker: A protective glove worn on the hand a goaltender uses to hold his stick so that the goalie can deflect pucks away from the net.

Blue lines: The lines, located 29 feet from each side of the center red line, which demarcate the beginning of the offensive zone.

Boarding: Riding or driving an opponent into the boards. A two- or five-minute penalty may be assessed, at the referee's discretion.

Boards: Wooden structures, 48 inches high, topped by plexiglass fencing, that enclose the 200 feet by 85 feet ice surface.

Bodycheck: Using the hips or shoulders to stop the progress of the puck carrier.

Breakaway: The puck carrier skating toward the opposition's net ahead of all the other players.

Butt-Ending: Striking an opponent with the top end of the hockey stick, a dangerously illegal act that brings a five-minute penalty.

Calder Memorial Trophy: Awarded to the goaltender, defenseman or forward judged to be the best first-year, or rookie, player.

Central Scouting Bureau: An NHL agency that compiles statistical and evaluative information on all players eligible for the Entry Draft. The information, which includes a rating system of all players, is distributed to all NHL teams.

Charging: Skating three strides or more and crashing into an opponent. Calls for a two-minute or five-minute penalty at the referee's discretion.

Conn Smythe Trophy: Awarded to the top performer throughout the Stanley Cup playoffs.

Crease: A six-foot semicircular area at the mouth of the goal that opponents may not enter. Only the goaltender may freeze the puck in this space.

Crossbar: A red, horizontal pipe, four feet above the ice and six feet long across the top of the goal cage.

Crosschecking: Hitting an opponent with both hands on the stick and no part of the stick on the ice. Warrants a two-minute penalty.

Defensemen: The two players who form the second line of defense, after the goalie. Defensemen try to strip opponents of the puck in their own zone and either pass to teammates or skate the puck up-ice themselves to start an attack. When retreating from the opponent's zone, defensemen move back toward their zone by skating backwards, facing the oncoming opponents.

Deflection: Placing the blade of the stick in the path of a shot on goal, causing the puck to change direction and deceive the goaltender. A puck may also deflect off a player's skate or pads.

Delay of game: Causing the play to stop by either propelling the puck outside the playing surface or covering it with the hand. Warrants a two-minute penalty.

Delayed penalty: An infraction, signaled by the referee's upraised right hand, but not whistled until the offending team regains possession of the puck. During the delay, the other team can launch a scoring attack, sometimes by replacing their goaltender with a skater. If the team scores during the delay, the penalized player does not sit out his penalty.

Elbowing: Striking an opponent with the elbow. Calls for a two-minute penalty.

Entry Draft: An annual event, at which all 26 NHL teams submit claims on young players who have not signed professional contracts. The talent pool consists of players from the Canadian junior leagues, U.S. high schools and universities and European elite and junior leagues.

Faceoff: A play that initiates all action in a hockey game, in which the referee or a linesman drops the puck onto a spot between the poised stick blades of two opponents. Marks the start of every period, also occurs after every goal and every play stoppage.

Fighting: Players dropping their gloves and striking each other with their fists. Calls for a five-minute penalty and ejection for the player who instigated the fisticuffs.

Forechecking: Harassing opponents in their own zone to try to gain possession of the puck.

Forwards: Three players—the center and the left and right wingers—comprise a hockey team's forward line. The forwards are primarily attackers whose aim is to score goals.

Frank J. Selke Trophy: Awarded to the player judged the best defensive forward in the NHL.

Goal: A goal is scored when the puck completely crosses the red goal line and enters the net.

Goals-Against-Average (GAA): Average number of goals a goaltender surrenders per game. Determined by multiplying the total